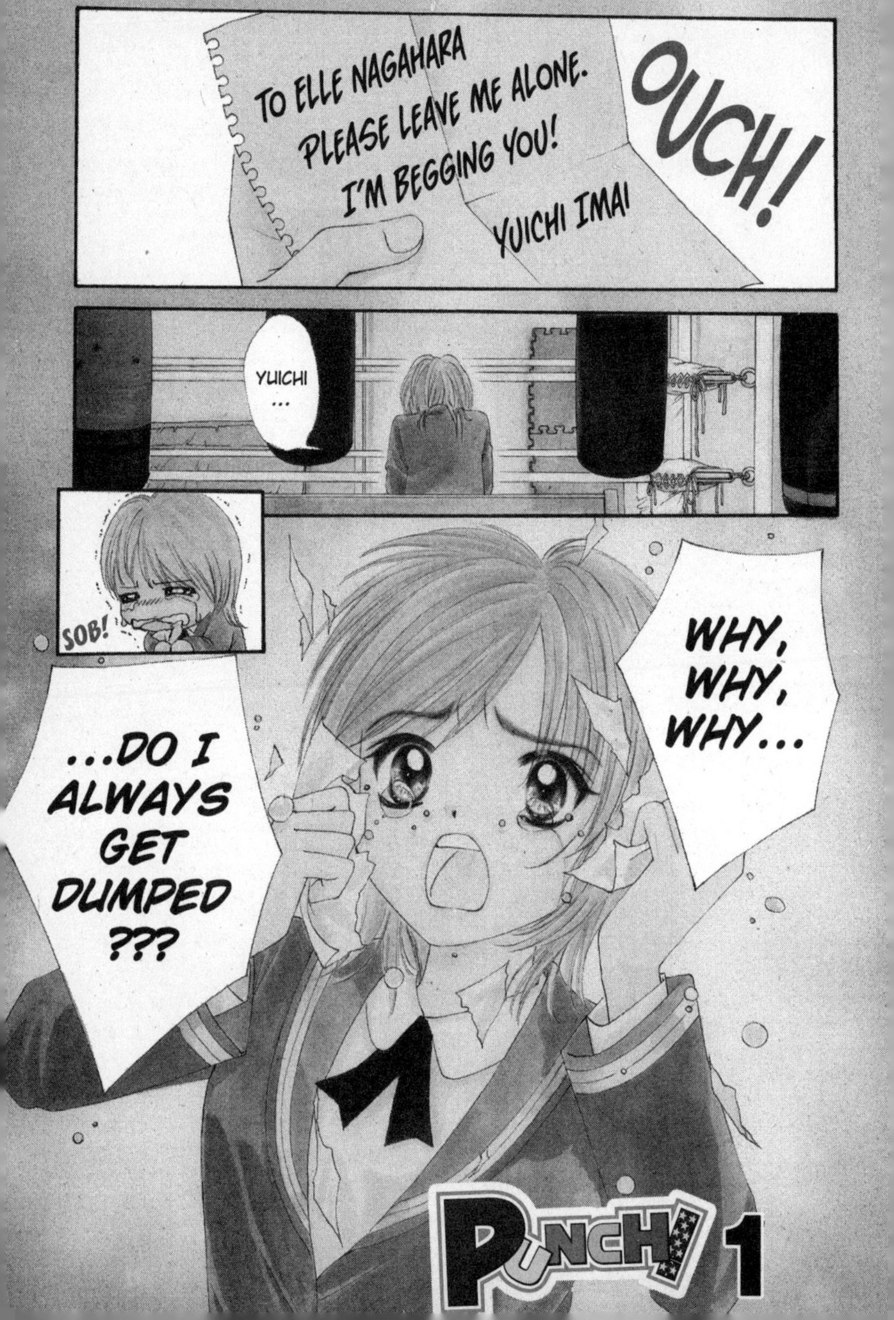
OUCH!
TO ELLE NAGAHARA
PLEASE LEAVE ME ALONE.
I'M BEGGING YOU!
YUICHI IMAI
YUICHI ...
SOB!
WHY, WHY, WHY...
...DO I ALWAYS GET DUMPED???
PUNCH! 1

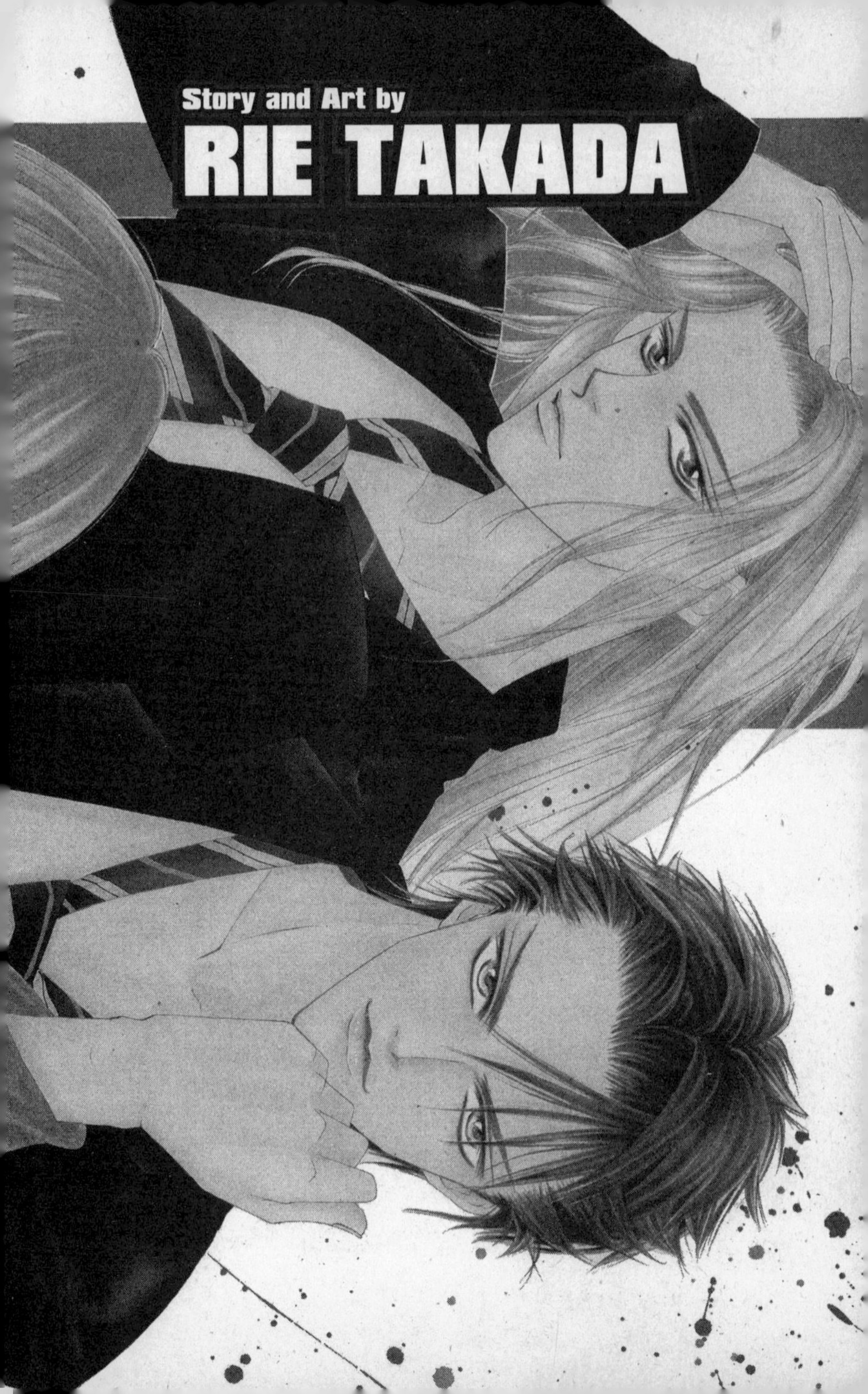
Story and Art by
RIE TAKADA

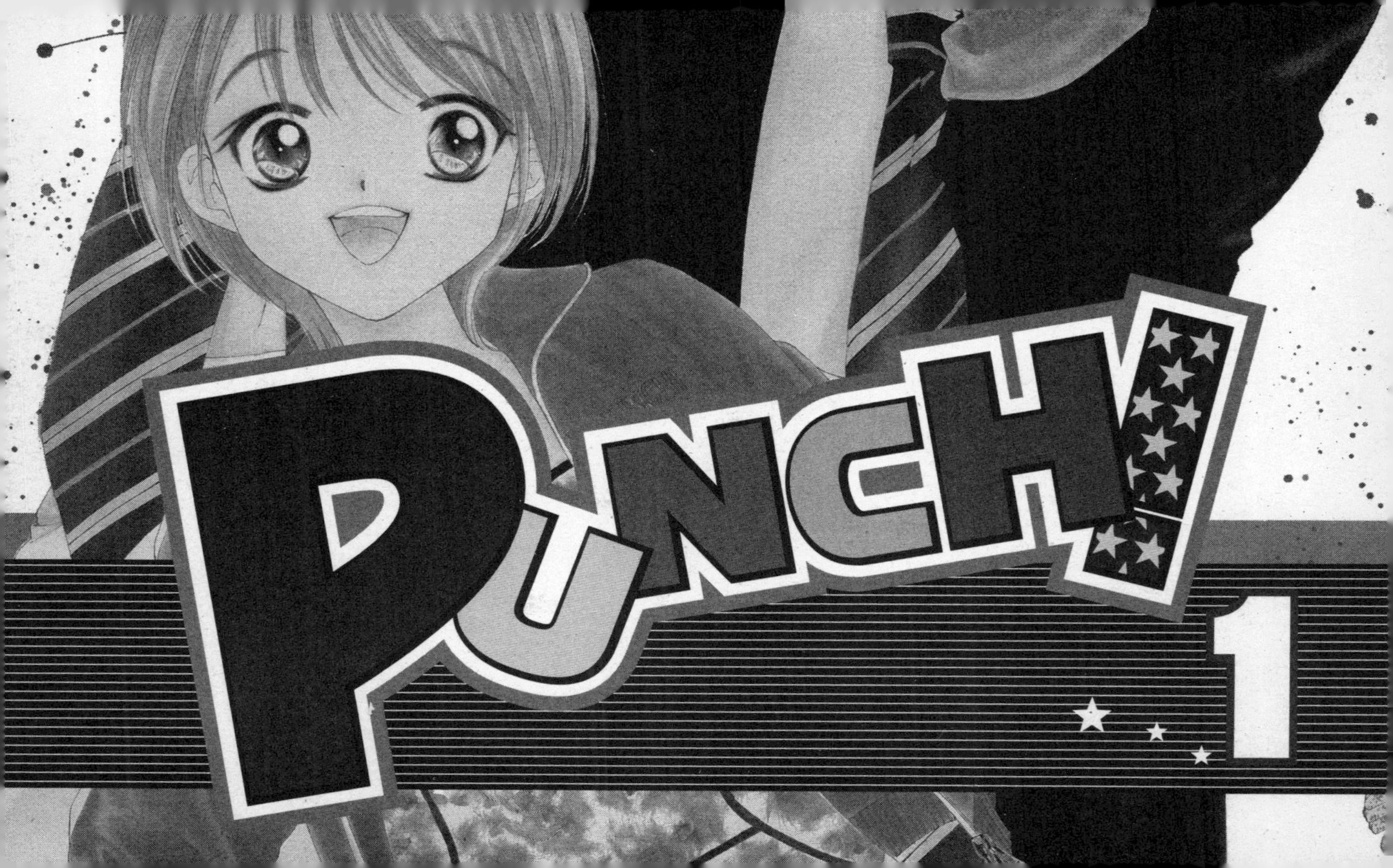
PUNCH!
1

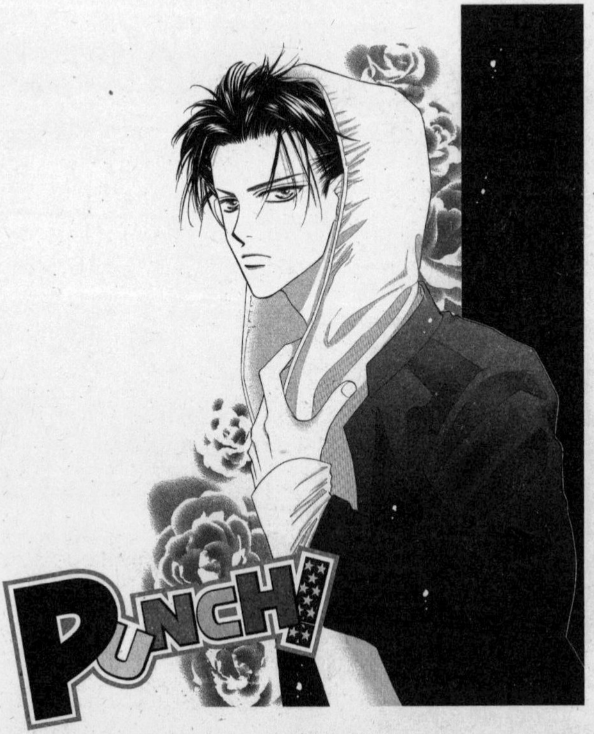
PUNCH!

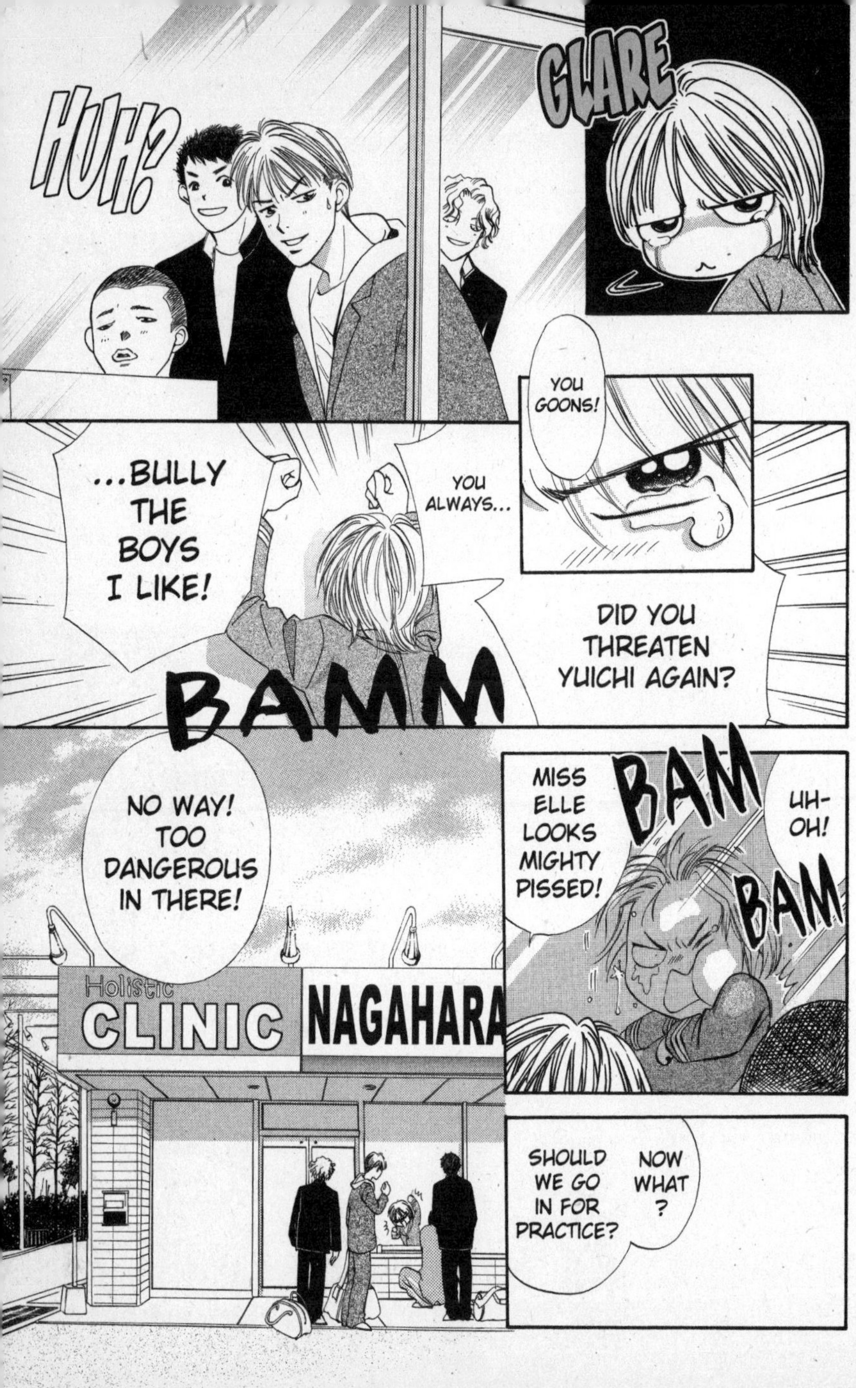
GLARE
HUH?
YOU GOONS!
DID YOU THREATEN YUICHI AGAIN?
YOU ALWAYS...
...BULLY THE BOYS I LIKE!
BAMM
UH-OH!
BAM
BAM
MISS ELLE LOOKS MIGHTY PISSED!
NOW WHAT?
SHOULD WE GO IN FOR PRACTICE?
NO WAY! TOO DANGEROUS IN THERE!
Holistic CLINIC NAGAHARA

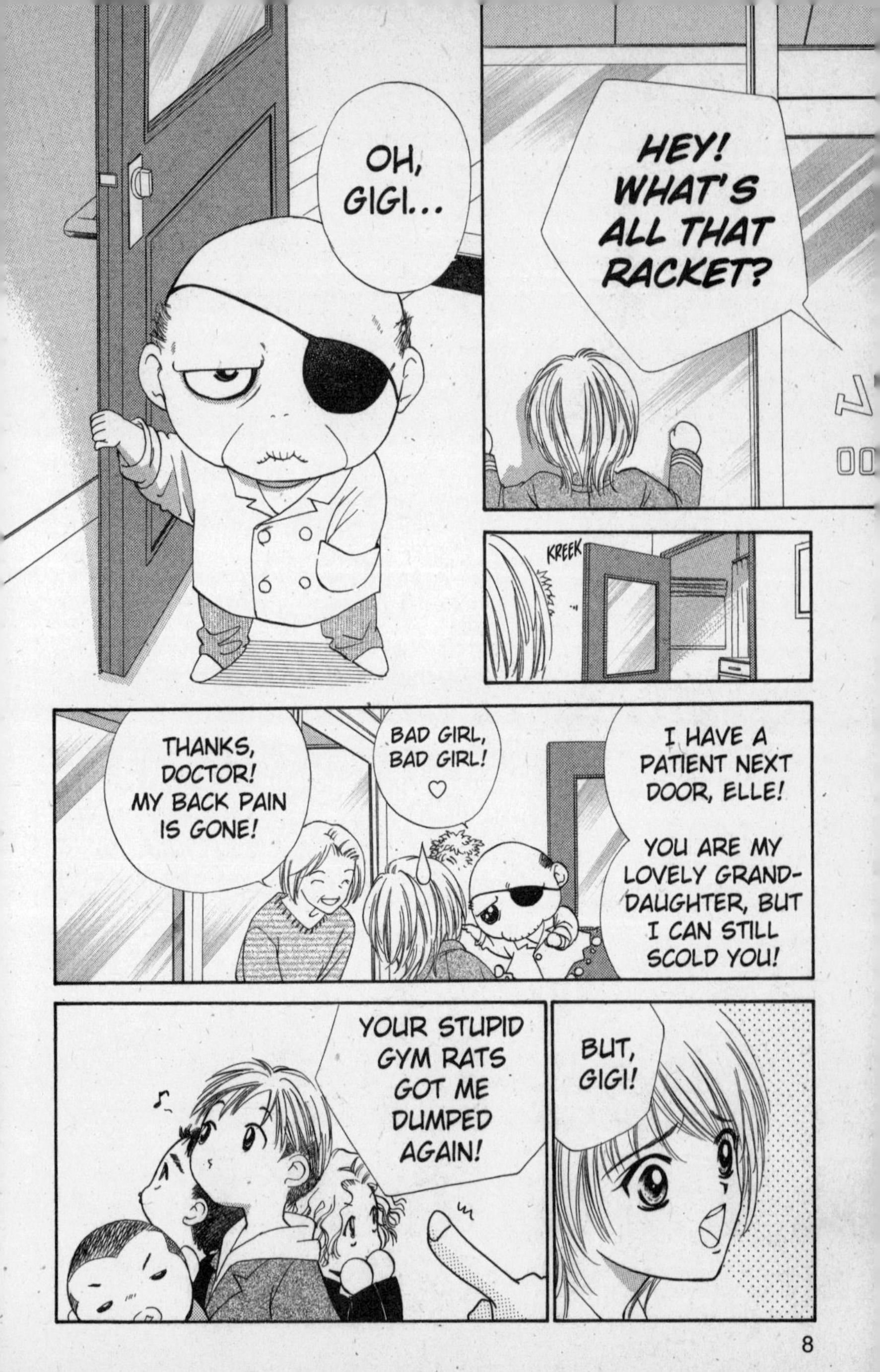
HEY! WHAT'S ALL THAT RACKET?
KREEK
OH, GIGI...
I HAVE A PATIENT NEXT DOOR, ELLE!
YOU ARE MY LOVELY GRAND-DAUGHTER, BUT I CAN STILL SCOLD YOU!
BAD GIRL, BAD GIRL! ♡
THANKS, DOCTOR! MY BACK PAIN IS GONE!
BUT, GIGI!
YOUR STUPID GYM RATS GOT ME DUMPED AGAIN!

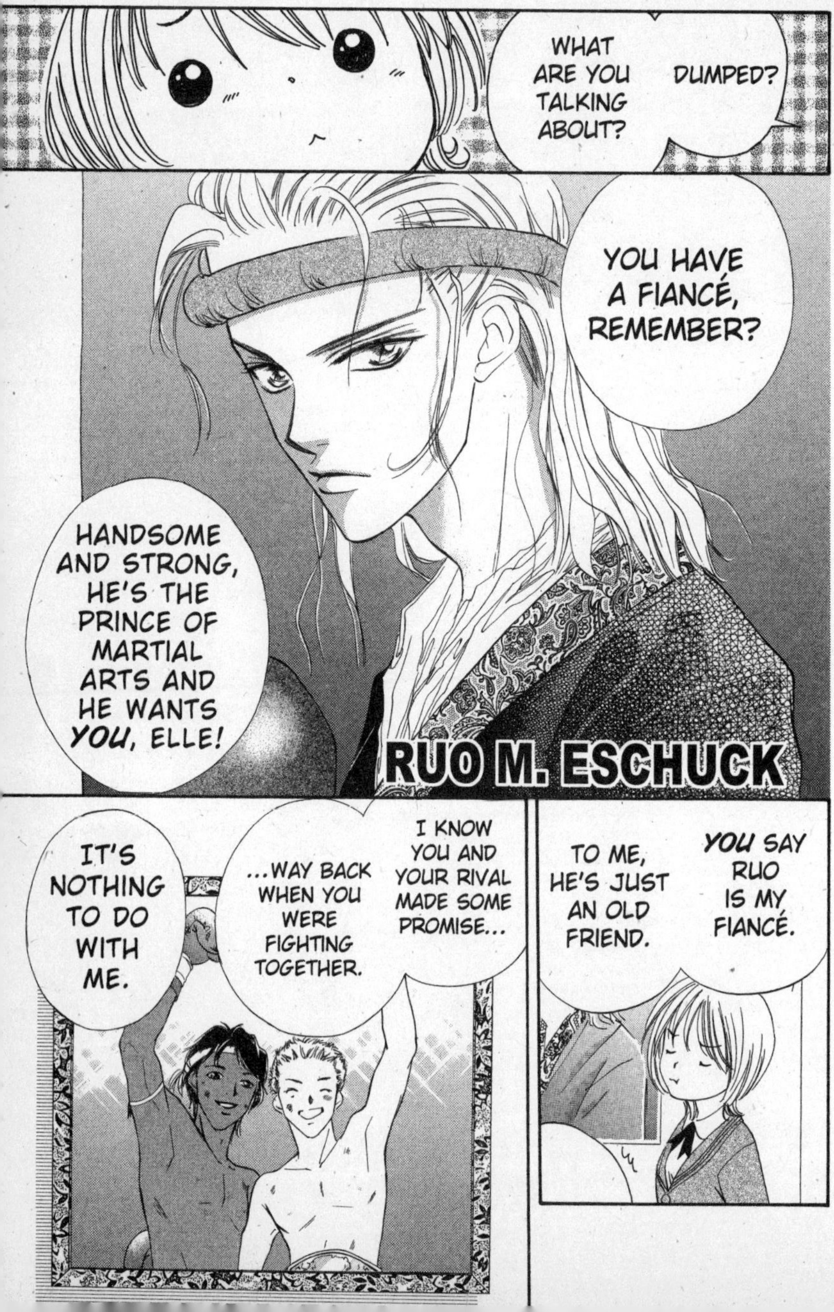
DUMPED?
WHAT ARE YOU TALKING ABOUT?
YOU HAVE A FIANCÉ, REMEMBER?
HANDSOME AND STRONG, HE'S THE PRINCE OF MARTIAL ARTS AND HE WANTS *YOU*, ELLE!
RUO M. ESCHUCK
YOU SAY RUO IS MY FIANCÉ.
TO ME, HE'S JUST AN OLD FRIEND.
I KNOW YOU AND YOUR RIVAL MADE SOME PROMISE...
...WAY BACK WHEN YOU WERE FIGHTING TOGETHER.
IT'S NOTHING TO DO WITH ME.

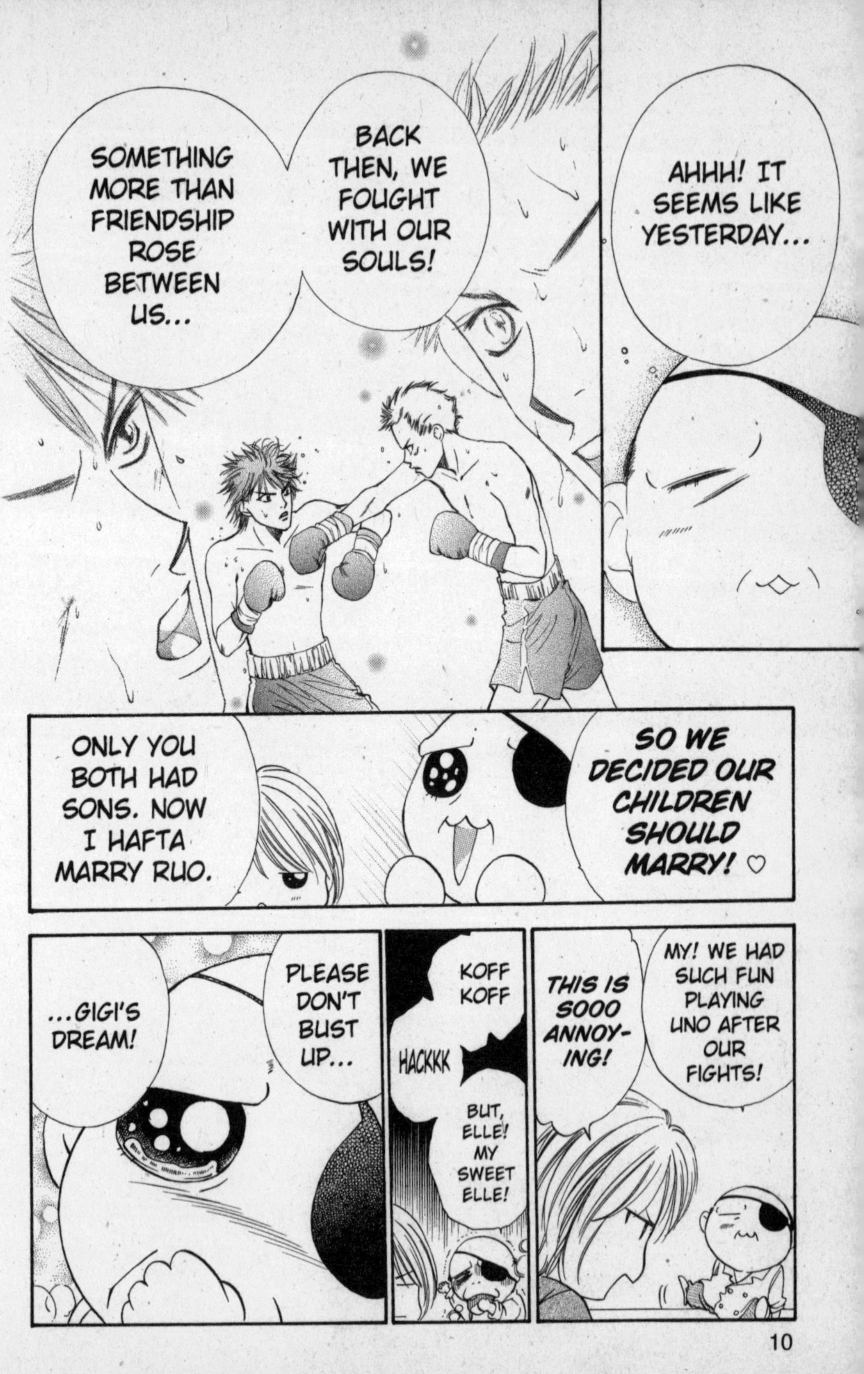
AHHH! IT SEEMS LIKE YESTERDAY...
BACK THEN, WE FOUGHT WITH OUR SOULS!
SOMETHING MORE THAN FRIENDSHIP ROSE BETWEEN US...
SO WE DECIDED OUR CHILDREN SHOULD MARRY! ♡
ONLY YOU BOTH HAD SONS. NOW I HAFTA MARRY RUO.
MY! WE HAD SUCH FUN PLAYING UNO AFTER OUR FIGHTS!
THIS IS SOOO ANNOY-ING!
KOFF KOFF
HACKKK
BUT, ELLE! MY SWEET ELLE!
PLEASE DON'T BUST UP...
...GIGI'S DREAM!

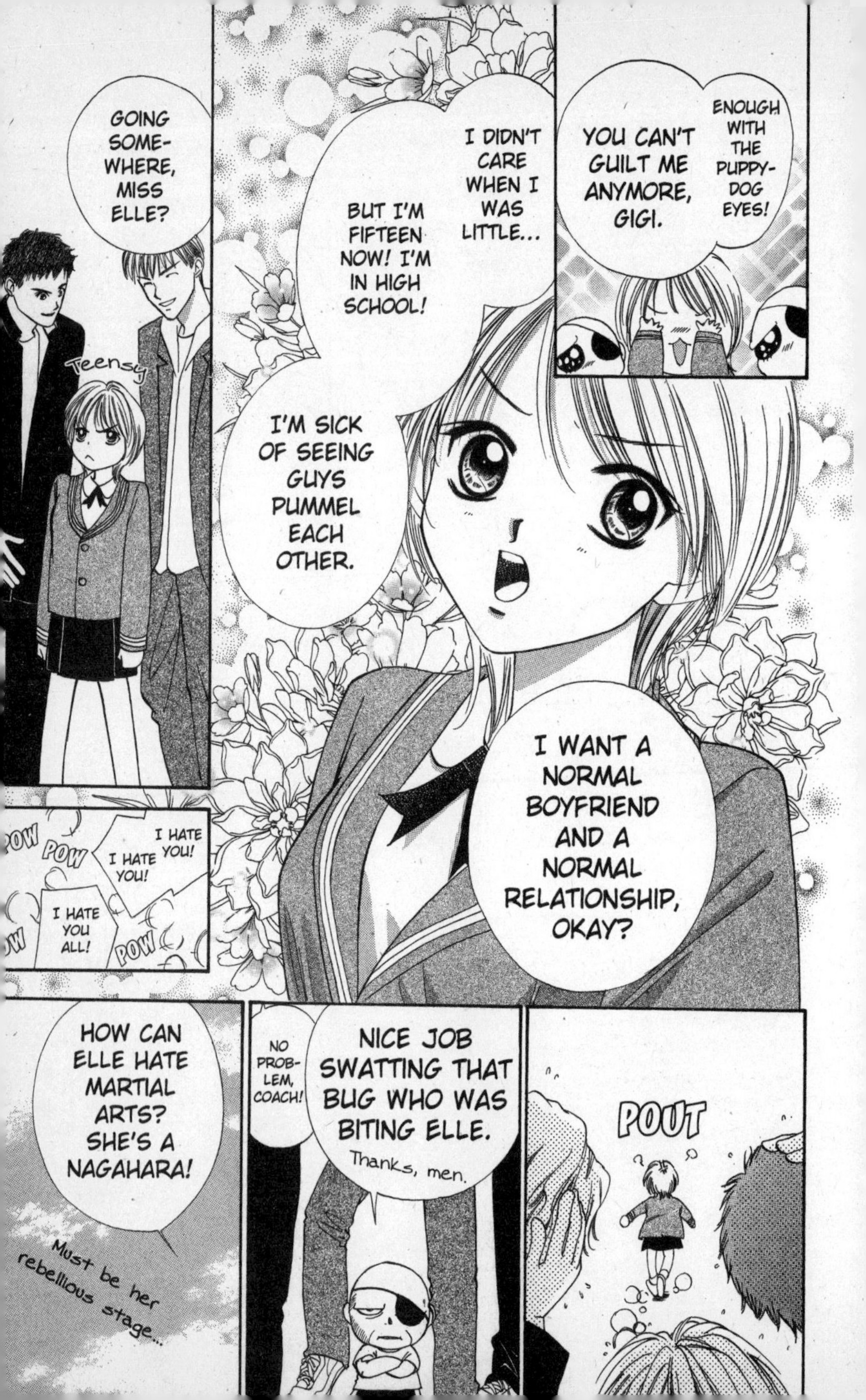
ENOUGH WITH THE PUPPY-DOG EYES!
YOU CAN'T GUILT ME ANYMORE, GIGI.
I DIDN'T CARE WHEN I WAS LITTLE...
BUT I'M FIFTEEN NOW! I'M IN HIGH SCHOOL!
I'M SICK OF SEEING GUYS PUMMEL EACH OTHER.
I WANT A NORMAL BOYFRIEND AND A NORMAL RELATIONSHIP, OKAY?
GOING SOME-WHERE, MISS ELLE?
Teensy
I HATE YOU!
I HATE YOU!
POW
POW
I HATE YOU ALL!
POW
POW
POUT
NICE JOB SWATTING THAT BUG WHO WAS BITING ELLE.
Thanks, men.
NO PROB-LEM, COACH!
HOW CAN ELLE HATE MARTIAL ARTS? SHE'S A NAGAHARA!
Must be her rebellious stage...

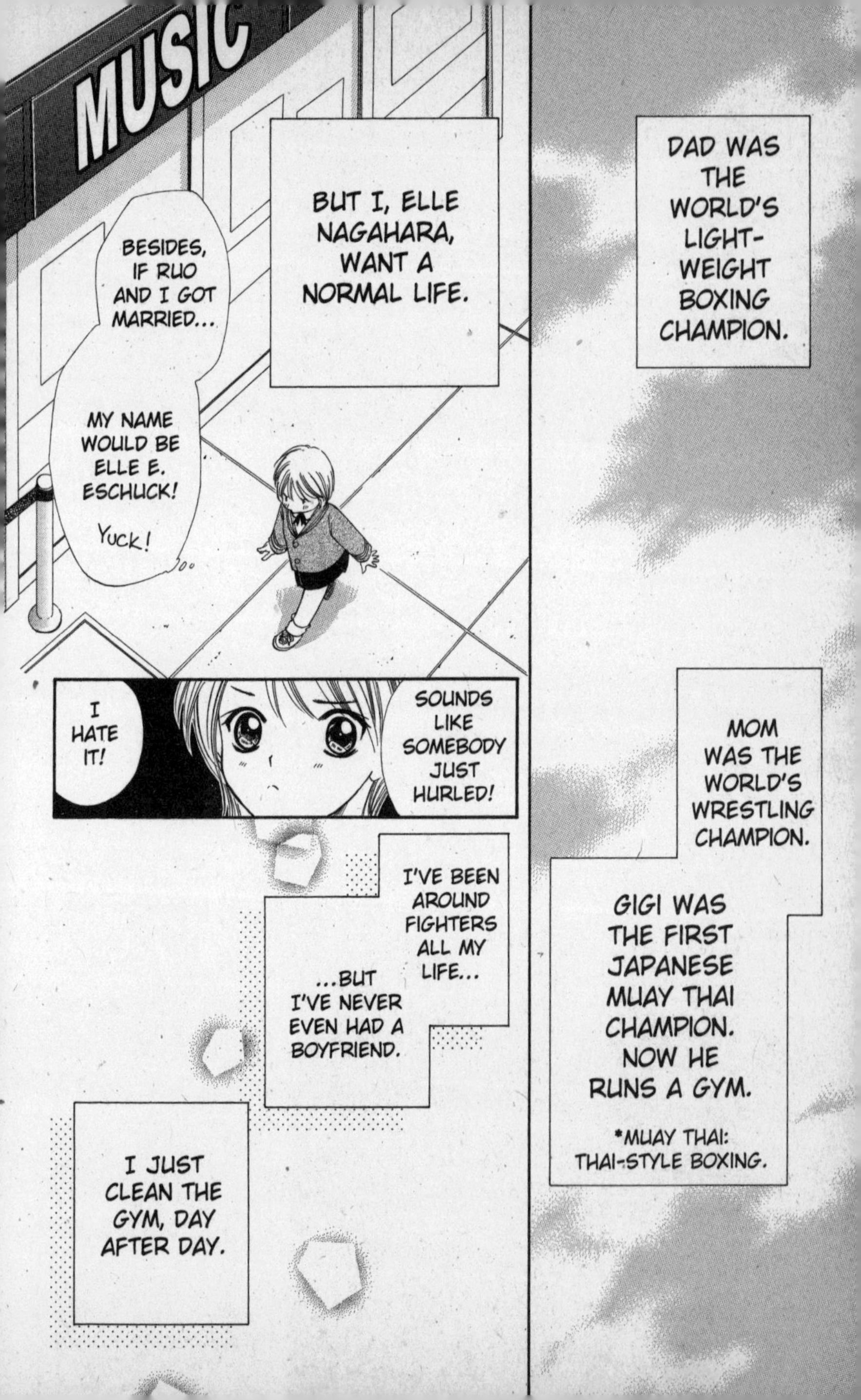
DAD WAS THE WORLD'S LIGHT-WEIGHT BOXING CHAMPION.
MOM WAS THE WORLD'S WRESTLING CHAMPION.
GIGI WAS THE FIRST JAPANESE MUAY THAI CHAMPION. NOW HE RUNS A GYM.
*MUAY THAI: THAI-STYLE BOXING.
MUSIC
BUT I, ELLE NAGAHARA, WANT A NORMAL LIFE.
BESIDES, IF RUO AND I GOT MARRIED...
MY NAME WOULD BE ELLE E. ESCHUCK!
YUCK!
SOUNDS LIKE SOMEBODY JUST HURLED!
I HATE IT!
I'VE BEEN AROUND FIGHTERS ALL MY LIFE...
...BUT I'VE NEVER EVEN HAD A BOYFRIEND.
I JUST CLEAN THE GYM, DAY AFTER DAY.

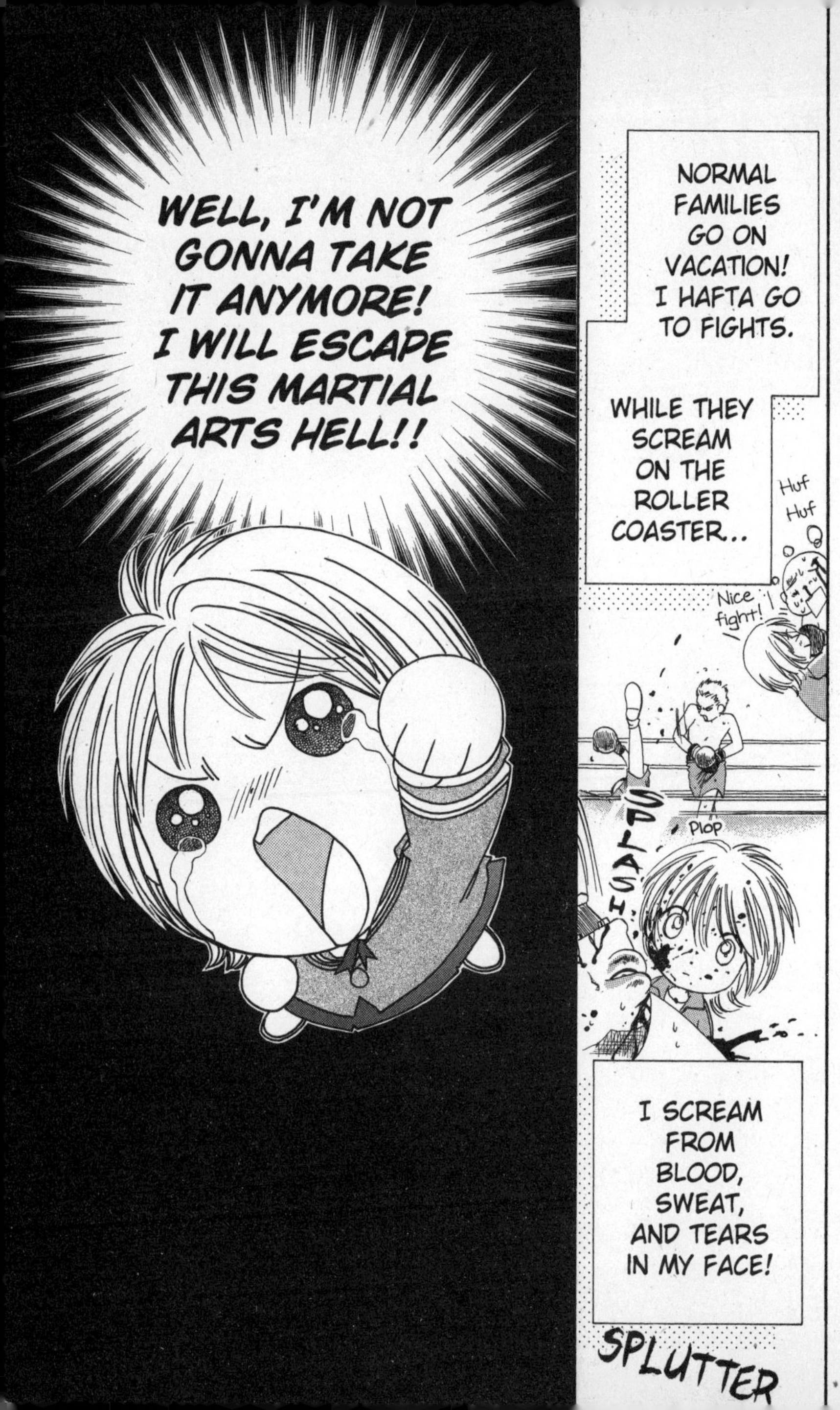
NORMAL FAMILIES GO ON VACATION! I HAFTA GO TO FIGHTS.
WHILE THEY SCREAM ON THE ROLLER COASTER...
Huf Huf
Nice fight!
SPLASH
Plop
I SCREAM FROM BLOOD, SWEAT, AND TEARS IN MY FACE!
SPLUTTER
WELL, I'M NOT GONNA TAKE IT ANYMORE! I WILL ESCAPE THIS MARTIAL ARTS HELL!!

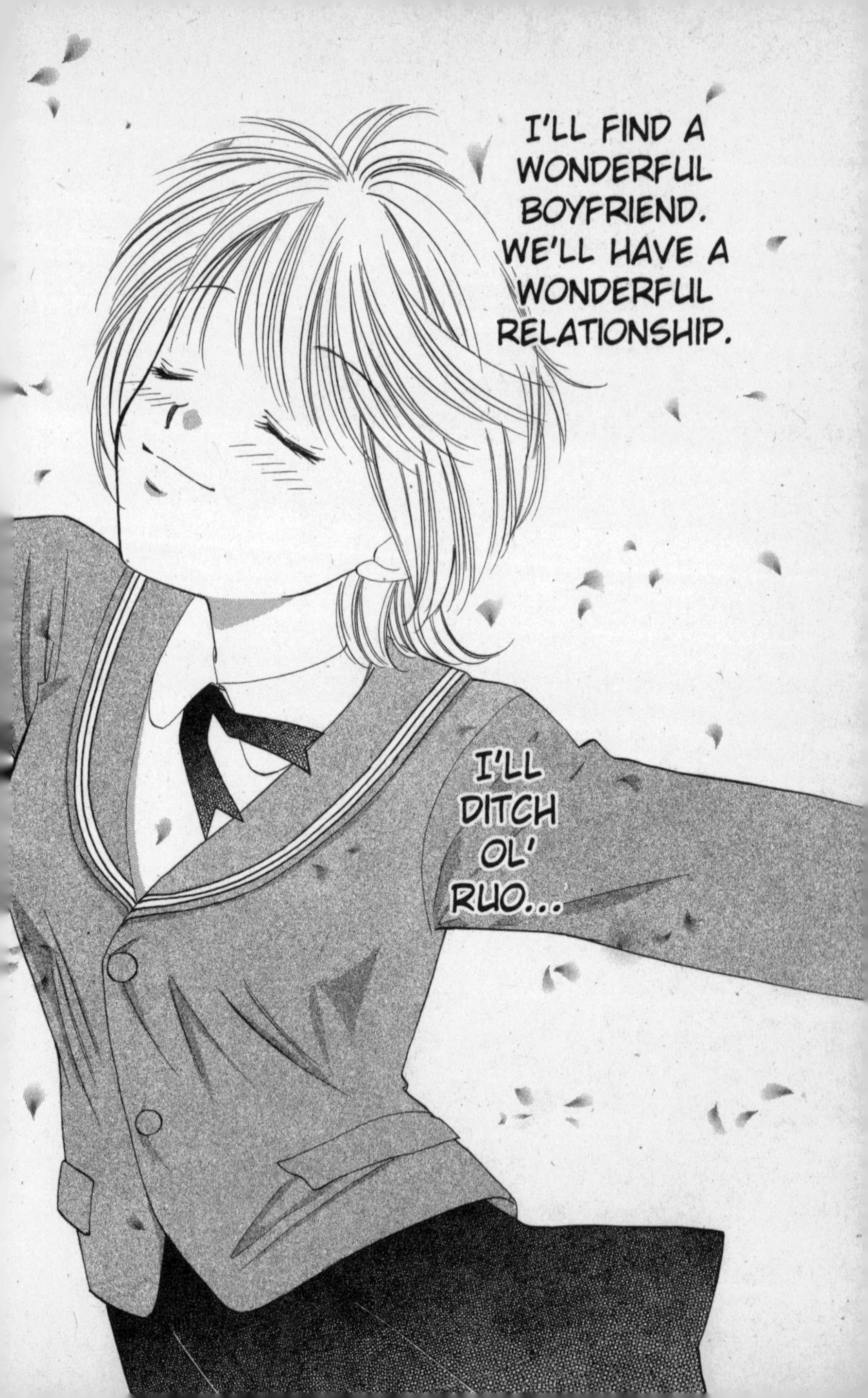
I'LL FIND A WONDERFUL BOYFRIEND. WE'LL HAVE A WONDERFUL RELATIONSHIP.
I'LL DITCH OL' RUO...

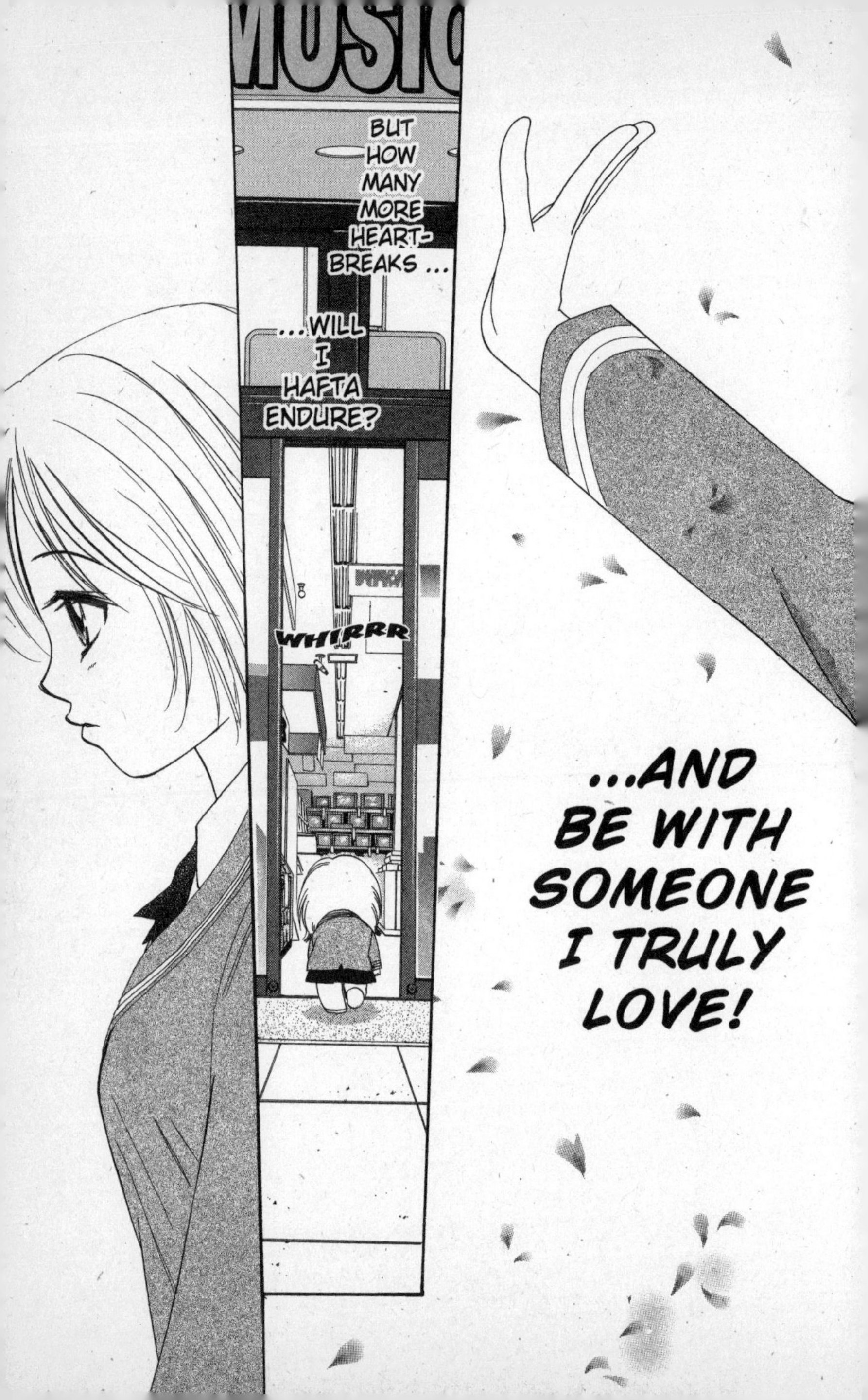
MUSIC
BUT HOW MANY MORE HEART-BREAKS ...
... WILL I HAFTA ENDURE?
WHIRRR
...AND BE WITH SOMEONE I TRULY LOVE!

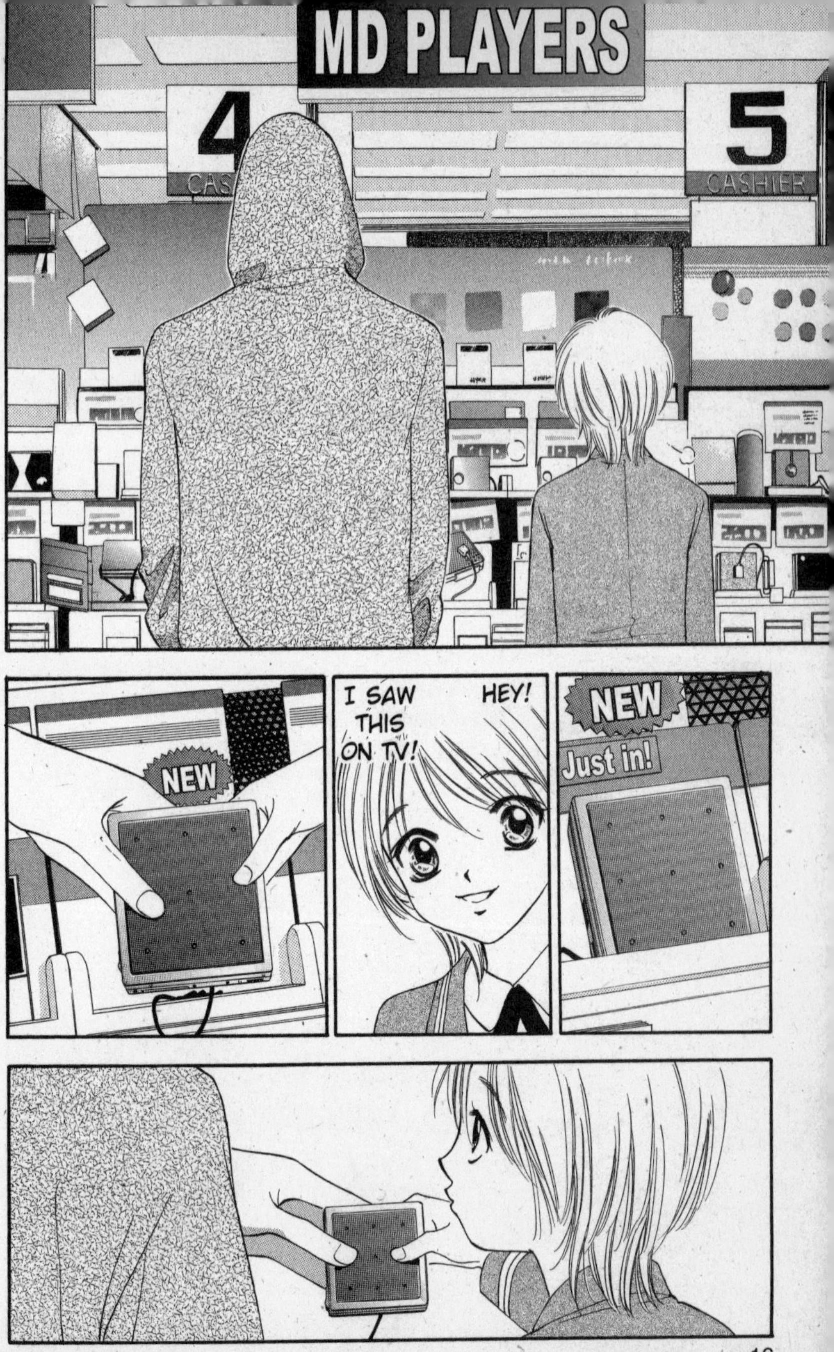
MD PLAYERS
4
5
CASHIER
NEW
Just in!
HEY!
I SAW THIS ON TV!
NEW

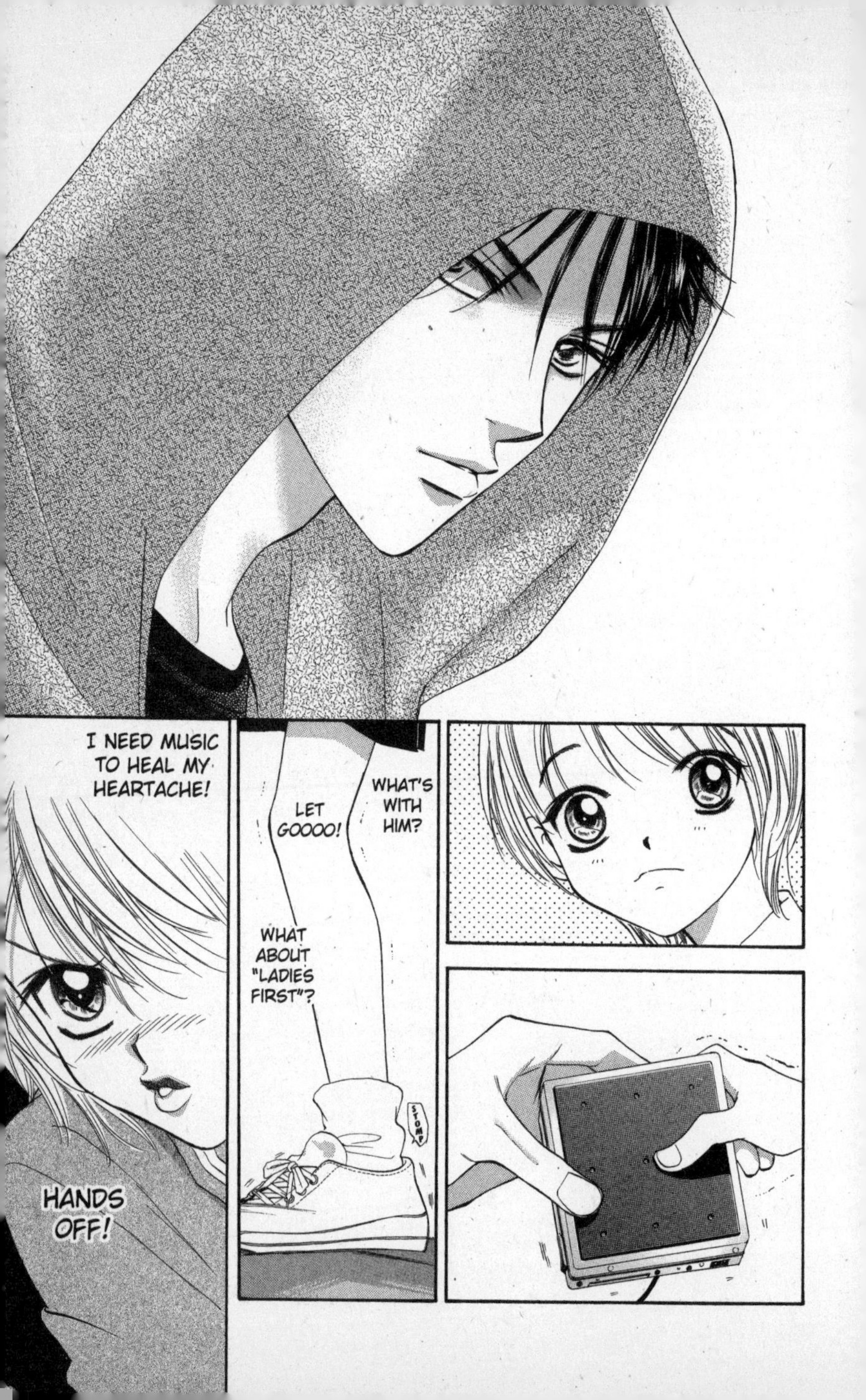
WHAT'S WITH HIM?
LET GOOOO!
WHAT ABOUT "LADIES FIRST"?
STOMP
I NEED MUSIC TO HEAL MY HEARTACHE!
HANDS OFF!

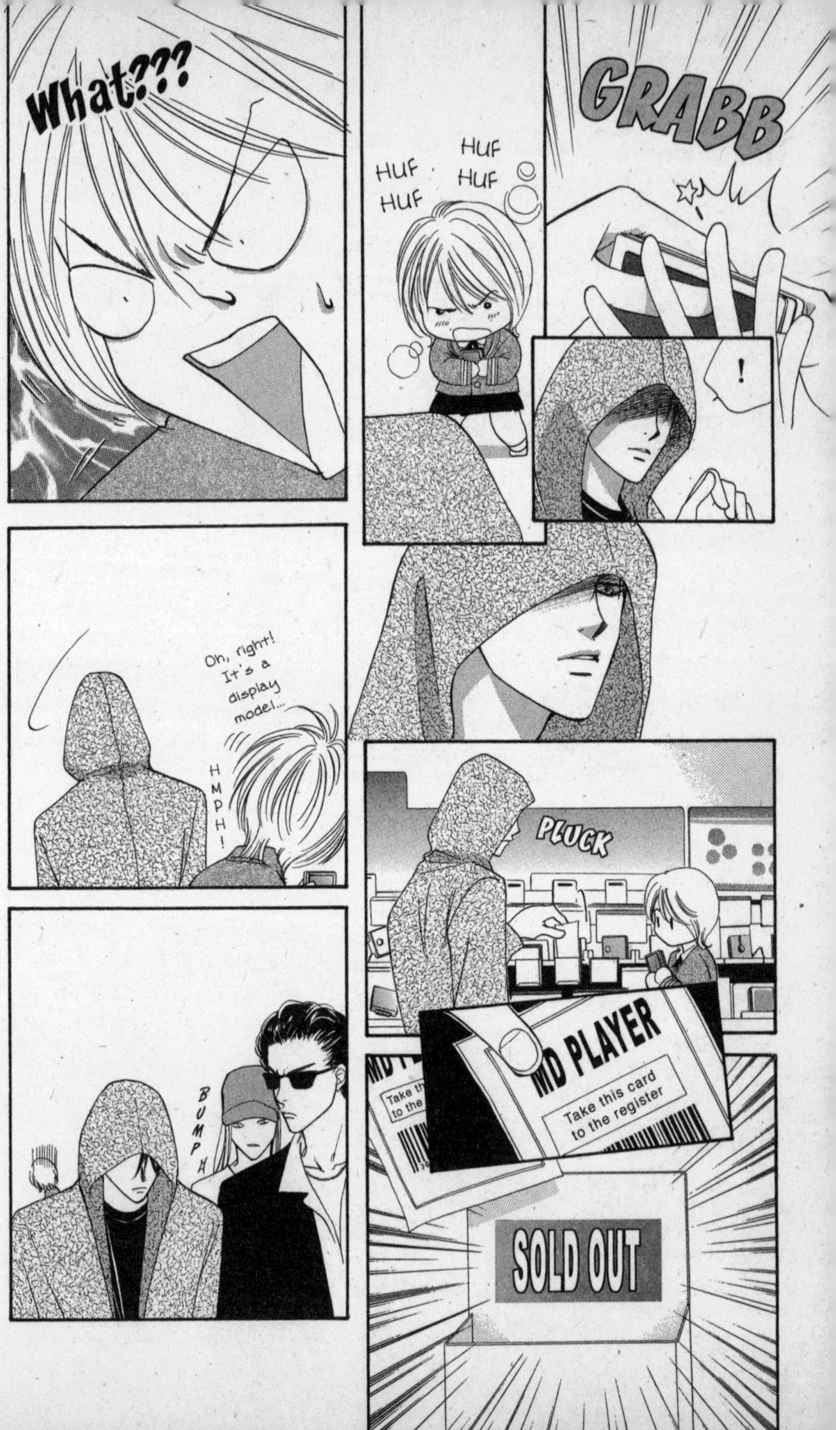
GRABB
!
HUF HUF HUF HUF
What???
Oh, right! It's a display model...
HMPH!
PLUCK
MD PLAYER
Take this card to the register
SOLD OUT
BUMP

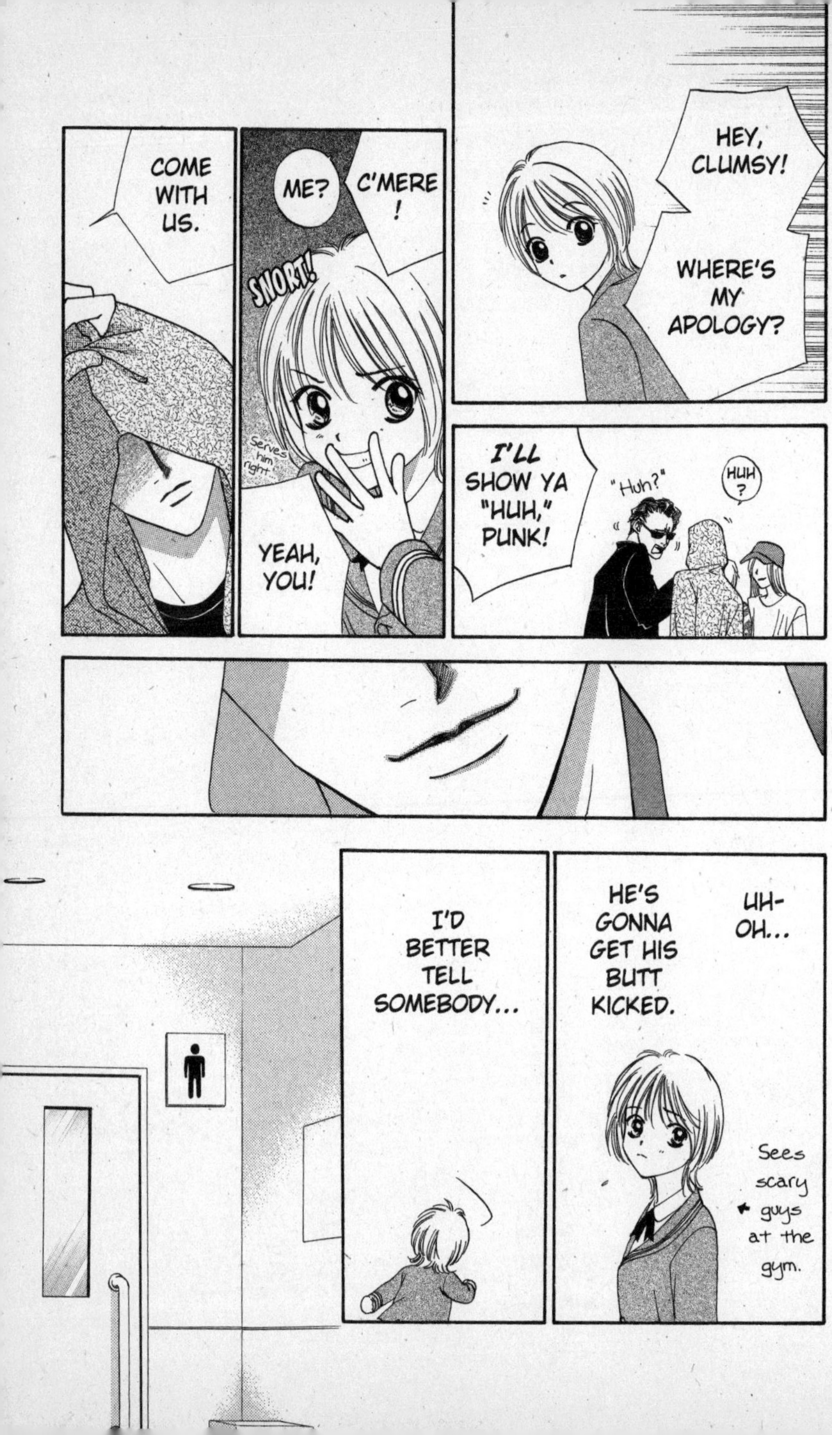
HEY, CLUMSY!
WHERE'S MY APOLOGY?
I'LL SHOW YA "HUH," PUNK!
"Huh?"
HUH?
C'MERE!
ME?
SNORT!
Serves him right...
YEAH, YOU!
COME WITH US.
UH-OH...
HE'S GONNA GET HIS BUTT KICKED.
Sees scary guys at the gym.
I'D BETTER TELL SOMEBODY...

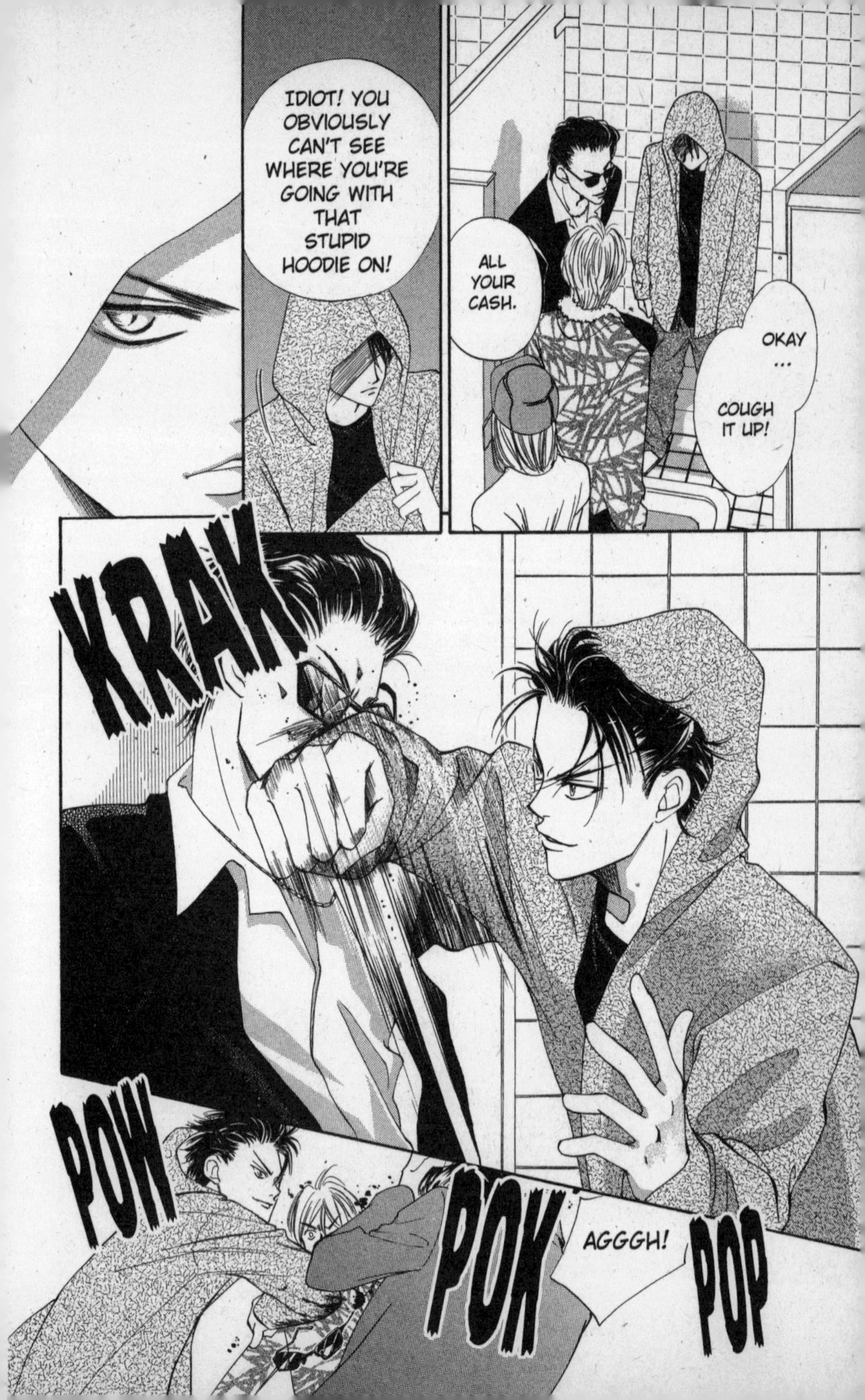
ALL YOUR CASH.
OKAY ... COUGH IT UP!
IDIOT! YOU OBVIOUSLY CAN'T SEE WHERE YOU'RE GOING WITH THAT STUPID HOODIE ON!
KRAK
POP
AGGGH!
POK
POW

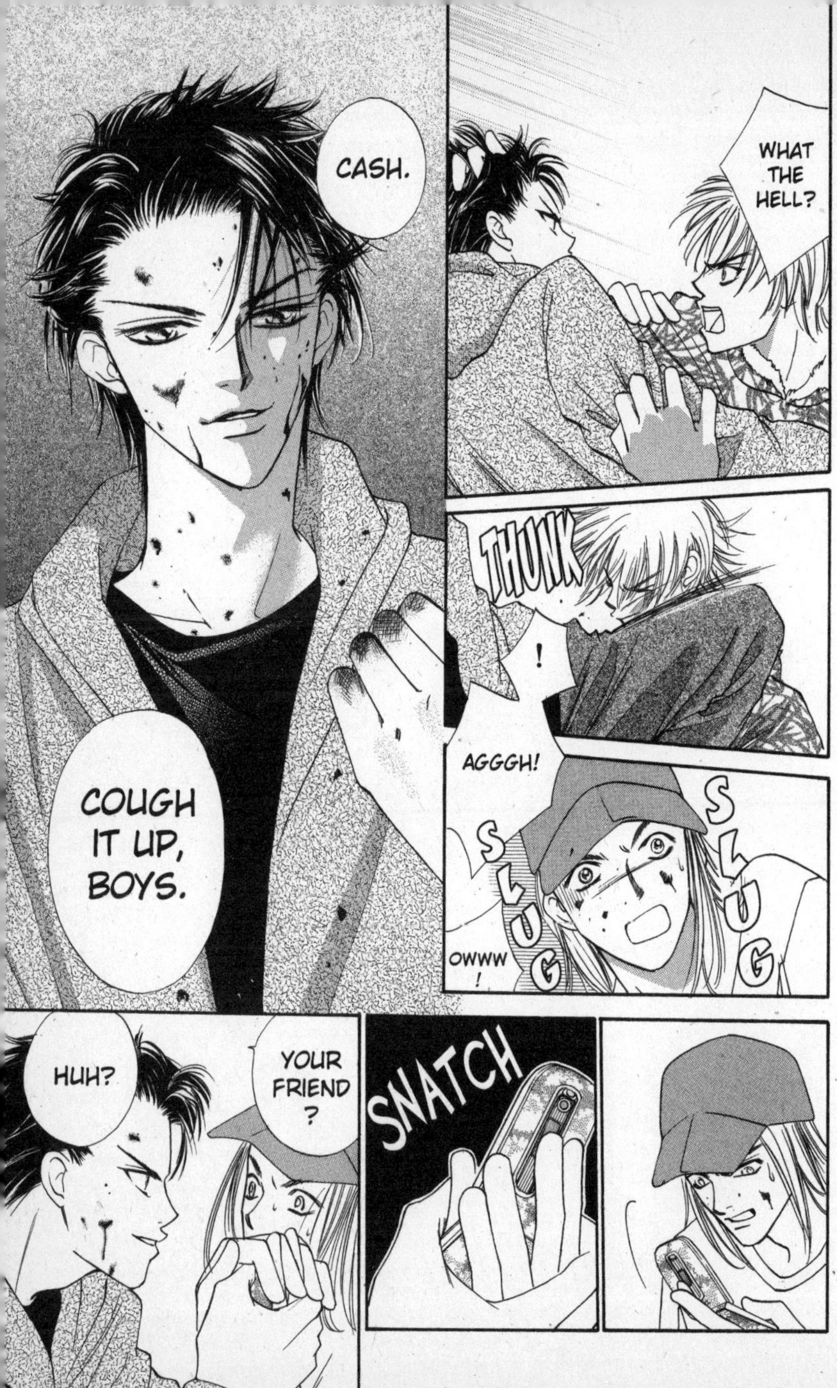
WHAT THE HELL?
THUNK
!
AGGGH!
SLUG SLUG
OWWW!
CASH.
COUGH IT UP, BOYS.
SNATCH
YOUR FRIEND?
HUH?

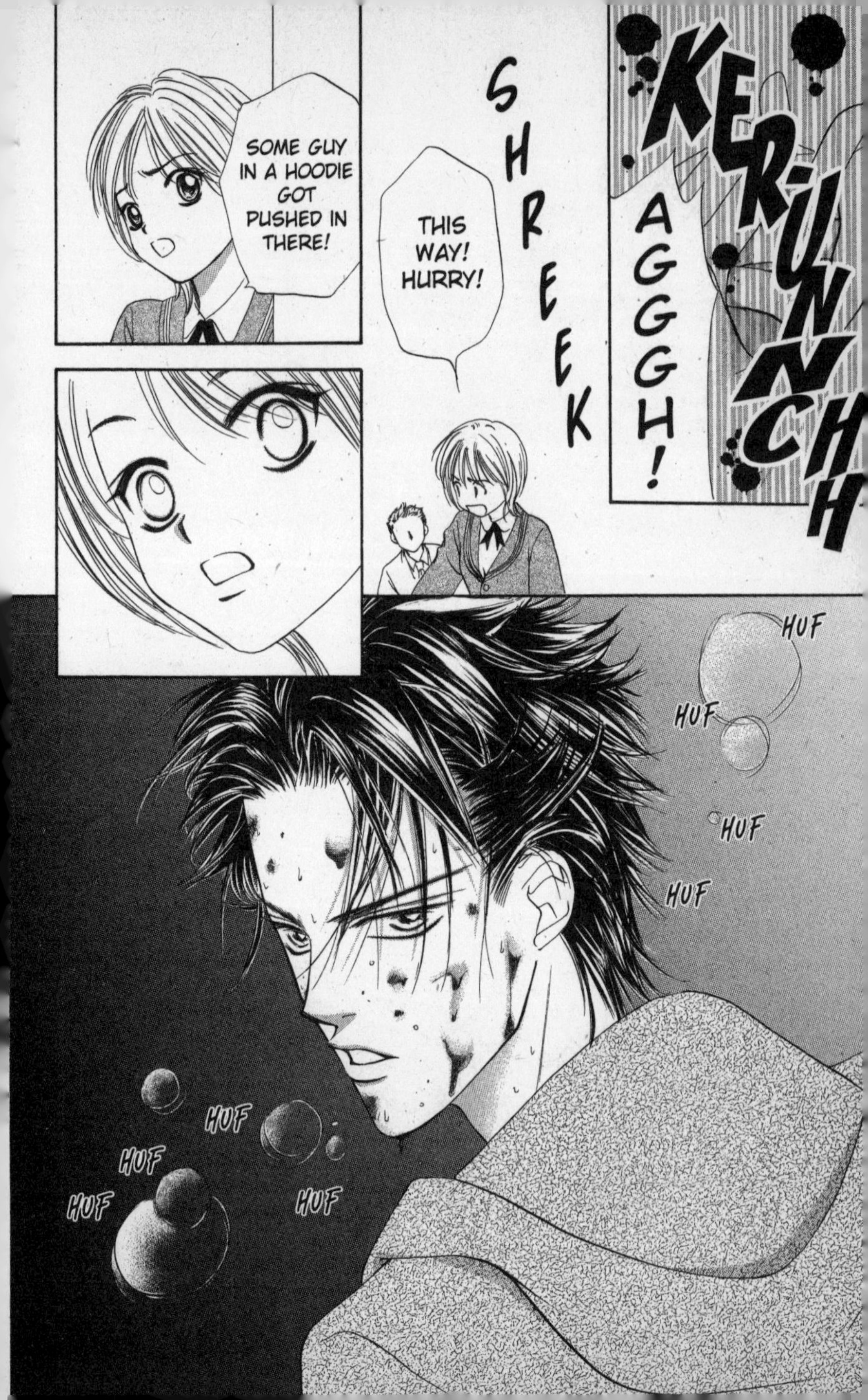
KER-RUNCHH
AGGGH!
SHREEK
THIS WAY! HURRY!
SOME GUY IN A HOODIE GOT PUSHED IN THERE!
HUF
HUF
HUF
HUF
HUF
HUF
HUF
HUF

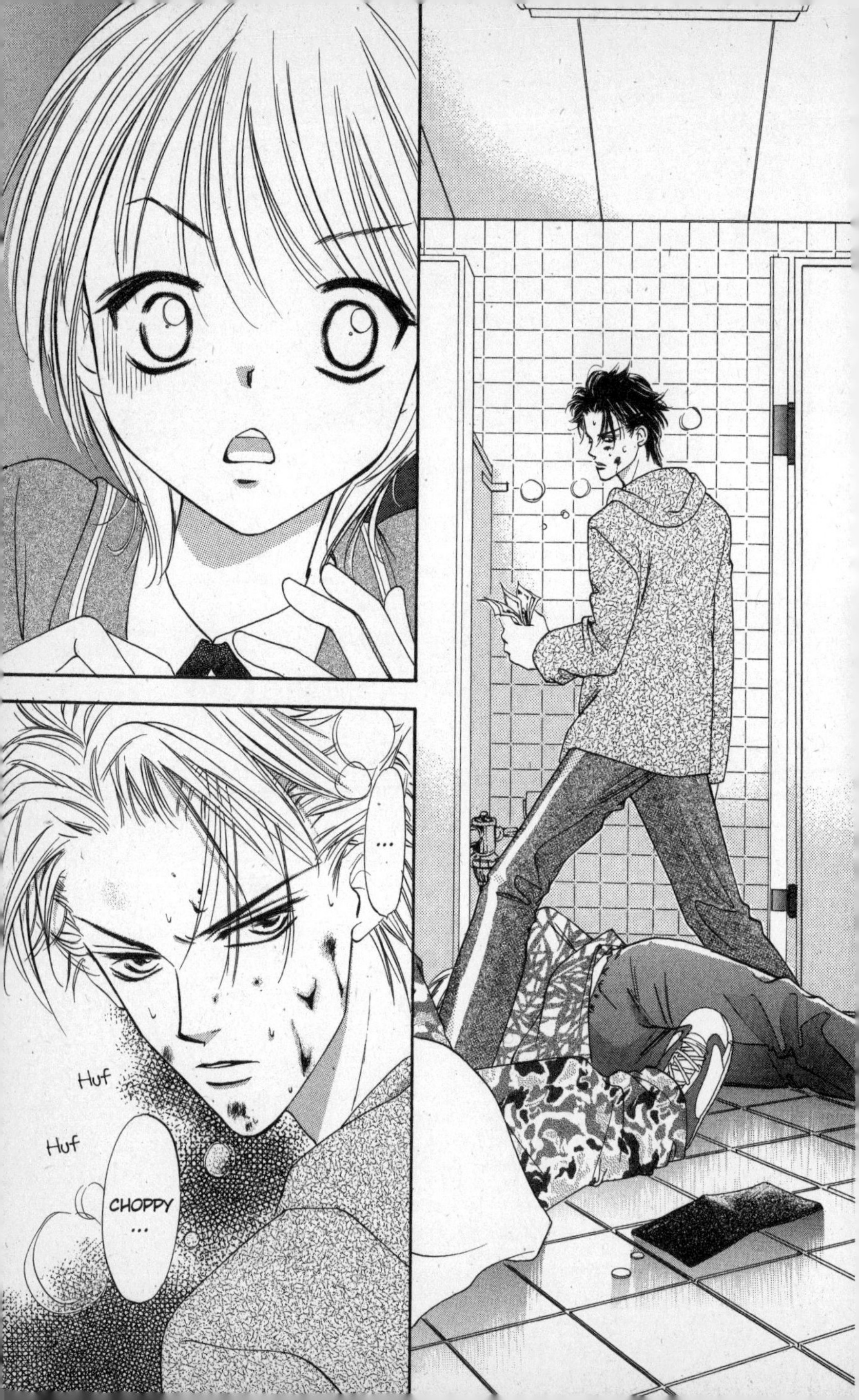
...
Huf
Huf
CHOPPY ...

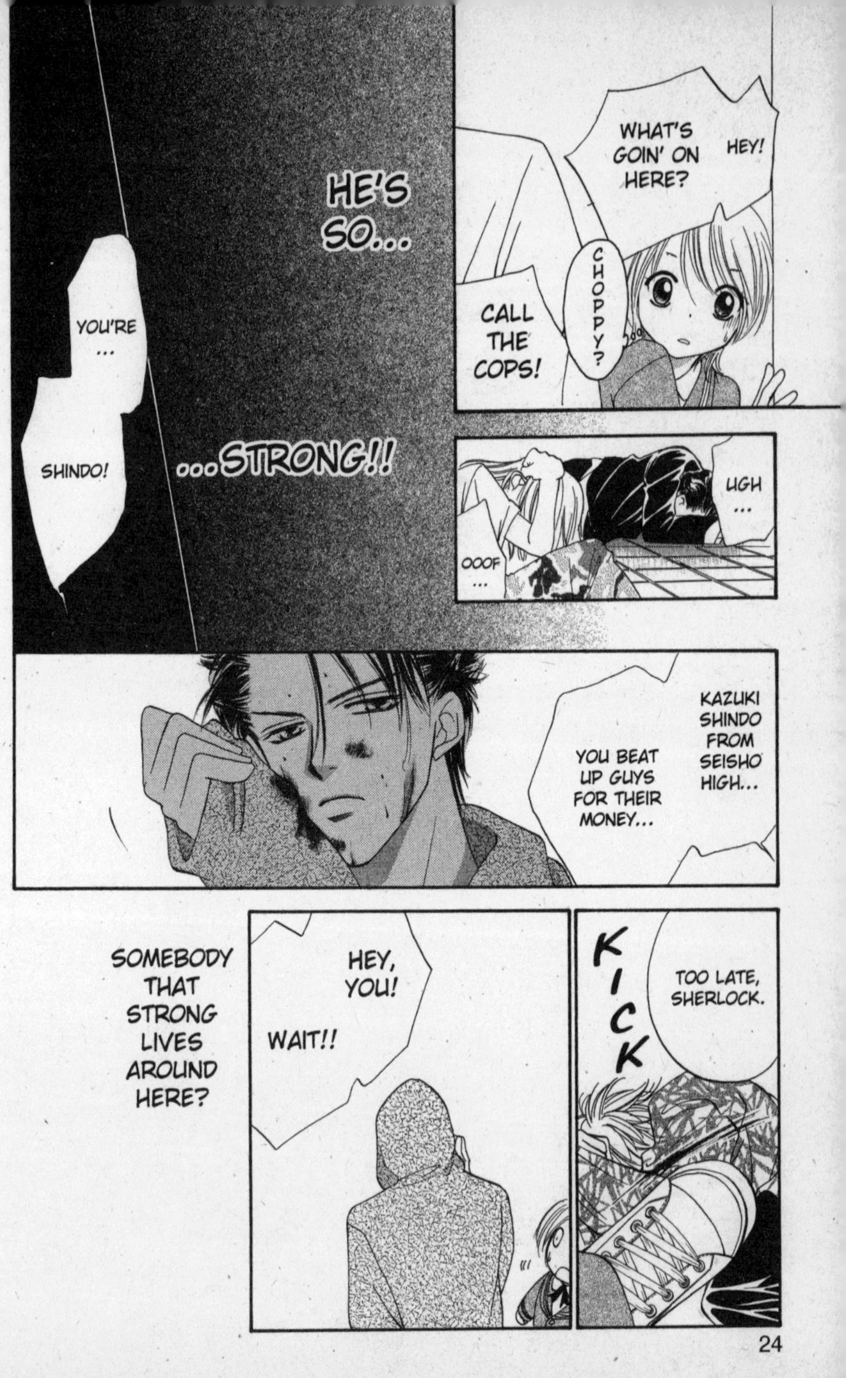
HEY!
WHAT'S GOIN' ON HERE?
CHOPPY?
CALL THE COPS!
UGH...
OOOF...
HE'S SO...
...STRONG!!
YOU'RE... SHINDO!
KAZUKI SHINDO FROM SEISHO HIGH...
YOU BEAT UP GUYS FOR THEIR MONEY...
TOO LATE, SHERLOCK.
KICK
HEY, YOU!
WAIT!!
SOMEBODY THAT STRONG LIVES AROUND HERE?

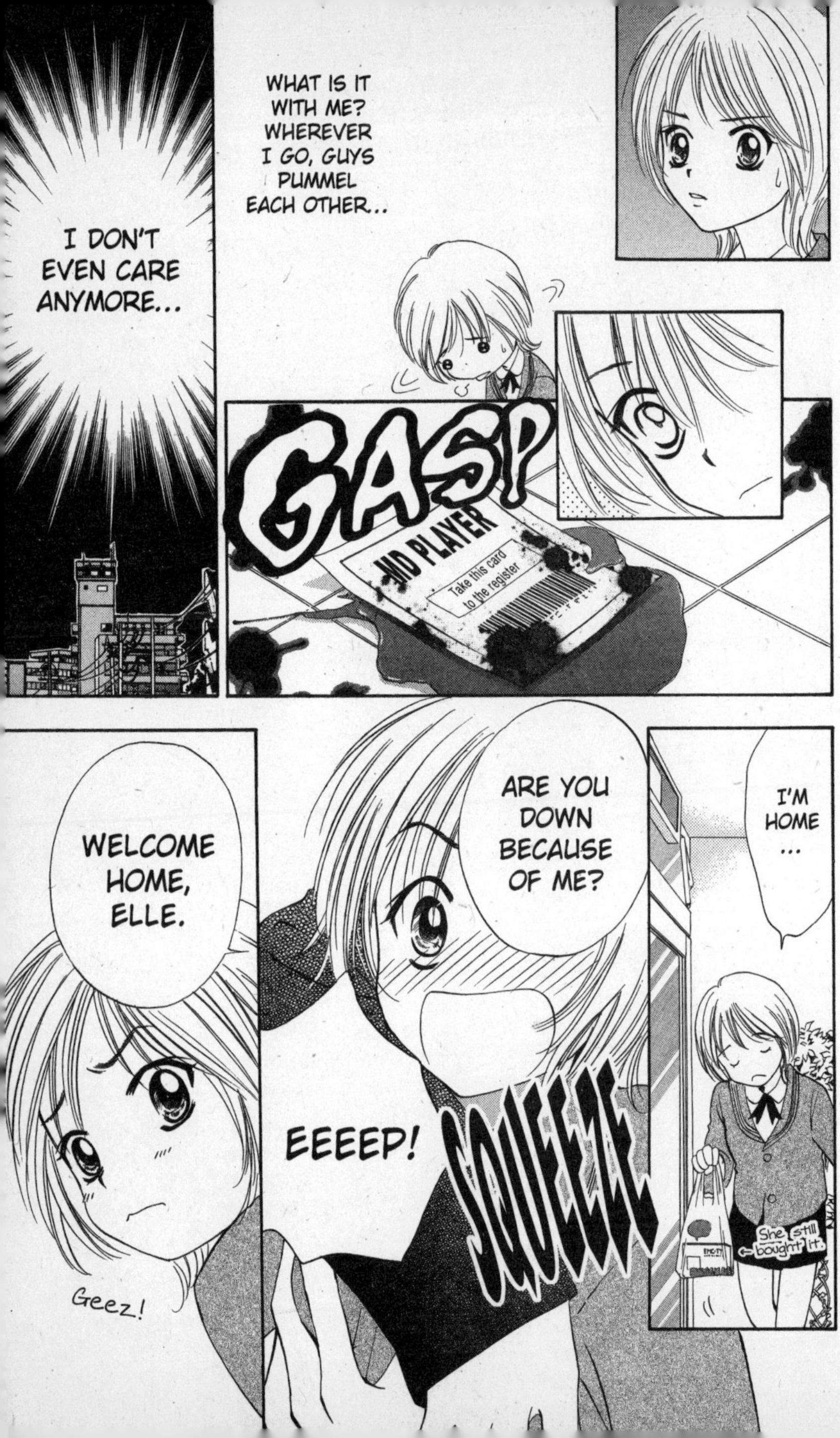

WHAT IS IT WITH ME? WHEREVER I GO, GUYS PUMMEL EACH OTHER...
GASP
MD PLAYER
Take this card to the register
I DON'T EVEN CARE ANYMORE...
I'M HOME...
She still bought it.
ARE YOU DOWN BECAUSE OF ME?
SQUEEZE
EEEEP!
WELCOME HOME, ELLE.
Geez!

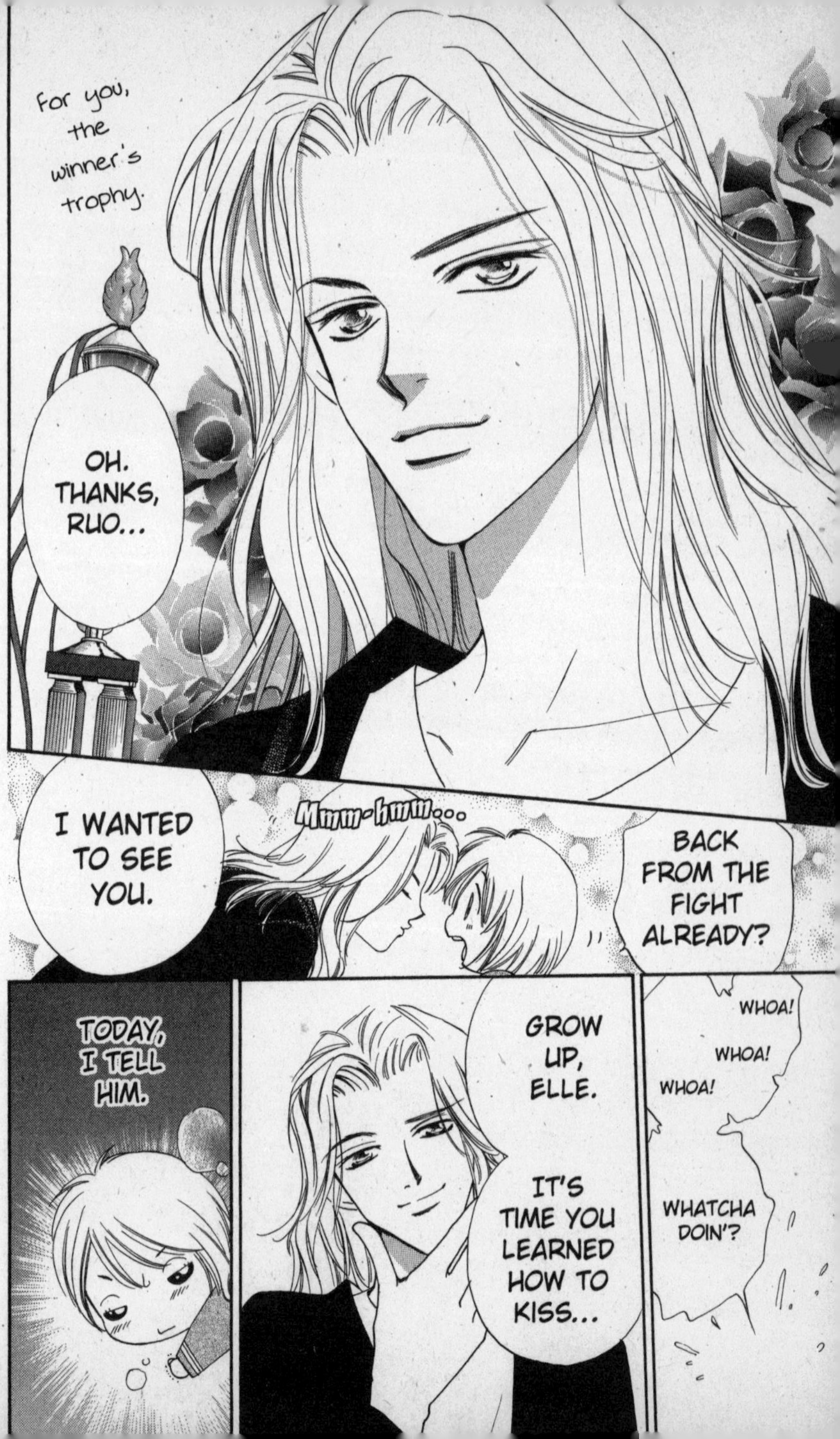
For you, the winner's trophy.
OH. THANKS, RUO...
BACK FROM THE FIGHT ALREADY?
Mmm-hmm...
I WANTED TO SEE YOU.
WHOA!
WHOA!
WHOA!
WHATCHA DOIN'?
GROW UP, ELLE.
IT'S TIME YOU LEARNED HOW TO KISS...
TODAY, I TELL HIM.

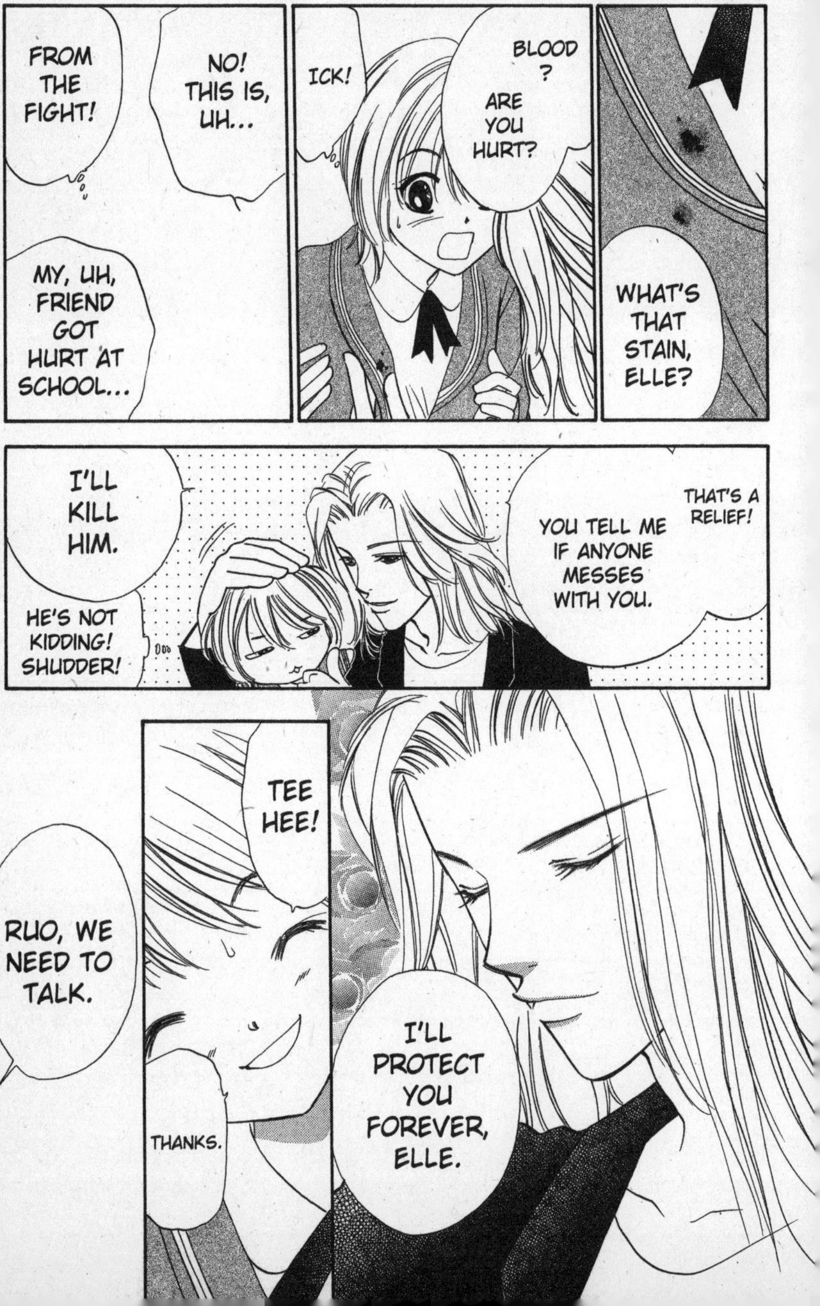
WHAT'S THAT STAIN, ELLE?
BLOOD? ARE YOU HURT?
ICK!
NO! THIS IS, UH...
FROM THE FIGHT!
MY, UH, FRIEND GOT HURT AT SCHOOL...
YOU TELL ME IF ANYONE MESSES WITH YOU.
THAT'S A RELIEF!
I'LL KILL HIM.
HE'S NOT KIDDING! SHUDDER!
I'LL PROTECT YOU FOREVER, ELLE.
TEE HEE!
THANKS.
RUO, WE NEED TO TALK.

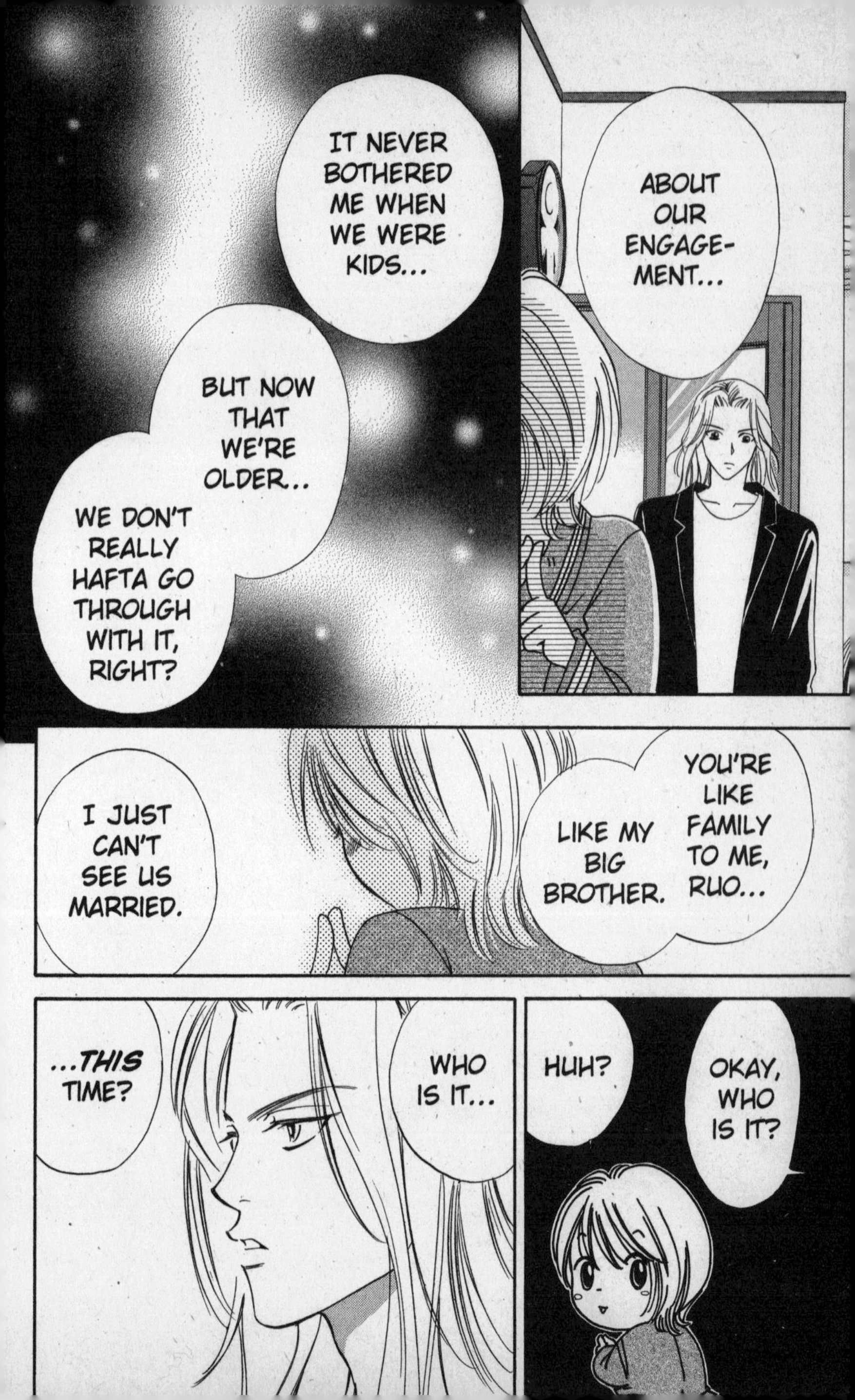
ABOUT OUR ENGAGEMENT...
IT NEVER BOTHERED ME WHEN WE WERE KIDS...
BUT NOW THAT WE'RE OLDER..
WE DON'T REALLY HAFTA GO THROUGH WITH IT, RIGHT?
YOU'RE LIKE FAMILY TO ME, RUO...
LIKE MY BIG BROTHER.
I JUST CAN'T SEE US MARRIED.
OKAY, WHO IS IT?
HUH?
WHO IS IT...
...*THIS* TIME?

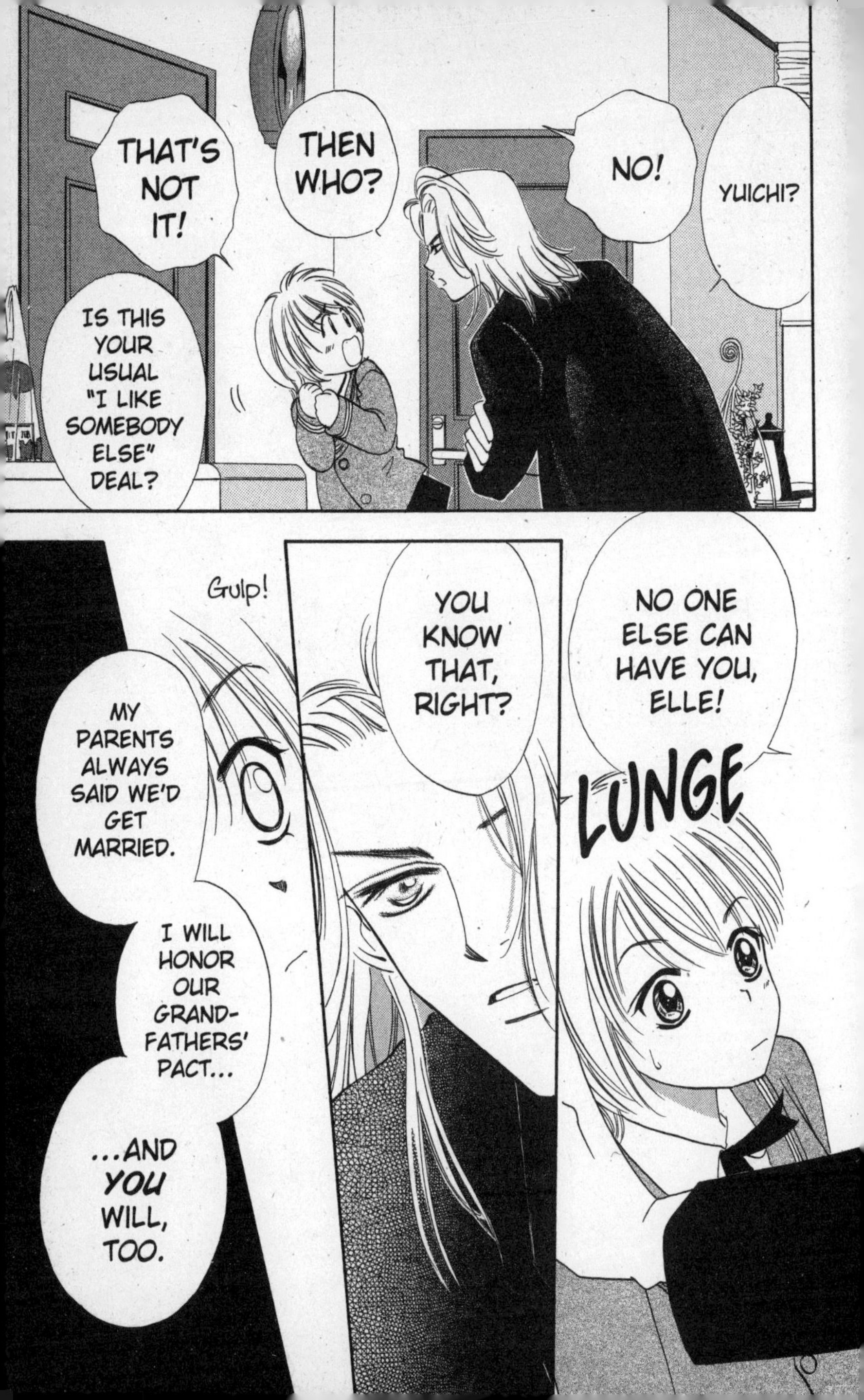
YUICHI?
NO!
THEN WHO?
THAT'S NOT IT!
IS THIS YOUR USUAL "I LIKE SOMEBODY ELSE" DEAL?
NO ONE ELSE CAN HAVE YOU, ELLE!
LUNGE
YOU KNOW THAT, RIGHT?
Gulp!
MY PARENTS ALWAYS SAID WE'D GET MARRIED.
I WILL HONOR OUR GRAND-FATHERS' PACT...
...AND *YOU* WILL, TOO.

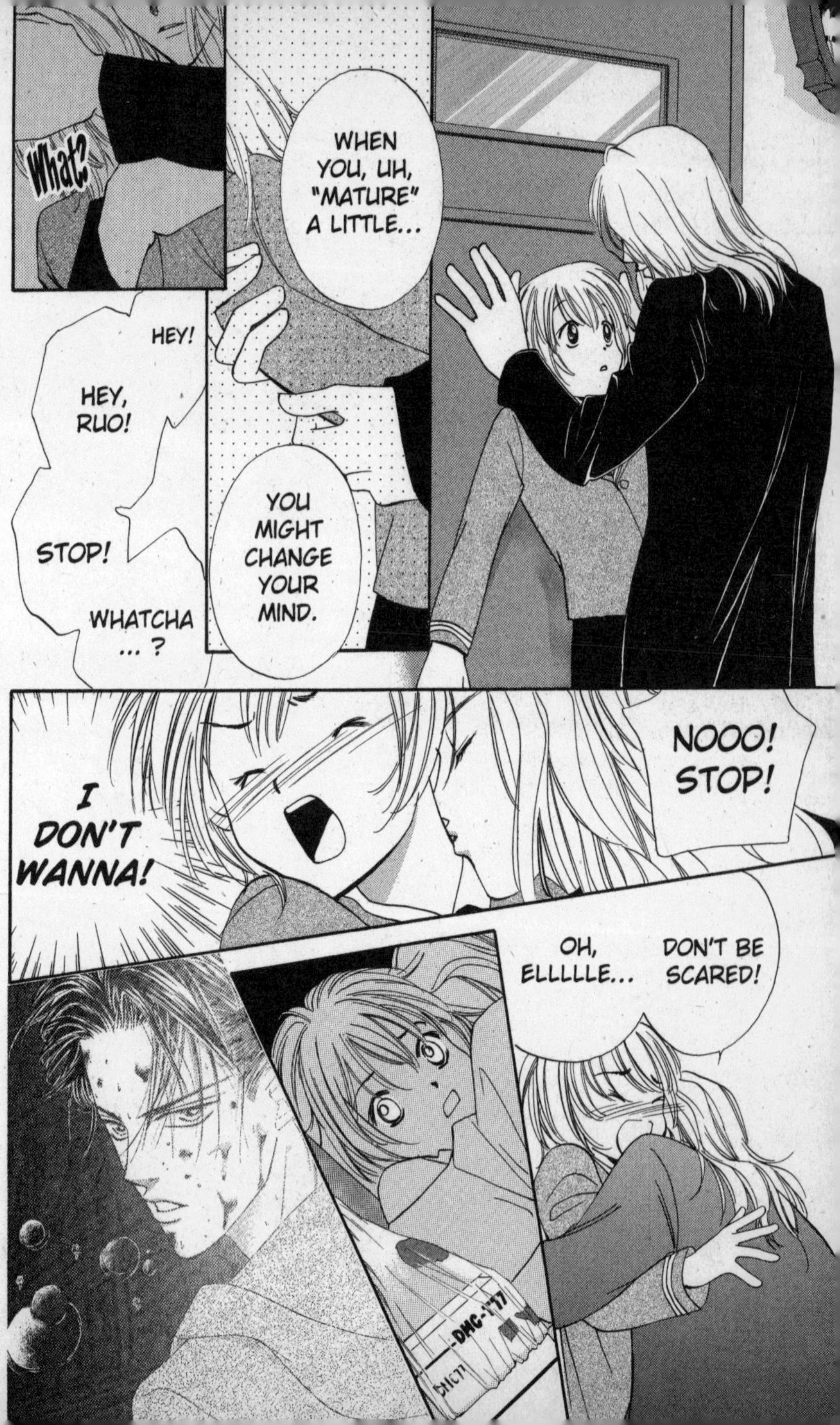
WHEN YOU, UH, "MATURE" A LITTLE...
YOU MIGHT CHANGE YOUR MIND.
What?
HEY!
HEY, RUO!
STOP!
WHATCHA ... ?
NOOO! STOP!
I DON'T WANNA!
OH, ELLLLLE... DON'T BE SCARED!
DMC-177

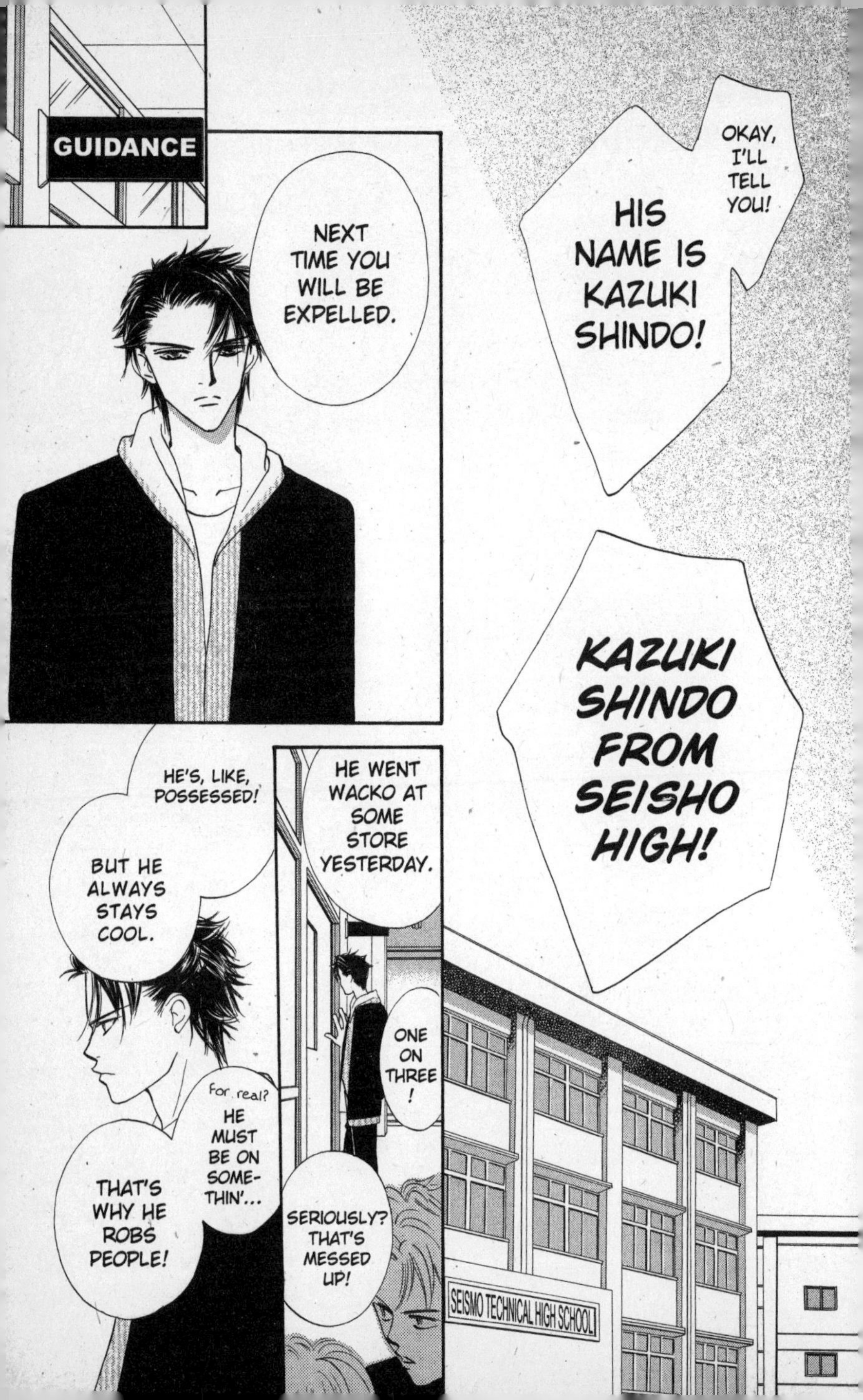
OKAY, I'LL TELL YOU!
HIS NAME IS KAZUKI SHINDO!
KAZUKI SHINDO FROM SEISHO HIGH!
SEISMO TECHNICAL HIGH SCHOOL
GUIDANCE
NEXT TIME YOU WILL BE EXPELLED.
HE WENT WACKO AT SOME STORE YESTERDAY.
ONE ON THREE!
SERIOUSLY? THAT'S MESSED UP!
HE'S, LIKE, POSSESSED!
BUT HE ALWAYS STAYS COOL.
For real?
HE MUST BE ON SOME-THIN'...
THAT'S WHY HE ROBS PEOPLE!

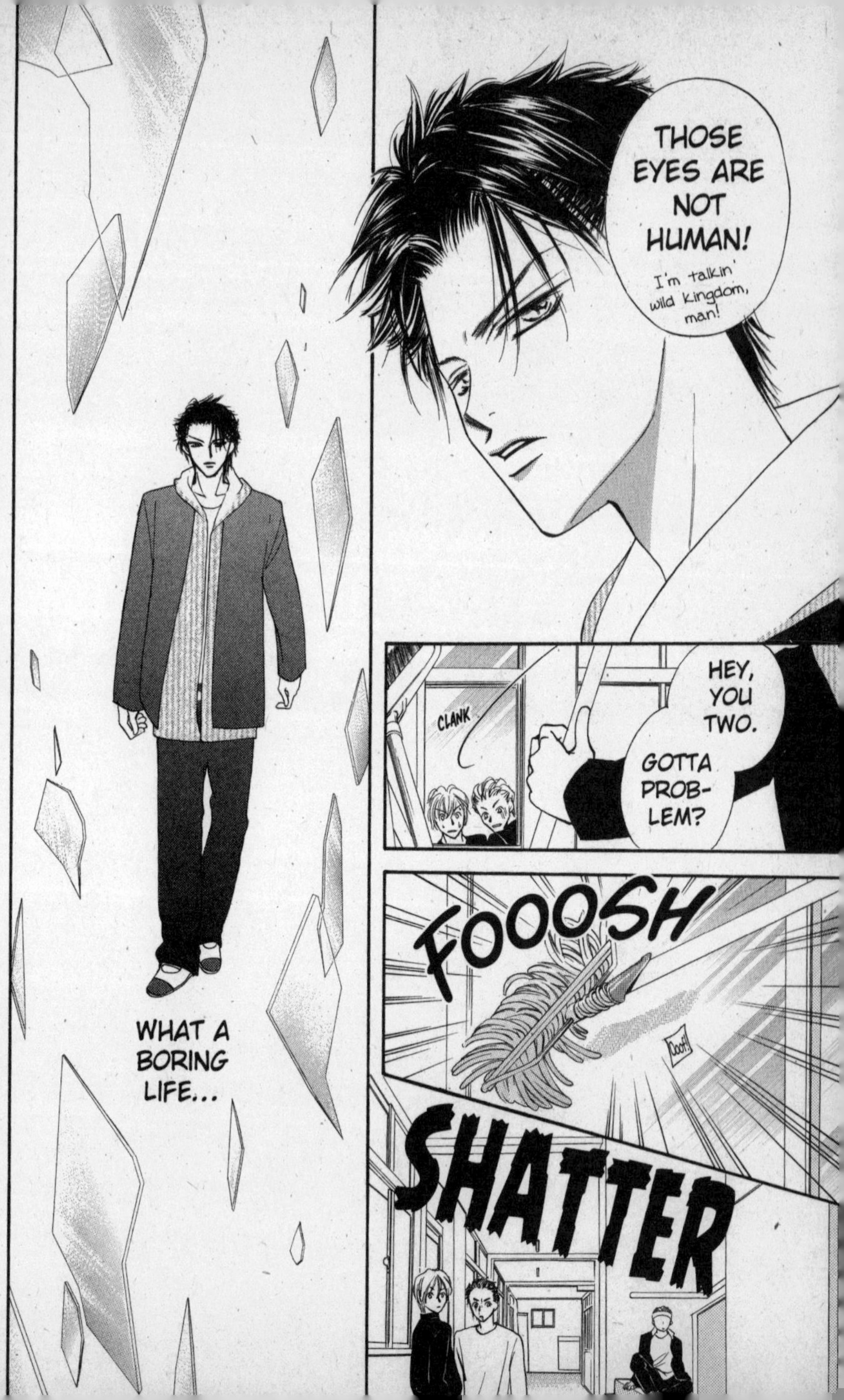
THOSE EYES ARE NOT HUMAN!
I'm talkin' wild kingdom, man!
CLANK
HEY, YOU TWO.
GOTTA PROB-LEM?
FOOOSH
Oof!
SHATTER
WHAT A BORING LIFE...

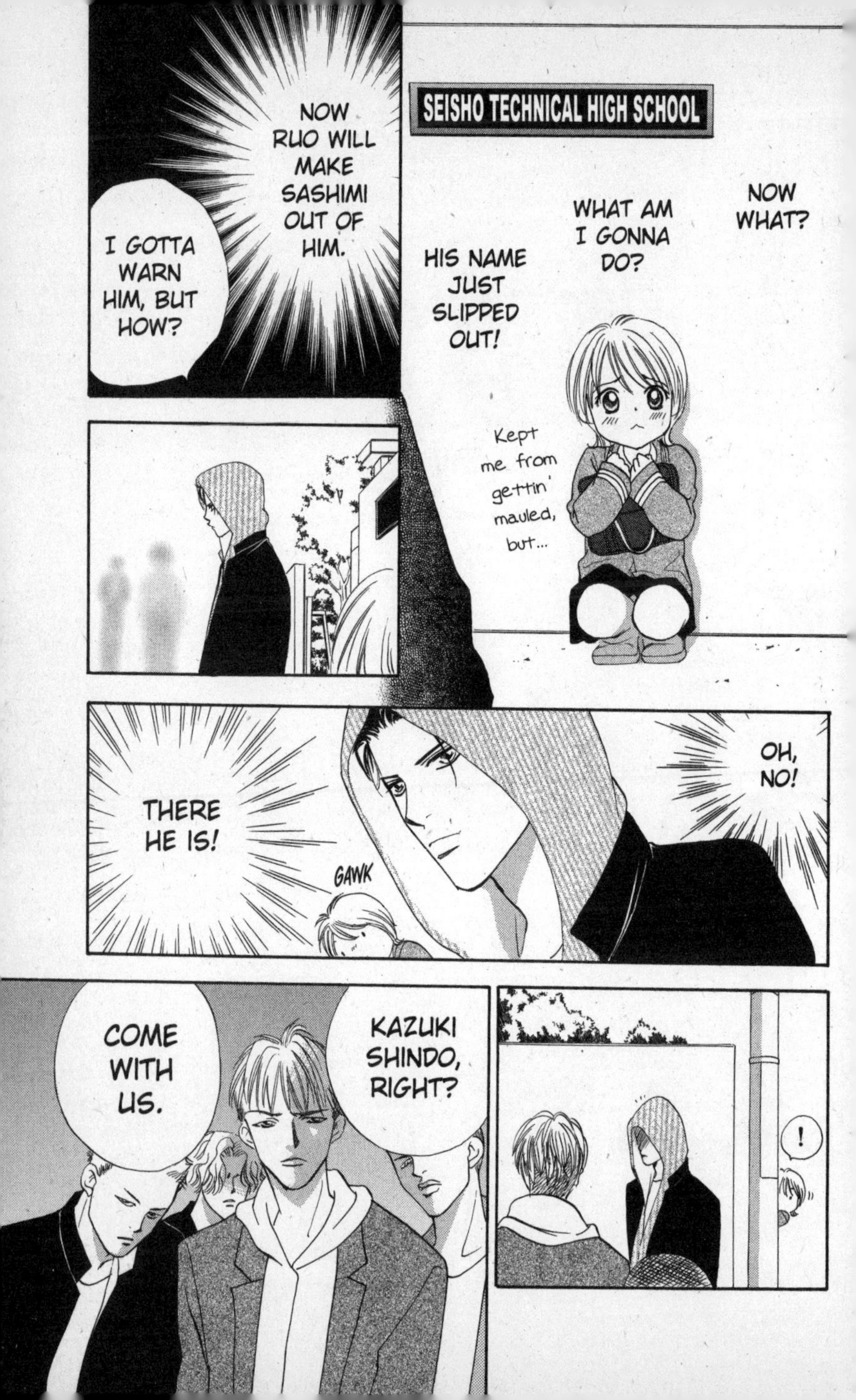
SEISHO TECHNICAL HIGH SCHOOL
NOW WHAT?
WHAT AM I GONNA DO?
HIS NAME JUST SLIPPED OUT!
Kept me from gettin' mauled, but...
NOW RUO WILL MAKE SASHIMI OUT OF HIM.
I GOTTA WARN HIM, BUT HOW?
OH, NO!
THERE HE IS!
GAWK
!
KAZUKI SHINDO, RIGHT?
COME WITH US.

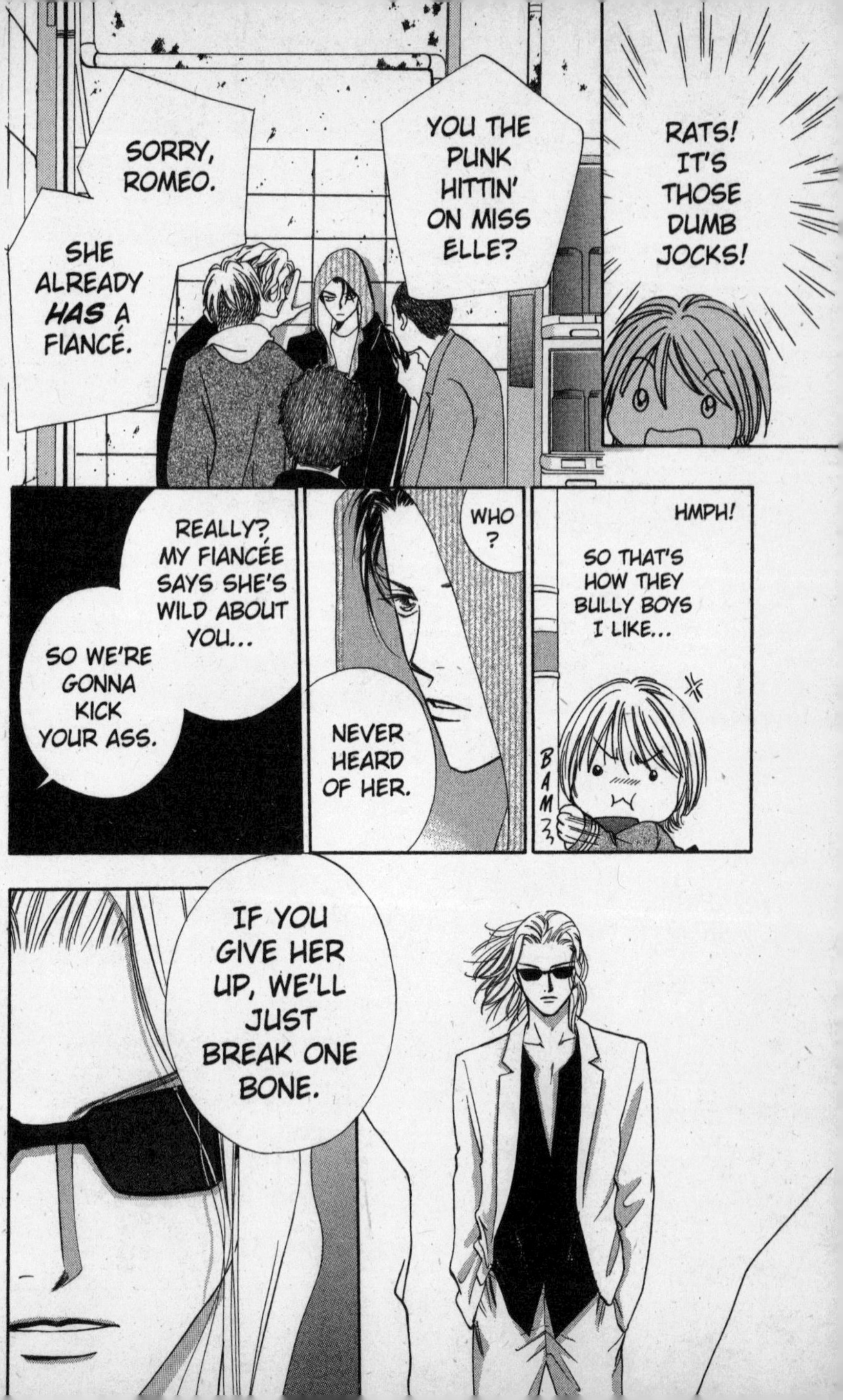
RATS! IT'S THOSE DUMB JOCKS!
YOU THE PUNK HITTIN' ON MISS ELLE?
SORRY, ROMEO.
SHE ALREADY **HAS** A FIANCÉ.
HMPH!
SO THAT'S HOW THEY BULLY BOYS I LIKE...
BAM
WHO?
NEVER HEARD OF HER.
REALLY? MY FIANCÉE SAYS SHE'S WILD ABOUT YOU...
SO WE'RE GONNA KICK YOUR ASS.
IF YOU GIVE HER UP, WE'LL JUST BREAK ONE BONE.

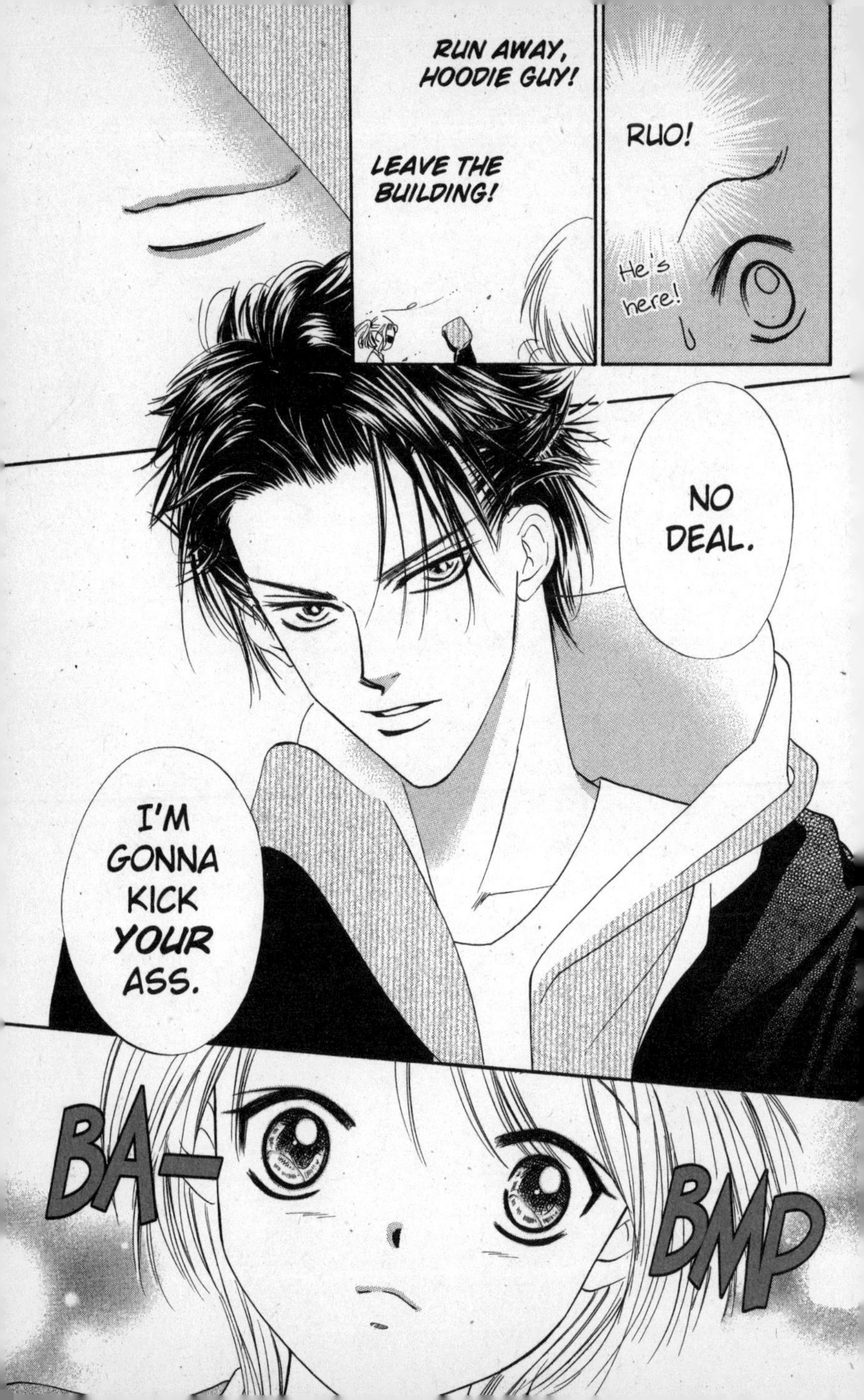
RUO!
He's here!
RUN AWAY, HOODIE GUY!
LEAVE THE BUILDING!
NO DEAL.
I'M GONNA KICK YOUR ASS.
BA-BMP

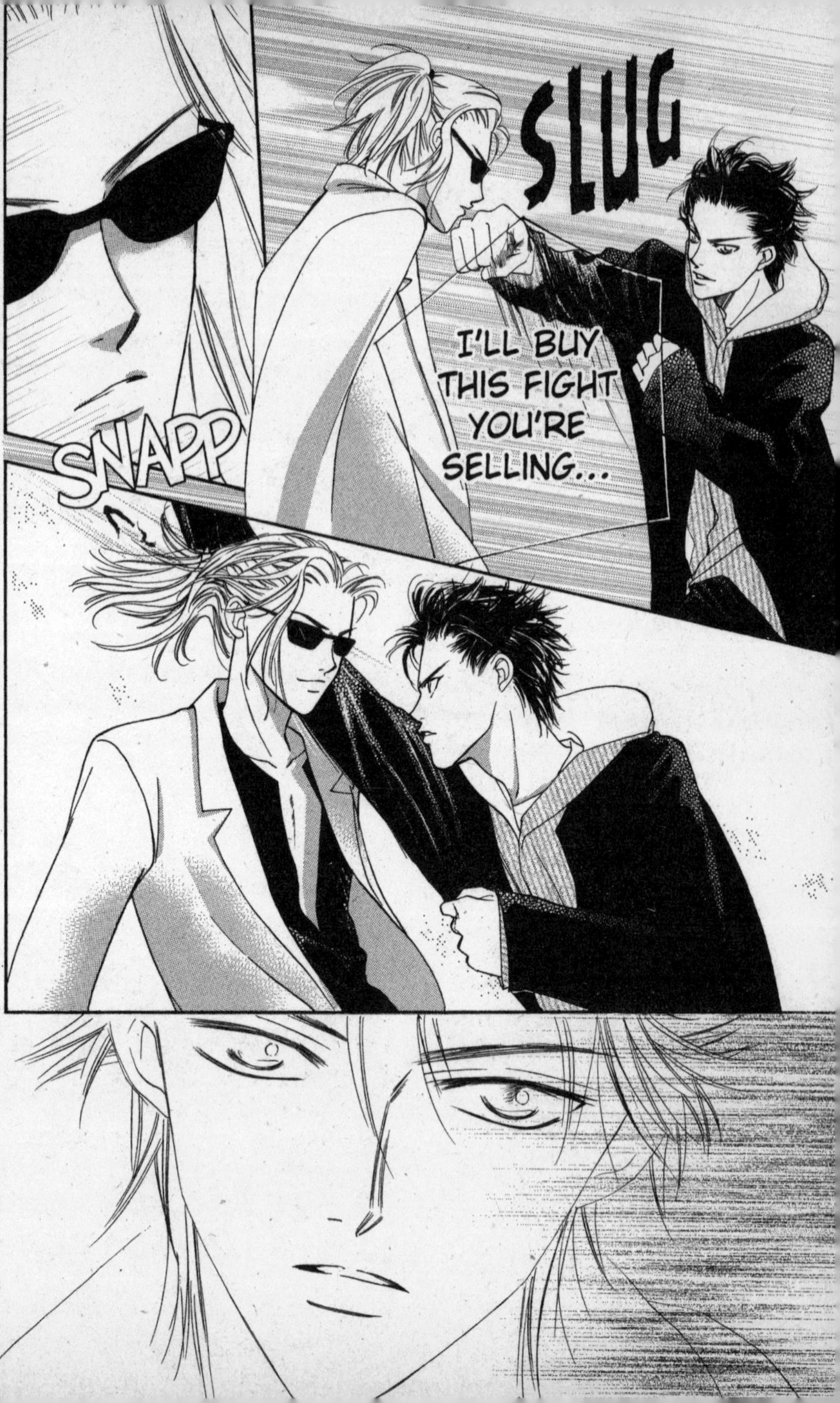
SLUG
I'LL BUY THIS FIGHT YOU'RE SELLING...
SNAPP

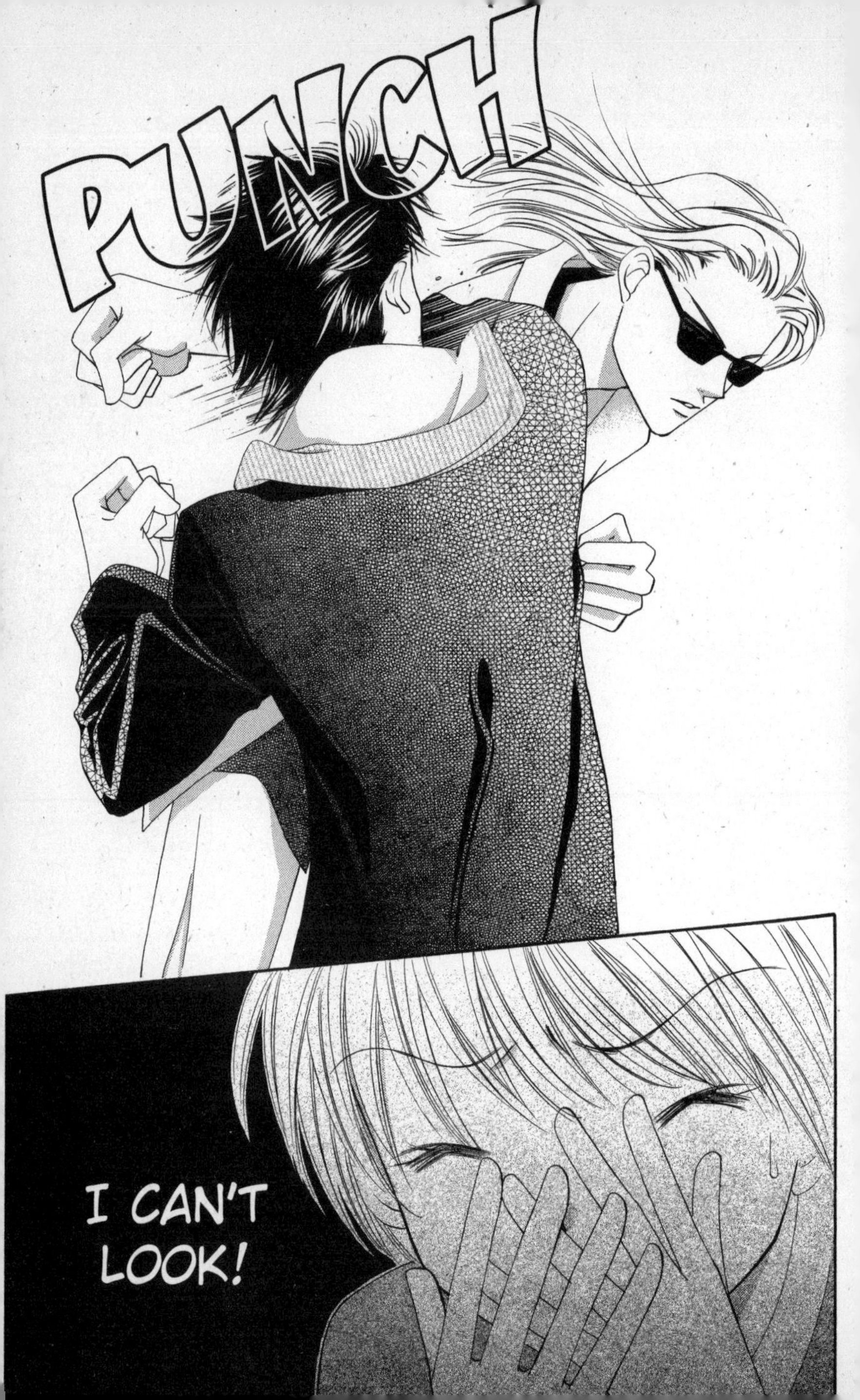
PUNCH
I CAN'T LOOK!

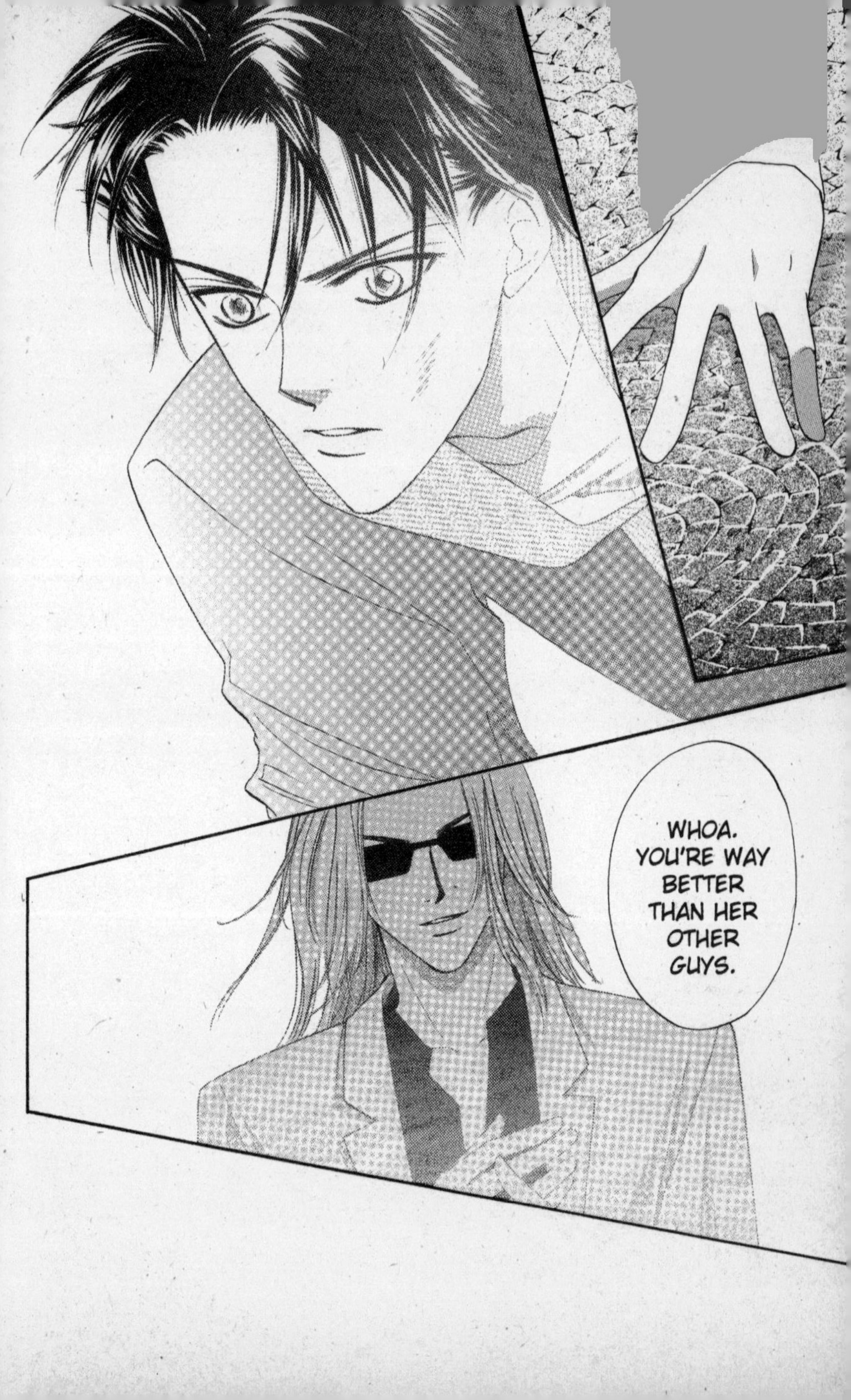
WHOA. YOU'RE WAY BETTER THAN HER OTHER GUYS.

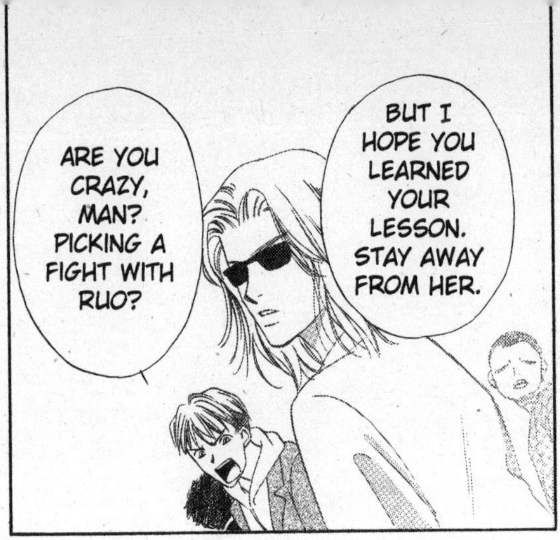
BUT I HOPE YOU LEARNED YOUR LESSON. STAY AWAY FROM HER.
ARE YOU CRAZY, MAN? PICKING A FIGHT WITH RUO?
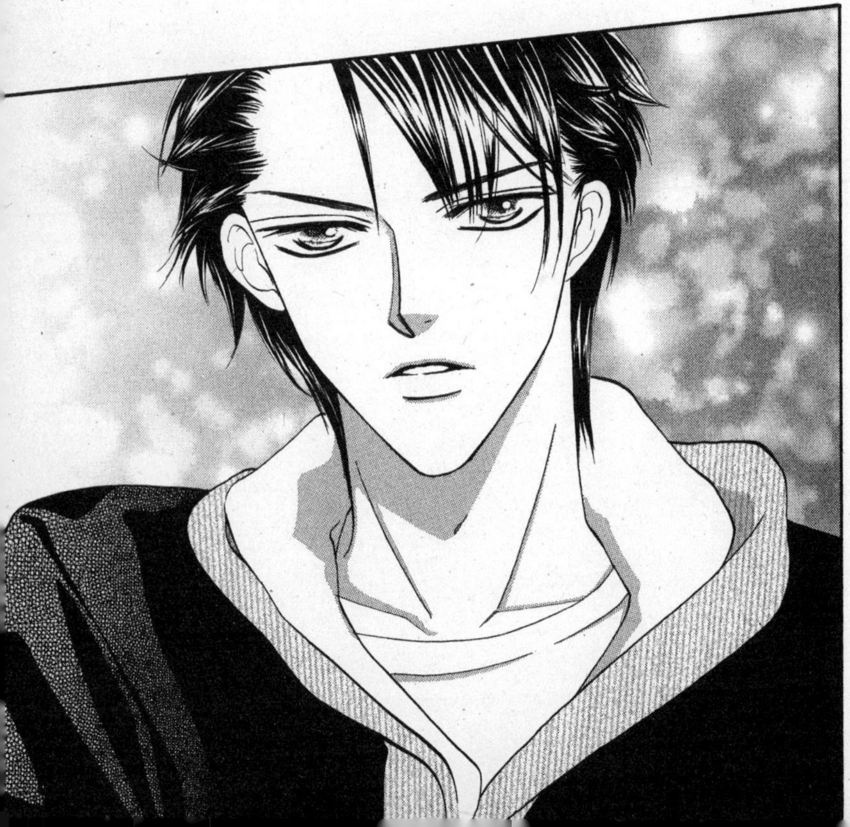

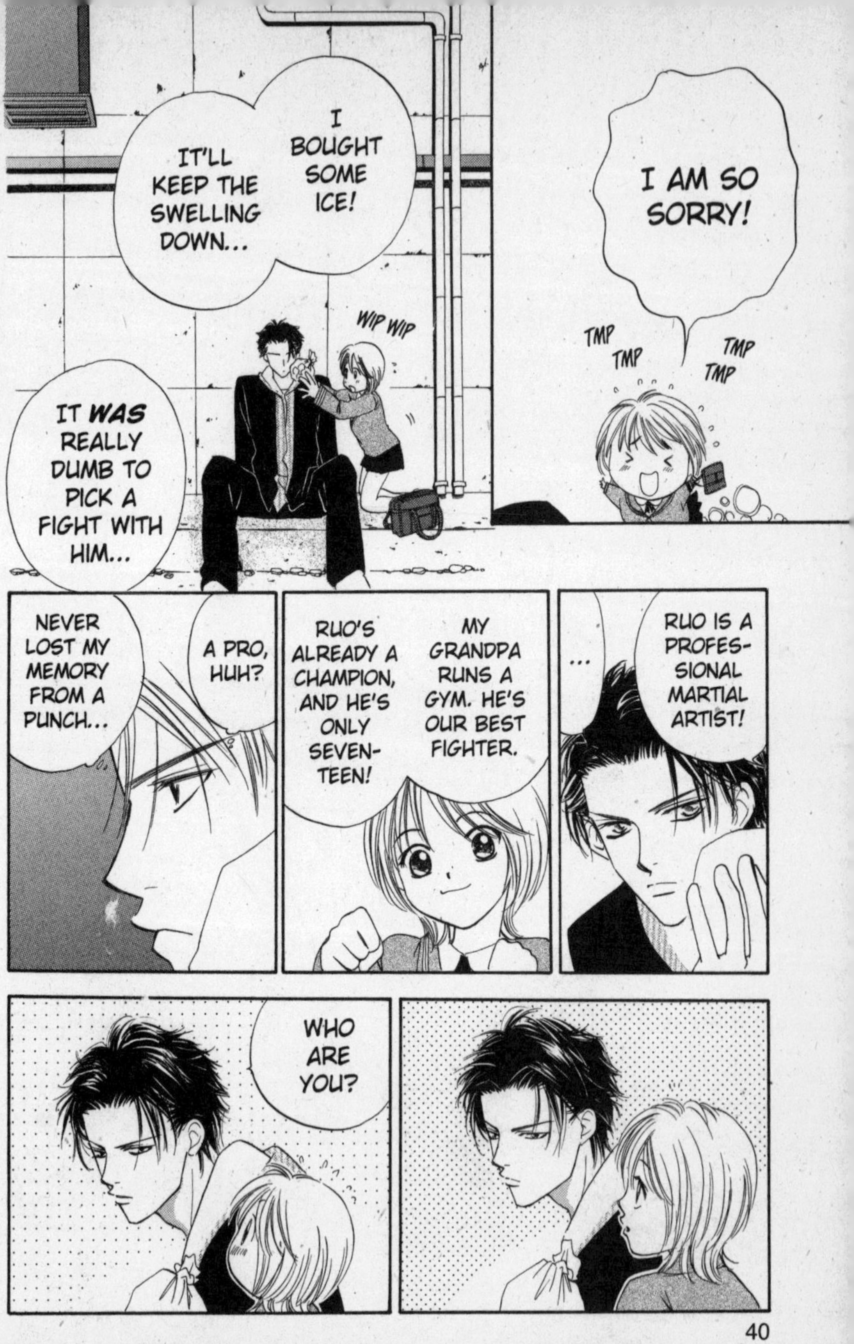
I AM SO SORRY!
TMP TMP TMP TMP
I BOUGHT SOME ICE!
IT'LL KEEP THE SWELLING DOWN...
WIP WIP
IT *WAS* REALLY DUMB TO PICK A FIGHT WITH HIM...
RUO IS A PROFES-SIONAL MARTIAL ARTIST!
...
MY GRANDPA RUNS A GYM. HE'S OUR BEST FIGHTER.
RUO'S ALREADY A CHAMPION, AND HE'S ONLY SEVEN-TEEN!
A PRO, HUH?
NEVER LOST MY MEMORY FROM A PUNCH...
WHO ARE YOU?

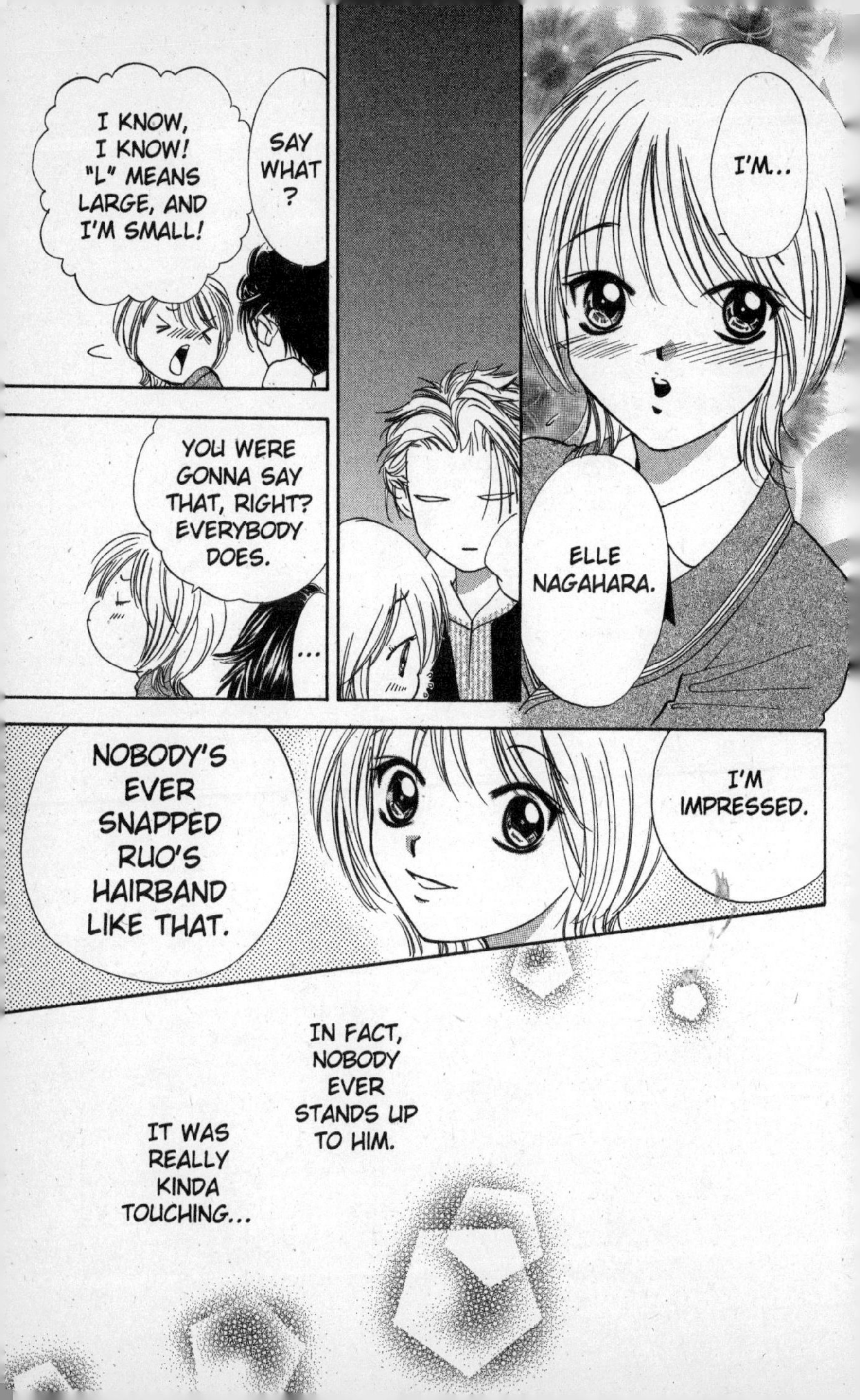
I'M...
ELLE NAGAHARA.
SAY WHAT?
I KNOW, I KNOW! "L" MEANS LARGE, AND I'M SMALL!
YOU WERE GONNA SAY THAT, RIGHT? EVERYBODY DOES.
...
I'M IMPRESSED.
NOBODY'S EVER SNAPPED RUO'S HAIRBAND LIKE THAT.
IN FACT, NOBODY EVER STANDS UP TO HIM.
IT WAS REALLY KINDA TOUCHING...

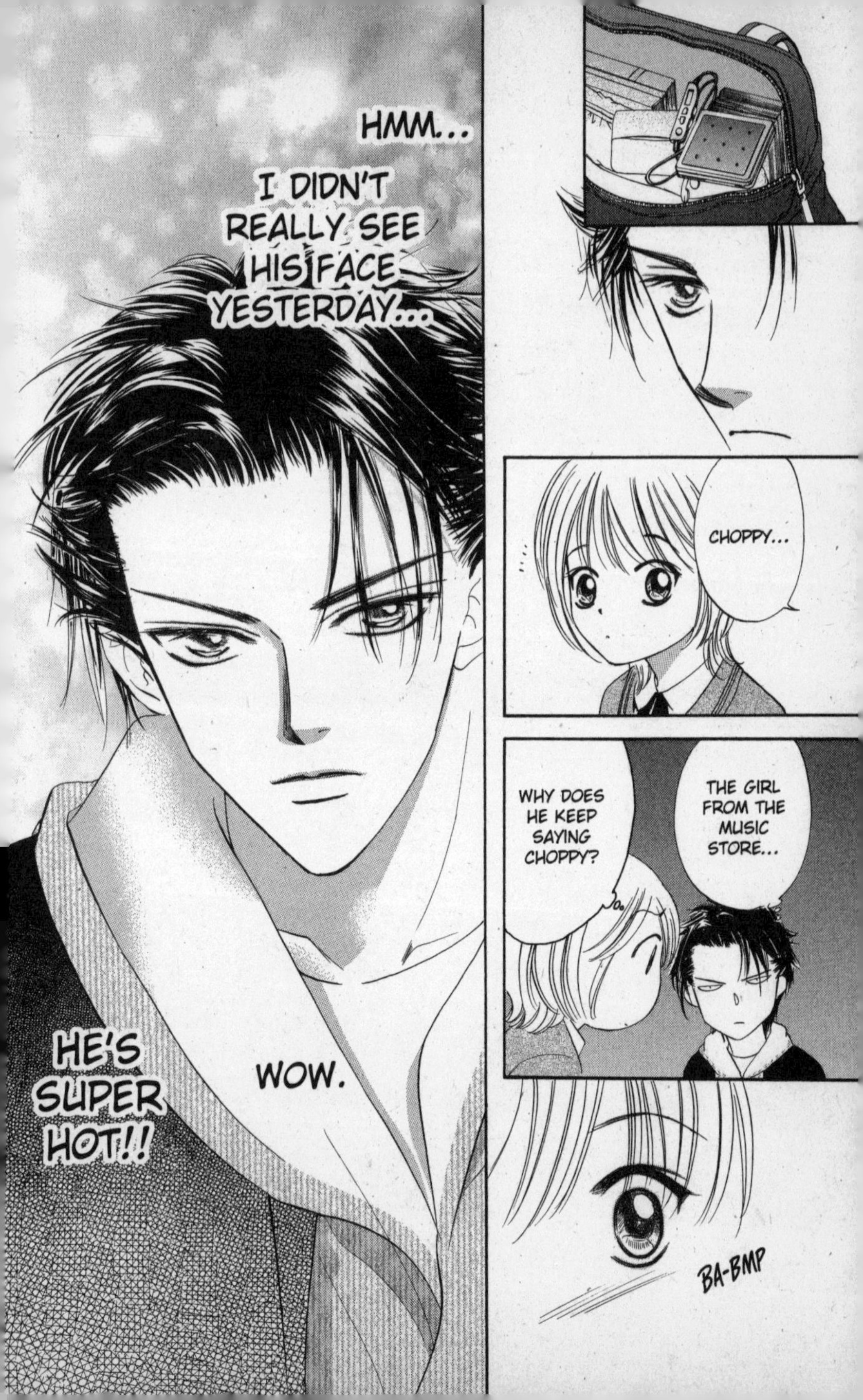

CHOPPY...
THE GIRL FROM THE MUSIC STORE...
WHY DOES HE KEEP SAYING CHOPPY?
BA-BMP
HMM...
I DIDN'T REALLY SEE HIS FACE YESTERDAY...
WOW.
HE'S SUPER HOT!!

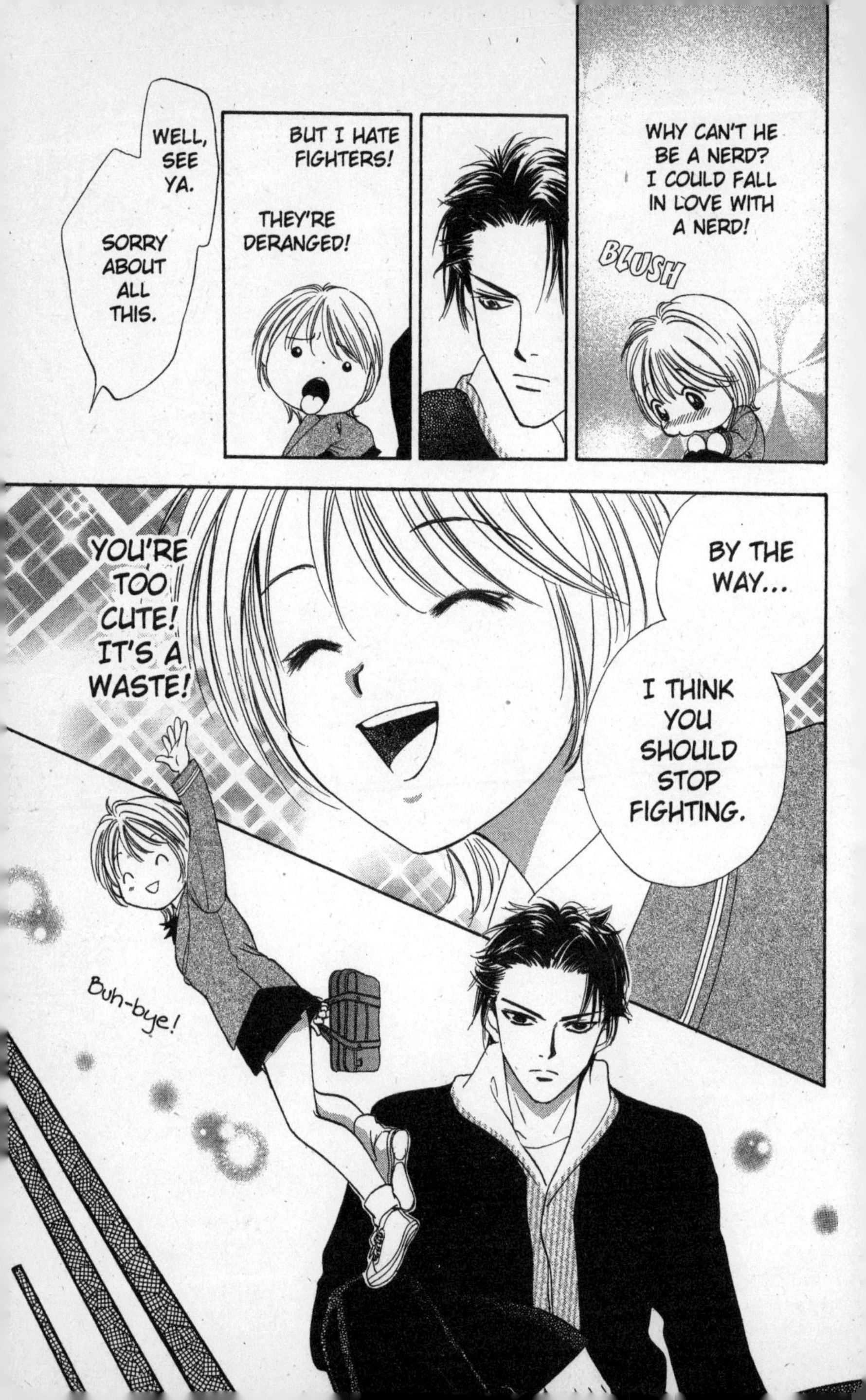
WHY CAN'T HE BE A NERD? I COULD FALL IN LOVE WITH A NERD!
BLUSH
BUT I HATE FIGHTERS!
THEY'RE DERANGED!
WELL, SEE YA.
SORRY ABOUT ALL THIS.
BY THE WAY...
I THINK YOU SHOULD STOP FIGHTING.
YOU'RE TOO CUTE! IT'S A WASTE!
Buh-bye!

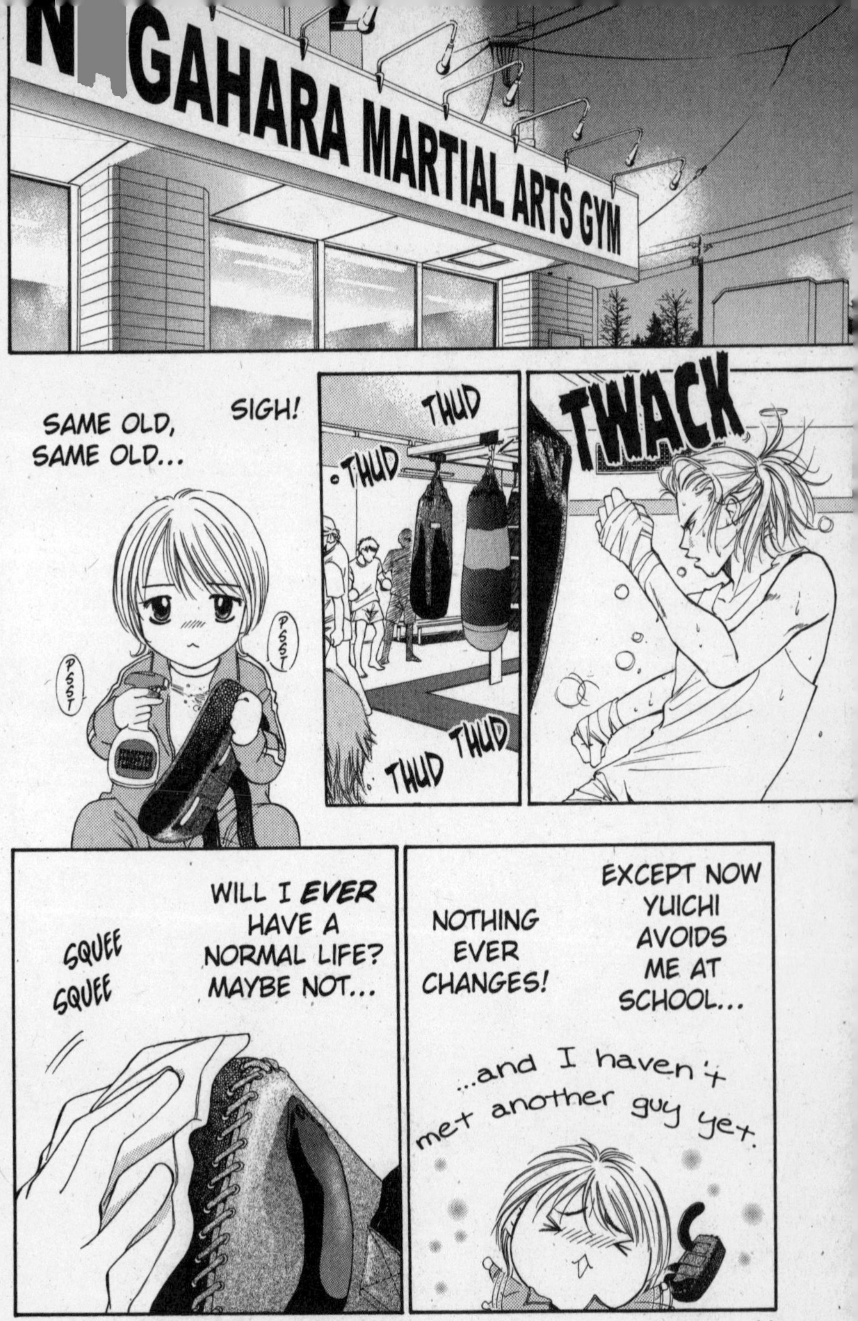

N GAHARA MARTIAL ARTS GYM
TWACK
THUD
THUD
THUD
THUD
SIGH!
SAME OLD, SAME OLD...
PSST
PSST
EXCEPT NOW YUICHI AVOIDS ME AT SCHOOL...
NOTHING EVER CHANGES!
...and I haven't met another guy yet.
WILL I *EVER* HAVE A NORMAL LIFE? MAYBE NOT...
SQUEE
SQUEE

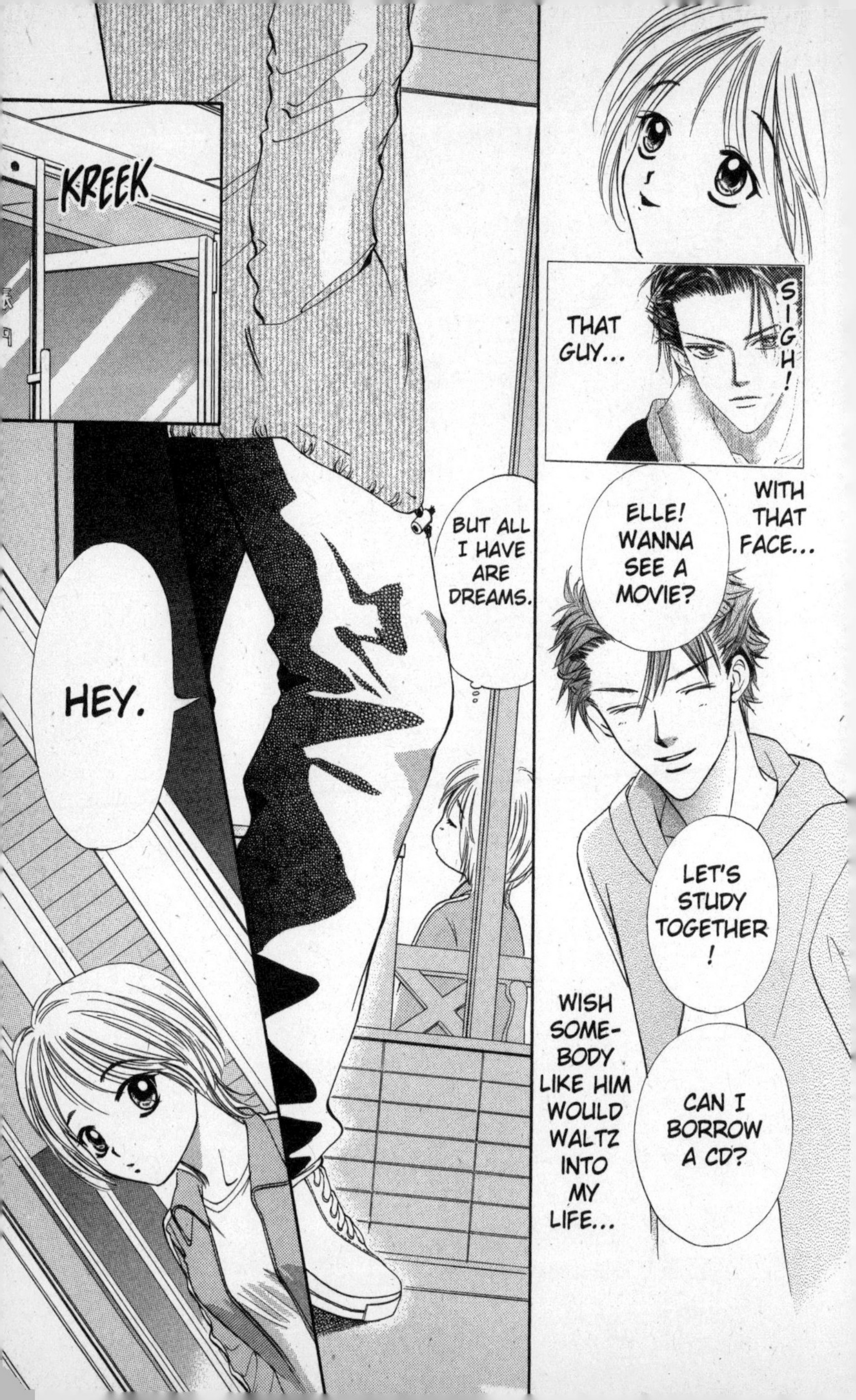
SIGH!
THAT GUY...
WITH THAT FACE...
ELLE! WANNA SEE A MOVIE?
LET'S STUDY TOGETHER!
WISH SOMEBODY LIKE HIM WOULD WALTZ INTO MY LIFE...
CAN I BORROW A CD?
KREEK
BUT ALL I HAVE ARE DREAMS.
HEY.

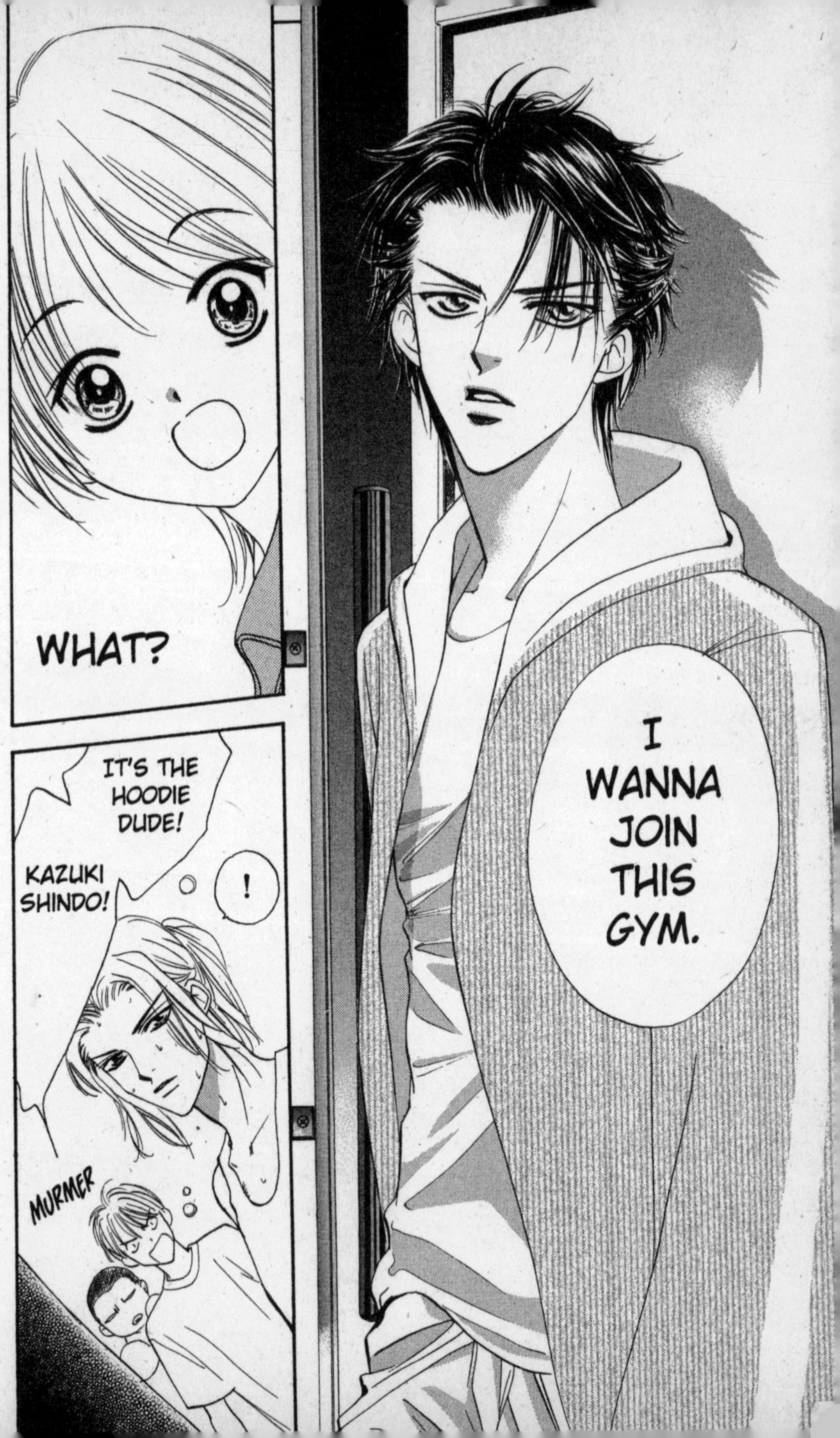
I WANNA JOIN THIS GYM.
WHAT?
IT'S THE HOODIE DUDE!
!
KAZUKI SHINDO!
MURMER

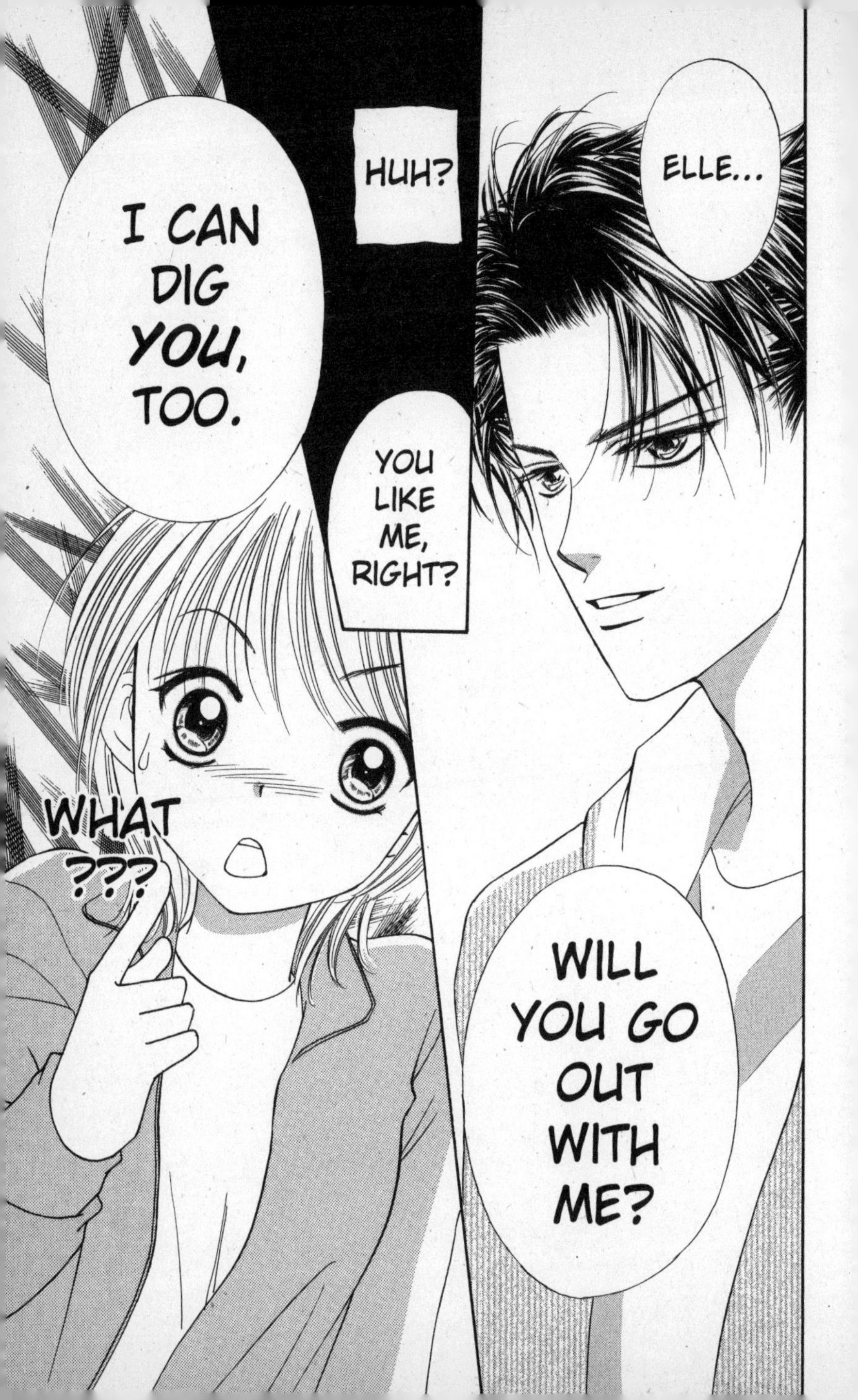
ELLE...
I CAN DIG YOU, TOO.
HUH?
YOU LIKE ME, RIGHT?
WILL YOU GO OUT WITH ME?
WHAT ???

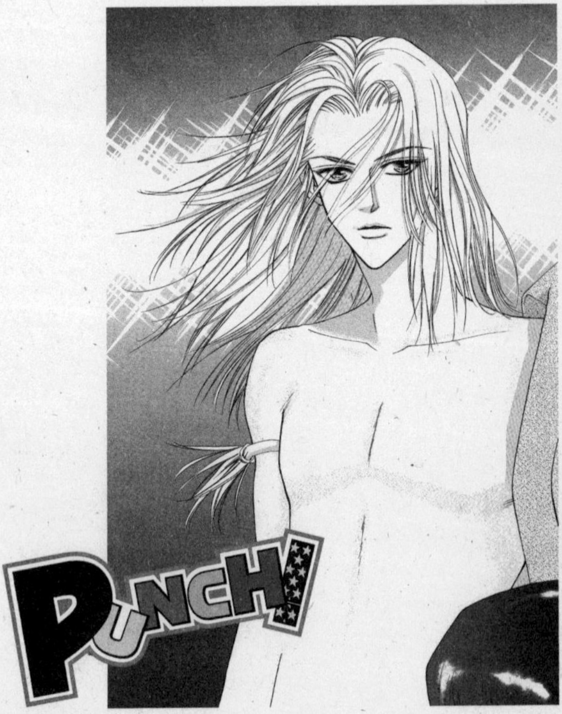
PUNCH!

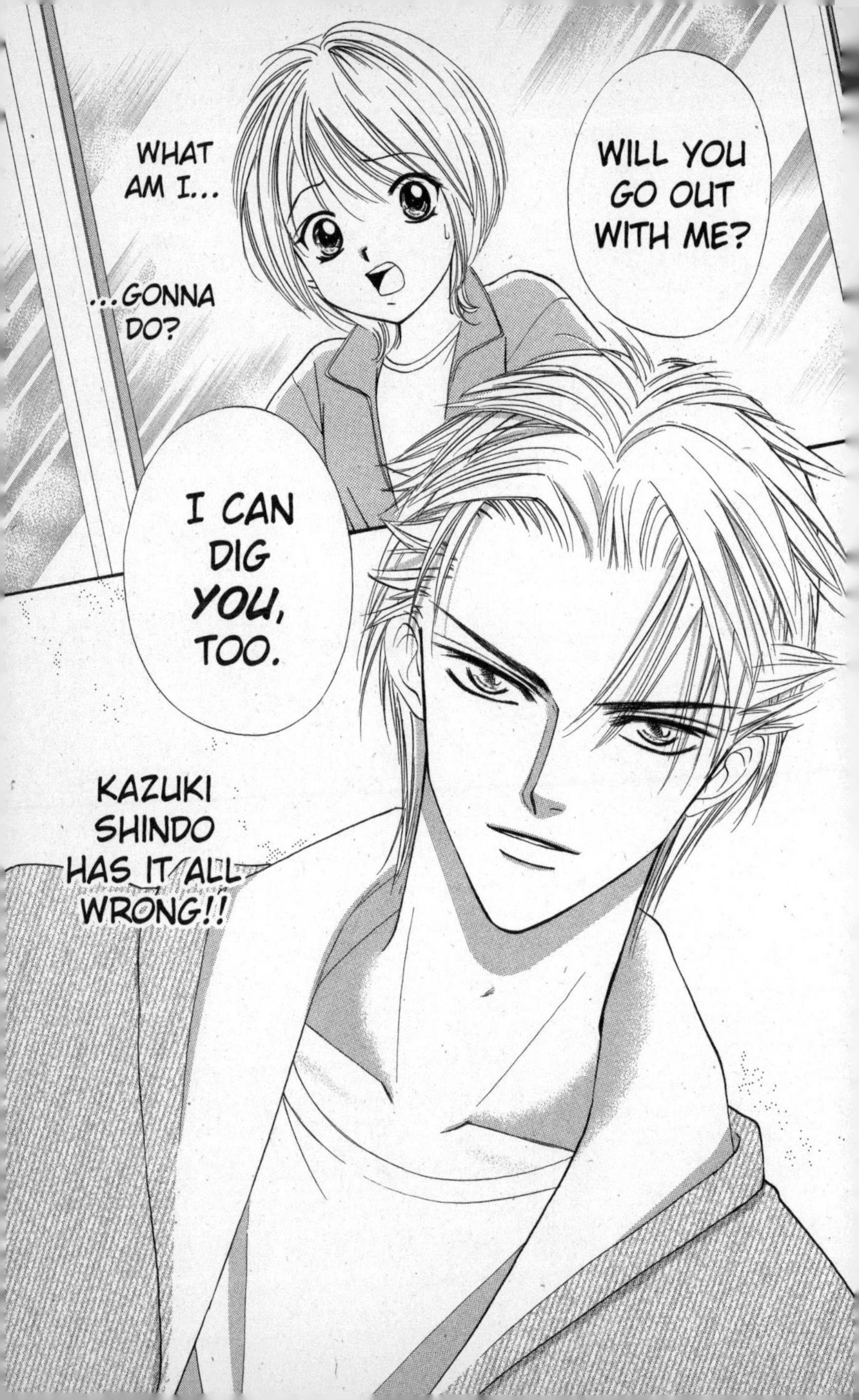
WILL YOU GO OUT WITH ME?
WHAT AM I...
...GONNA DO?
I CAN DIG *YOU*, TOO.
KAZUKI SHINDO HAS IT ALL WRONG!!

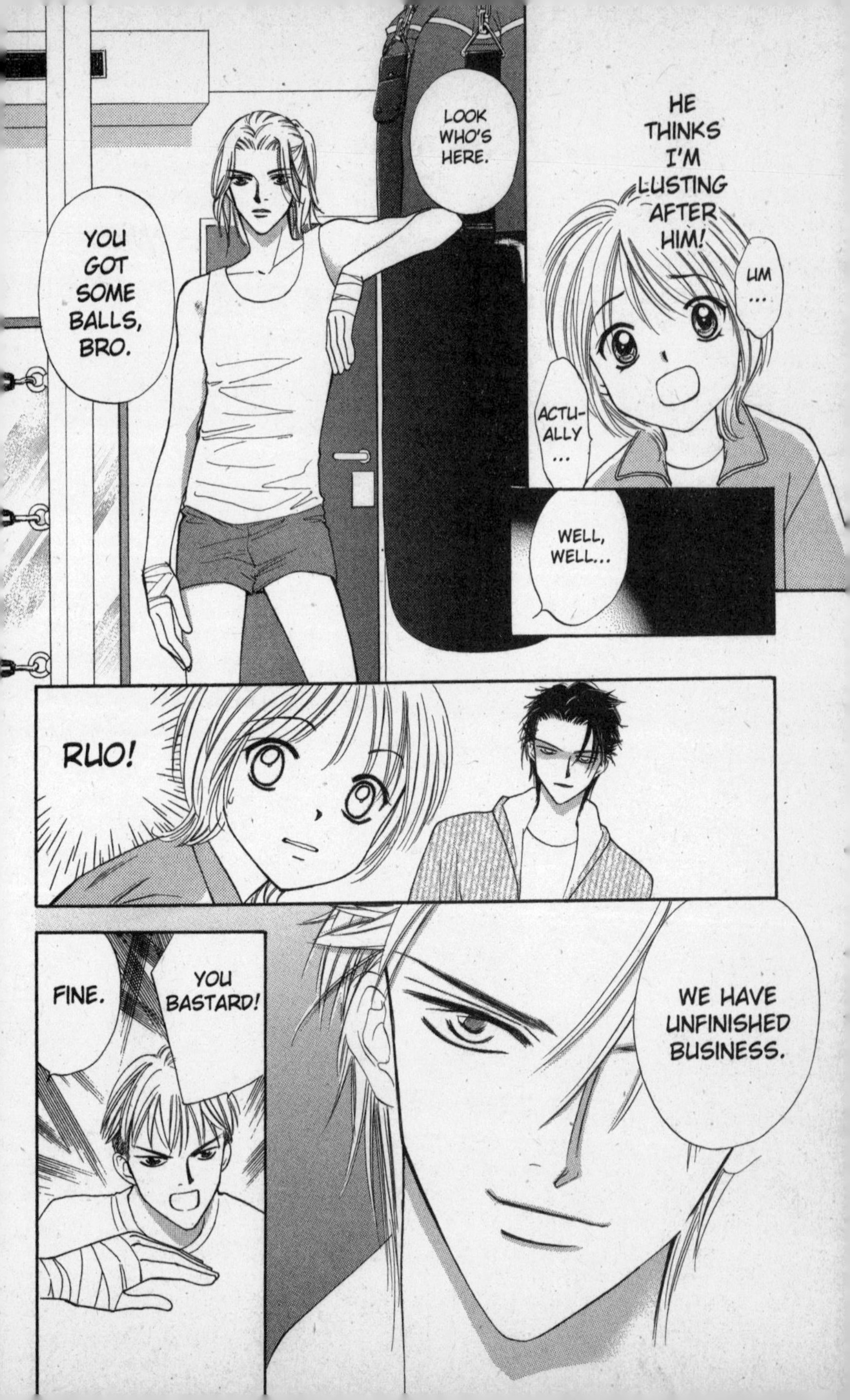
HE THINKS I'M LUSTING AFTER HIM!
UM ...
ACTU-ALLY ...
WELL, WELL...
LOOK WHO'S HERE.
YOU GOT SOME BALLS, BRO.
RUO!
WE HAVE UNFINISHED BUSINESS.
YOU BASTARD!
FINE.

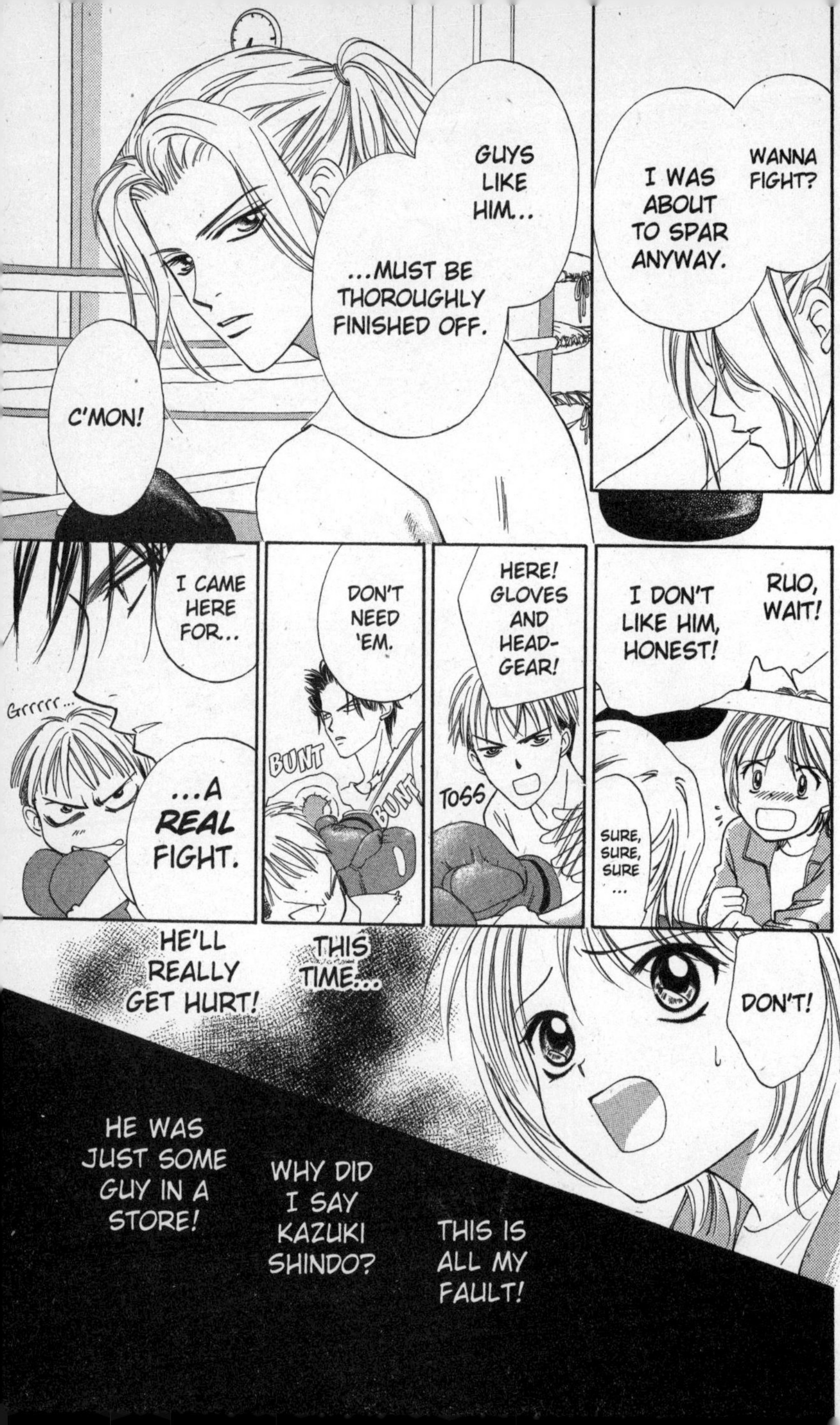
WANNA FIGHT?
I WAS ABOUT TO SPAR ANYWAY.
GUYS LIKE HIM...
...MUST BE THOROUGHLY FINISHED OFF.
C'MON!
RUO, WAIT!
I DON'T LIKE HIM, HONEST!
SURE, SURE, SURE ...
HERE! GLOVES AND HEAD-GEAR!
TOSS
DON'T NEED 'EM.
BUNT
BUNT
I CAME HERE FOR...
Grrrrr...
...A *REAL* FIGHT.
DON'T!
THIS TIME...
HE'LL REALLY GET HURT!
HE WAS JUST SOME GUY IN A STORE!
WHY DID I SAY KAZUKI SHINDO?
THIS IS ALL MY FAULT!

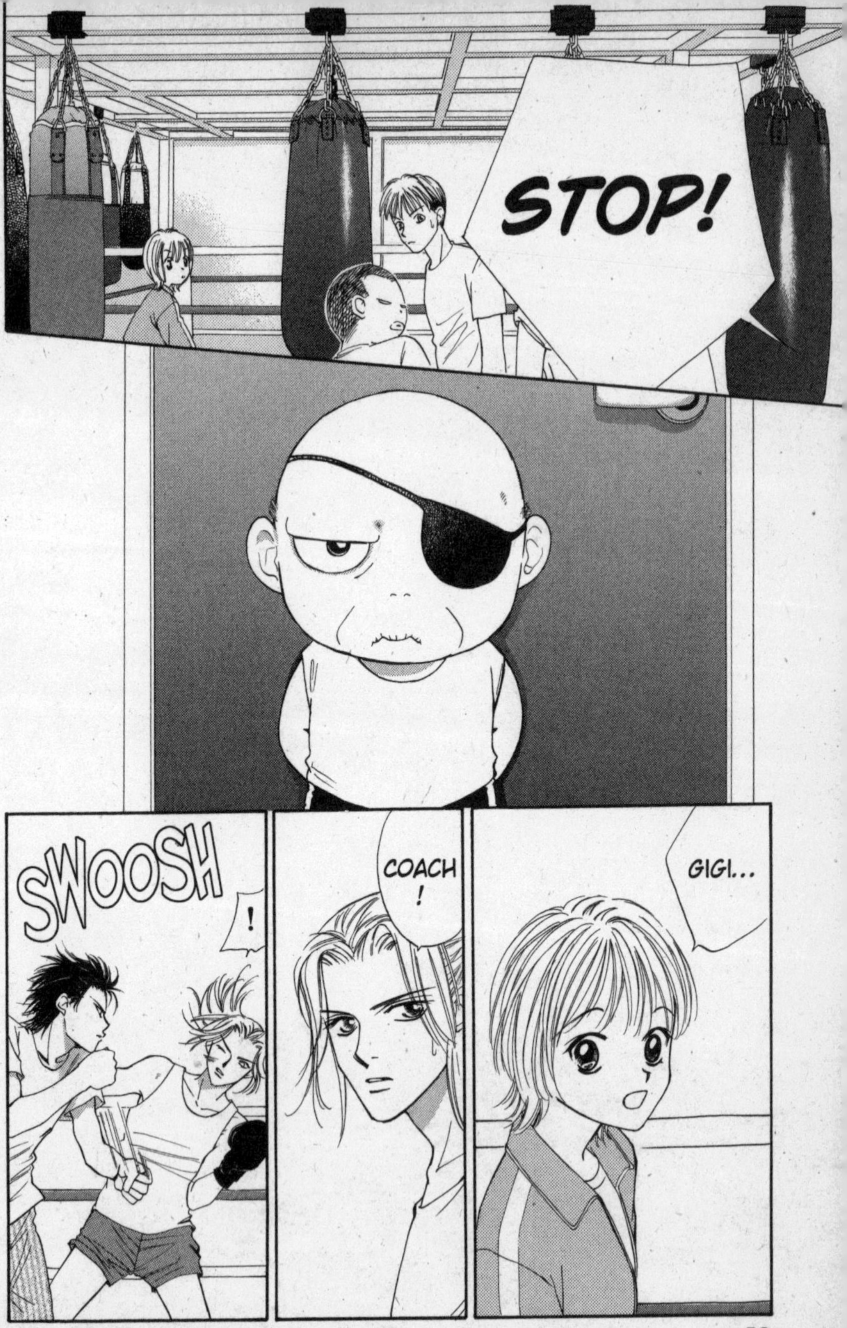
STOP!
GIGI...
COACH!
SWOOSH
!

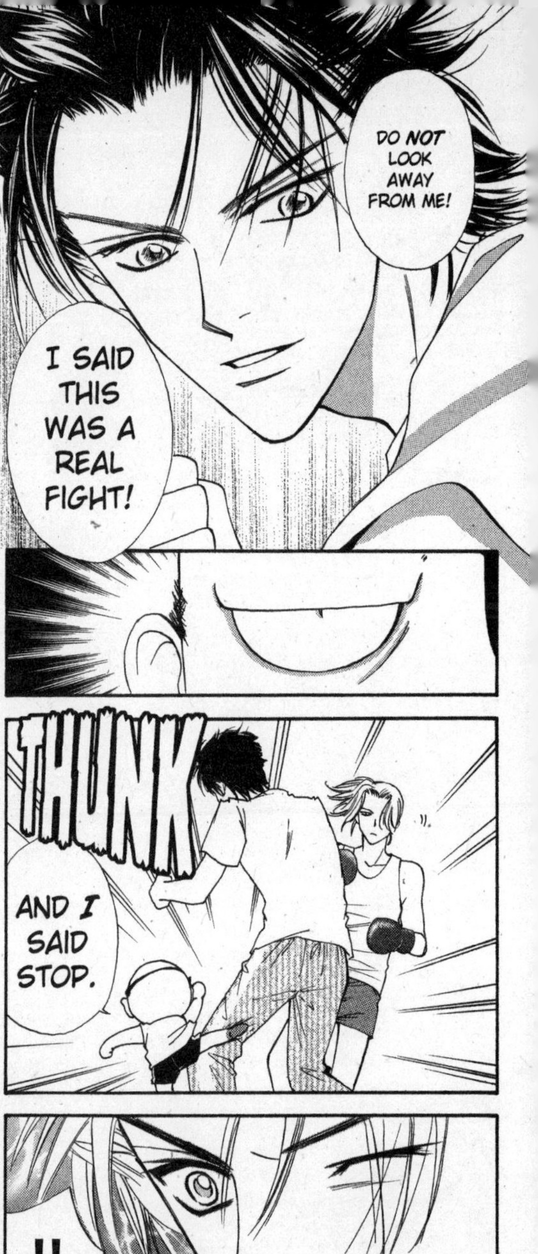
DO NOT LOOK AWAY FROM ME!
I SAID THIS WAS A REAL FIGHT!
THUNK
AND I SAID STOP.
!!

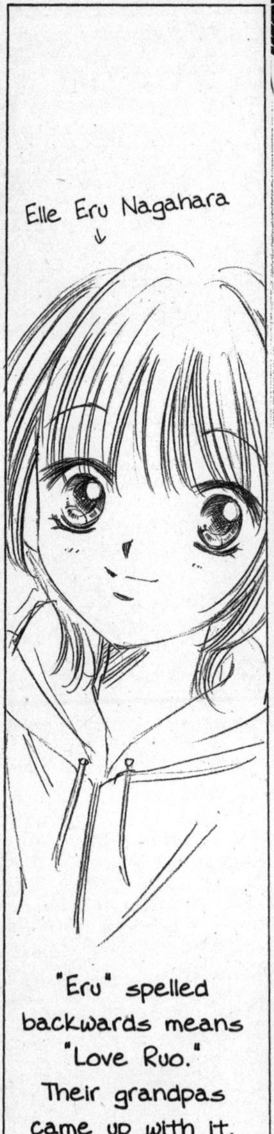
Elle Eru Nagahara
"Eru" spelled backwards means "Love Ruo." Their grandpas came up with it.

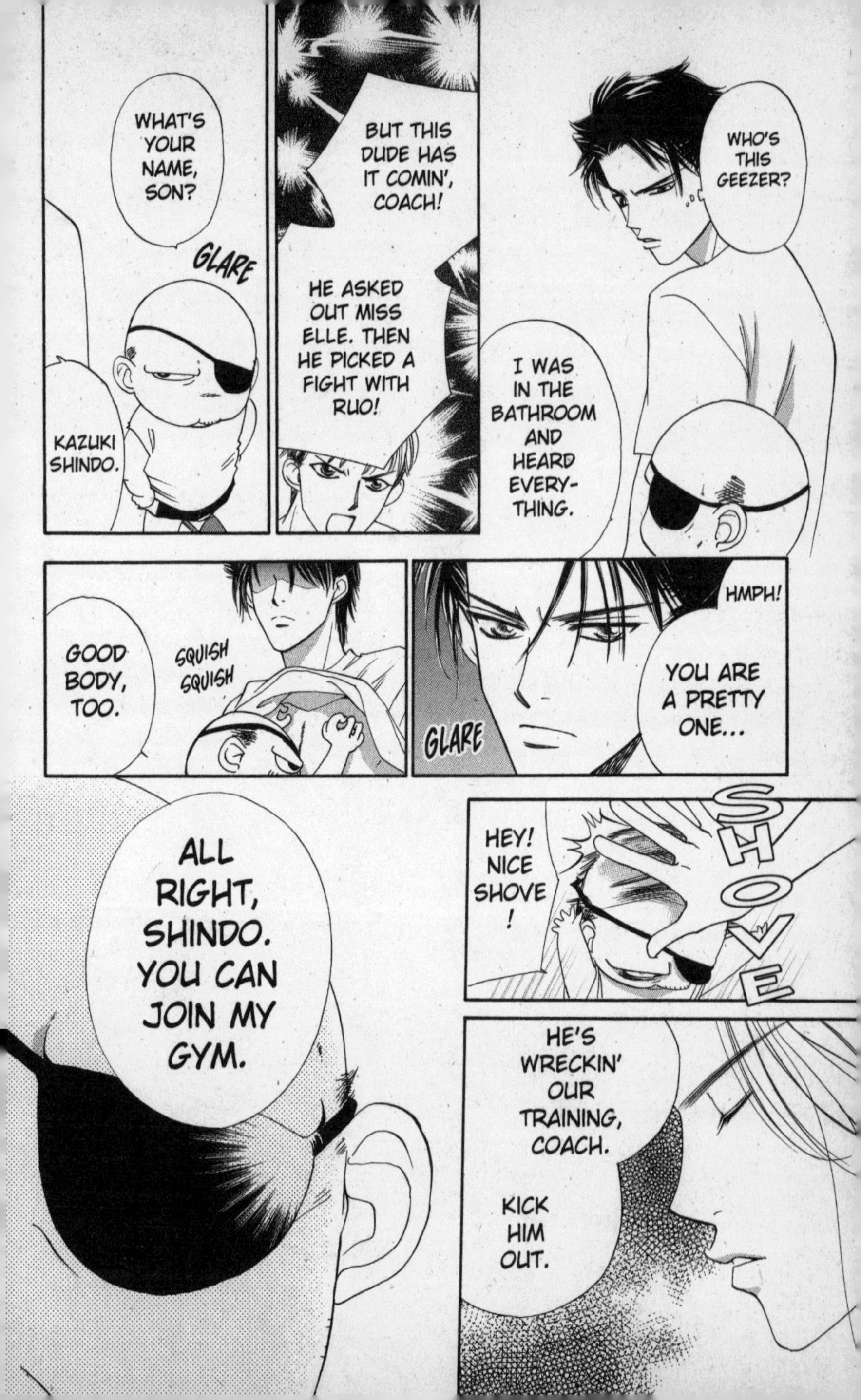
WHO'S THIS GEEZER?
I WAS IN THE BATHROOM AND HEARD EVERY-THING.
BUT THIS DUDE HAS IT COMIN', COACH!
HE ASKED OUT MISS ELLE. THEN HE PICKED A FIGHT WITH RUO!
WHAT'S YOUR NAME, SON?
GLARE
KAZUKI SHINDO.
HMPH!
YOU ARE A PRETTY ONE...
GLARE
GOOD BODY, TOO.
SQUISH SQUISH
SHOVE
HEY! NICE SHOVE!
HE'S WRECKIN' OUR TRAINING, COACH.
KICK HIM OUT.
ALL RIGHT, SHINDO. YOU CAN JOIN MY GYM.

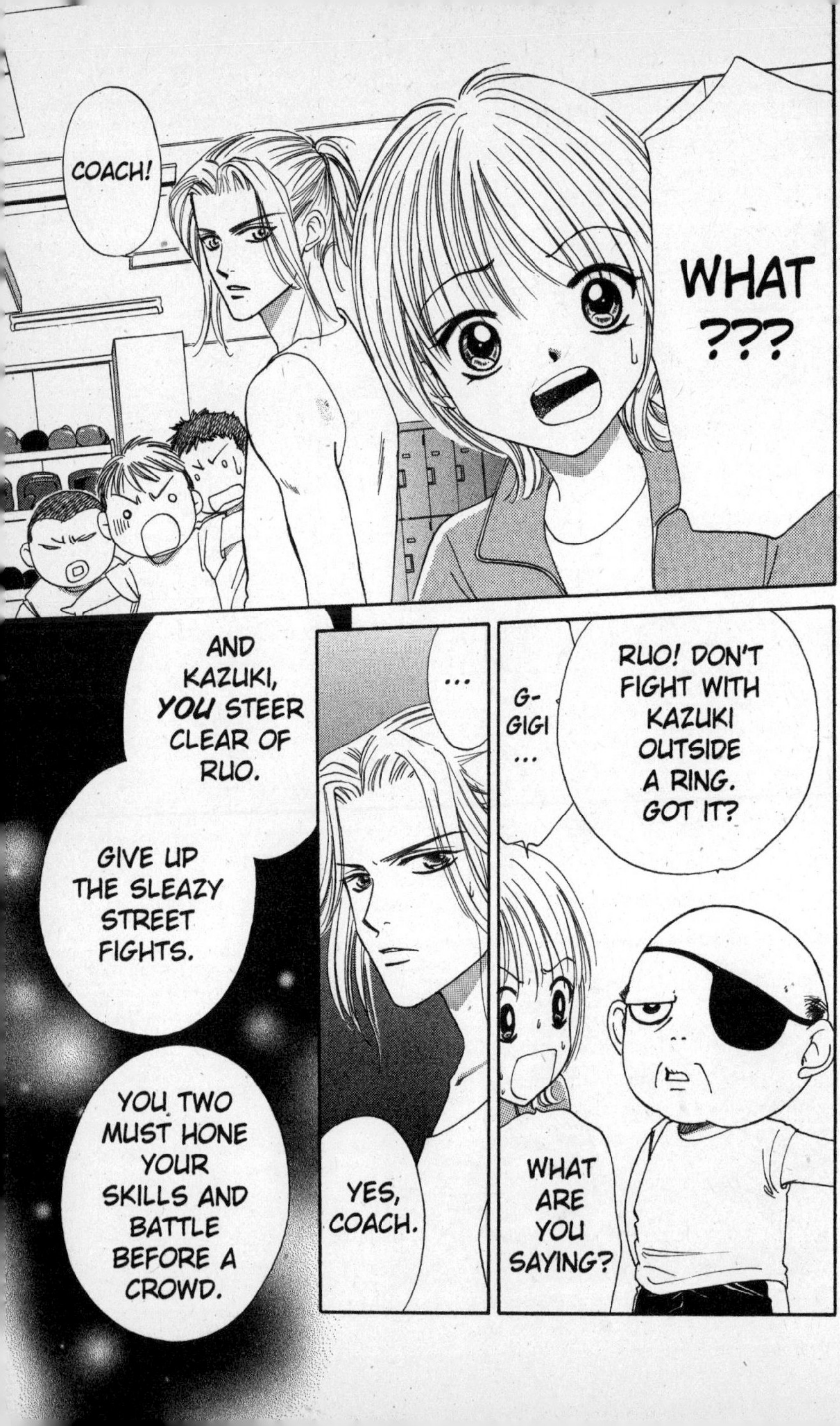
WHAT ???
COACH!
RUO! DON'T FIGHT WITH KAZUKI OUTSIDE A RING. GOT IT?
G-GIGI ...
WHAT ARE YOU SAYING?
...
YES, COACH.
AND KAZUKI, *YOU* STEER CLEAR OF RUO.
GIVE UP THE SLEAZY STREET FIGHTS.
YOU TWO MUST HONE YOUR SKILLS AND BATTLE BEFORE A CROWD.

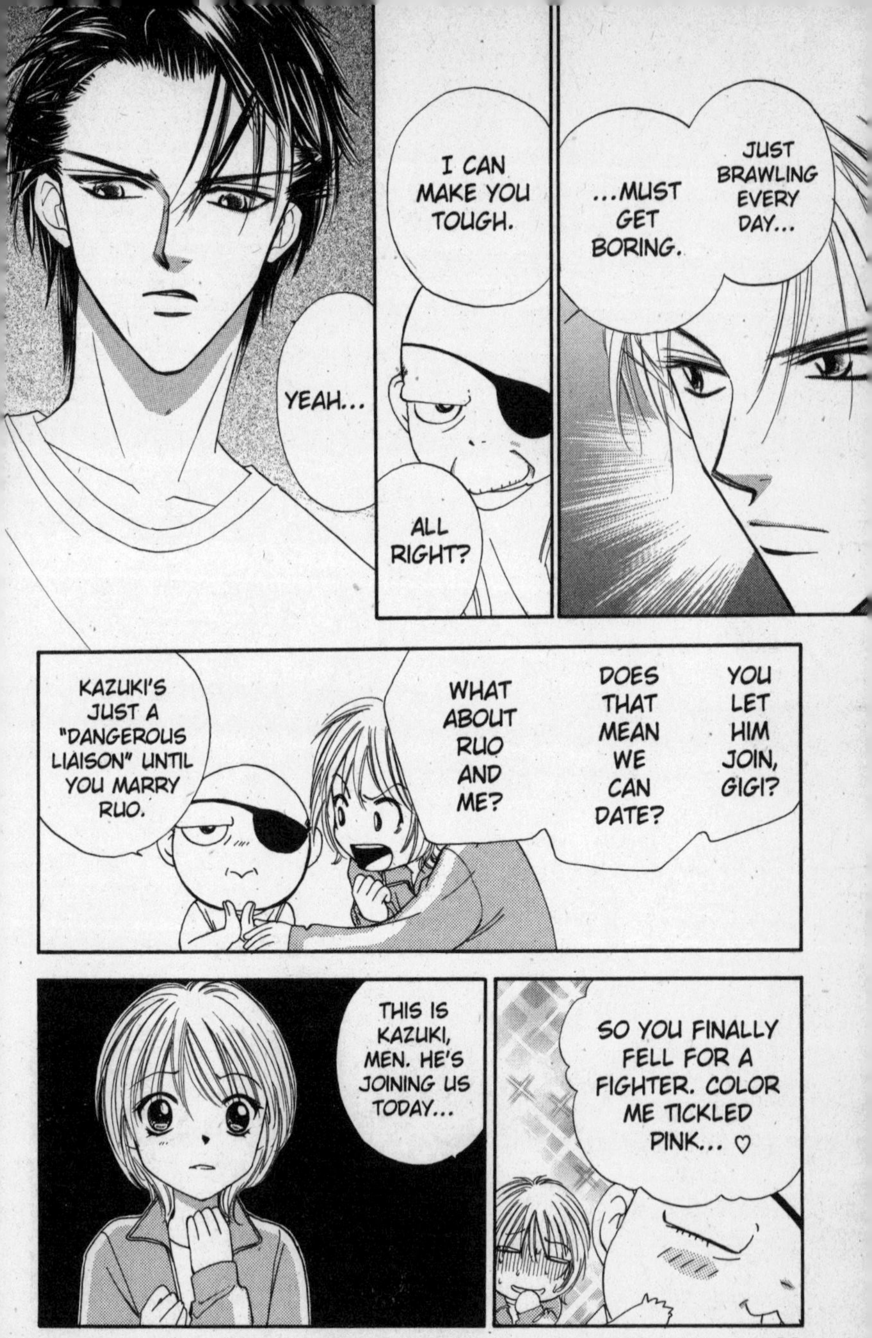
JUST BRAWLING EVERY DAY...
...MUST GET BORING.
I CAN MAKE YOU TOUGH.
ALL RIGHT?
YEAH...
YOU LET HIM JOIN, GIGI?
DOES THAT MEAN WE CAN DATE?
WHAT ABOUT RUO AND ME?
KAZUKI'S JUST A "DANGEROUS LIAISON" UNTIL YOU MARRY RUO.
SO YOU FINALLY FELL FOR A FIGHTER. COLOR ME TICKLED PINK... ♡
THIS IS KAZUKI, MEN. HE'S JOINING US TODAY...

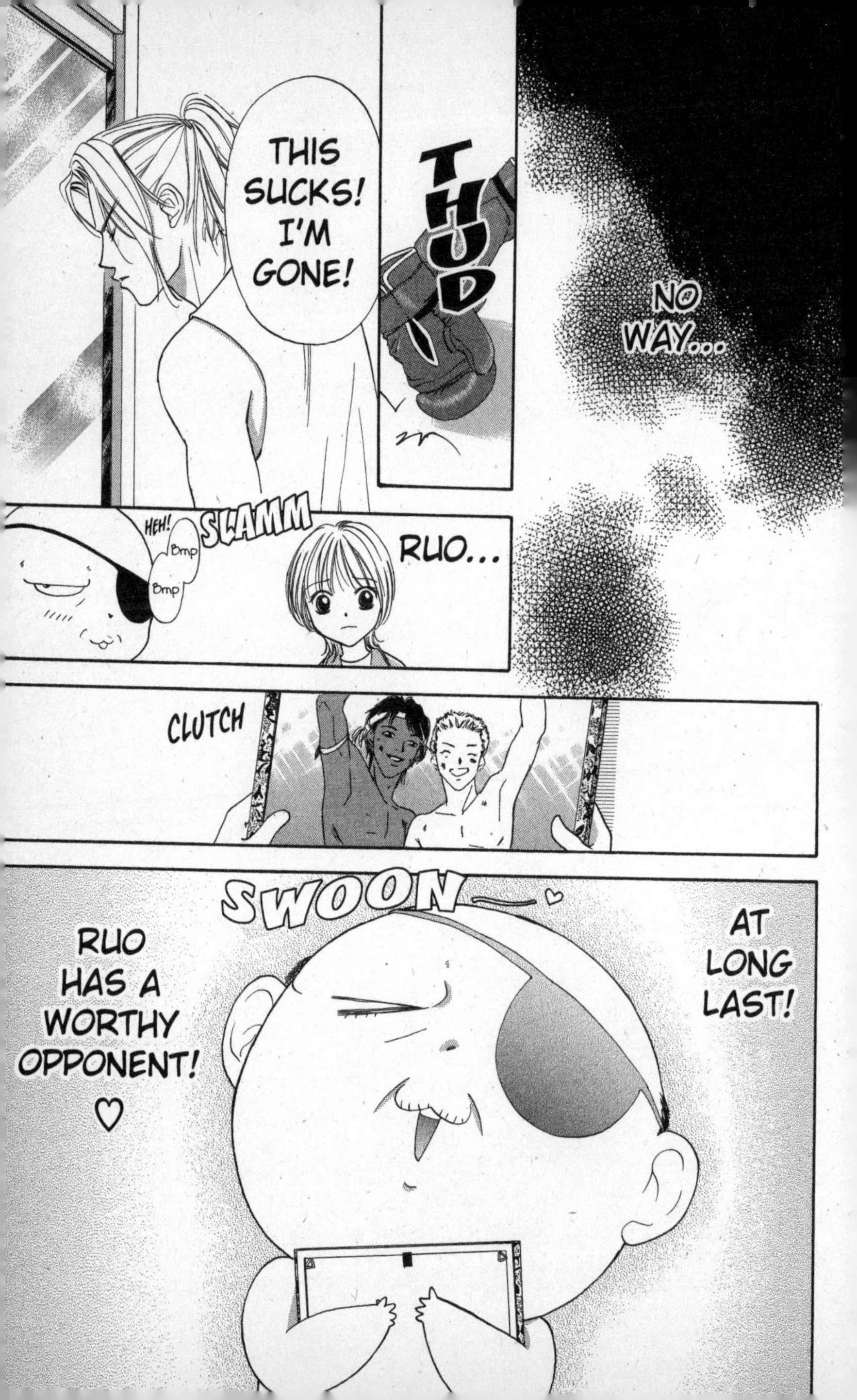
NO WAY...
THUD
THIS SUCKS! I'M GONE!
RUO...
SLAMM
Bmp
Bmp
HEH!
CLUTCH
SWOON ♡
AT LONG LAST!
RUO HAS A WORTHY OPPONENT! ♡

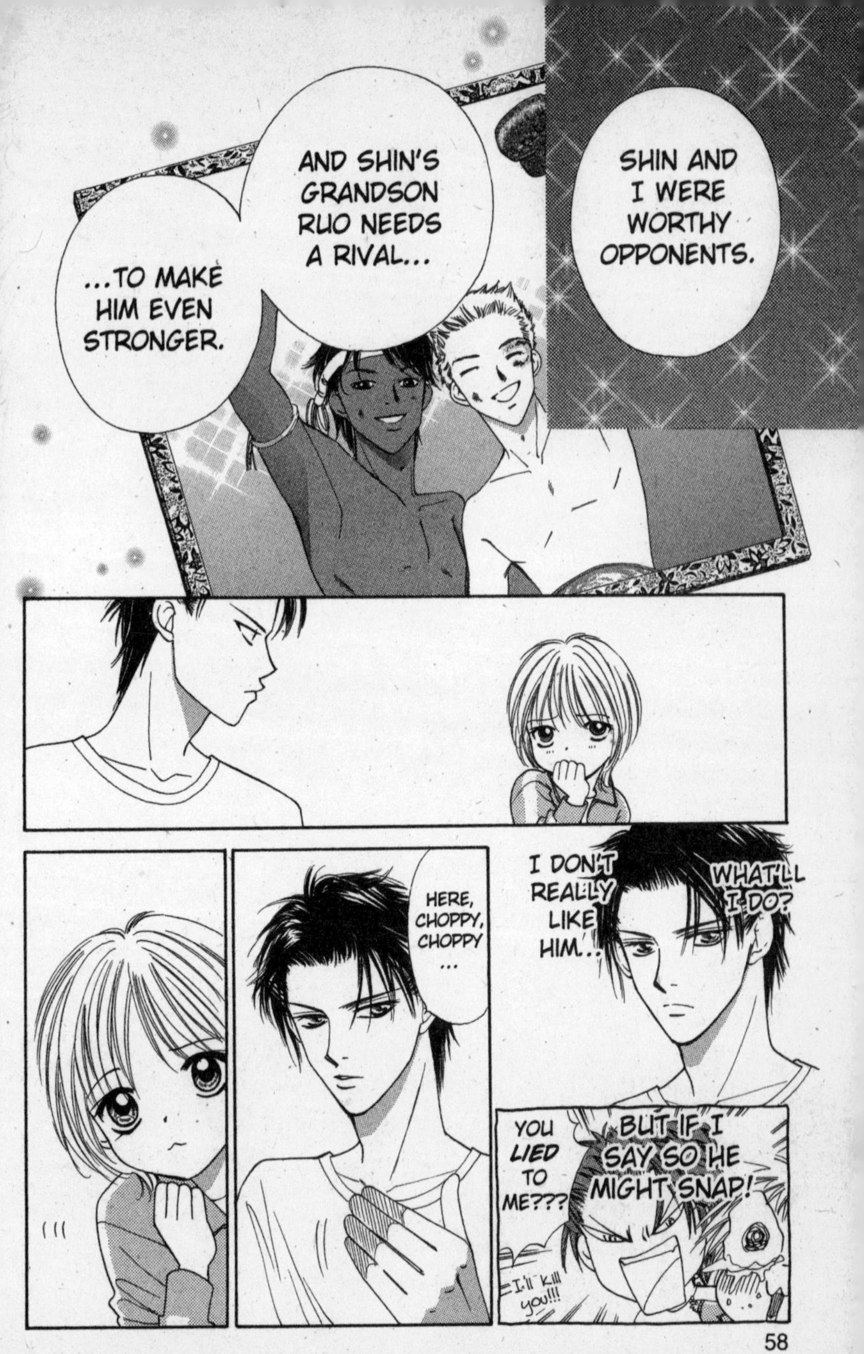
SHIN AND I WERE WORTHY OPPONENTS.
AND SHIN'S GRANDSON RUO NEEDS A RIVAL...
...TO MAKE HIM EVEN STRONGER.
WHAT'LL I DO?
I DON'T REALLY LIKE HIM...
BUT IF I SAY SO HE MIGHT SNAP!
YOU LIED TO ME???
I'll kill you!!!
HERE, CHOPPY, CHOPPY ...

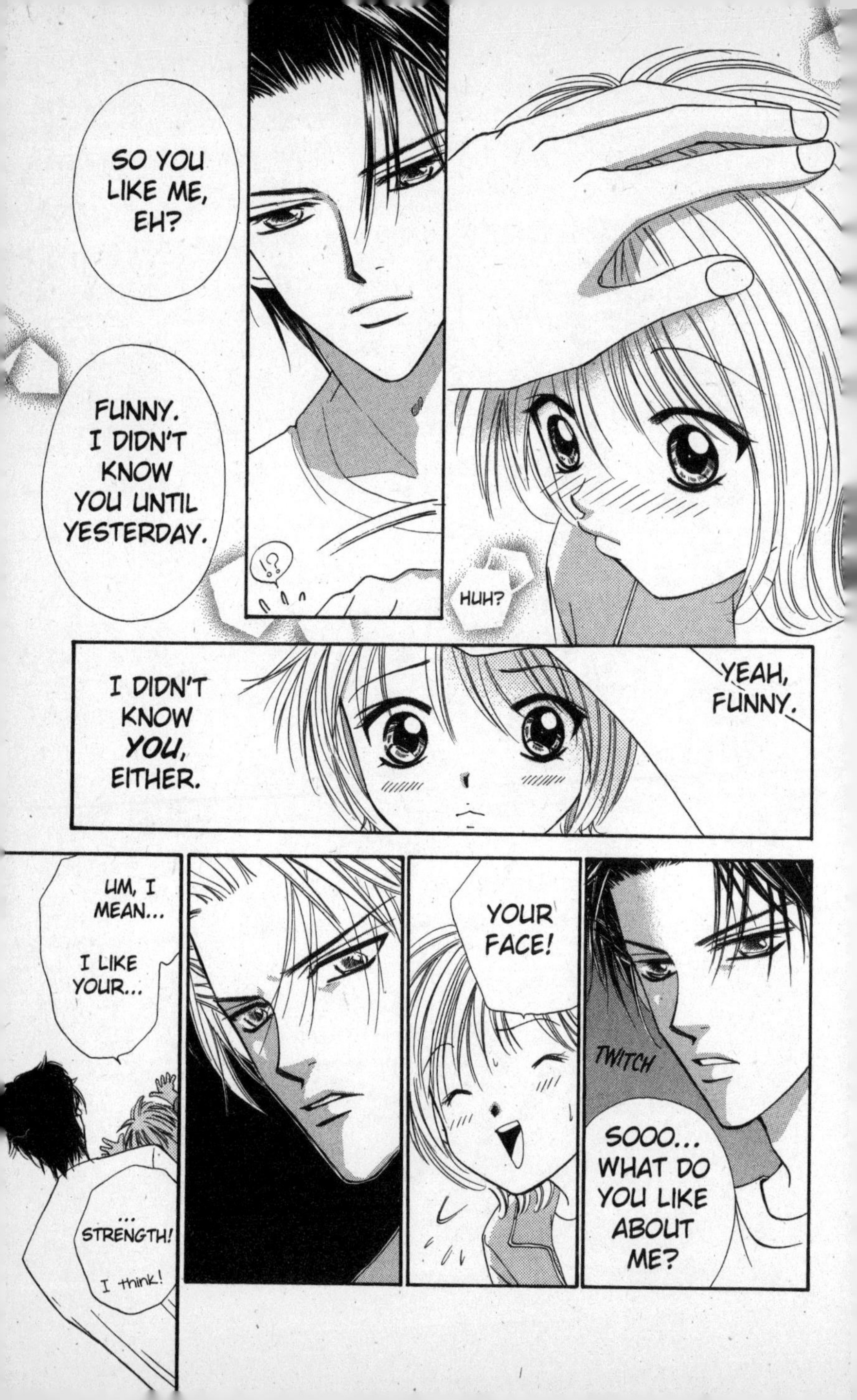
SO YOU LIKE ME, EH?
FUNNY. I DIDN'T KNOW YOU UNTIL YESTERDAY.
!?
HUH?
YEAH, FUNNY.
I DIDN'T KNOW *YOU*, EITHER.
TWITCH
SOOO... WHAT DO YOU LIKE ABOUT ME?
YOUR FACE!
UM, I MEAN...
I LIKE YOUR...
...STRENGTH!
I think!

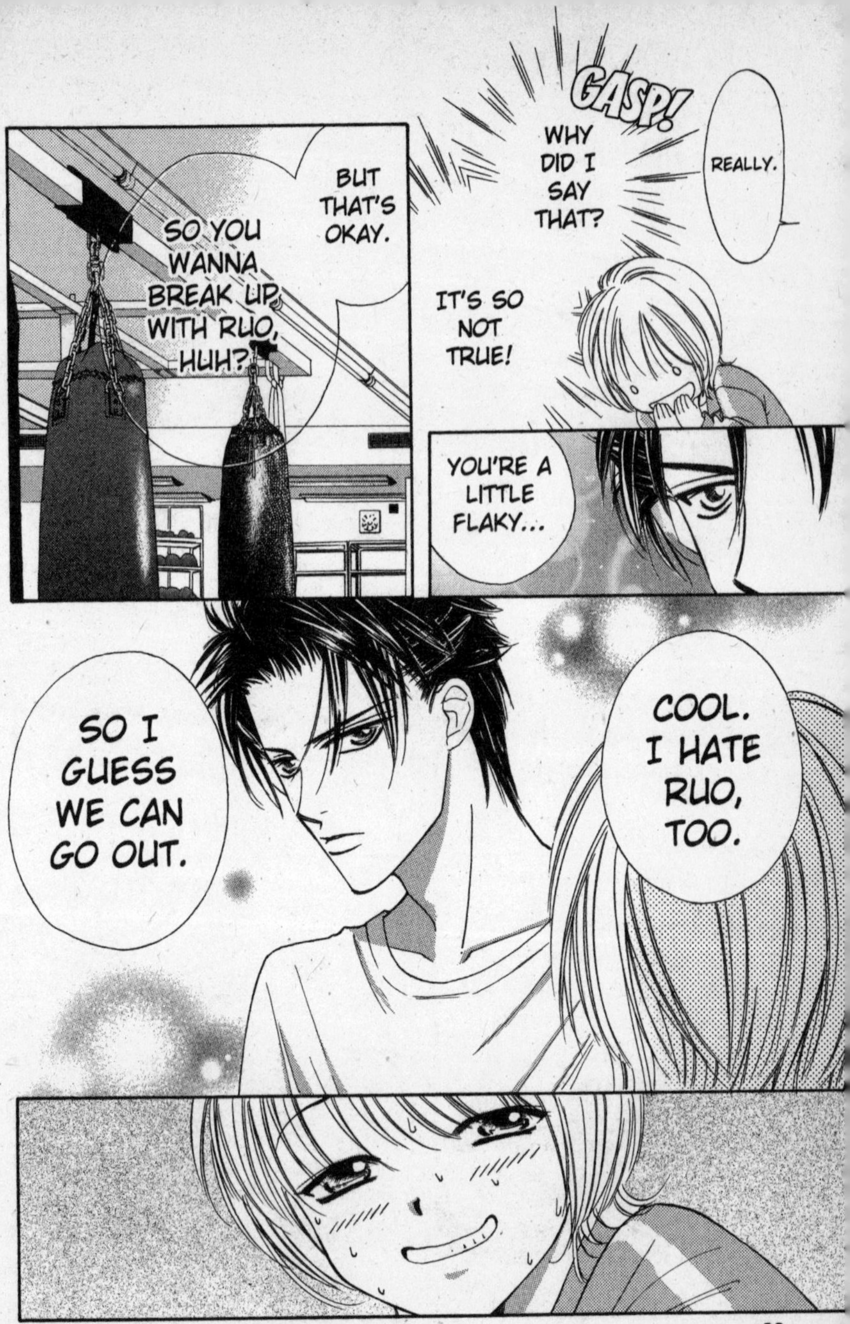
REALLY.
GASP!
WHY DID I SAY THAT?
IT'S SO NOT TRUE!
YOU'RE A LITTLE FLAKY...
SO YOU WANNA BREAK UP WITH RUO, HUH?
BUT THAT'S OKAY.
COOL. I HATE RUO, TOO.
SO I GUESS WE CAN GO OUT.

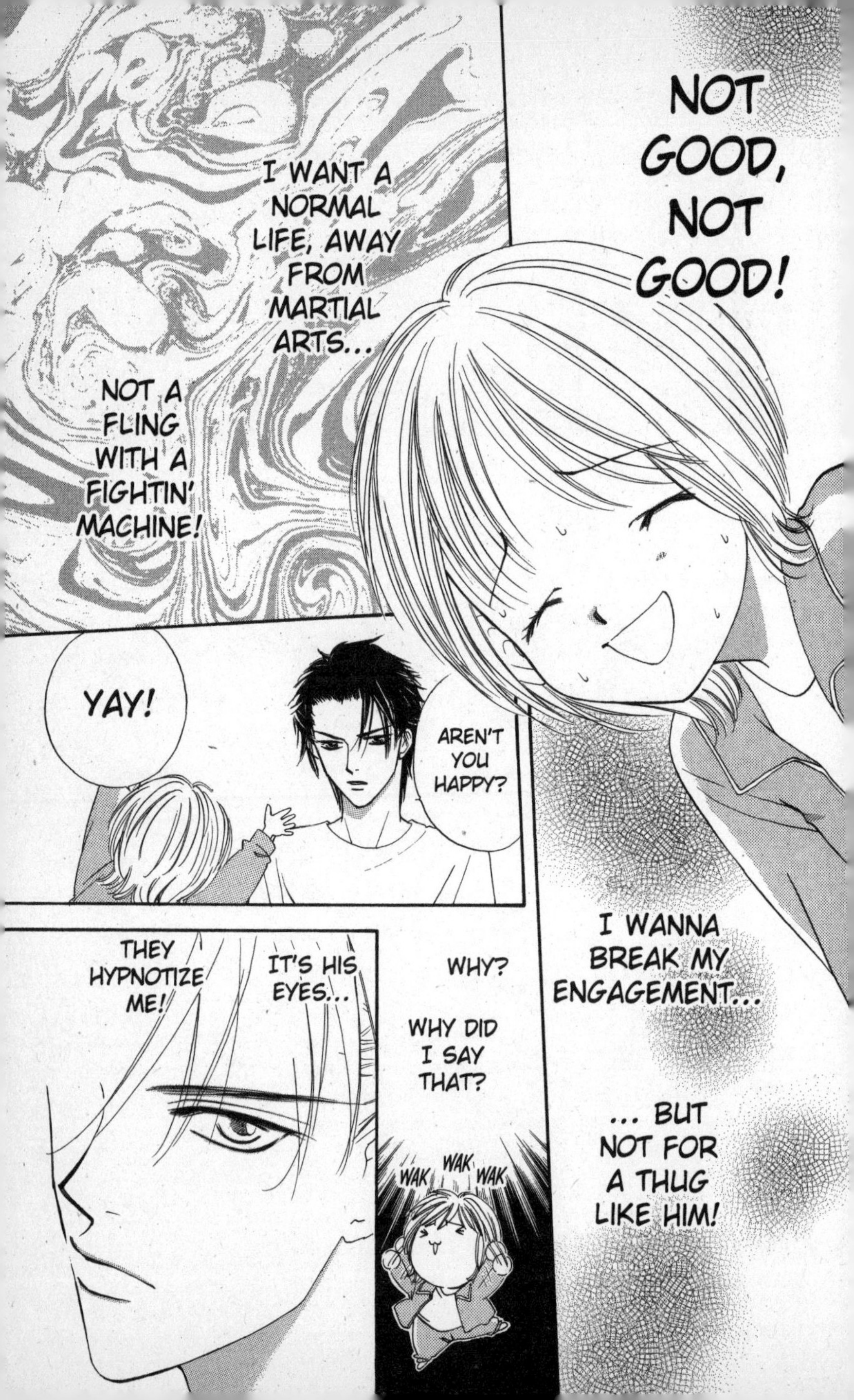
NOT GOOD, NOT GOOD!
I WANNA BREAK MY ENGAGEMENT...
... BUT NOT FOR A THUG LIKE HIM!
I WANT A NORMAL LIFE, AWAY FROM MARTIAL ARTS...
NOT A FLING WITH A FIGHTIN' MACHINE!
AREN'T YOU HAPPY?
YAY!
WHY?
WHY DID I SAY THAT?
WAK WAK WAK
IT'S HIS EYES...
THEY HYPNOTIZE ME!

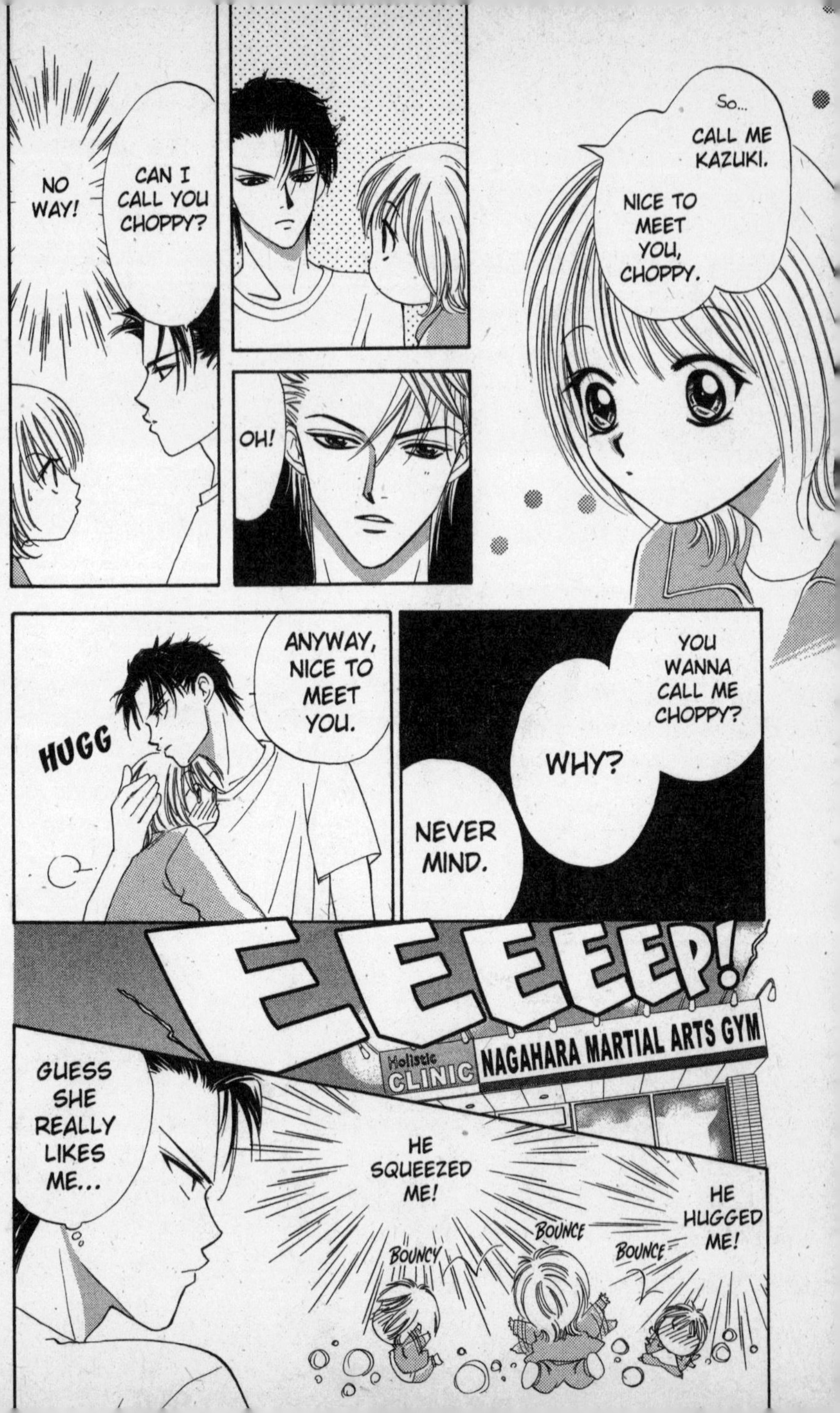
So... CALL ME KAZUKI.
NICE TO MEET YOU, CHOPPY.
OH!
CAN I CALL YOU CHOPPY?
NO WAY!
YOU WANNA CALL ME CHOPPY?
WHY?
NEVER MIND.
ANYWAY, NICE TO MEET YOU.
HUGG
EEEEEP!
NAGAHARA MARTIAL ARTS GYM
Holistic CLINIC
HE HUGGED ME!
BOUNCE
BOUNCE
HE SQUEEZED ME!
BOUNCY
GUESS SHE REALLY LIKES ME...

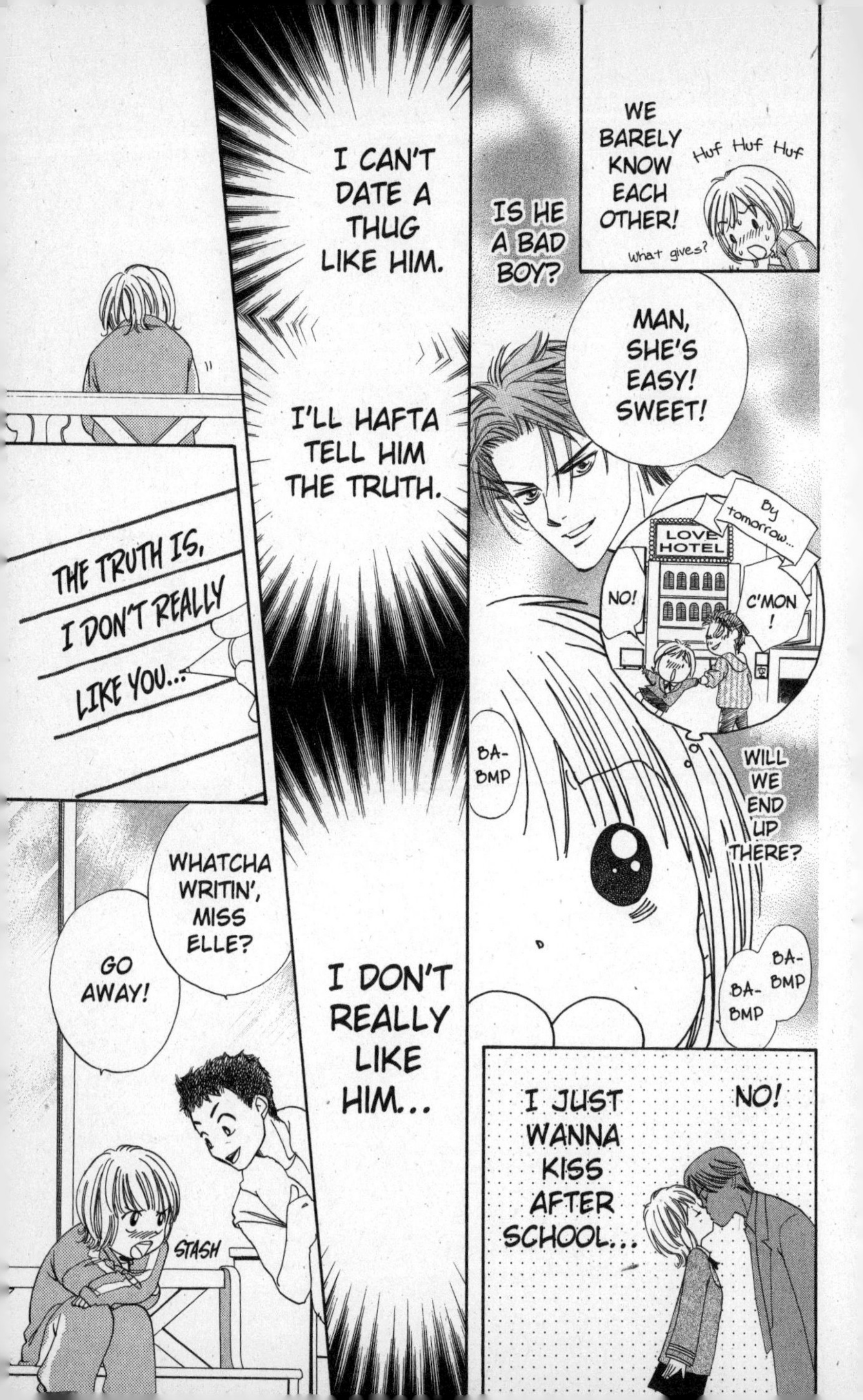
WE BARELY KNOW EACH OTHER!
Huf Huf Huf
What gives?
IS HE A BAD BOY?
MAN, SHE'S EASY! SWEET!
By tomorrow...
LOVE HOTEL
C'MON!
NO!
BA-BMP
WILL WE END UP THERE?
BA-BMP
BA-BMP
NO!
I JUST WANNA KISS AFTER SCHOOL...
I CAN'T DATE A THUG LIKE HIM.
I'LL HAFTA TELL HIM THE TRUTH.
I DON'T REALLY LIKE HIM...
THE TRUTH IS, I DON'T REALLY LIKE YOU...
WHATCHA WRITIN', MISS ELLE?
GO AWAY!
STASH

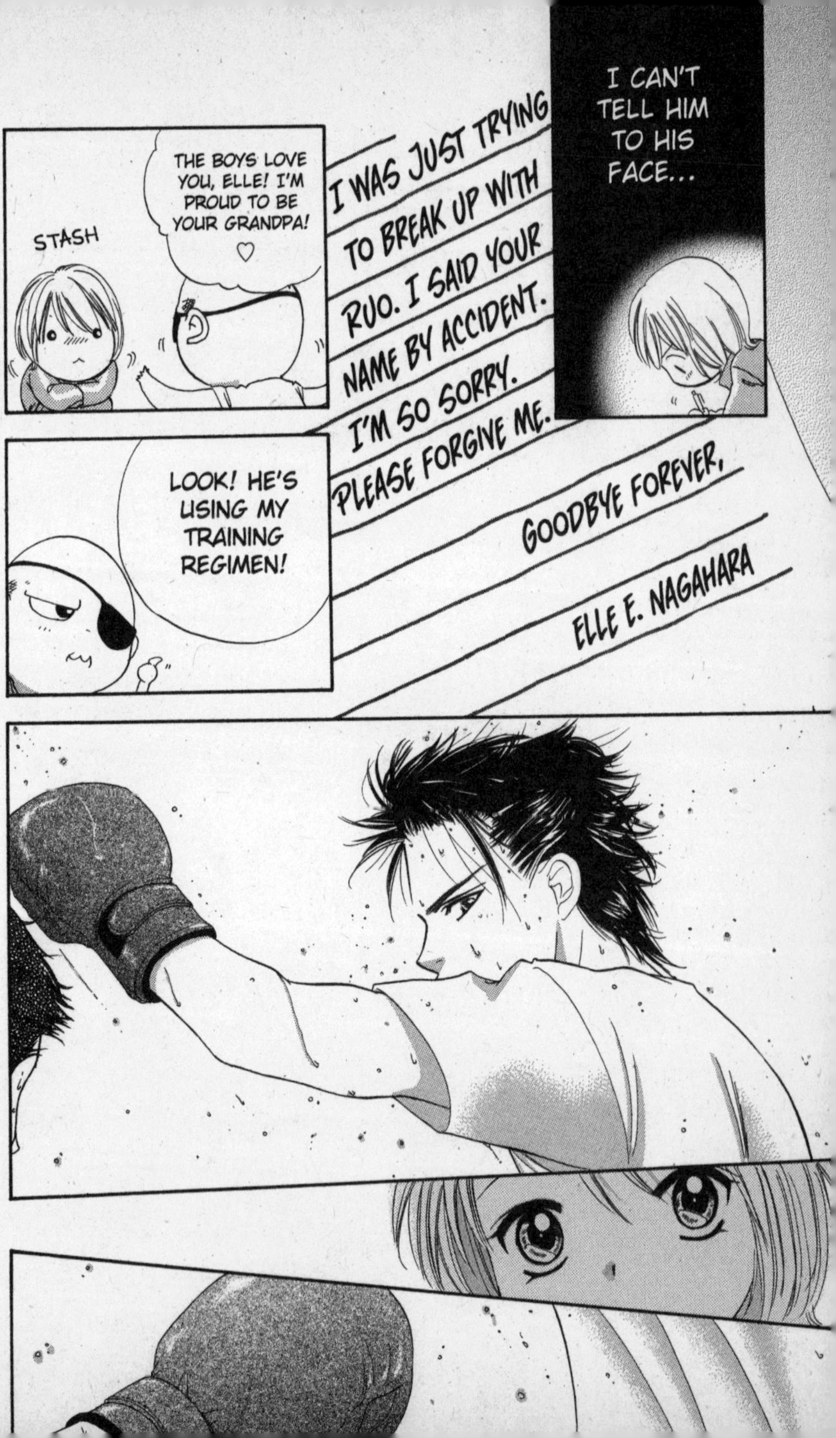
I CAN'T TELL HIM TO HIS FACE...
I WAS JUST TRYING TO BREAK UP WITH RUO. I SAID YOUR NAME BY ACCIDENT. I'M SO SORRY. PLEASE FORGIVE ME.
GOODBYE FOREVER,
ELLE E. NAGAHARA
THE BOYS LOVE YOU, ELLE! I'M PROUD TO BE YOUR GRANDPA! ♡
STASH
LOOK! HE'S USING MY TRAINING REGIMEN!

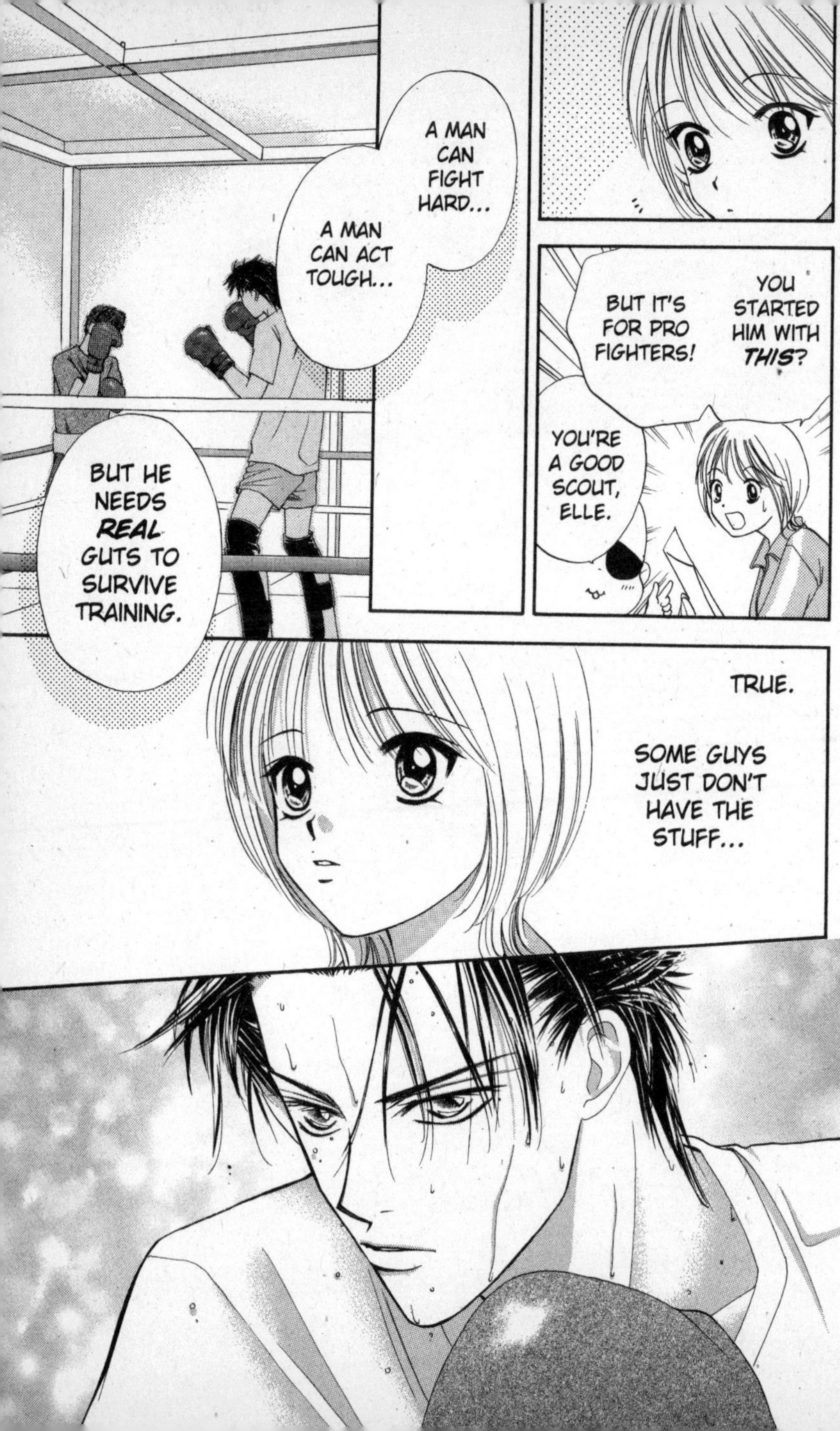
YOU STARTED HIM WITH *THIS*?
BUT IT'S FOR PRO FIGHTERS!
YOU'RE A GOOD SCOUT, ELLE.
A MAN CAN FIGHT HARD...
A MAN CAN ACT TOUGH...
BUT HE NEEDS *REAL* GUTS TO SURVIVE TRAINING.
TRUE.
SOME GUYS JUST DON'T HAVE THE STUFF...

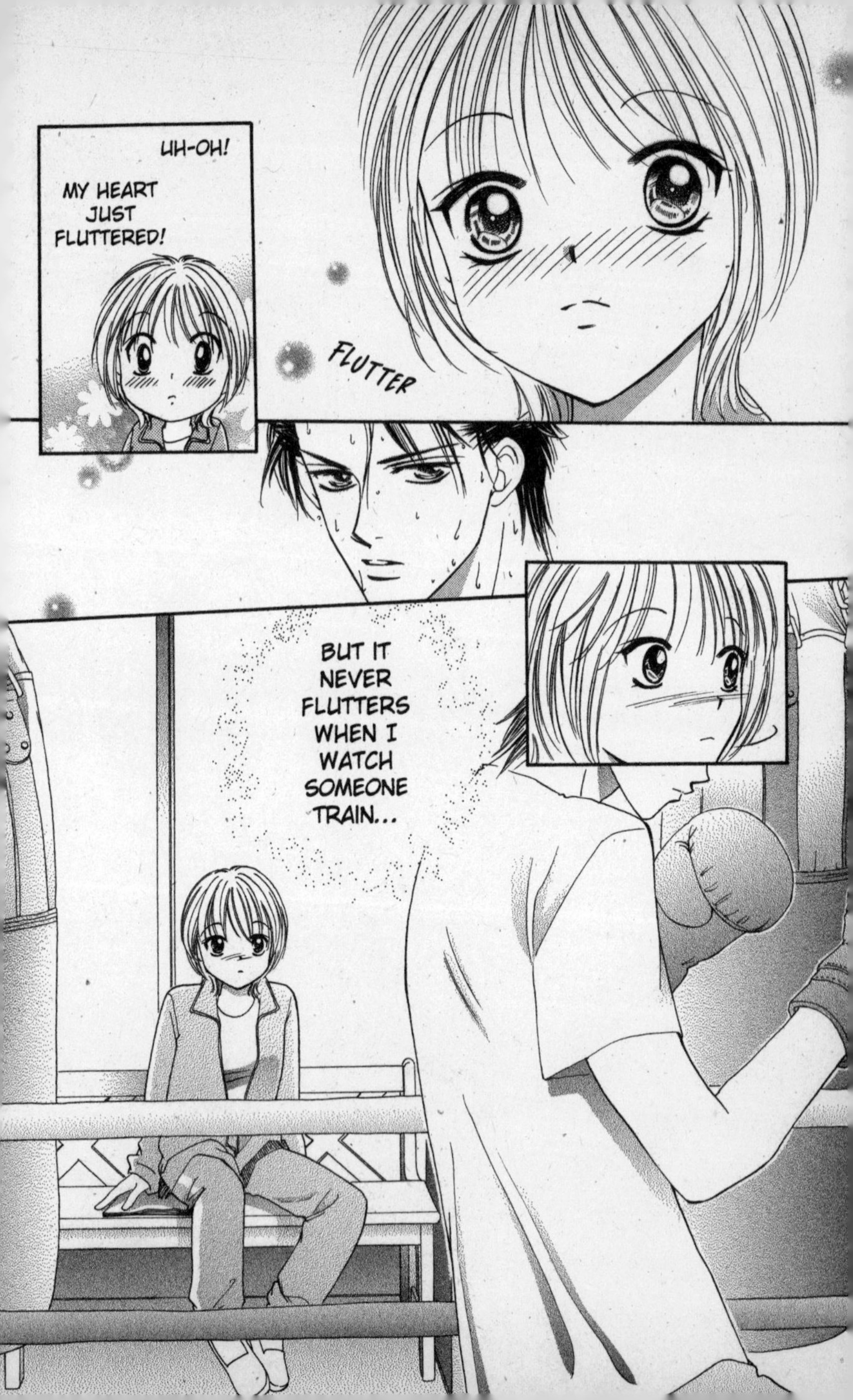
FLUTTER
UH-OH!
MY HEART JUST FLUTTERED!
BUT IT NEVER FLUTTERS WHEN I WATCH SOMEONE TRAIN...

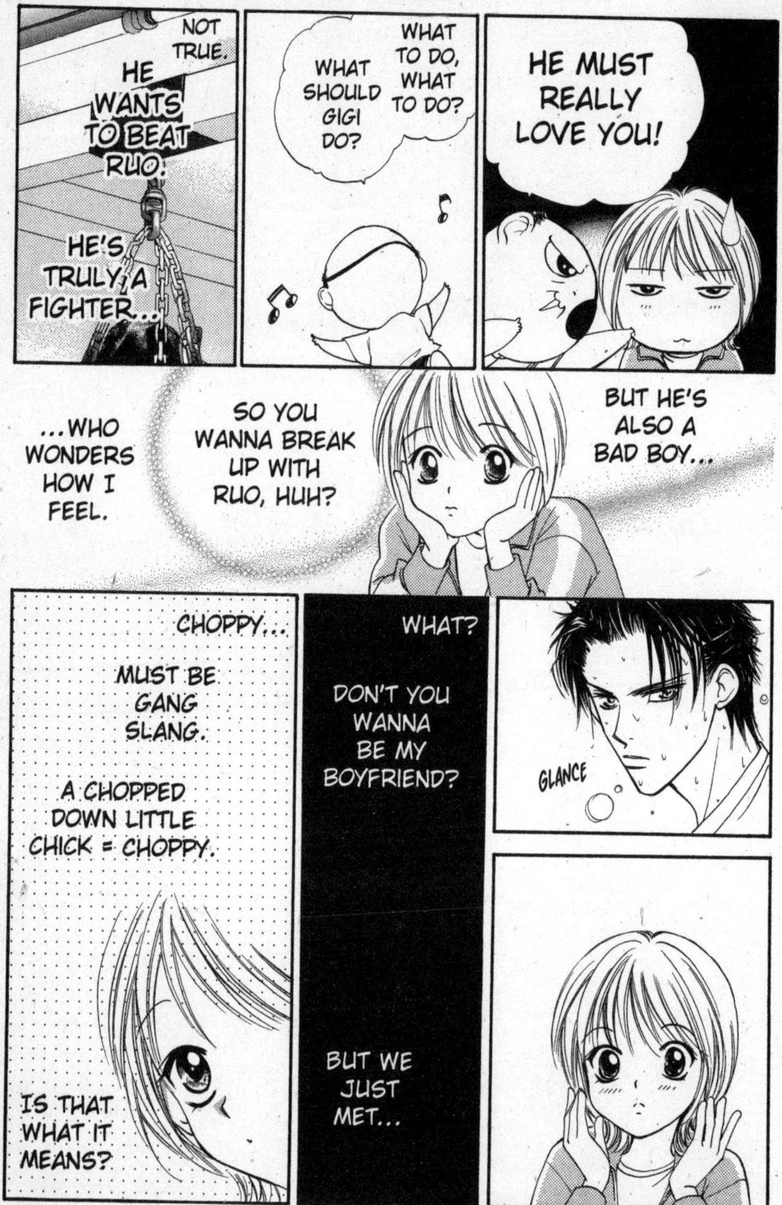
HE MUST REALLY LOVE YOU!
WHAT TO DO, WHAT TO DO?
WHAT SHOULD GIGI DO?
NOT TRUE.
HE WANTS TO BEAT RUO.
HE'S TRULY A FIGHTER...
BUT HE'S ALSO A BAD BOY...
SO YOU WANNA BREAK UP WITH RUO, HUH?
...WHO WONDERS HOW I FEEL.
GLANCE
WHAT?
DON'T YOU WANNA BE MY BOYFRIEND?
BUT WE JUST MET...
CHOPPY...
MUST BE GANG SLANG.
A CHOPPED DOWN LITTLE CHICK = CHOPPY.
IS THAT WHAT IT MEANS?

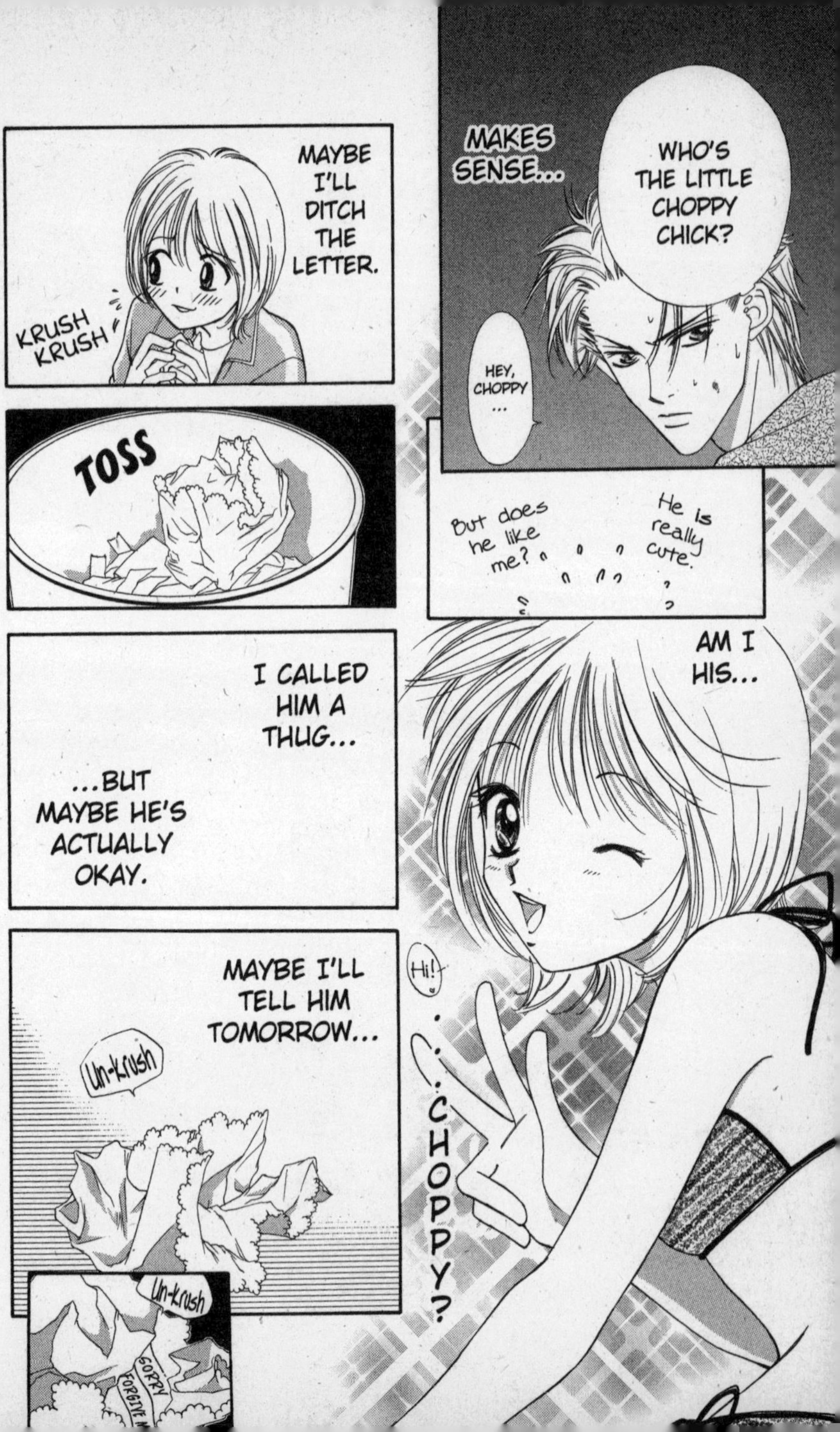
WHO'S THE LITTLE CHOPPY CHICK?
MAKES SENSE...
HEY, CHOPPY...
He is really cute.
But does he like me?
AM I HIS...
Hi!
...CHOPPY?
MAYBE I'LL DITCH THE LETTER.
KRUSH KRUSH
TOSS
I CALLED HIM A THUG...
...BUT MAYBE HE'S ACTUALLY OKAY.
MAYBE I'LL TELL HIM TOMORROW...
Un-krush
Un-krush
SORRY
FORGIVE

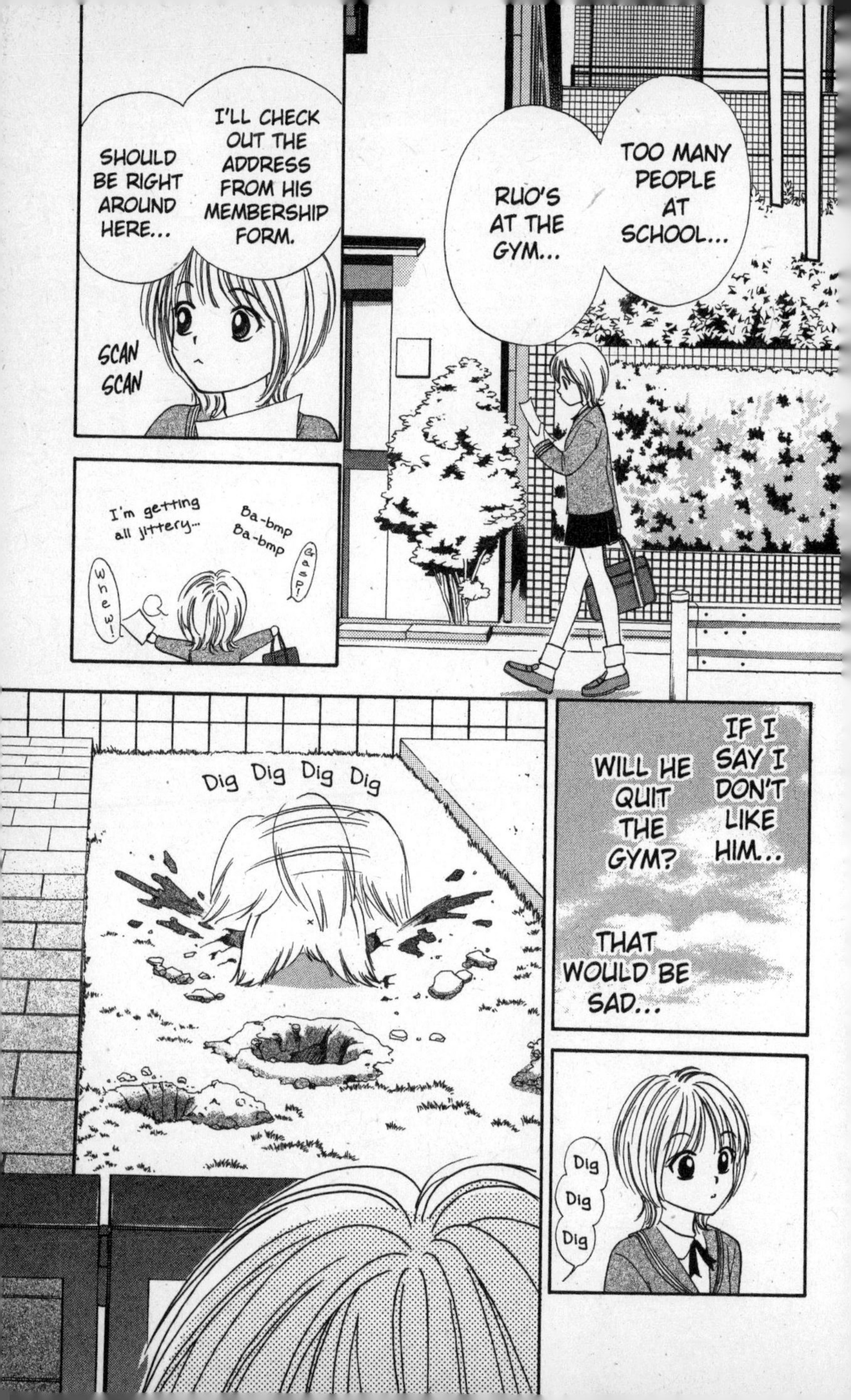
TOO MANY PEOPLE AT SCHOOL...
RUO'S AT THE GYM...
I'LL CHECK OUT THE ADDRESS FROM HIS MEMBERSHIP FORM.
SHOULD BE RIGHT AROUND HERE...
SCAN SCAN
Ba-bmp Ba-bmp
Gasp!
I'm getting all jittery...
Whew!
IF I SAY I DON'T LIKE HIM...
WILL HE QUIT THE GYM?
THAT WOULD BE SAD...
Dig Dig Dig
Dig Dig Dig Dig

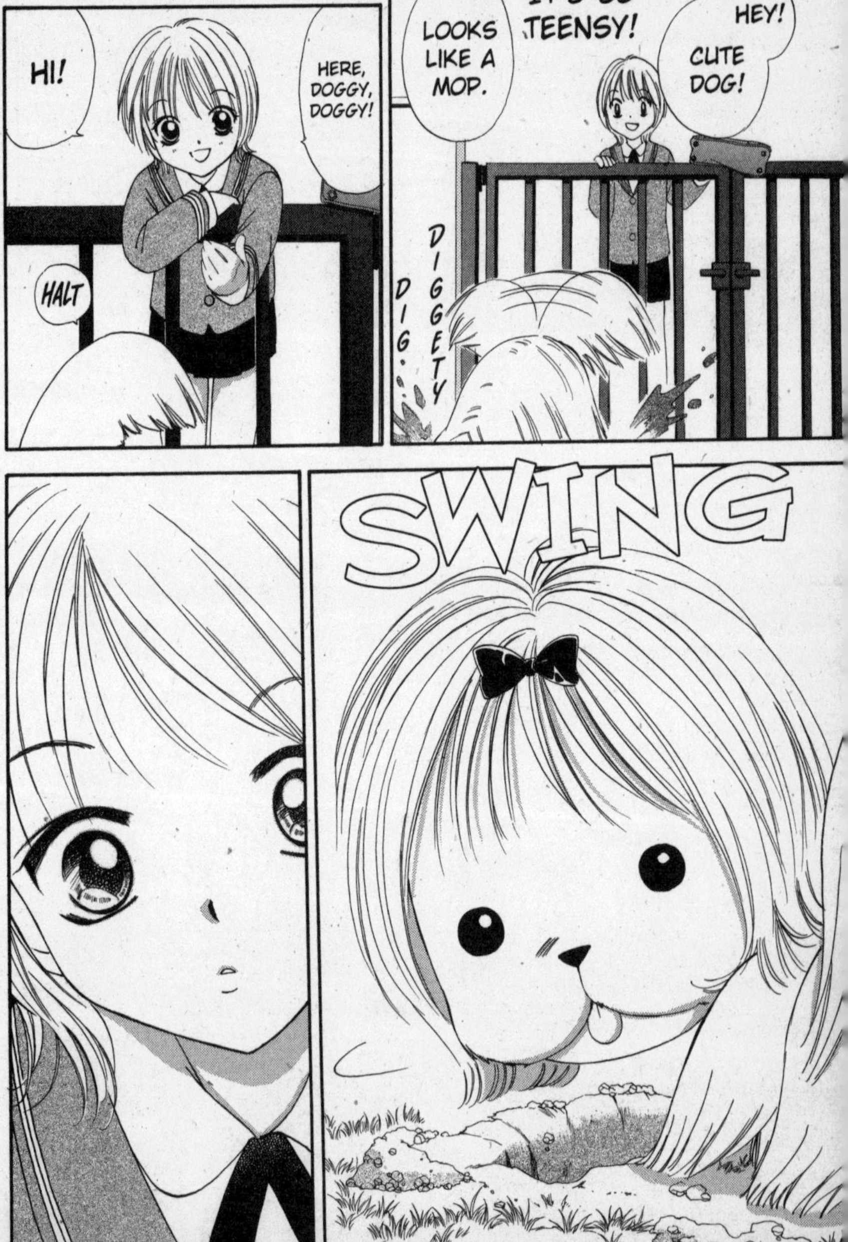
HEY!
CUTE DOG!
IT'S SO TEENSY!
LOOKS LIKE A MOP.
DIGGETY
DIG
HERE, DOGGY, DOGGY!
HI!
HALT
SWING

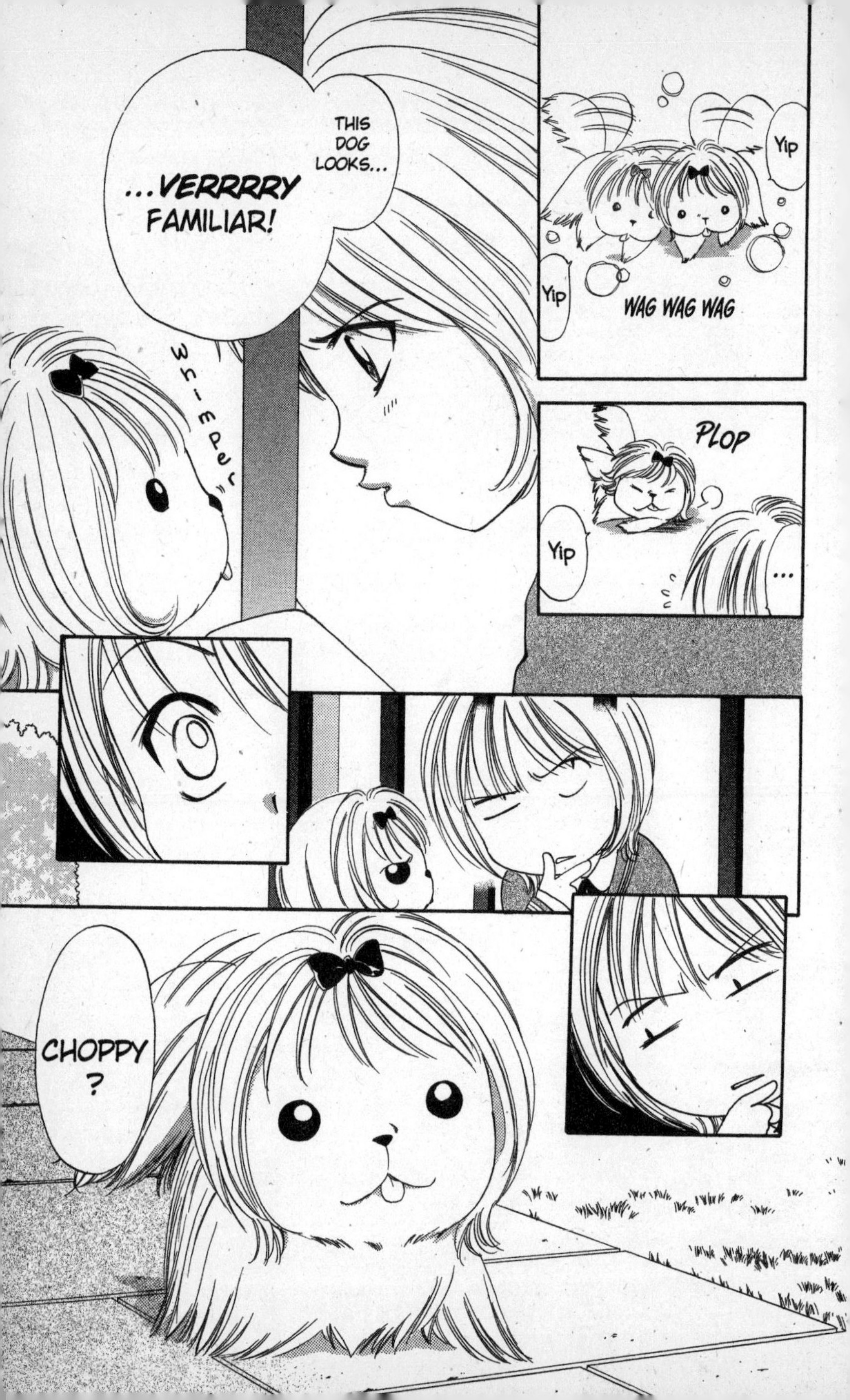
Yip
Yip
WAG WAG WAG
PLOP
Yip
...
THIS DOG LOOKS...
...VERRRRY FAMILIAR!
whimper
CHOPPY ?

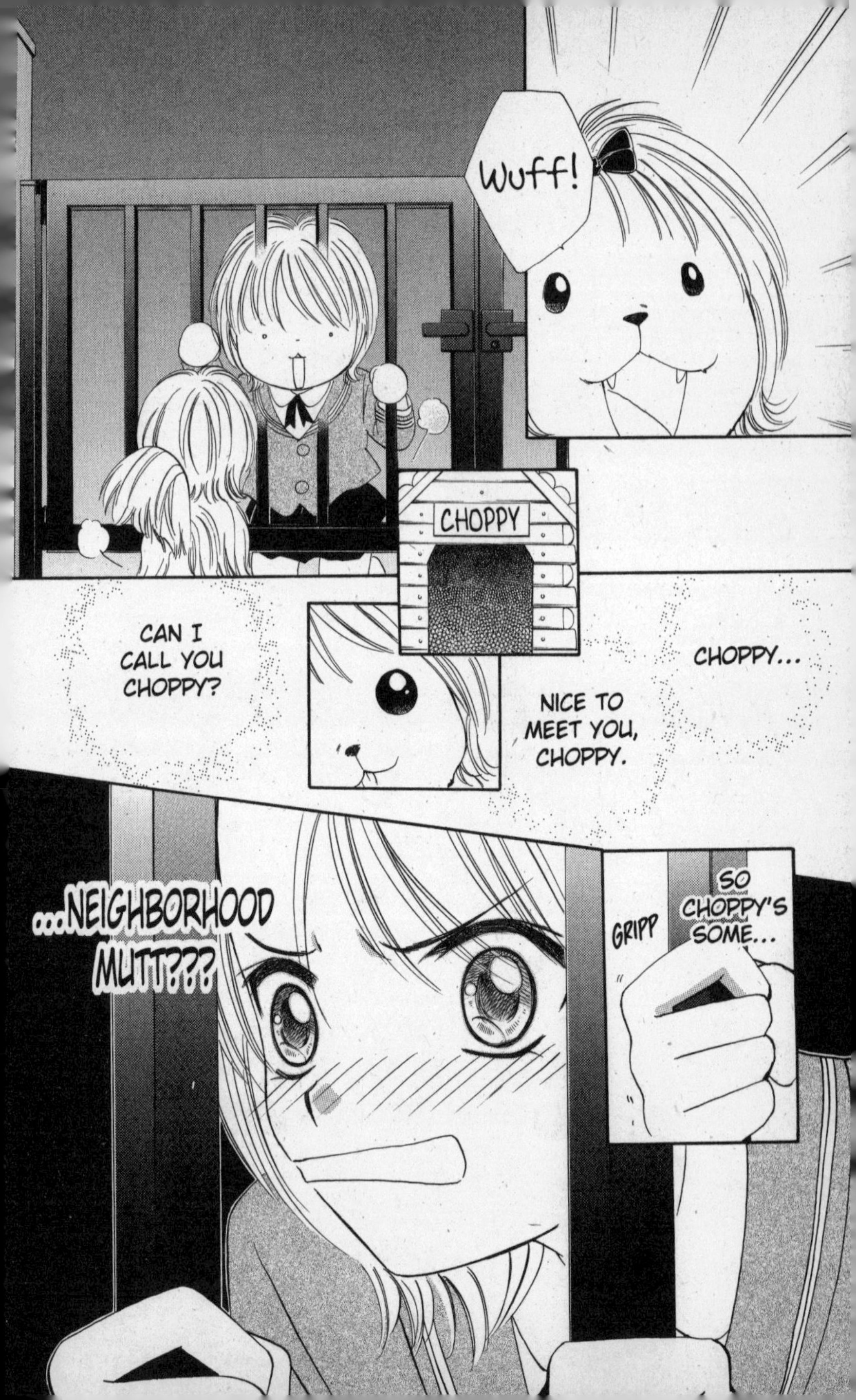
Wuff!
CHOPPY
CHOPPY...
NICE TO MEET YOU, CHOPPY.
CAN I CALL YOU CHOPPY?
SO CHOPPY'S SOME...
GRIPP
...NEIGHBORHOOD MUTT???

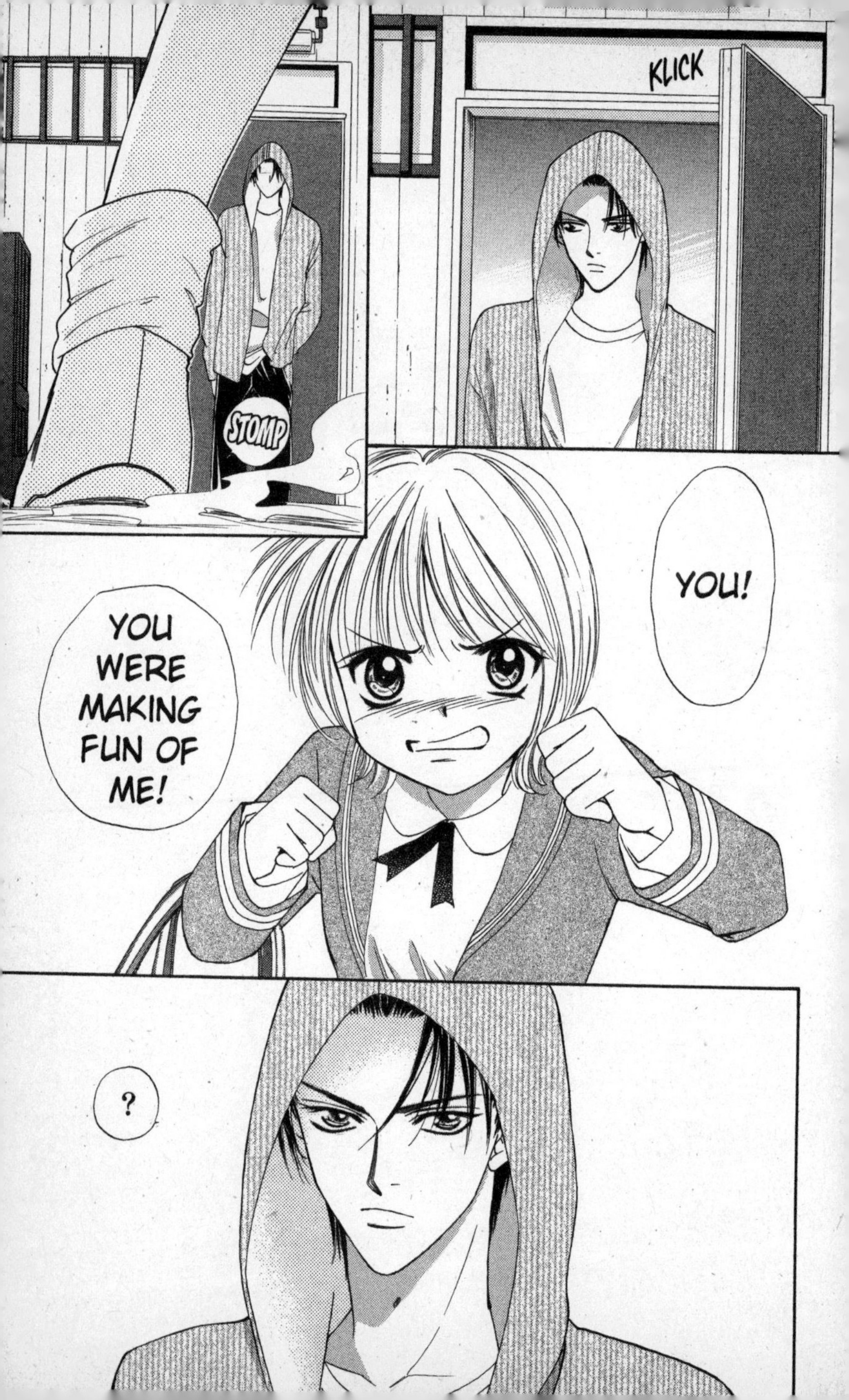
KLICK
STOMP
YOU!
YOU WERE MAKING FUN OF ME!
?

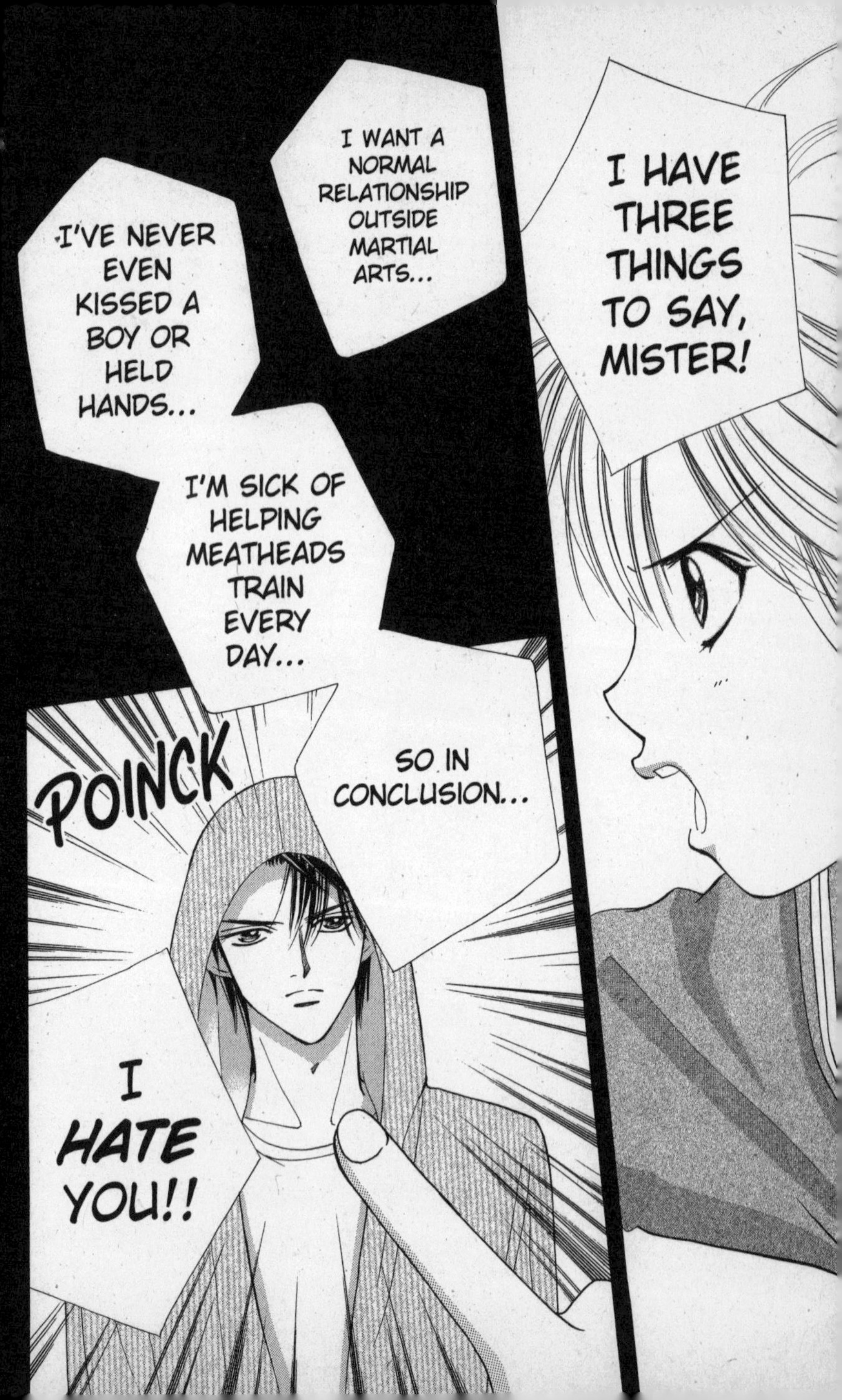
I HAVE THREE THINGS TO SAY, MISTER!
I WANT A NORMAL RELATIONSHIP OUTSIDE MARTIAL ARTS...
I'VE NEVER EVEN KISSED A BOY OR HELD HANDS...
I'M SICK OF HELPING MEATHEADS TRAIN EVERY DAY...
SO IN CONCLUSION...
POINCK
I HATE YOU!!

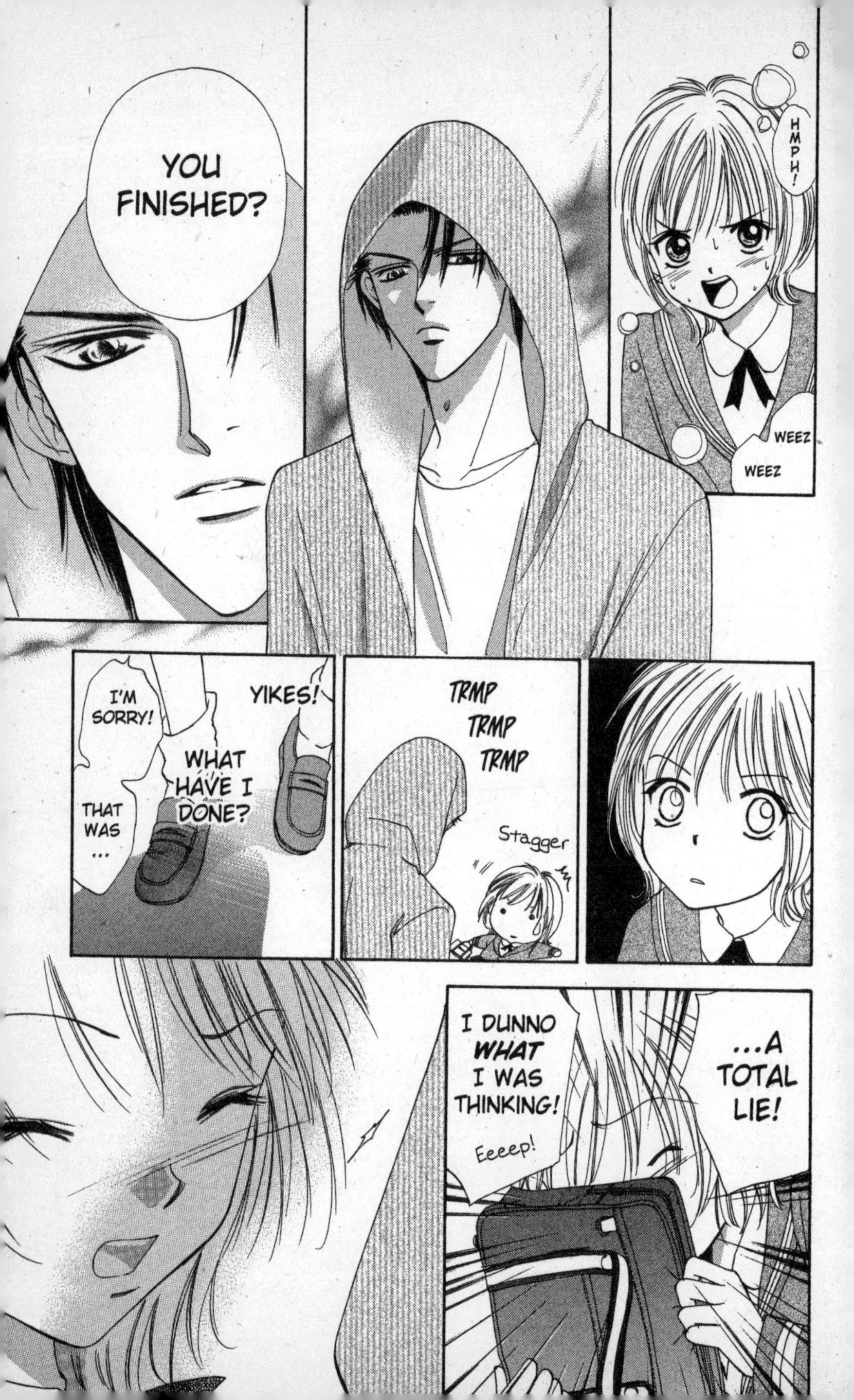
HMPH!
WEEZ
WEEZ
YOU FINISHED?
TRMP
TRMP
TRMP
Stagger
YIKES!
I'M SORRY!
WHAT HAVE I DONE?
THAT WAS ...
...A TOTAL LIE!
I DUNNO **WHAT** I WAS THINKING!
Eeeep!

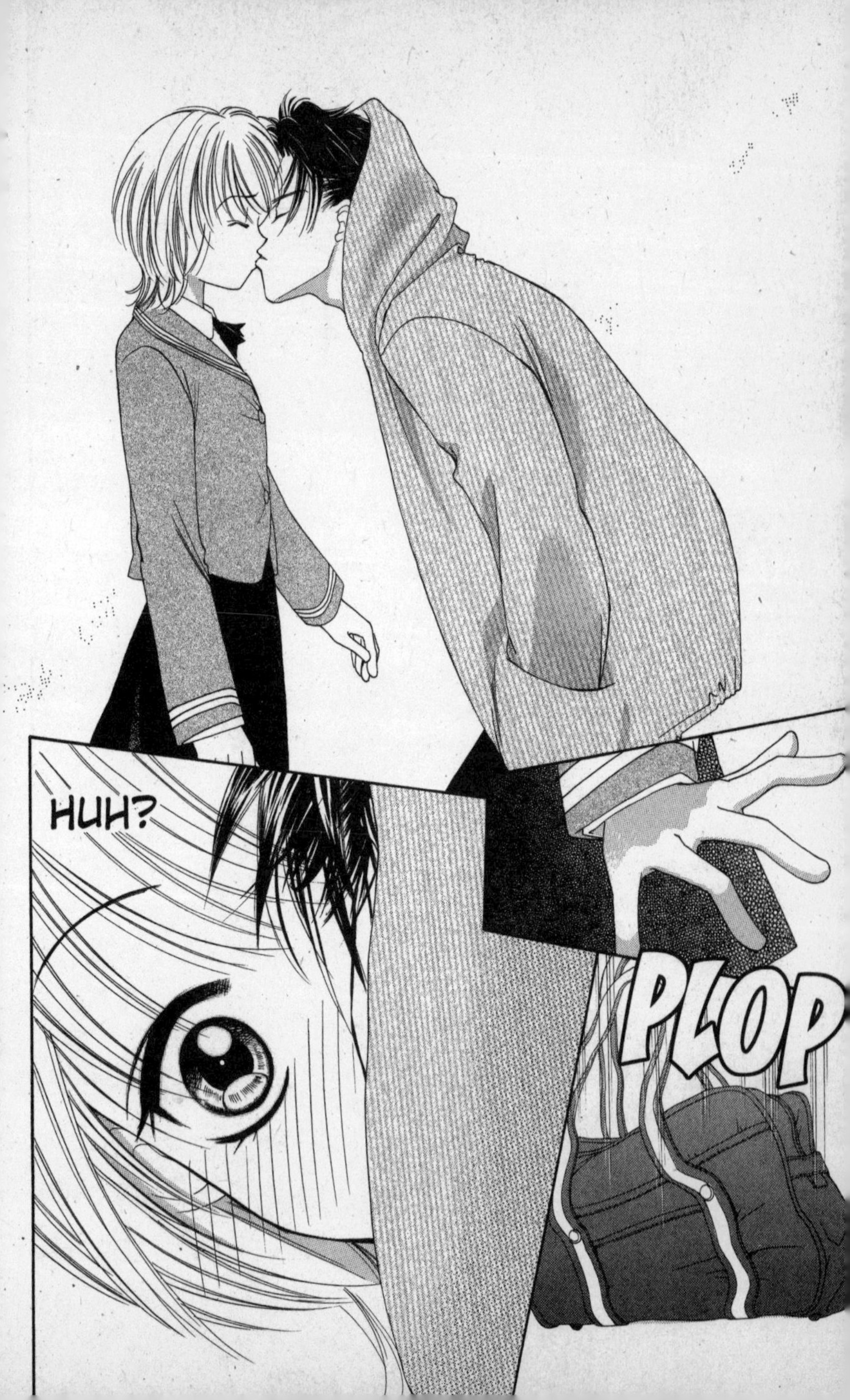
PLOP
HUH?

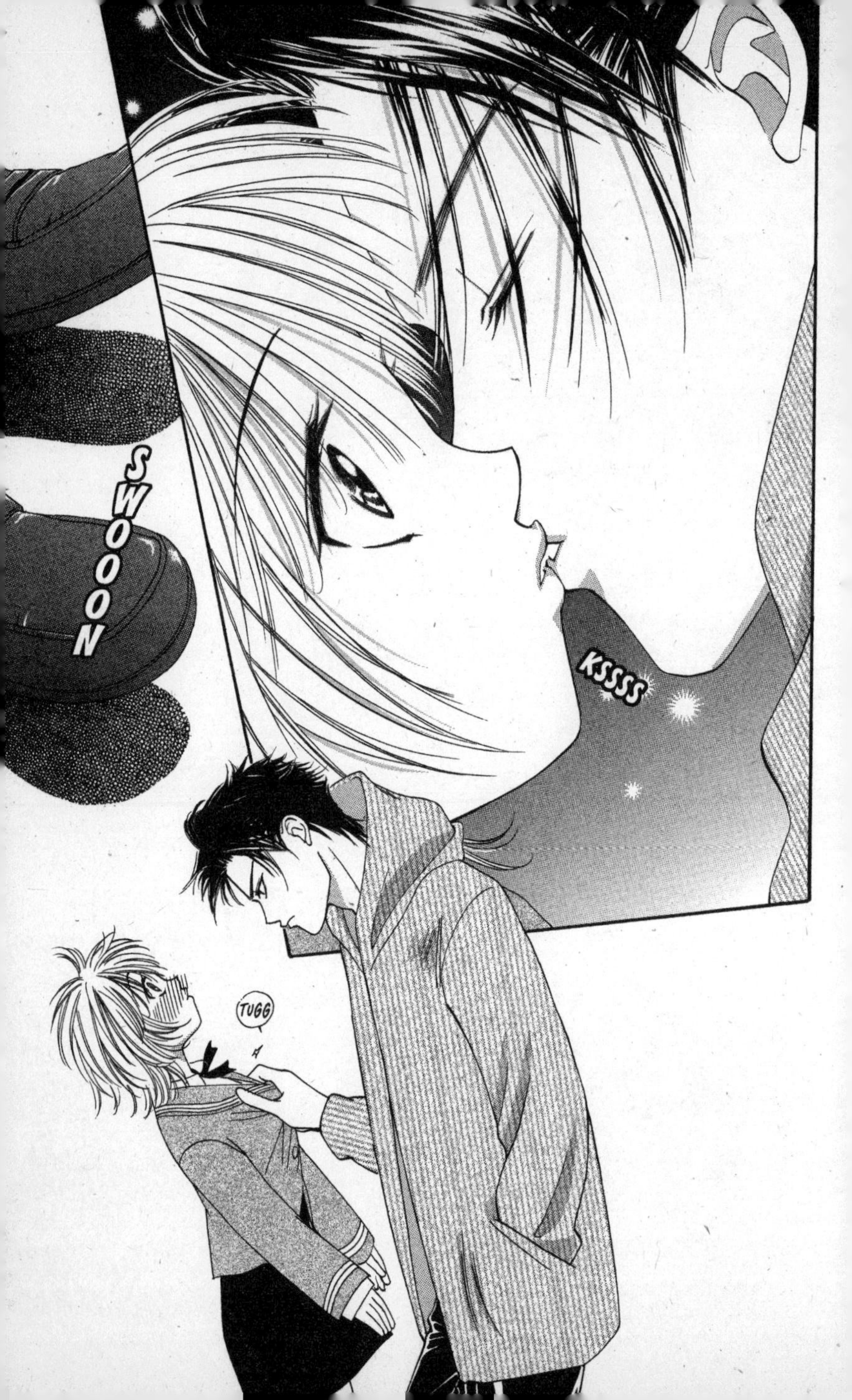
KSSSS
SWOOOON
TUGG

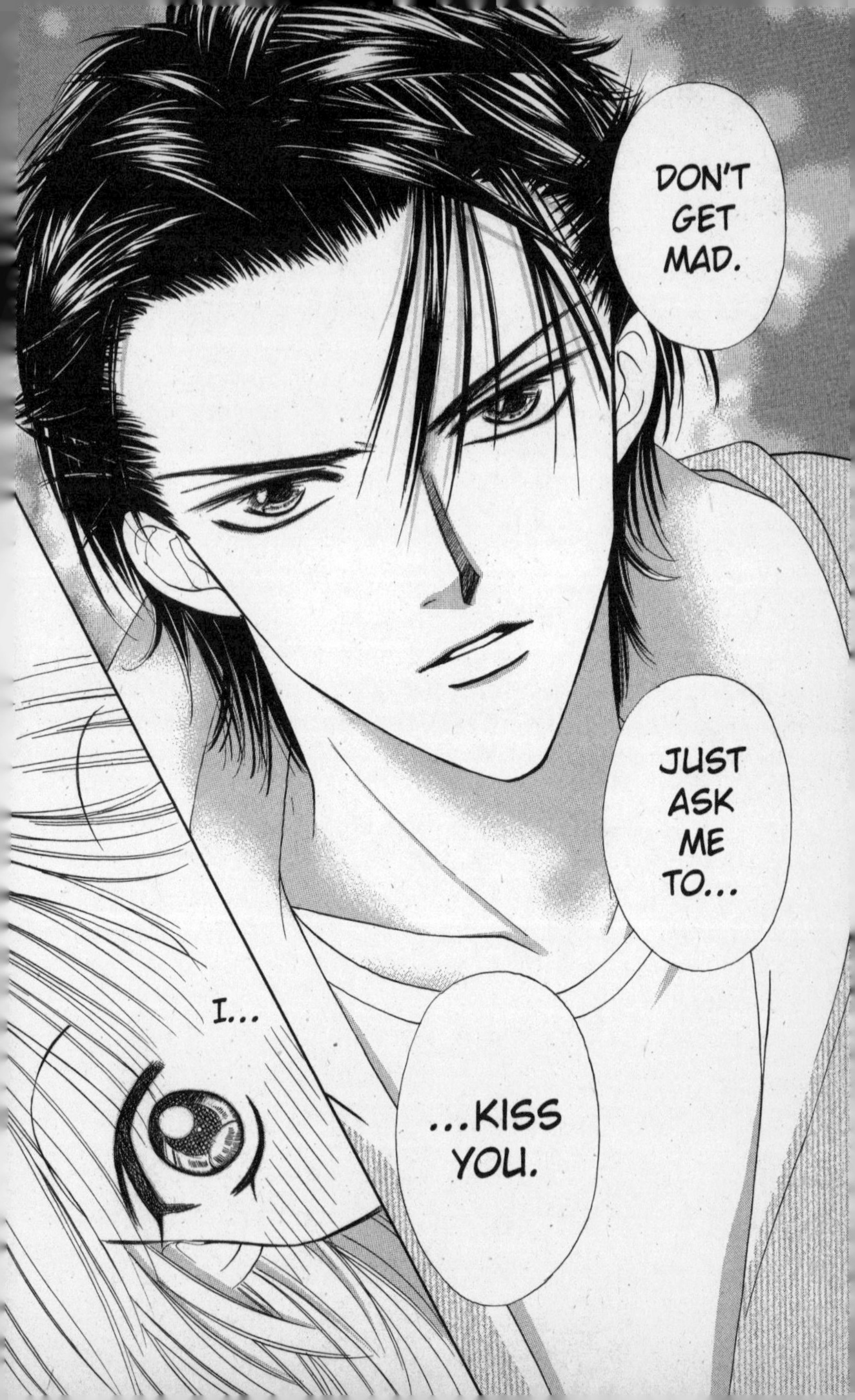
DON'T GET MAD.
JUST ASK ME TO...
...KISS YOU.
I...

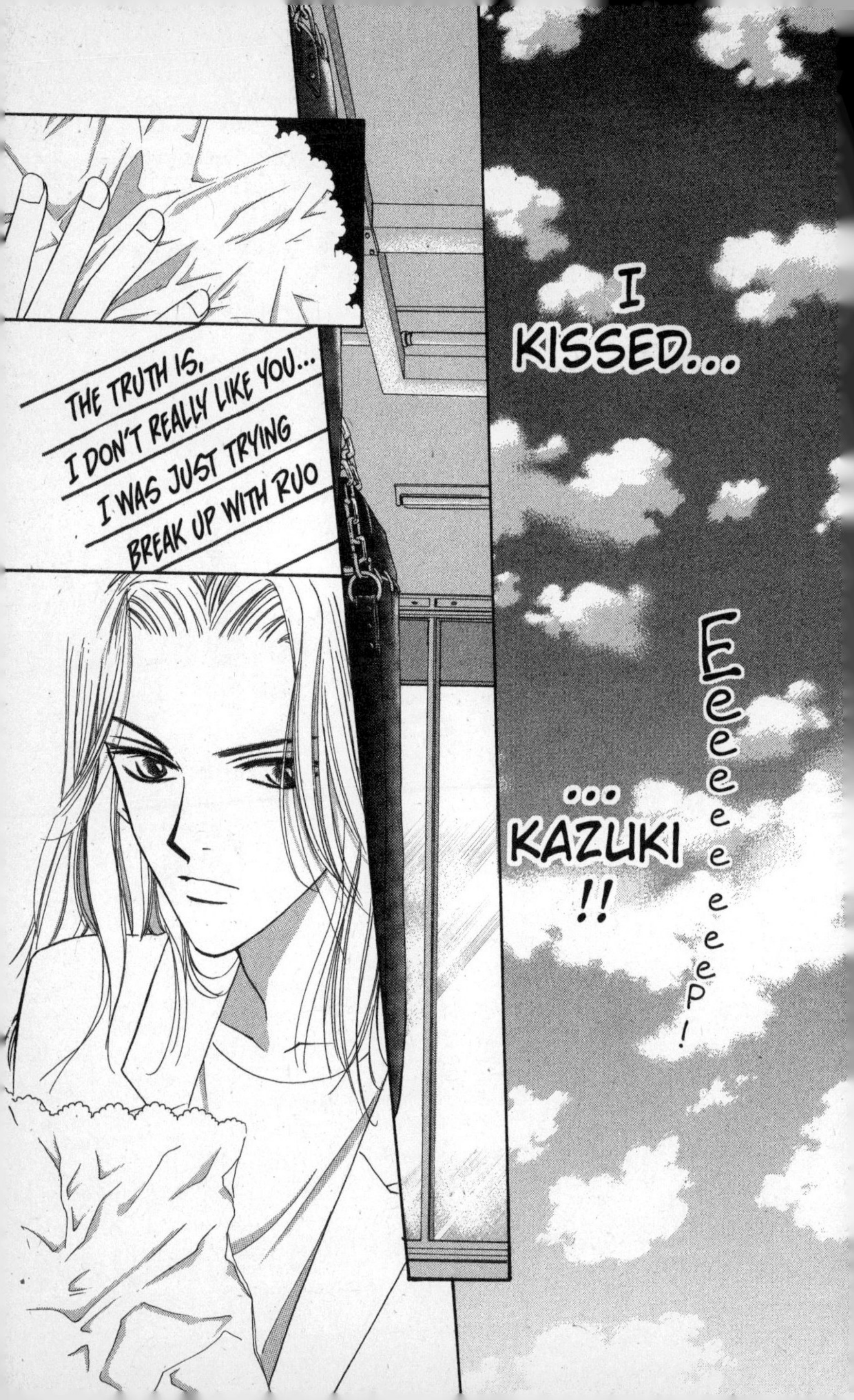
I KISSED...
...KAZUKI!!
Eeeeeeeeeep!
THE TRUTH IS,
I DON'T REALLY LIKE YOU...
I WAS JUST TRYING
BREAK UP WITH RUO

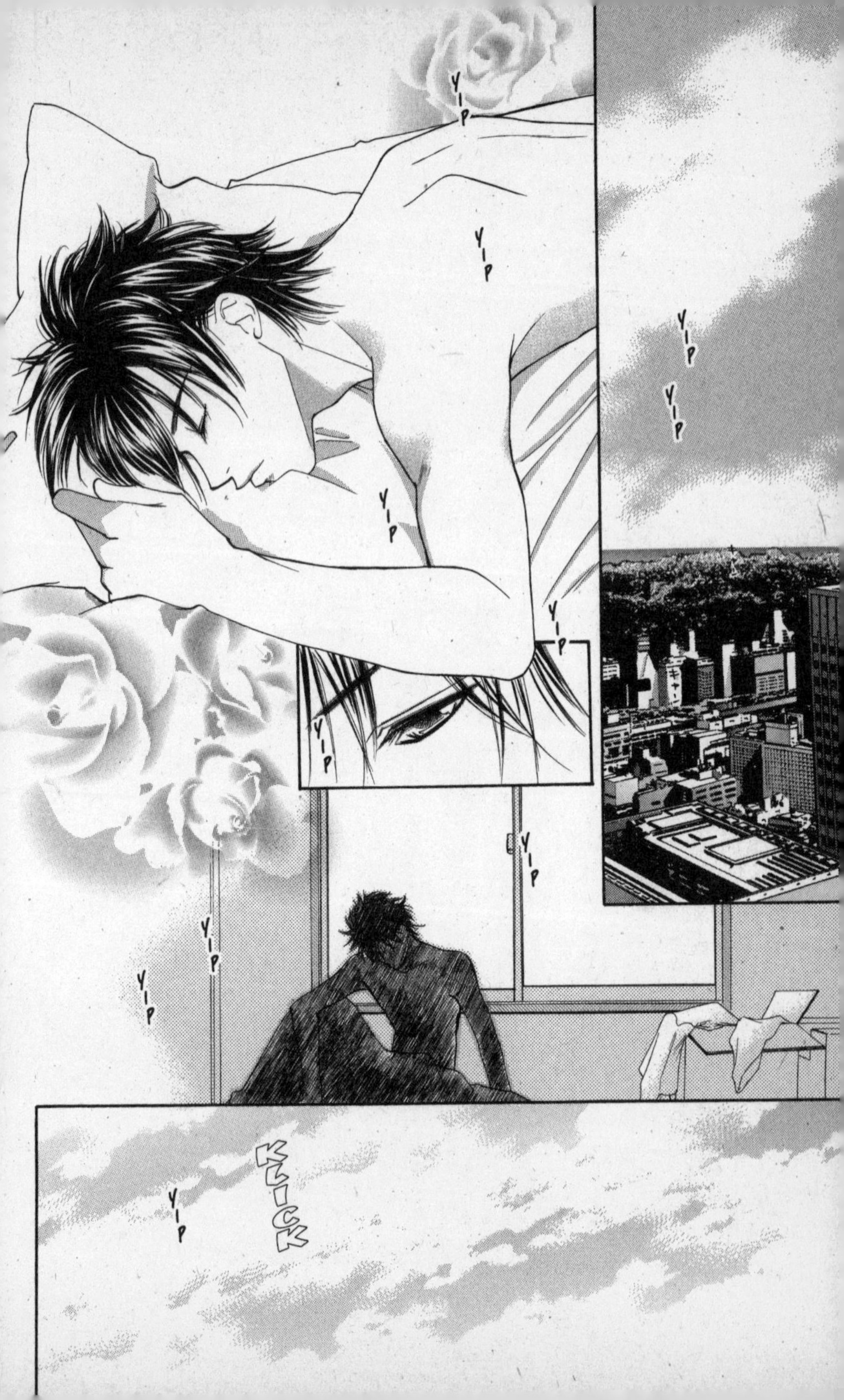
YIP
YIP
YIP
YIP
YIP
YIP
YIP
YIP
YIP
YIP
KLICK
YIP

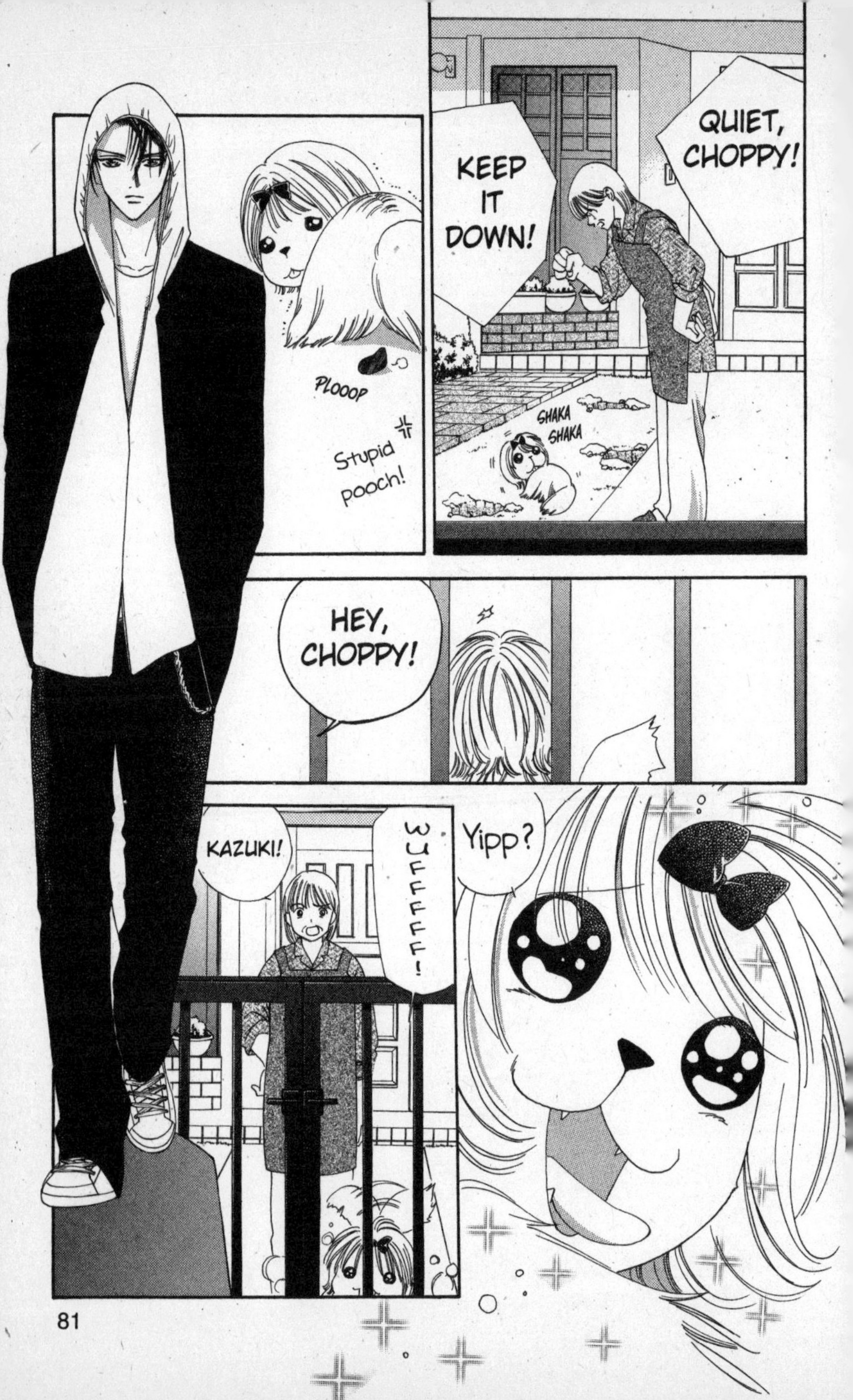
QUIET, CHOPPY!
KEEP IT DOWN!
SHAKA SHAKA
PLOOOP
Stupid pooch!
HEY, CHOPPY!
Yipp?
WUFFFFF!
KAZUKI!

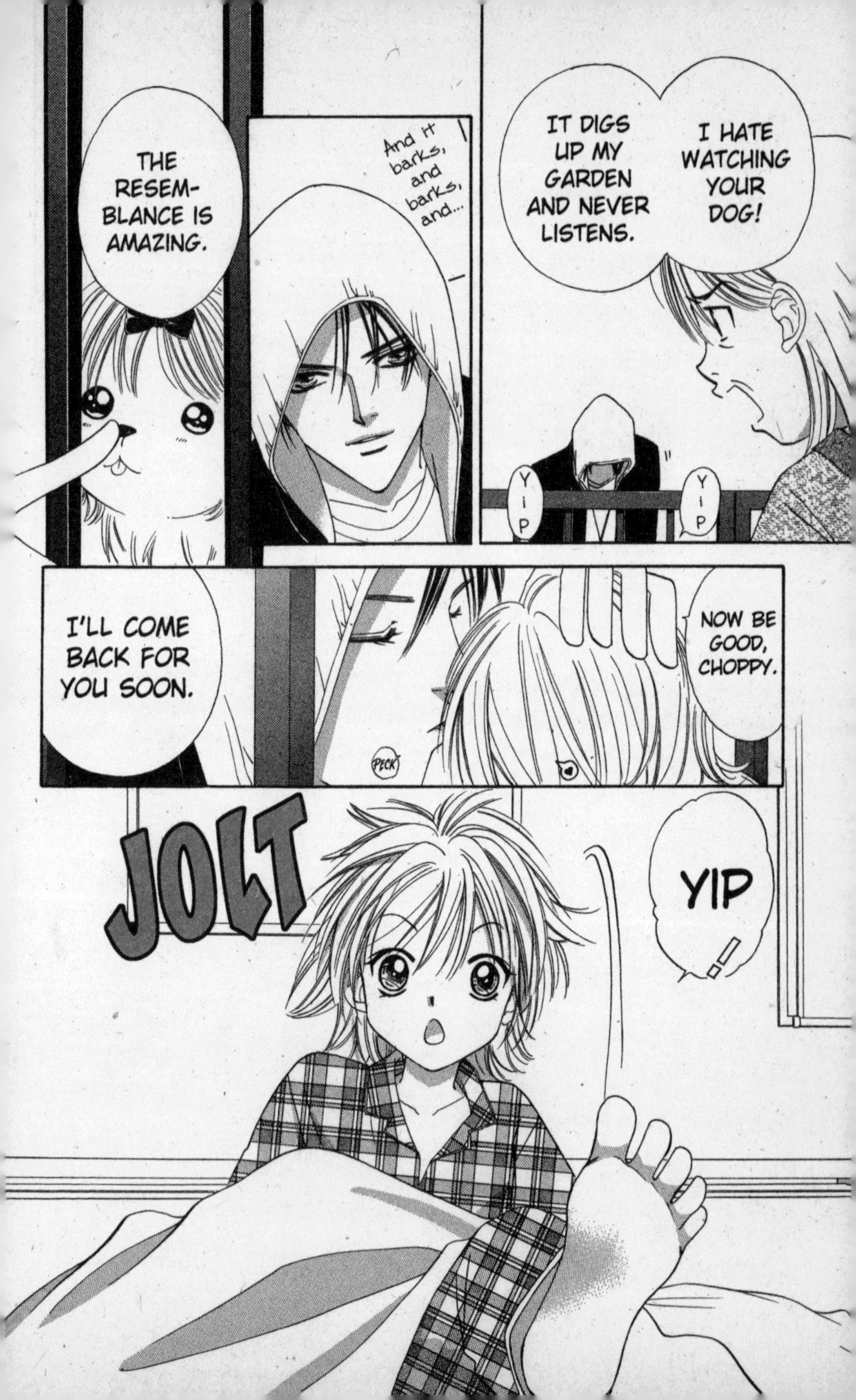
I HATE WATCHING YOUR DOG!
IT DIGS UP MY GARDEN AND NEVER LISTENS.
YiP
YiP
And it barks, and barks, and...
THE RESEM-BLANCE IS AMAZING.
NOW BE GOOD, CHOPPY.
PECK
I'LL COME BACK FOR YOU SOON.
YIP
!
JOLT

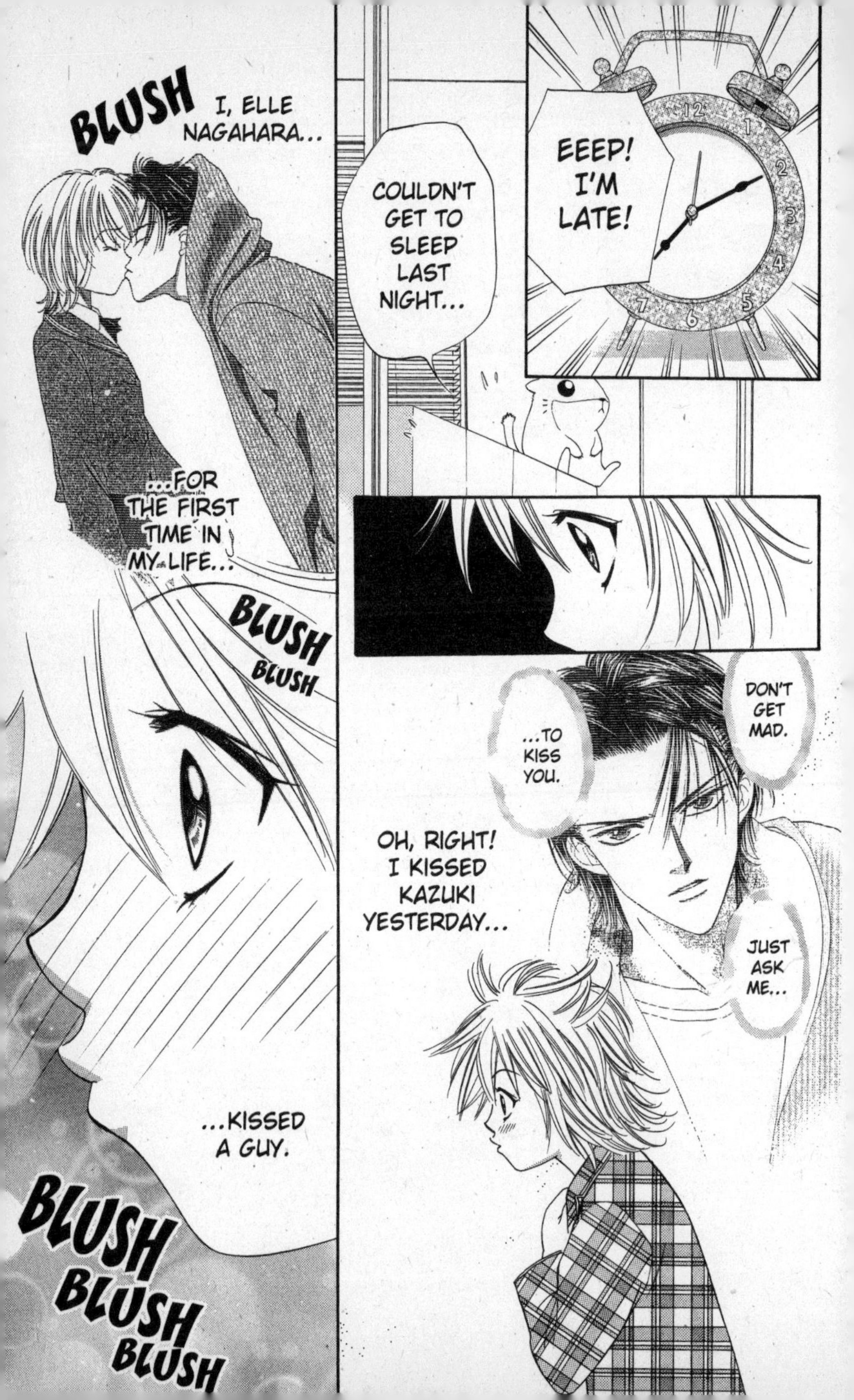
EEEP! I'M LATE!
COULDN'T GET TO SLEEP LAST NIGHT...
DON'T GET MAD.
JUST ASK ME...
...TO KISS YOU.
OH, RIGHT! I KISSED KAZUKI YESTERDAY...
BLUSH
I, ELLE NAGAHARA...
...FOR THE FIRST TIME IN MY LIFE...
BLUSH
BLUSH
...KISSED A GUY.
BLUSH
BLUSH
BLUSH

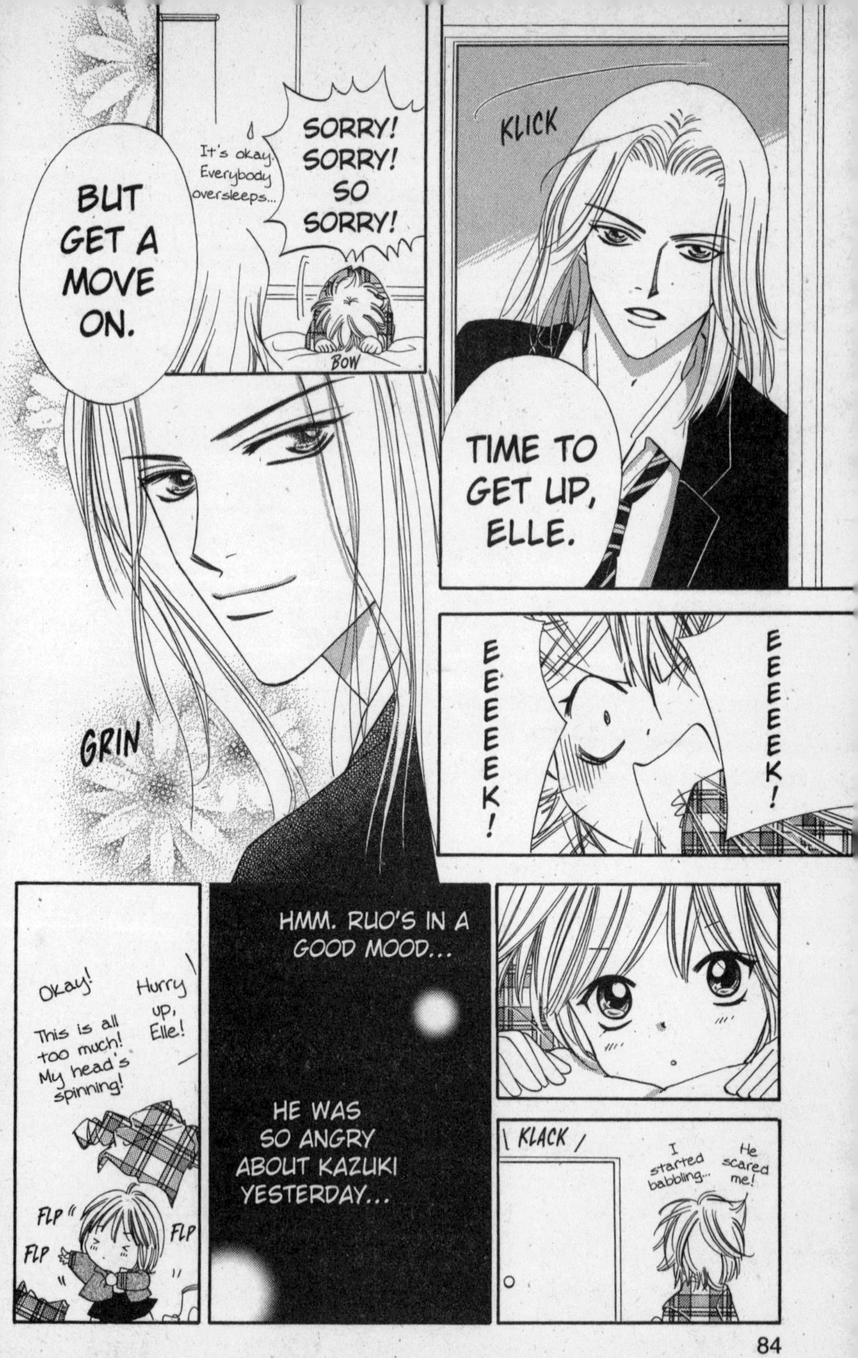
KLICK
TIME TO GET UP, ELLE.
SORRY! SORRY! SO SORRY!
It's okay. Everybody oversleeps...
BOW
BUT GET A MOVE ON.
GRIN
EEEEEEK!
EEEEEEK!
KLACK
He scared me!
I started babbling...
HMM. RUO'S IN A GOOD MOOD...
HE WAS SO ANGRY ABOUT KAZUKI YESTERDAY...
Hurry up, Elle!
Okay!
This is all too much! My head's spinning!
FLP
FLP
FLP

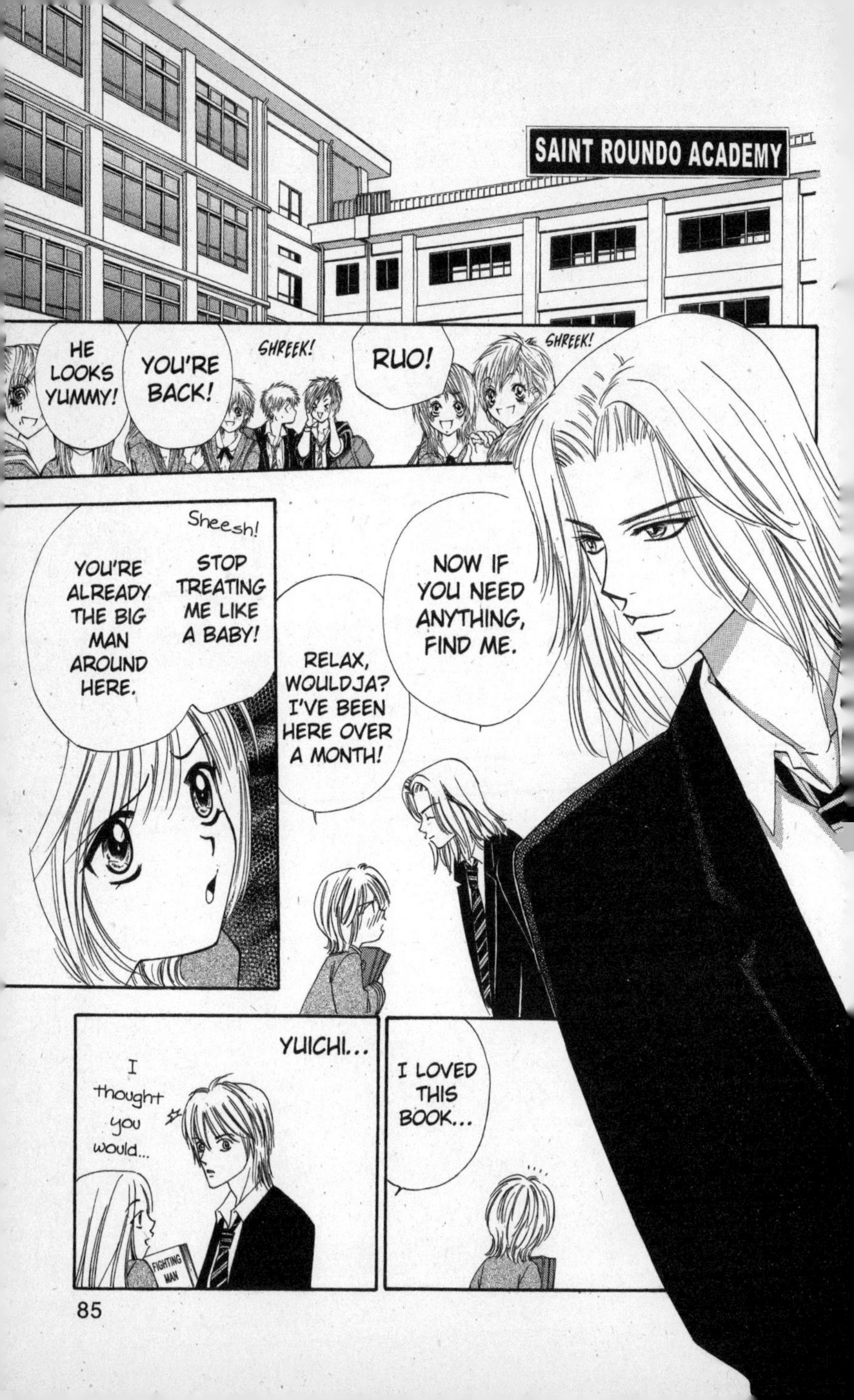
SAINT ROUNDO ACADEMY
SHREEK!
RUO!
SHREEK!
YOU'RE BACK!
HE LOOKS YUMMY!
NOW IF YOU NEED ANYTHING, FIND ME.
RELAX, WOULDJA? I'VE BEEN HERE OVER A MONTH!
Sheesh!
STOP TREATING ME LIKE A BABY!
YOU'RE ALREADY THE BIG MAN AROUND HERE.
I LOVED THIS BOOK...
YUICHI...
I thought you would...
FIGHTING MAN

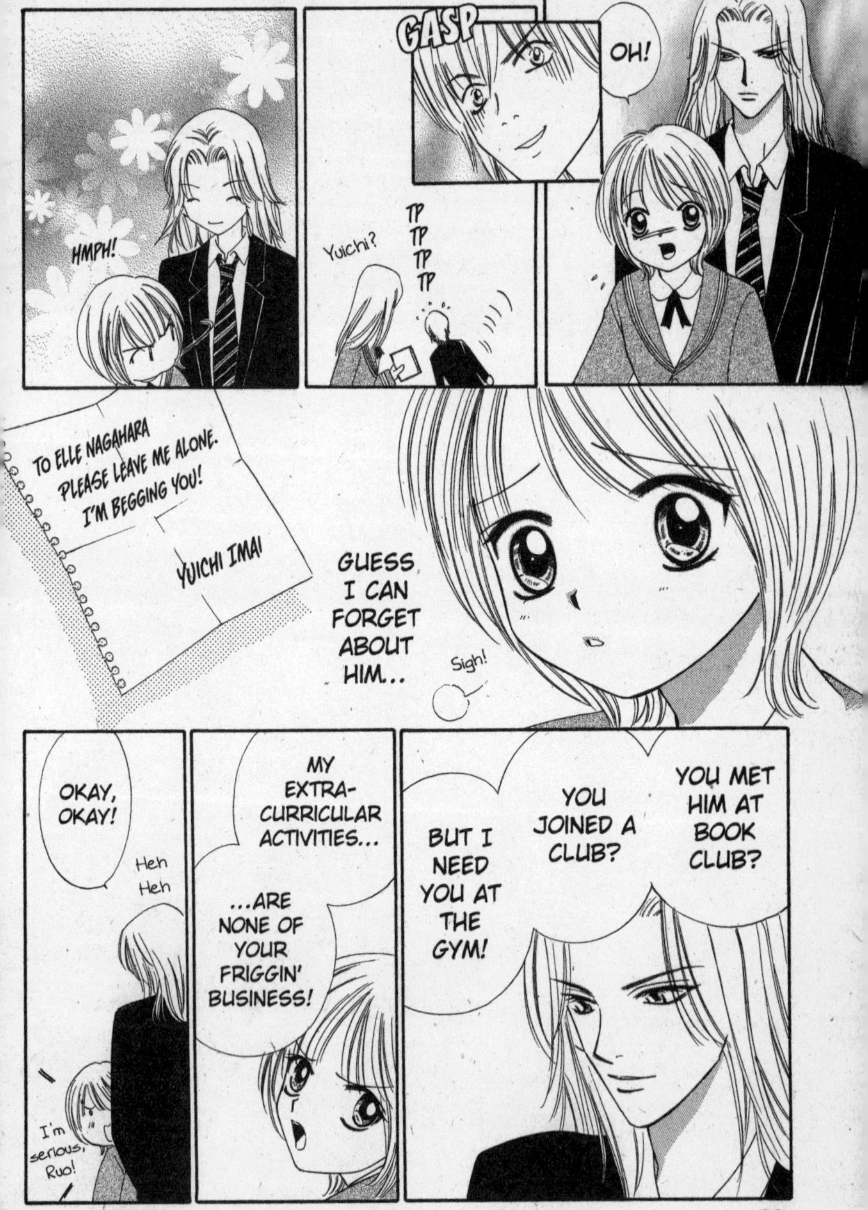
OH!
GASP
Yuichi?
TP TP TP TP
HMPH!
GUESS I CAN FORGET ABOUT HIM...
Sigh!
TO ELLE NAGAHARA
PLEASE LEAVE ME ALONE.
I'M BEGGING YOU!
YUICHI IMAI
YOU MET HIM AT BOOK CLUB?
YOU JOINED A CLUB?
BUT I NEED YOU AT THE GYM!
MY EXTRA-CURRICULAR ACTIVITIES...
...ARE NONE OF YOUR FRIGGIN' BUSINESS!
OKAY, OKAY!
Heh Heh
I'm serious, Ruo!

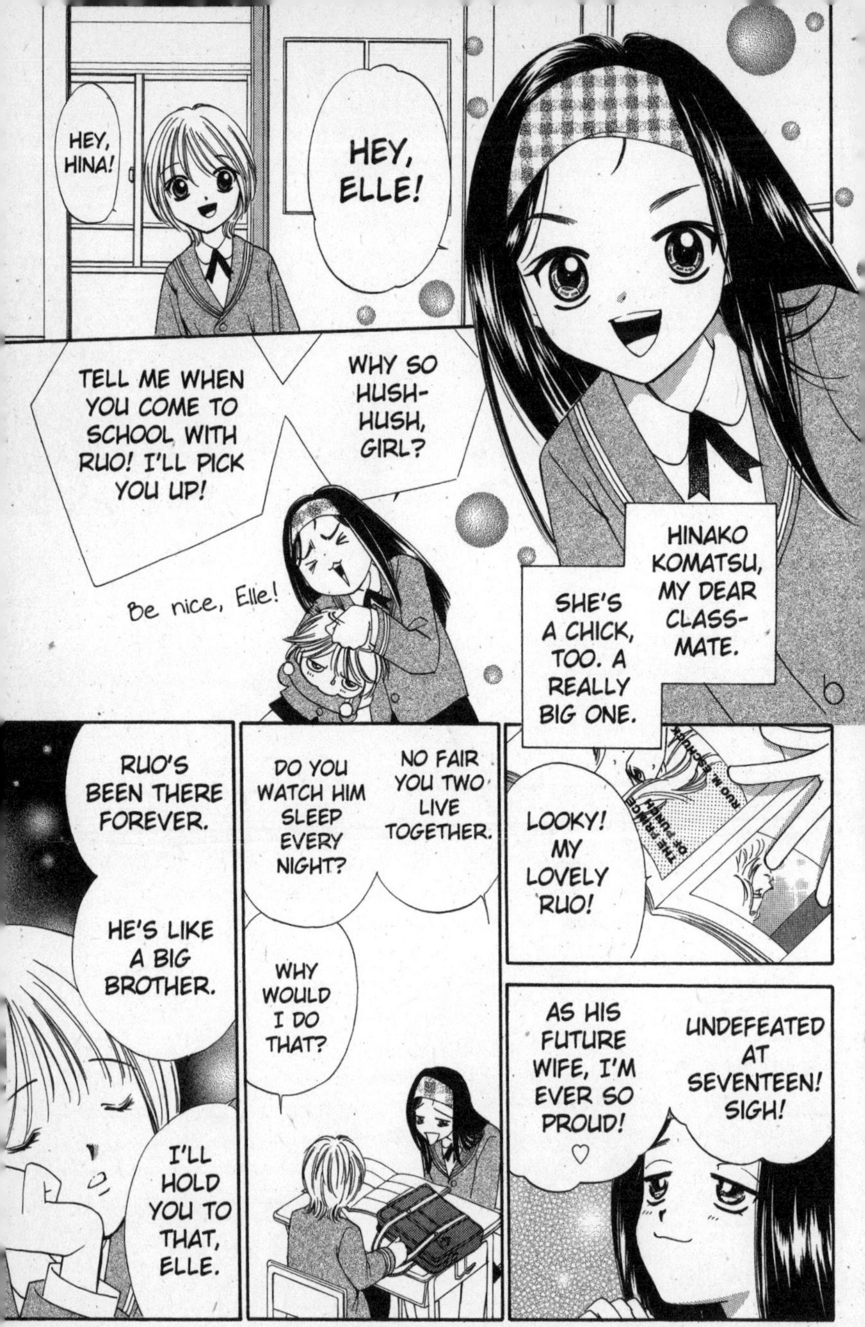
HINAKO KOMATSU, MY DEAR CLASSMATE.
SHE'S A CHICK, TOO. A REALLY BIG ONE.
HEY, ELLE!
HEY, HINA!
WHY SO HUSH-HUSH, GIRL?
TELL ME WHEN YOU COME TO SCHOOL WITH RUO! I'LL PICK YOU UP!
Be nice, Elle!
LOOKY! MY LOVELY RUO!
UNDEFEATED AT SEVENTEEN! SIGH!
AS HIS FUTURE WIFE, I'M EVER SO PROUD! ♡
NO FAIR YOU TWO LIVE TOGETHER.
DO YOU WATCH HIM SLEEP EVERY NIGHT?
WHY WOULD I DO THAT?
RUO'S BEEN THERE FOREVER.
HE'S LIKE A BIG BROTHER.
I'LL HOLD YOU TO THAT, ELLE.

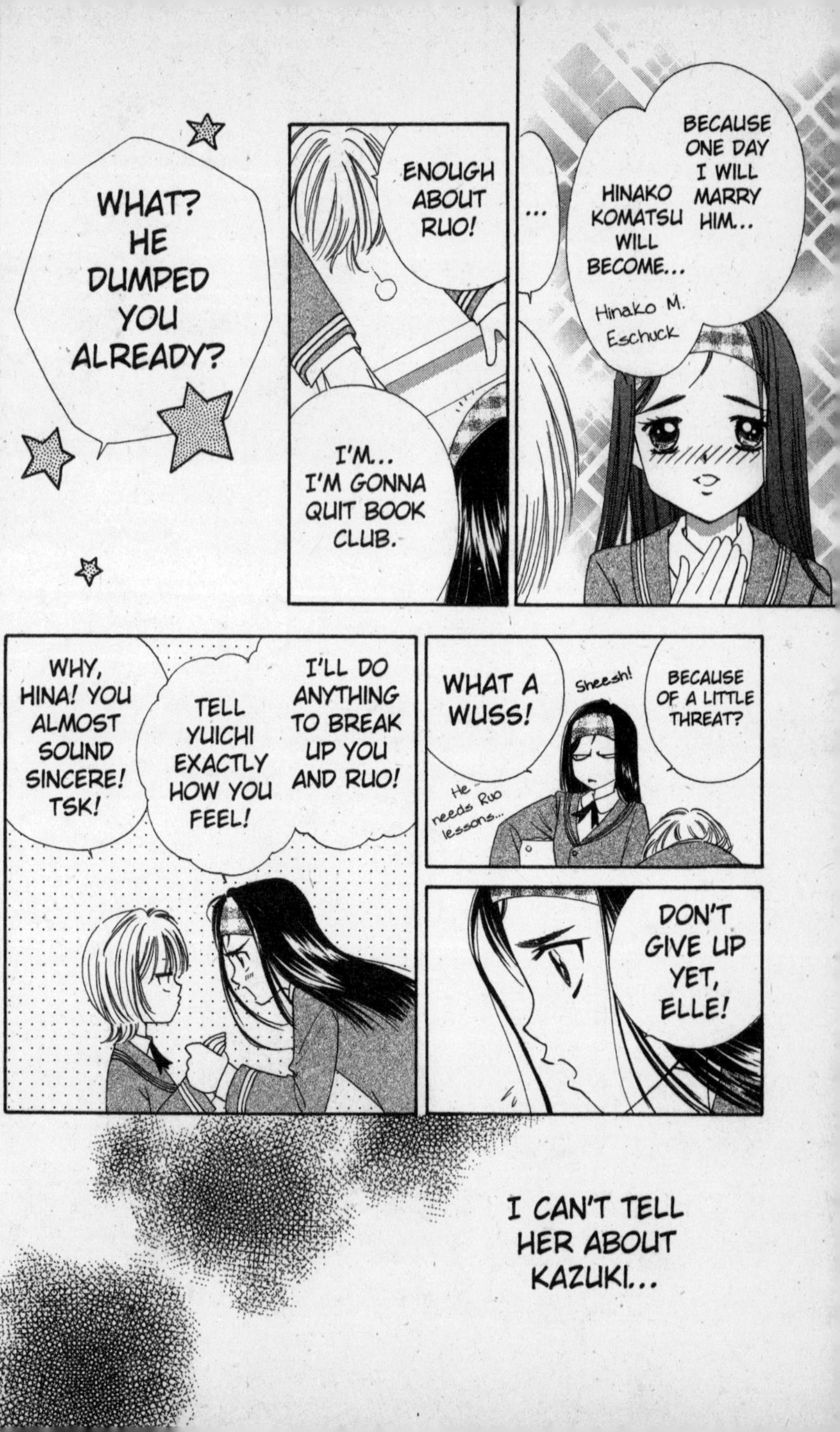
BECAUSE ONE DAY I WILL MARRY HIM... HINAKO KOMATSU WILL BECOME...
Hinako M. Eschuck
...
ENOUGH ABOUT RUO!
I'M... I'M GONNA QUIT BOOK CLUB.
WHAT? HE DUMPED YOU ALREADY?
BECAUSE OF A LITTLE THREAT?
Sheesh!
WHAT A WUSS!
He needs Ruo lessons...
DON'T GIVE UP YET, ELLE!
I'LL DO ANYTHING TO BREAK UP YOU AND RUO!
TELL YUICHI EXACTLY HOW YOU FEEL!
WHY, HINA! YOU ALMOST SOUND SINCERE! TSK!
I CAN'T TELL HER ABOUT KAZUKI...

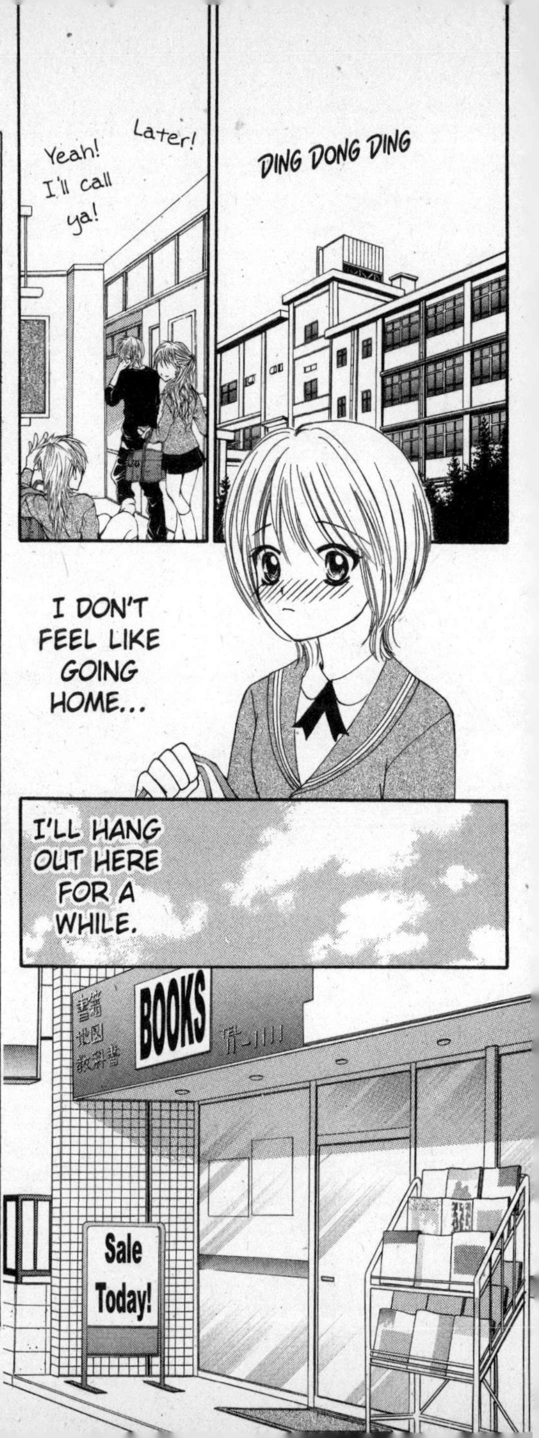
DING DONG DING
Later!
Yeah! I'll call ya!
I DON'T FEEL LIKE GOING HOME...
I'LL HANG OUT HERE FOR A WHILE.
BOOKS
Sale Today!

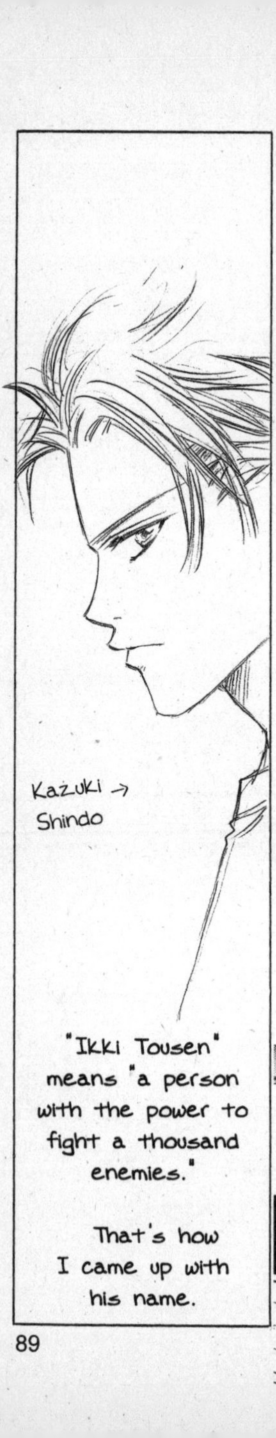
Kazuki → Shindo

"Ikki Tousen" means "a person with the power to fight a thousand enemies."

That's how I came up with his name.

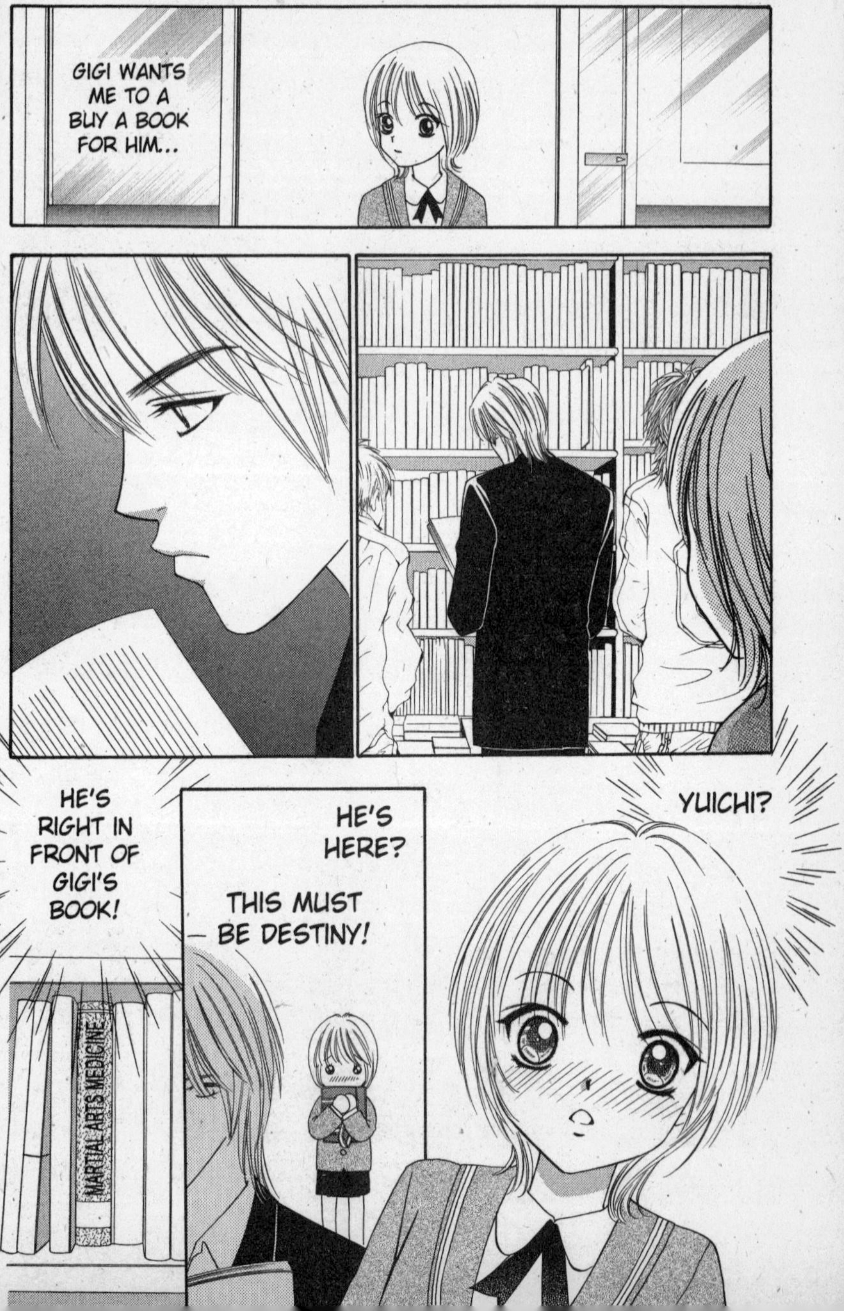
GIGI WANTS ME TO A BUY A BOOK FOR HIM...
YUICHI?
HE'S HERE?
THIS MUST BE DESTINY!
HE'S RIGHT IN FRONT OF GIGI'S BOOK!
MARTIAL ARTS MEDICINE

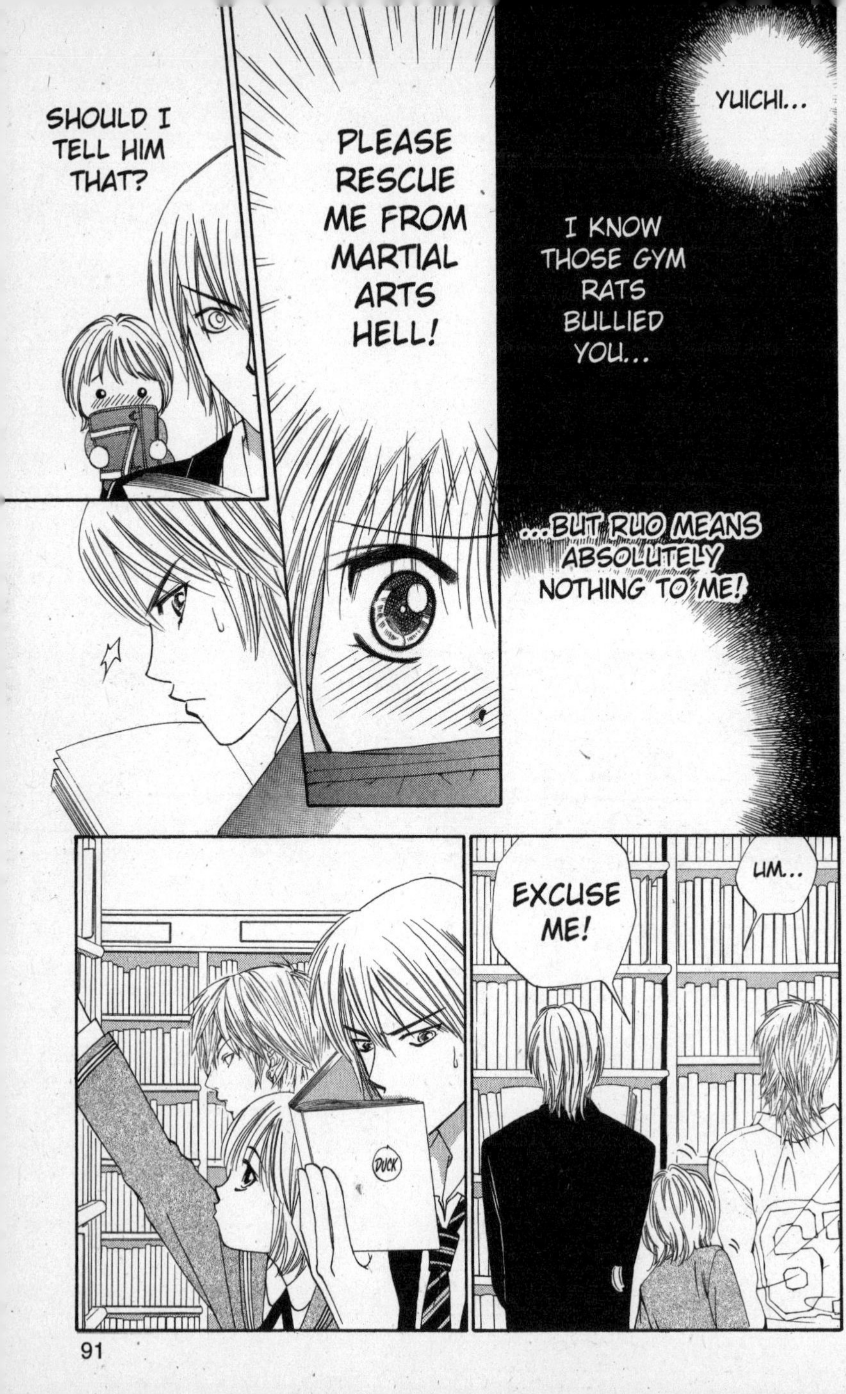

YUICHI...
I KNOW THOSE GYM RATS BULLIED YOU...
PLEASE RESCUE ME FROM MARTIAL ARTS HELL!
SHOULD I TELL HIM THAT?
...BUT RUO MEANS ABSOLUTELY NOTHING TO ME!
UM...
EXCUSE ME!
DUCK

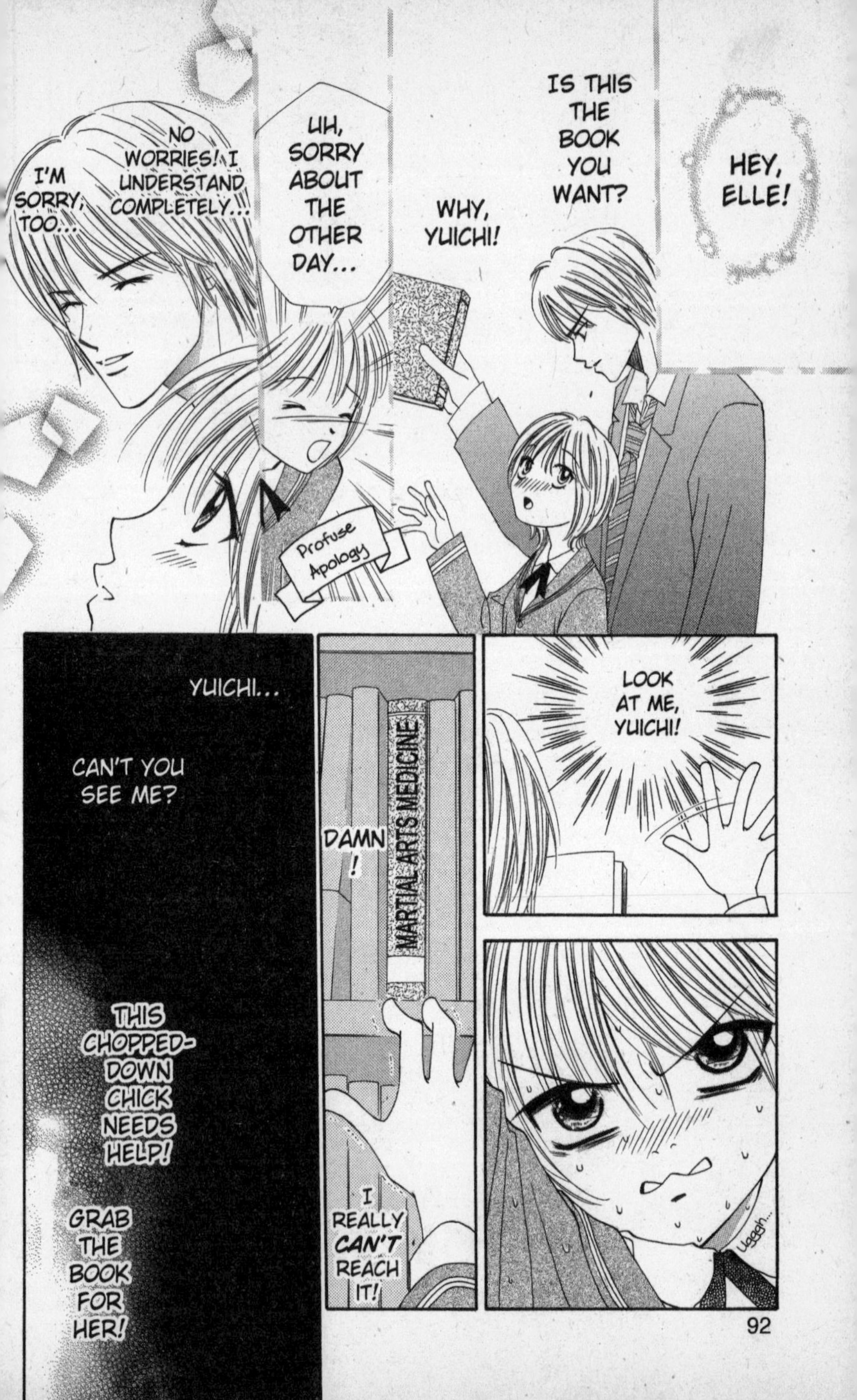
HEY, ELLE!
IS THIS THE BOOK YOU WANT?
WHY, YUICHI!
UH, SORRY ABOUT THE OTHER DAY...
Profuse Apology
NO WORRIES! I UNDERSTAND COMPLETELY...
I'M SORRY, TOO...
LOOK AT ME, YUICHI!
Ugggh...
DAMN!
MARTIAL ARTS MEDICINE
I REALLY CAN'T REACH IT!
YUICHI...
CAN'T YOU SEE ME?
THIS CHOPPED-DOWN CHICK NEEDS HELP!
GRAB THE BOOK FOR HER!

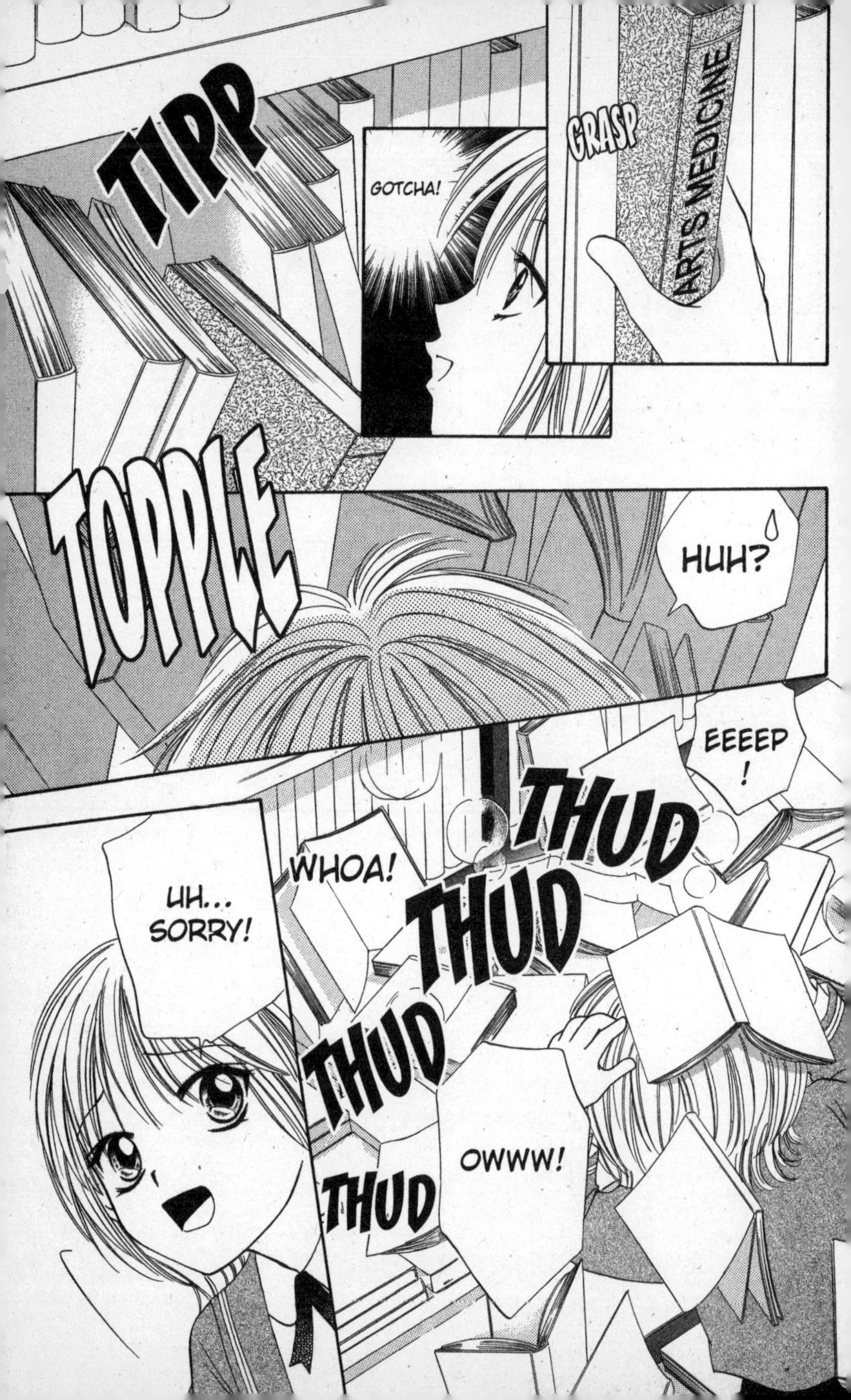

ARTS MEDICINE
GRASP
GOTCHA!
TIPP
TOPPLE
HUH?
EEEEP!
THUD
THUD
THUD
THUD
WHOA!
OWWW!
UH... SORRY!

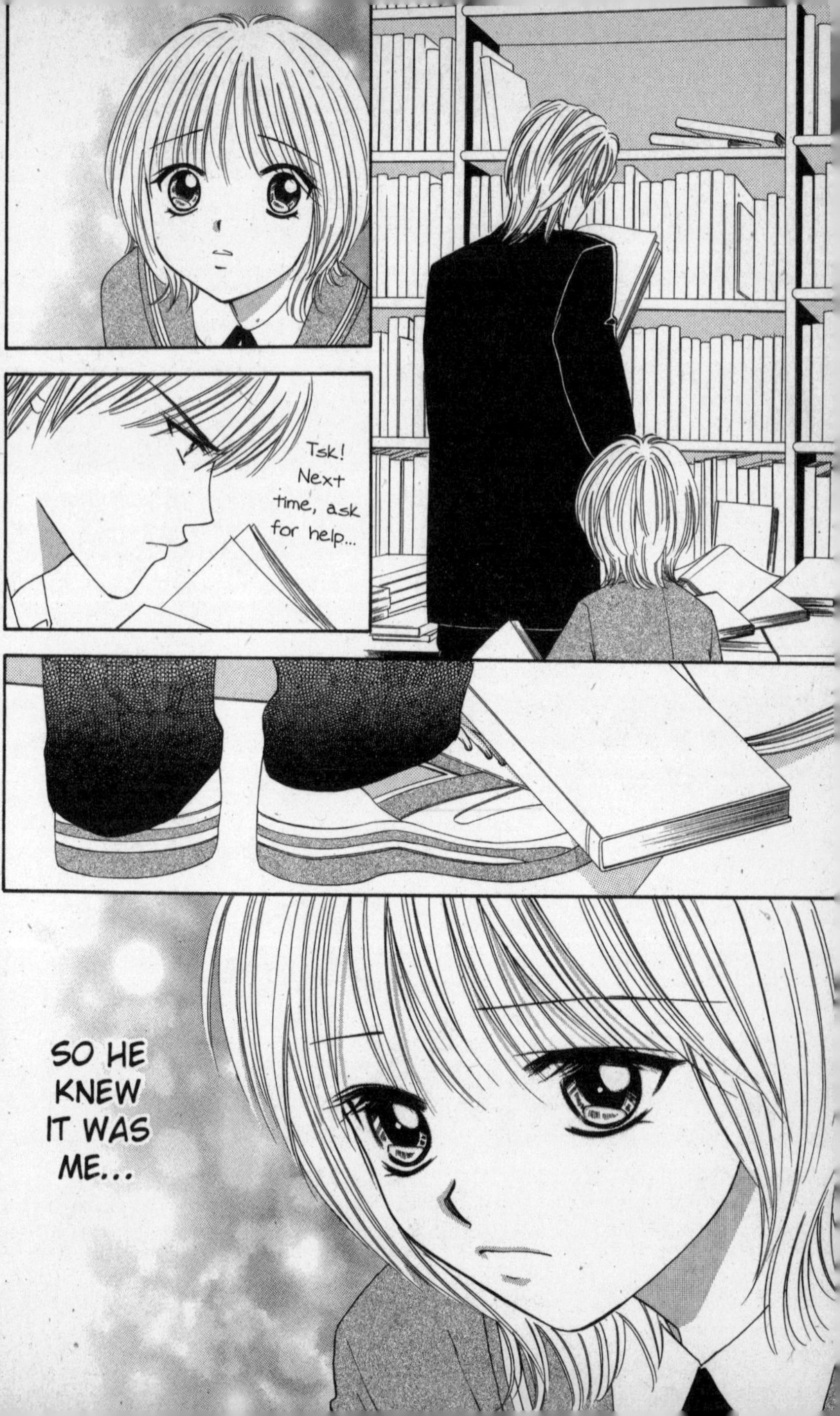
Tsk! Next time, ask for help...
SO HE KNEW IT WAS ME...

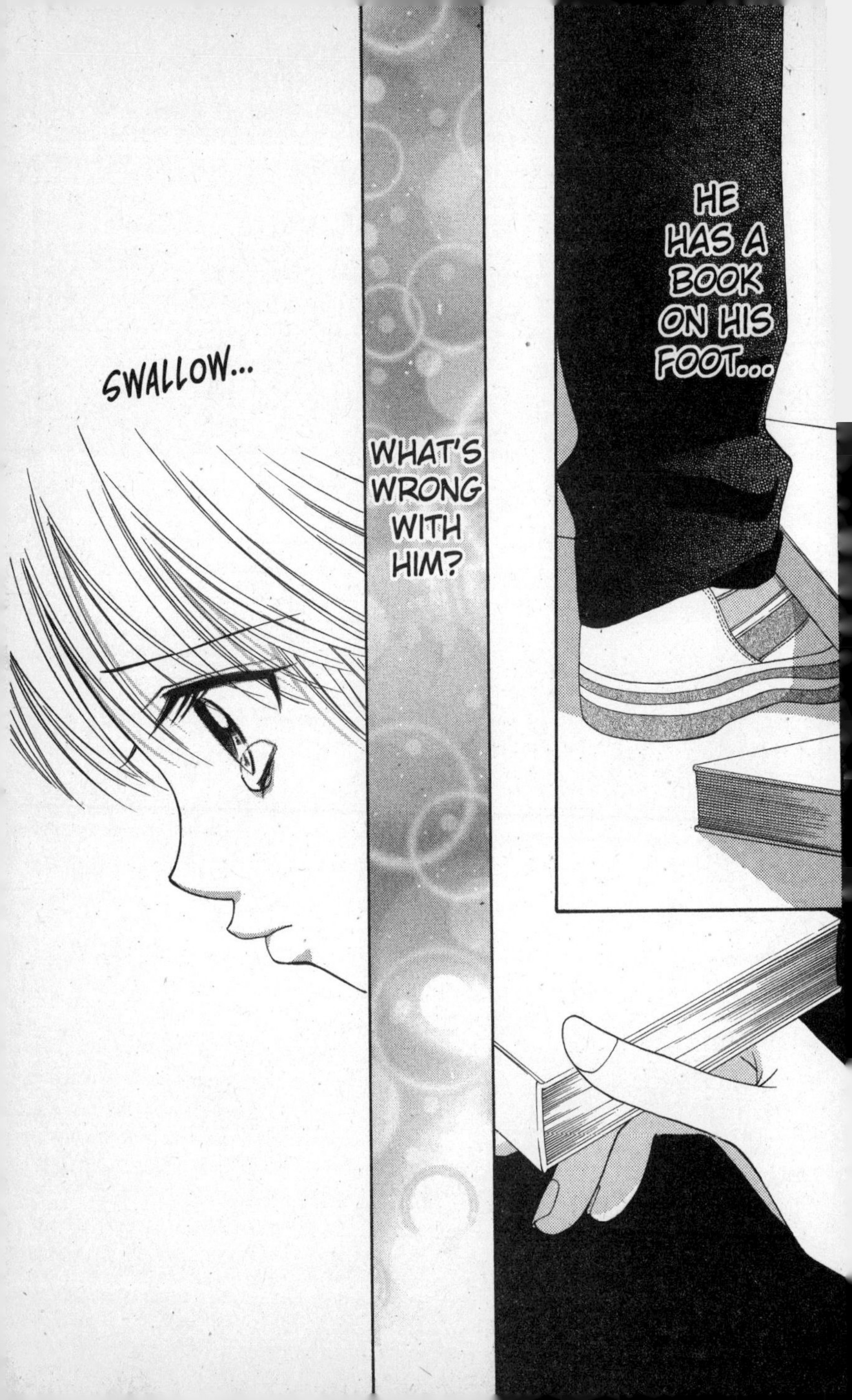
HE HAS A BOOK ON HIS FOOT...
WHAT'S WRONG WITH HIM?
SWALLOW...

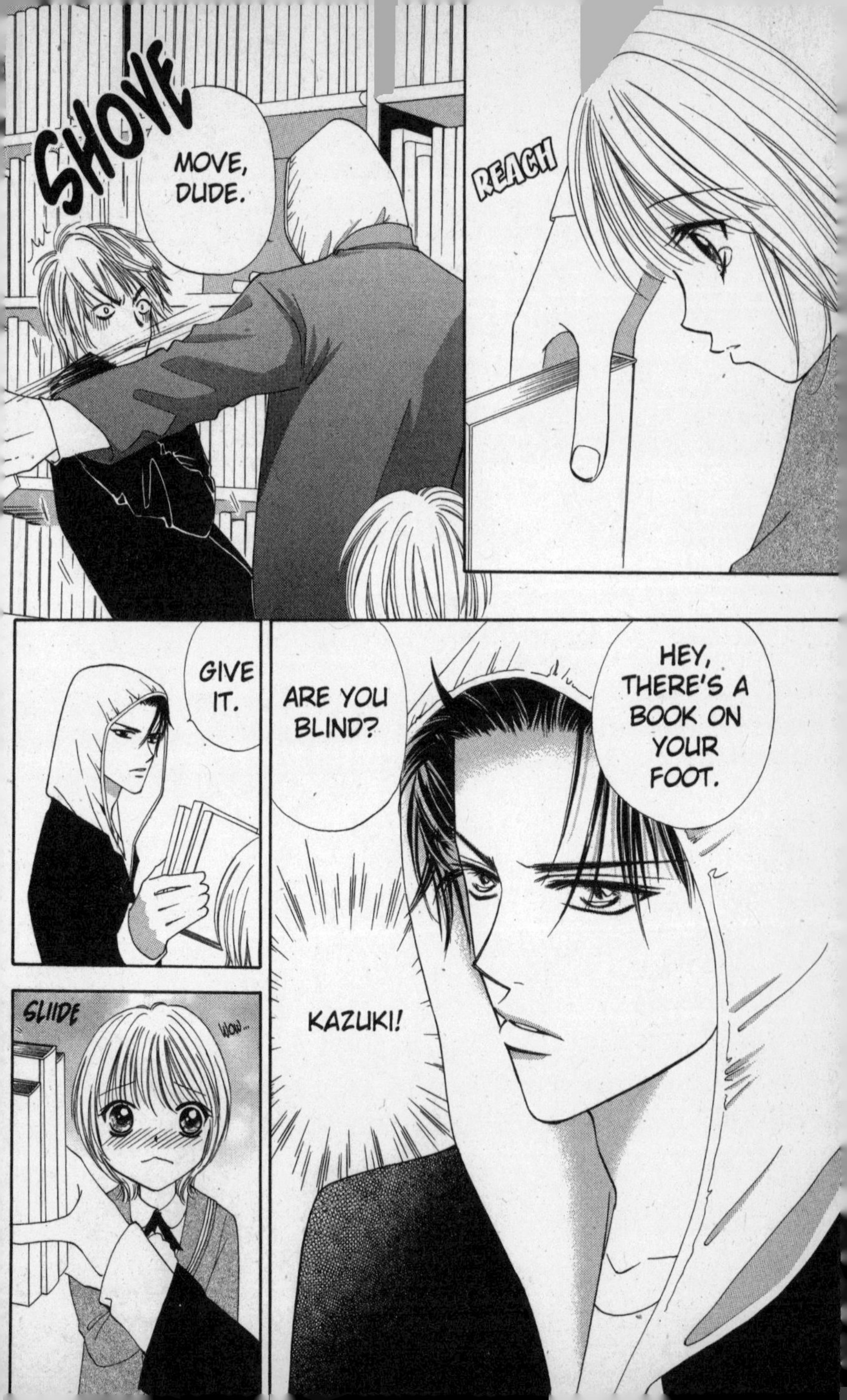
REACH
SHOVE
MOVE, DUDE.
HEY, THERE'S A BOOK ON YOUR FOOT.
ARE YOU BLIND?
KAZUKI!
GIVE IT.
SLIIDE
WOW...

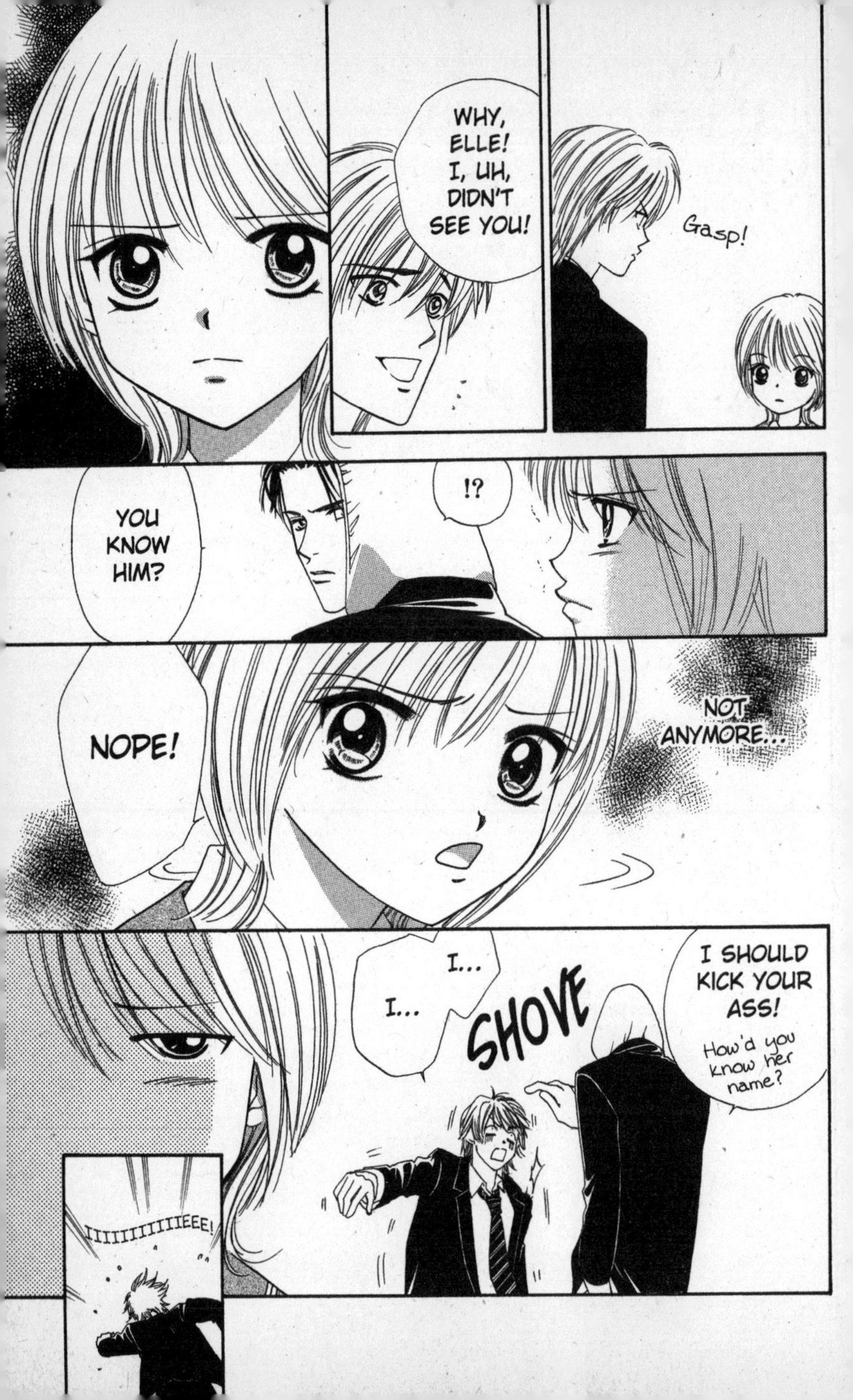
Gasp!
WHY, ELLE! I, UH, DIDN'T SEE YOU!
!?
YOU KNOW HIM?
NOT ANYMORE...
NOPE!
I SHOULD KICK YOUR ASS!
How'd you know her name?
SHOVE
I...
I...
IIIIIIIIIIIEEE!

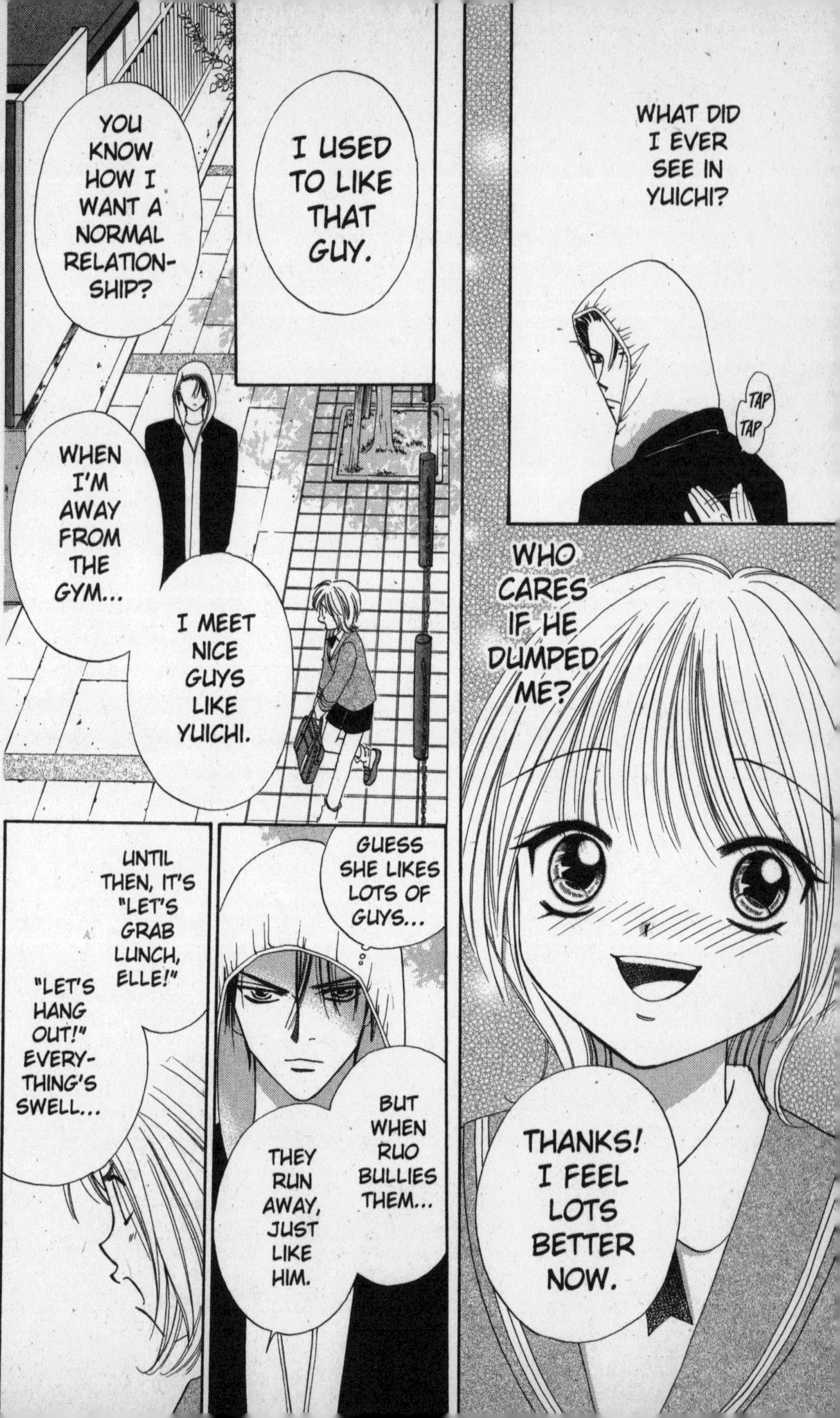
WHAT DID I EVER SEE IN YUICHI?
TAP TAP
WHO CARES IF HE DUMPED ME?
THANKS! I FEEL LOTS BETTER NOW.
I USED TO LIKE THAT GUY.
YOU KNOW HOW I WANT A NORMAL RELATION-SHIP?
WHEN I'M AWAY FROM THE GYM...
I MEET NICE GUYS LIKE YUICHI.
GUESS SHE LIKES LOTS OF GUYS...
UNTIL THEN, IT'S "LET'S GRAB LUNCH, ELLE!"
"LET'S HANG OUT!" EVERY-THING'S SWELL...
BUT WHEN RUO BULLIES THEM...
THEY RUN AWAY, JUST LIKE HIM.

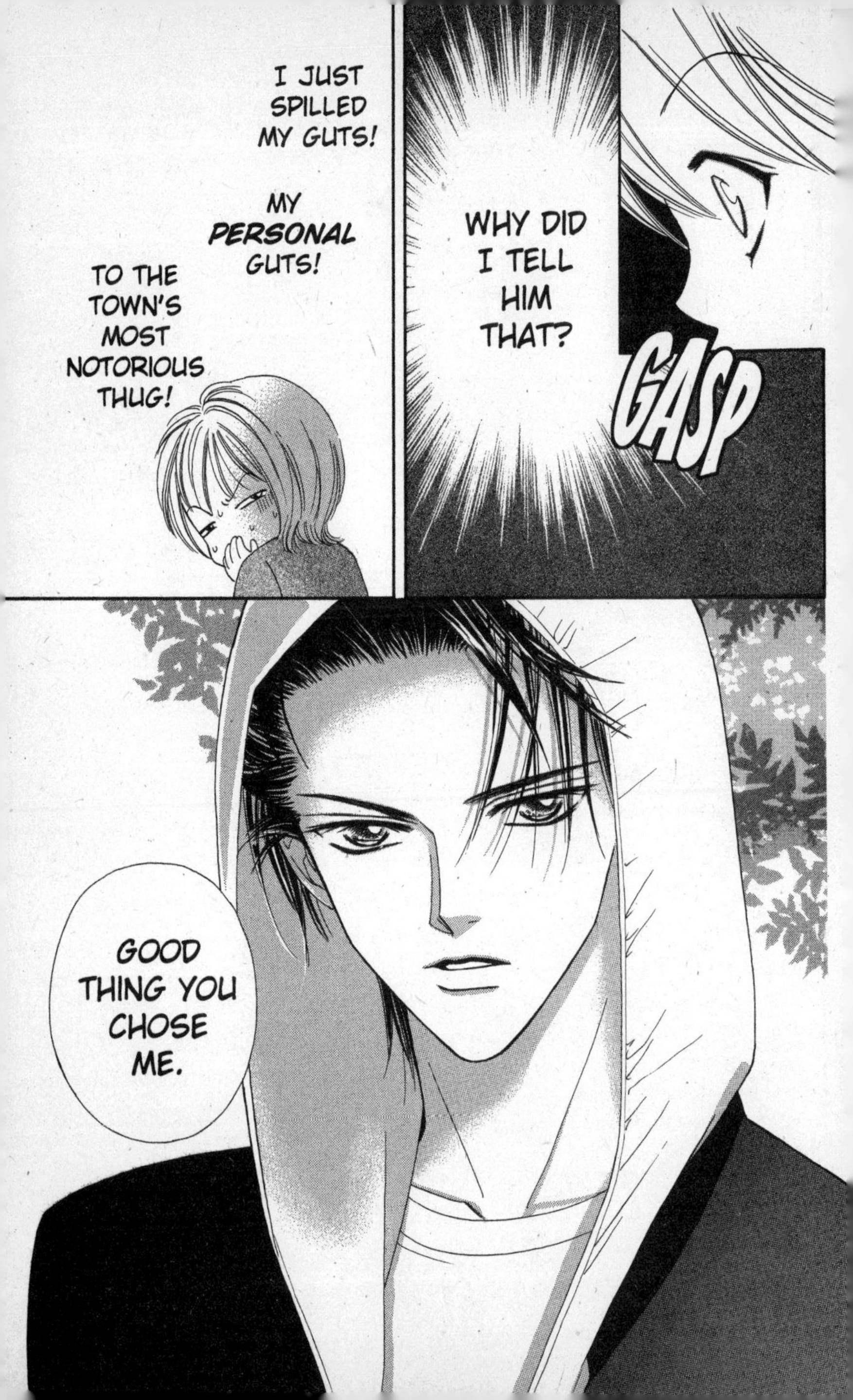
GASP
WHY DID I TELL HIM THAT?
I JUST SPILLED MY GUTS!
MY PERSONAL GUTS!
TO THE TOWN'S MOST NOTORIOUS THUG!
GOOD THING YOU CHOSE ME.

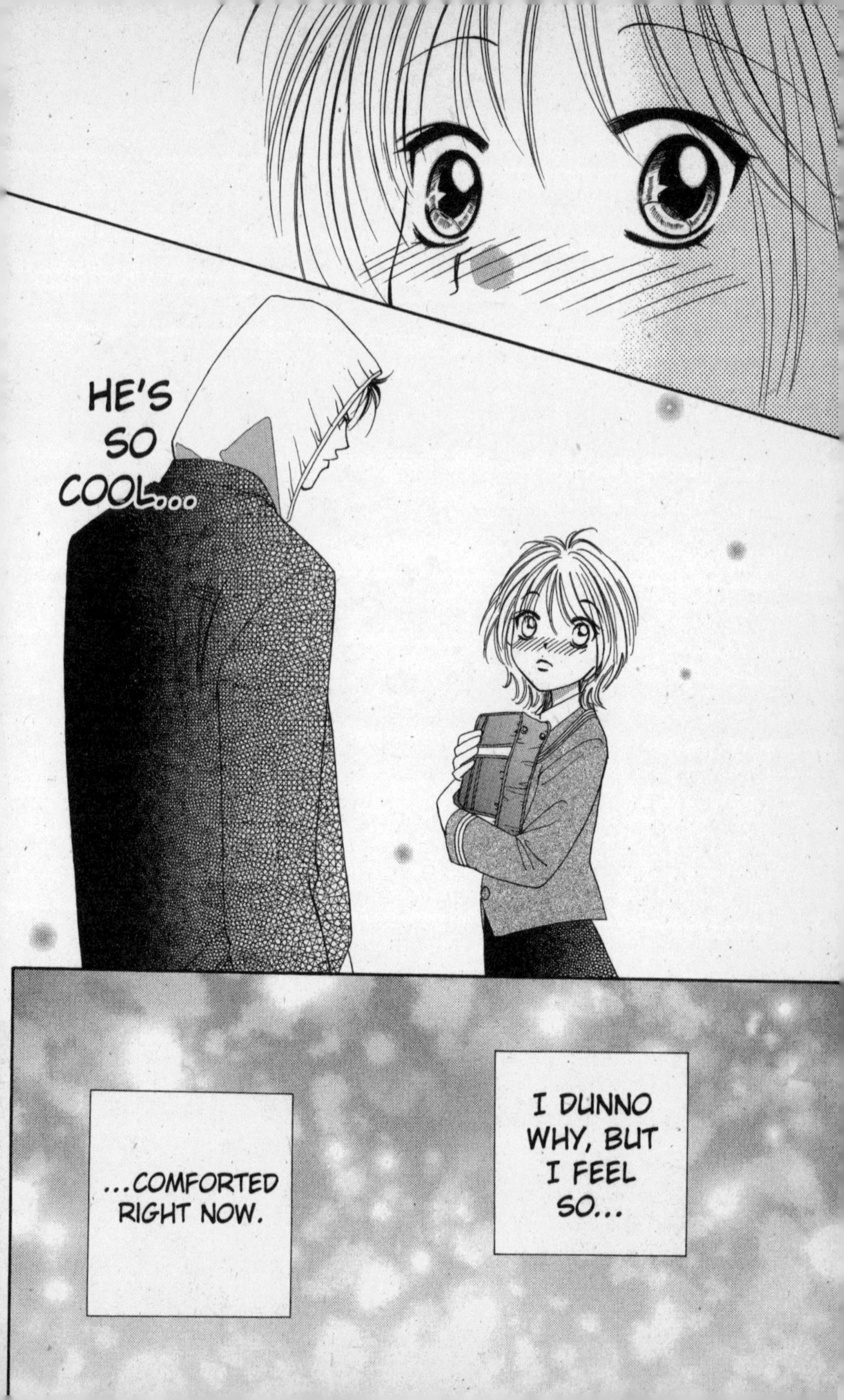
HE'S SO COOL...
I DUNNO WHY, BUT I FEEL SO...
...COMFORTED RIGHT NOW.

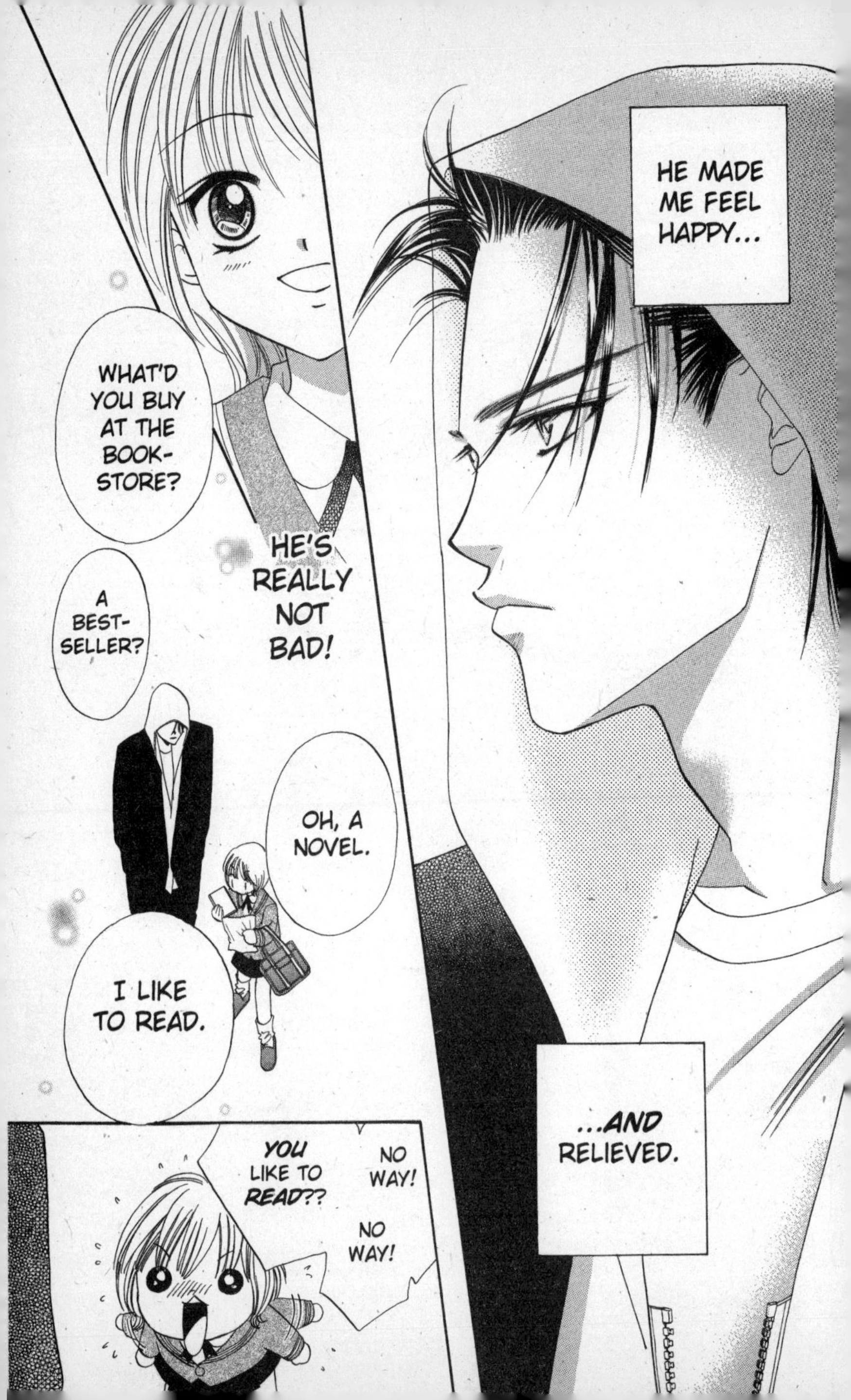
HE MADE ME FEEL HAPPY...
...AND RELIEVED.
WHAT'D YOU BUY AT THE BOOK-STORE?
A BEST-SELLER?
HE'S REALLY NOT BAD!
OH, A NOVEL.
I LIKE TO READ.
NO WAY!
NO WAY!
YOU LIKE TO READ??

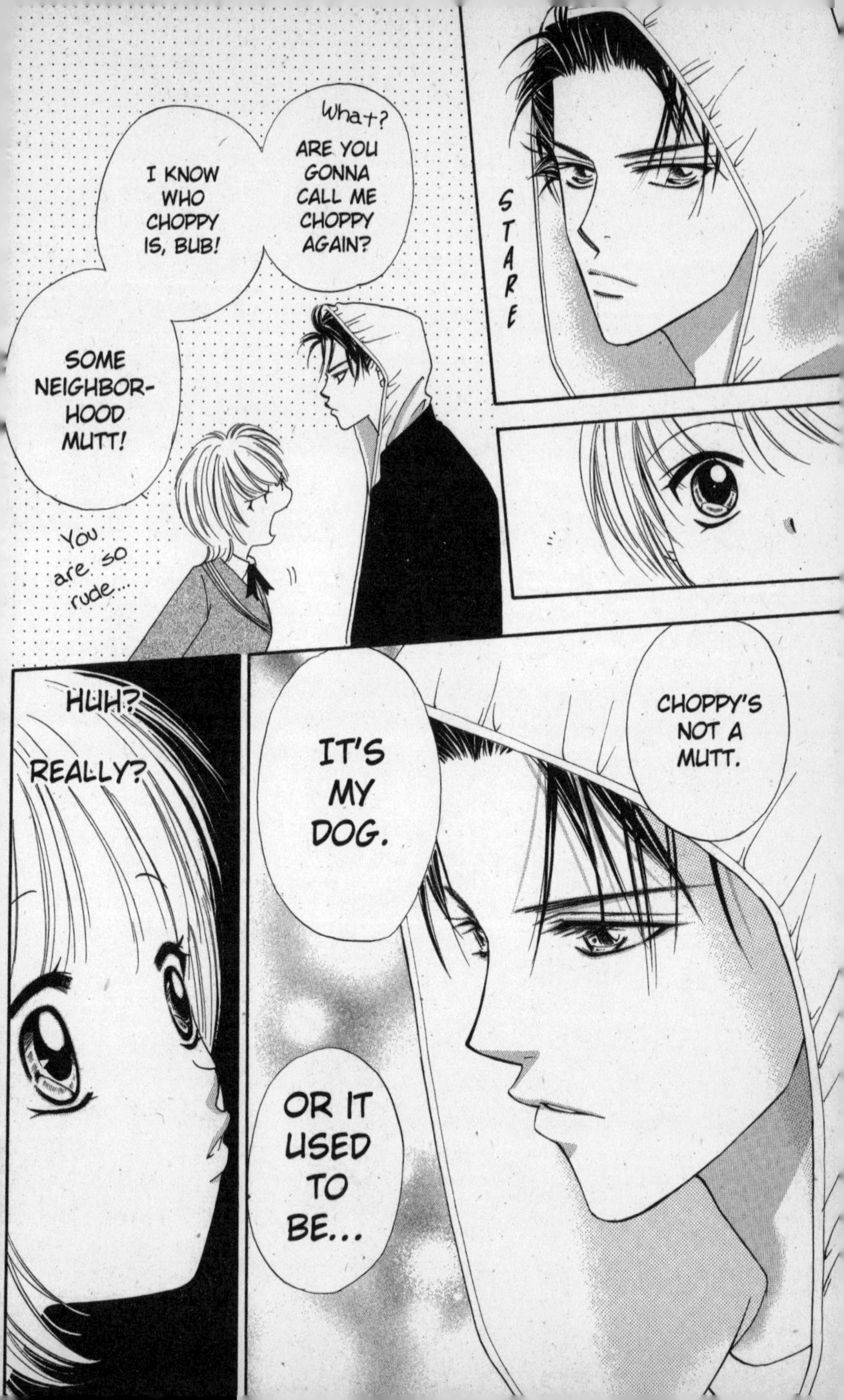
STARE
What?
ARE YOU GONNA CALL ME CHOPPY AGAIN?
I KNOW WHO CHOPPY IS, BUB!
SOME NEIGHBOR-HOOD MUTT!
You are so rude...
CHOPPY'S NOT A MUTT.
IT'S MY DOG.
OR IT USED TO BE...
HUH?
REALLY?

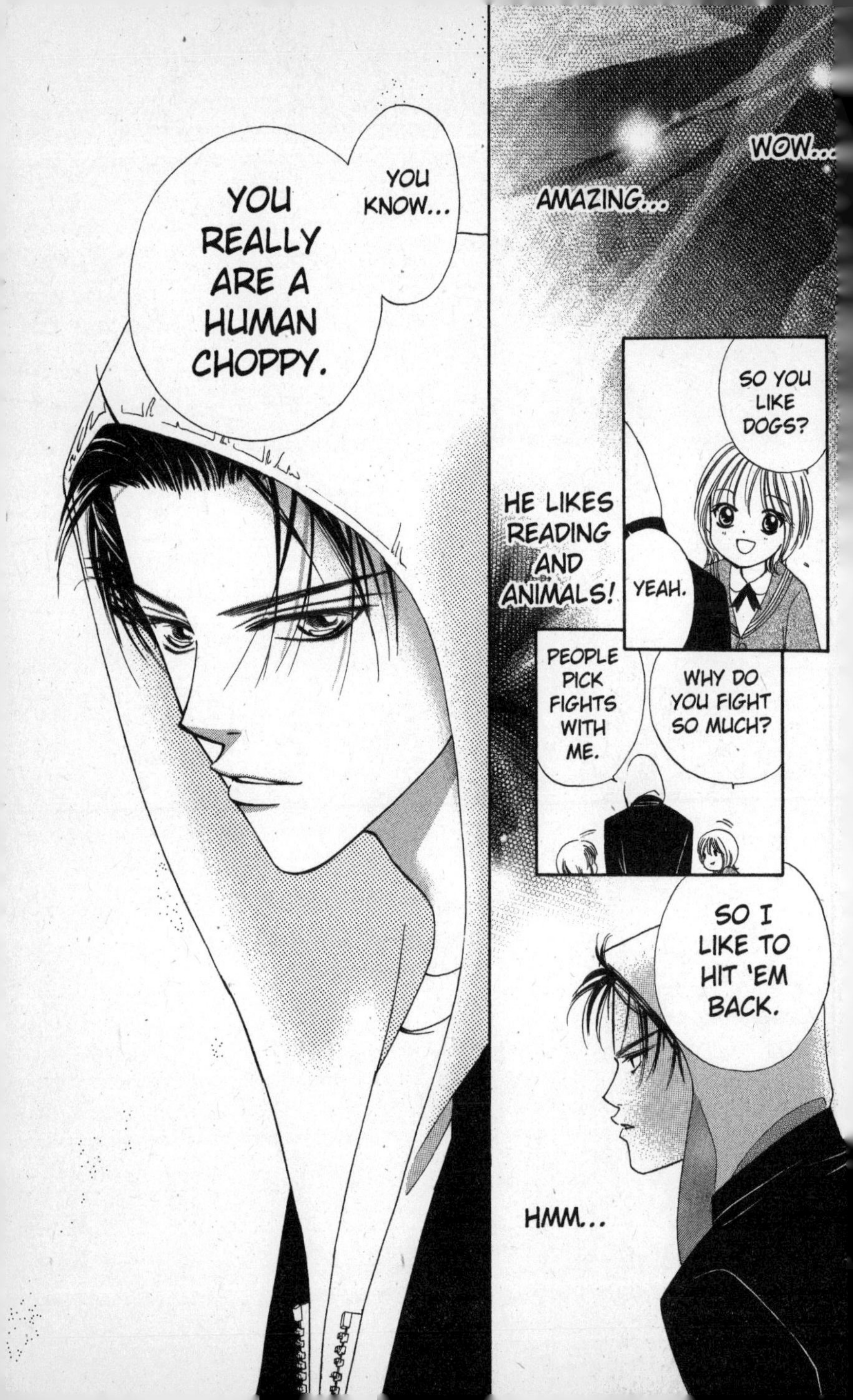
WOW...
AMAZING...
SO YOU LIKE DOGS?
YEAH.
HE LIKES READING AND ANIMALS!
WHY DO YOU FIGHT SO MUCH?
PEOPLE PICK FIGHTS WITH ME.
SO I LIKE TO HIT 'EM BACK.
HMM..
YOU KNOW...
YOU REALLY ARE A HUMAN CHOPPY.

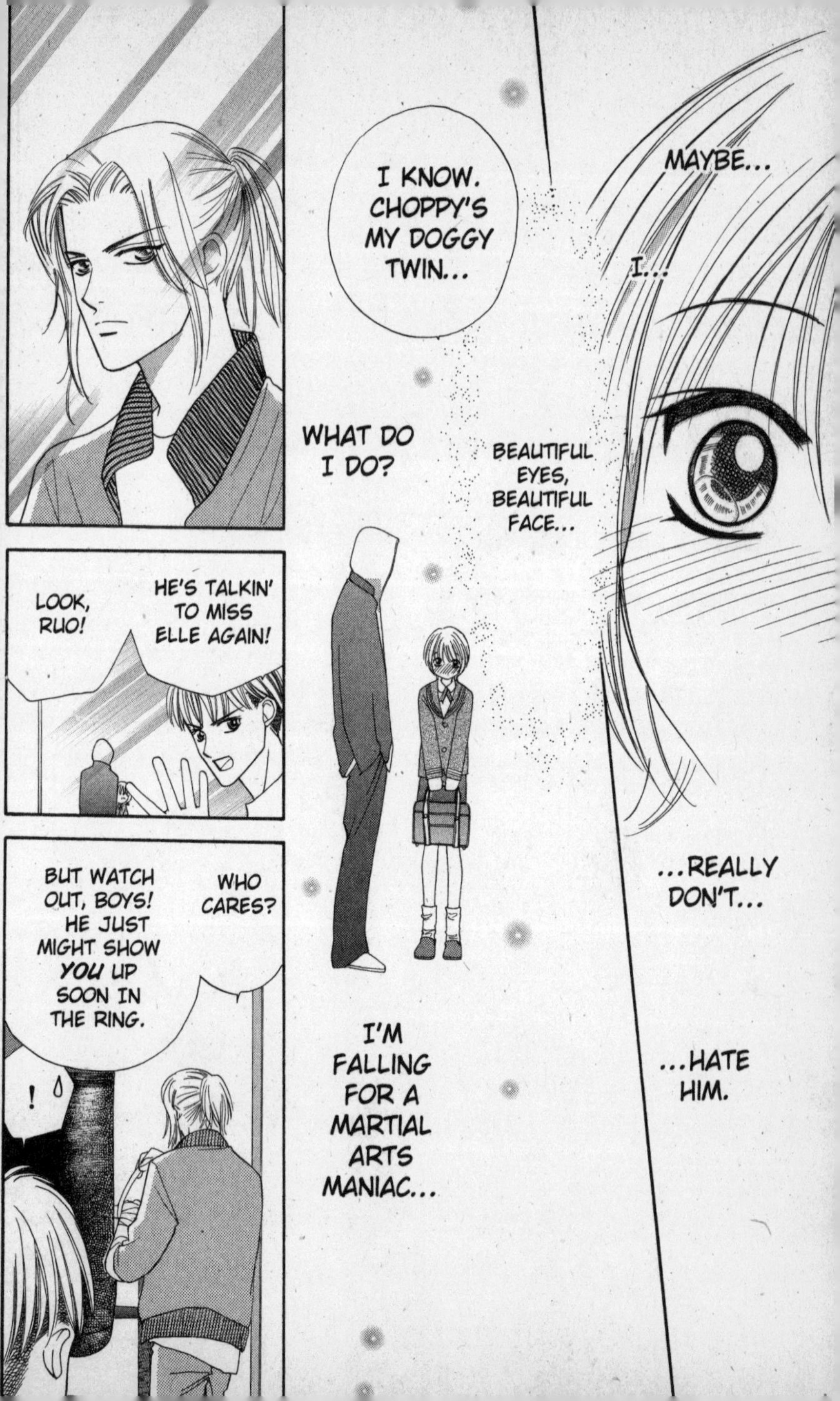
MAYBE...
I...
...REALLY DON'T...
...HATE HIM.
I KNOW. CHOPPY'S MY DOGGY TWIN...
BEAUTIFUL EYES, BEAUTIFUL FACE...
WHAT DO I DO?
I'M FALLING FOR A MARTIAL ARTS MANIAC...
LOOK, RUO!
HE'S TALKIN' TO MISS ELLE AGAIN!
WHO CARES?
BUT WATCH OUT, BOYS! HE JUST MIGHT SHOW ***YOU*** UP SOON IN THE RING.
!

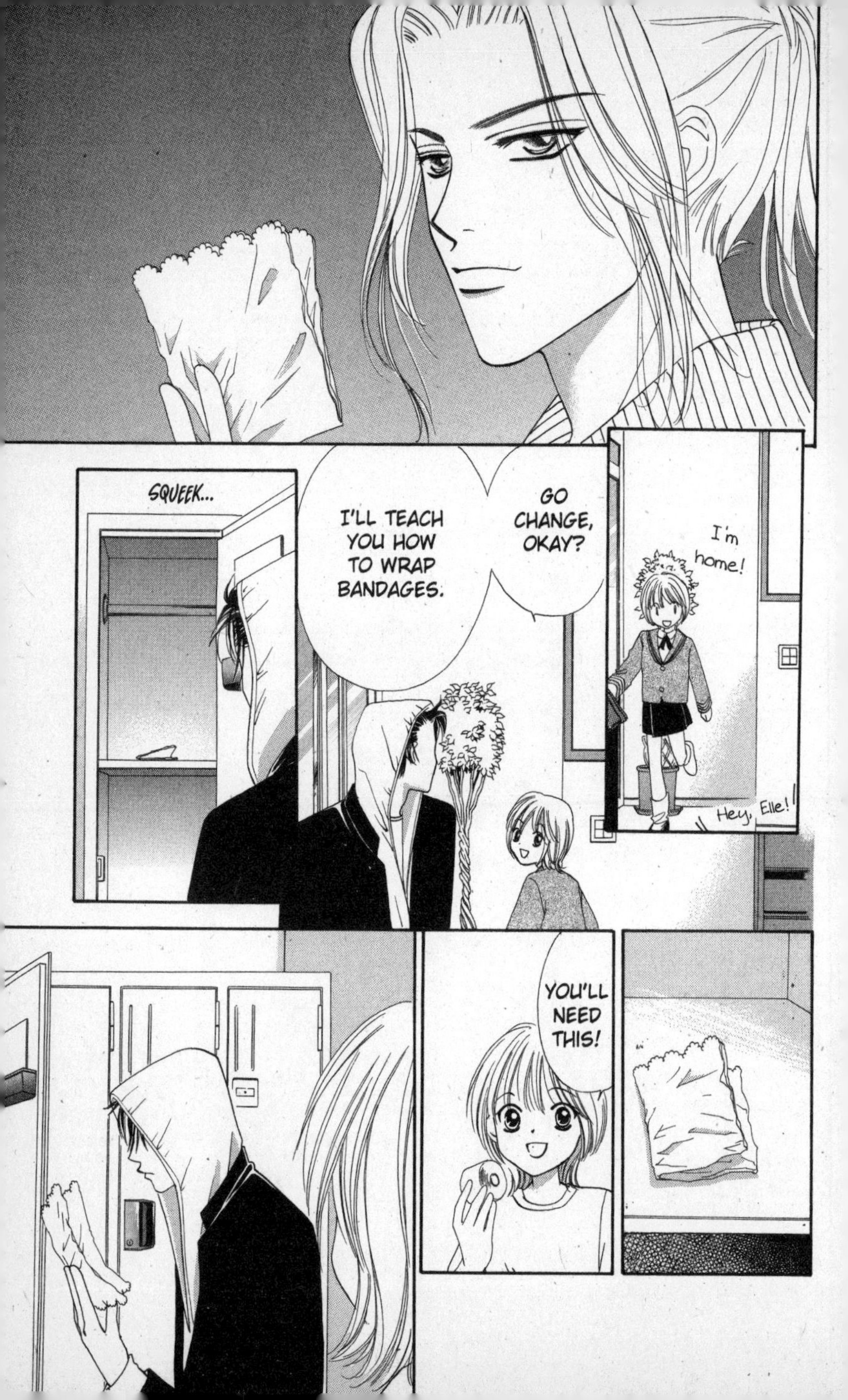
I'm home!
Hey, Elle!
GO CHANGE, OKAY?
I'LL TEACH YOU HOW TO WRAP BANDAGES.
SQUEEK...
YOU'LL NEED THIS!

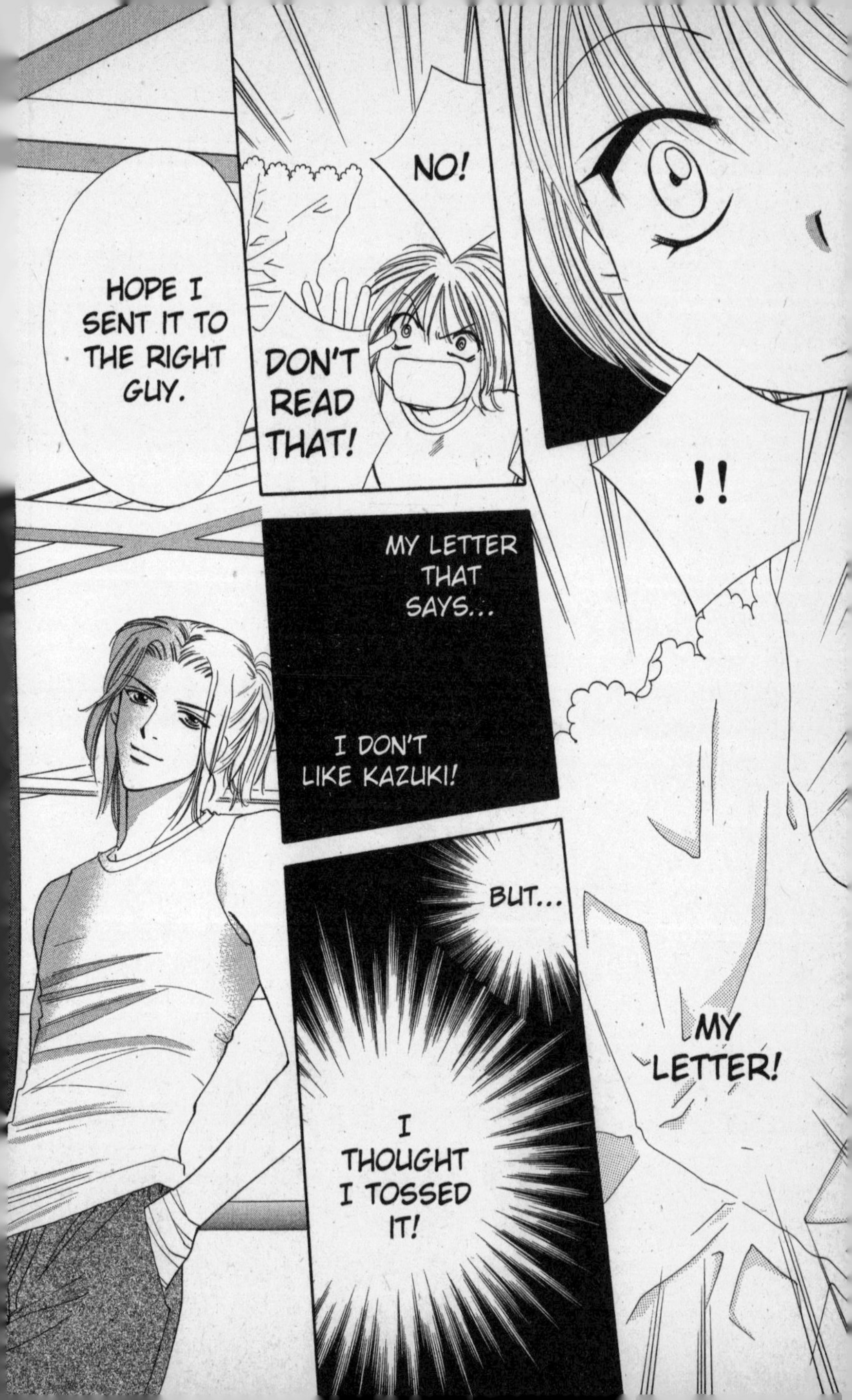
!!
MY LETTER!
NO!
DON'T READ THAT!
MY LETTER THAT SAYS...
I DON'T LIKE KAZUKI!
BUT...
I THOUGHT I TOSSED IT!
HOPE I SENT IT TO THE RIGHT GUY.

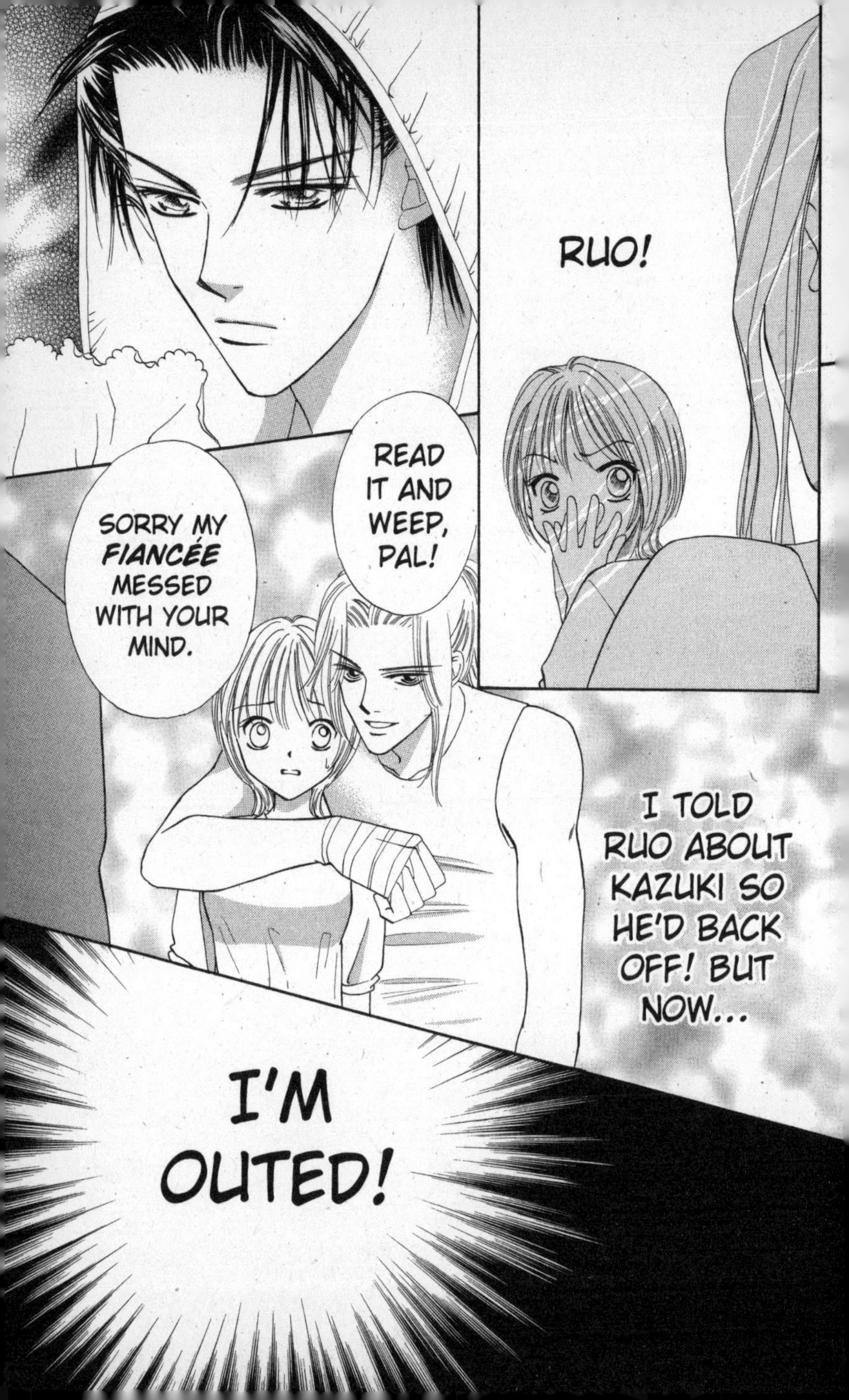
RUO!
READ IT AND WEEP, PAL!
SORRY MY *FIANCÉE* MESSED WITH YOUR MIND.
I TOLD RUO ABOUT KAZUKI SO HE'D BACK OFF! BUT NOW...
I'M OUTED!

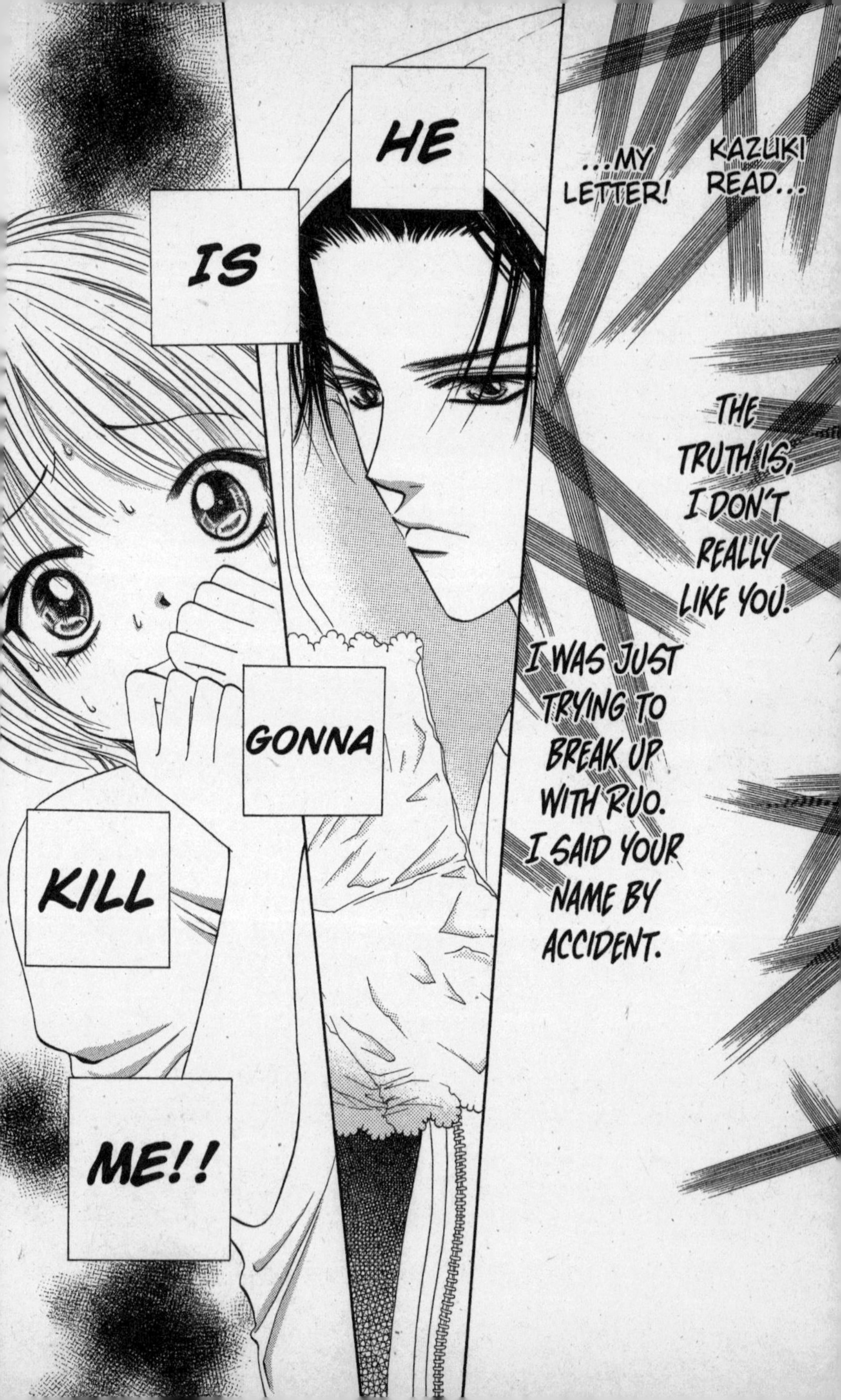
KAZUKI READ...
...MY LETTER!
THE TRUTH IS, I DON'T REALLY LIKE YOU.
I WAS JUST TRYING TO BREAK UP WITH RUO. I SAID YOUR NAME BY ACCIDENT.
HE
IS
GONNA
KILL
ME!!

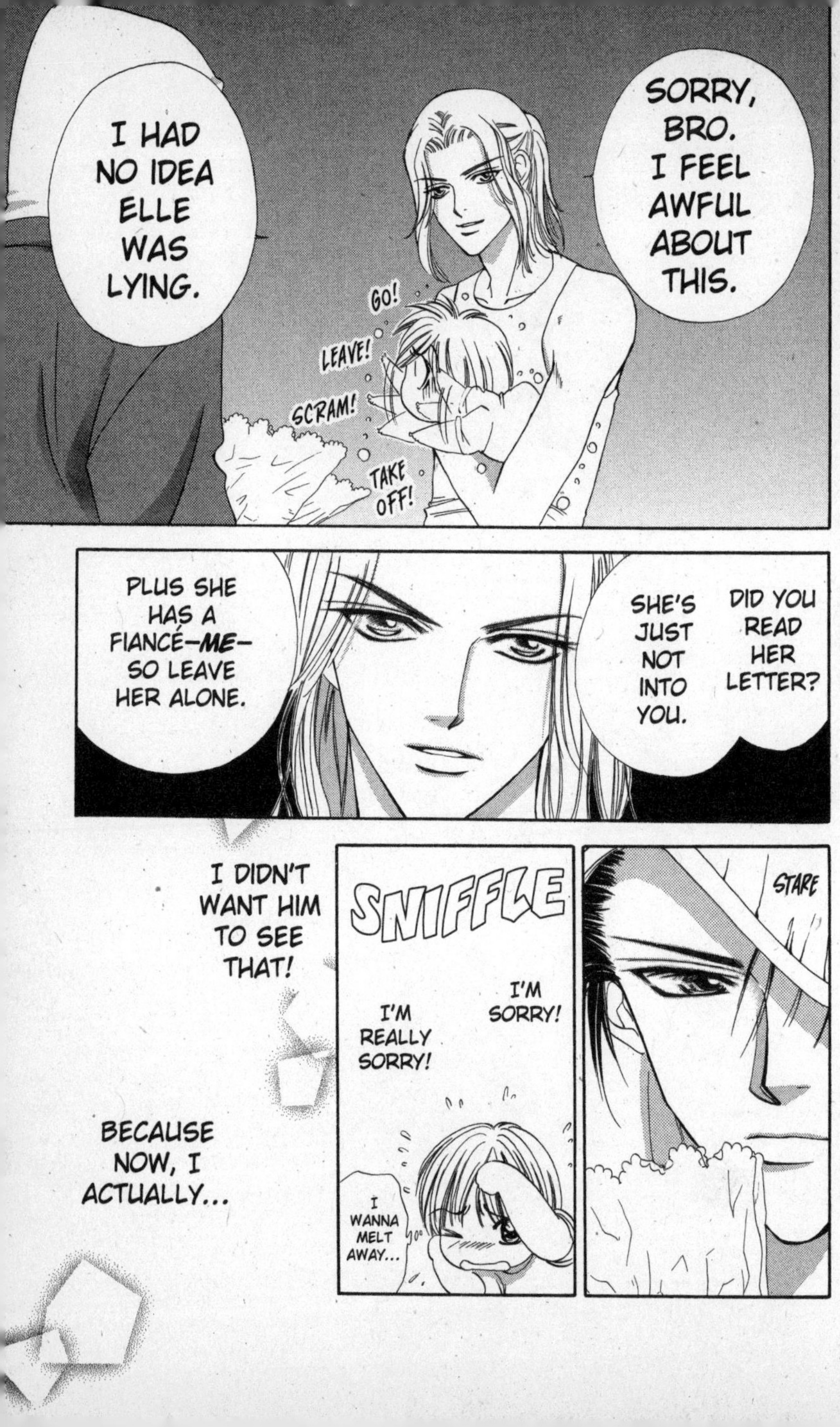
SORRY, BRO. I FEEL AWFUL ABOUT THIS.
I HAD NO IDEA ELLE WAS LYING.
GO!
LEAVE!
SCRAM!
TAKE OFF!
DID YOU READ HER LETTER?
SHE'S JUST NOT INTO YOU.
PLUS SHE HAS A FIANCÉ—*ME*—SO LEAVE HER ALONE.
STARE
SNIFFLE
I'M SORRY!
I'M REALLY SORRY!
I WANNA MELT AWAY...
I DIDN'T WANT HIM TO SEE THAT!
BECAUSE NOW, I ACTUALLY...

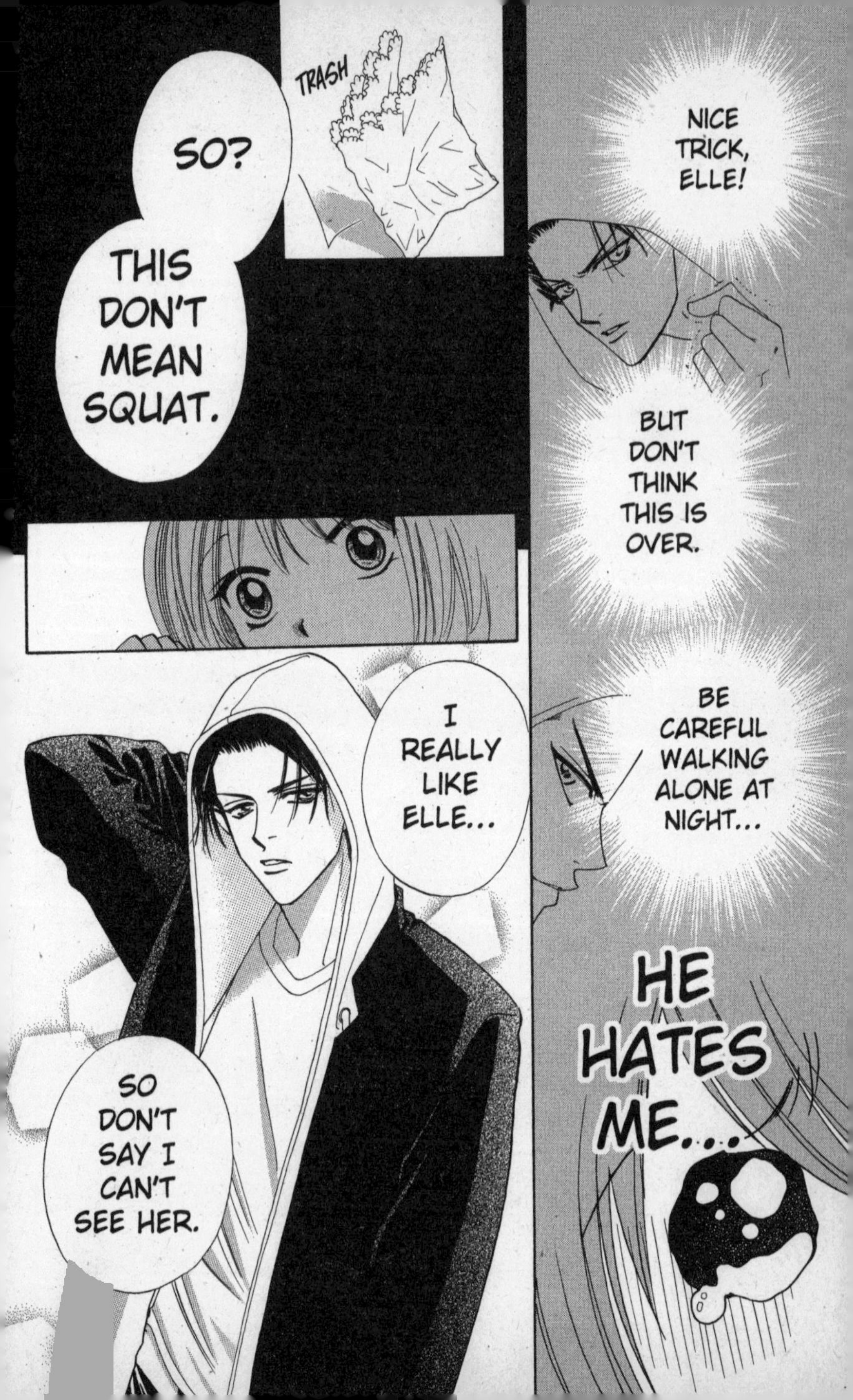
NICE TRICK, ELLE!
BUT DON'T THINK THIS IS OVER.
BE CAREFUL WALKING ALONE AT NIGHT...
HE HATES ME...
TRASH
SO?
THIS DON'T MEAN SQUAT.
I REALLY LIKE ELLE...
SO DON'T SAY I CAN'T SEE HER.

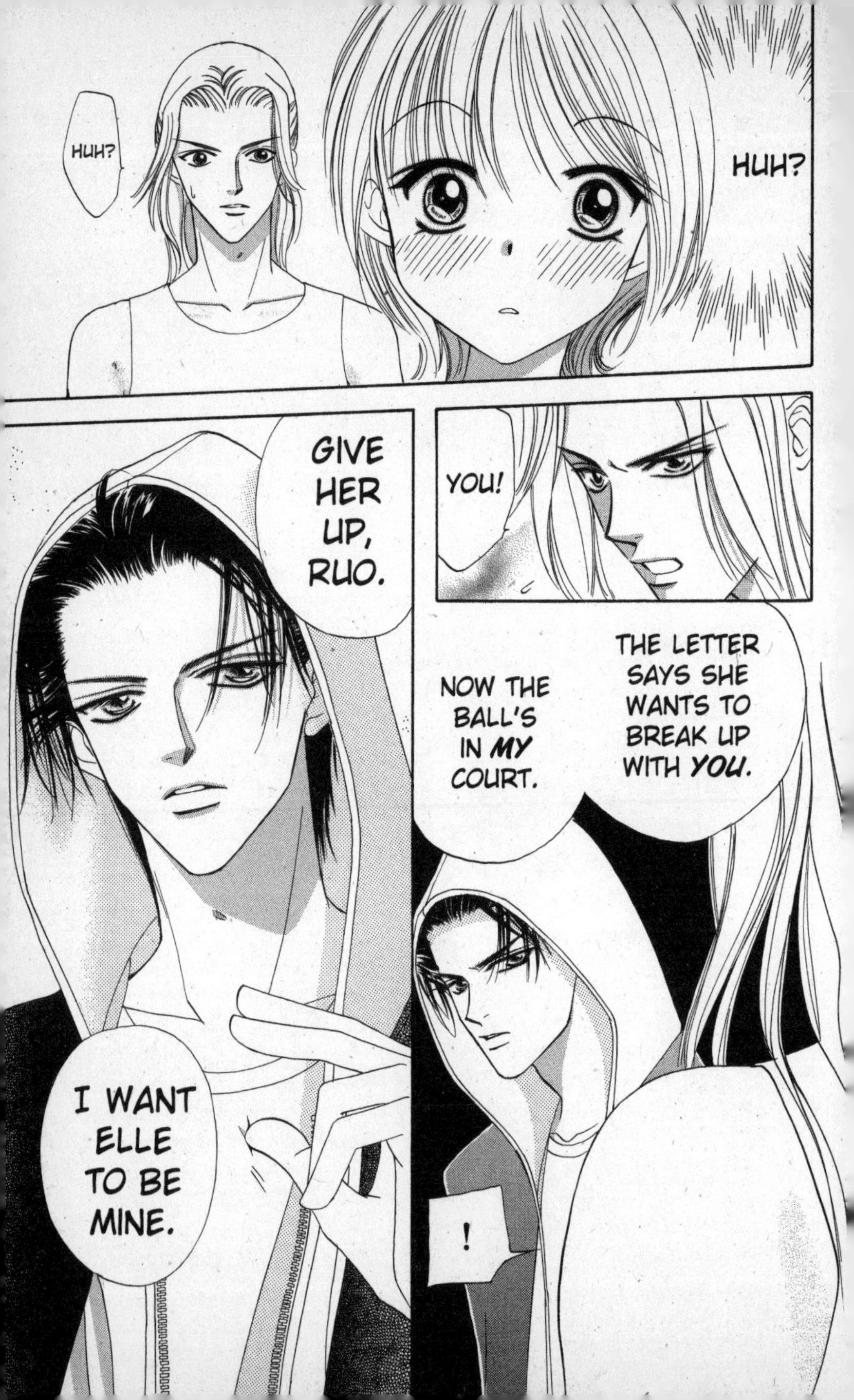
HUH?
HUH?
YOU!
THE LETTER SAYS SHE WANTS TO BREAK UP WITH *YOU*.
NOW THE BALL'S IN *MY* COURT.
!
GIVE HER UP, RUO.
I WANT ELLE TO BE MINE.

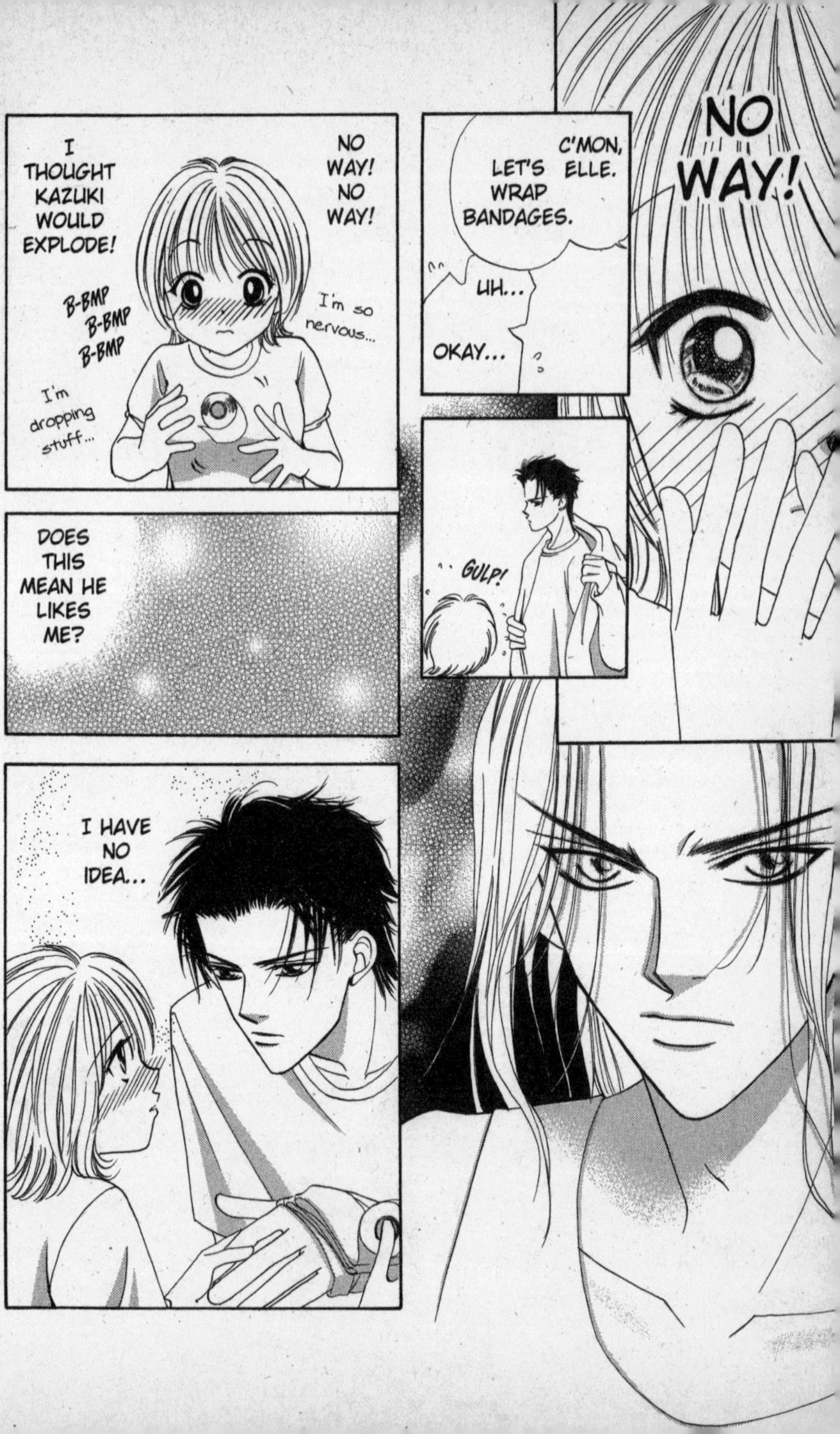
NO WAY!
C'MON, ELLE. LET'S WRAP BANDAGES.
UH...
OKAY...
GULP!
NO WAY! NO WAY!
I THOUGHT KAZUKI WOULD EXPLODE!
I'm so nervous...
B-BMP B-BMP B-BMP
I'm dropping stuff...
DOES THIS MEAN HE LIKES ME?
I HAVE NO IDEA...

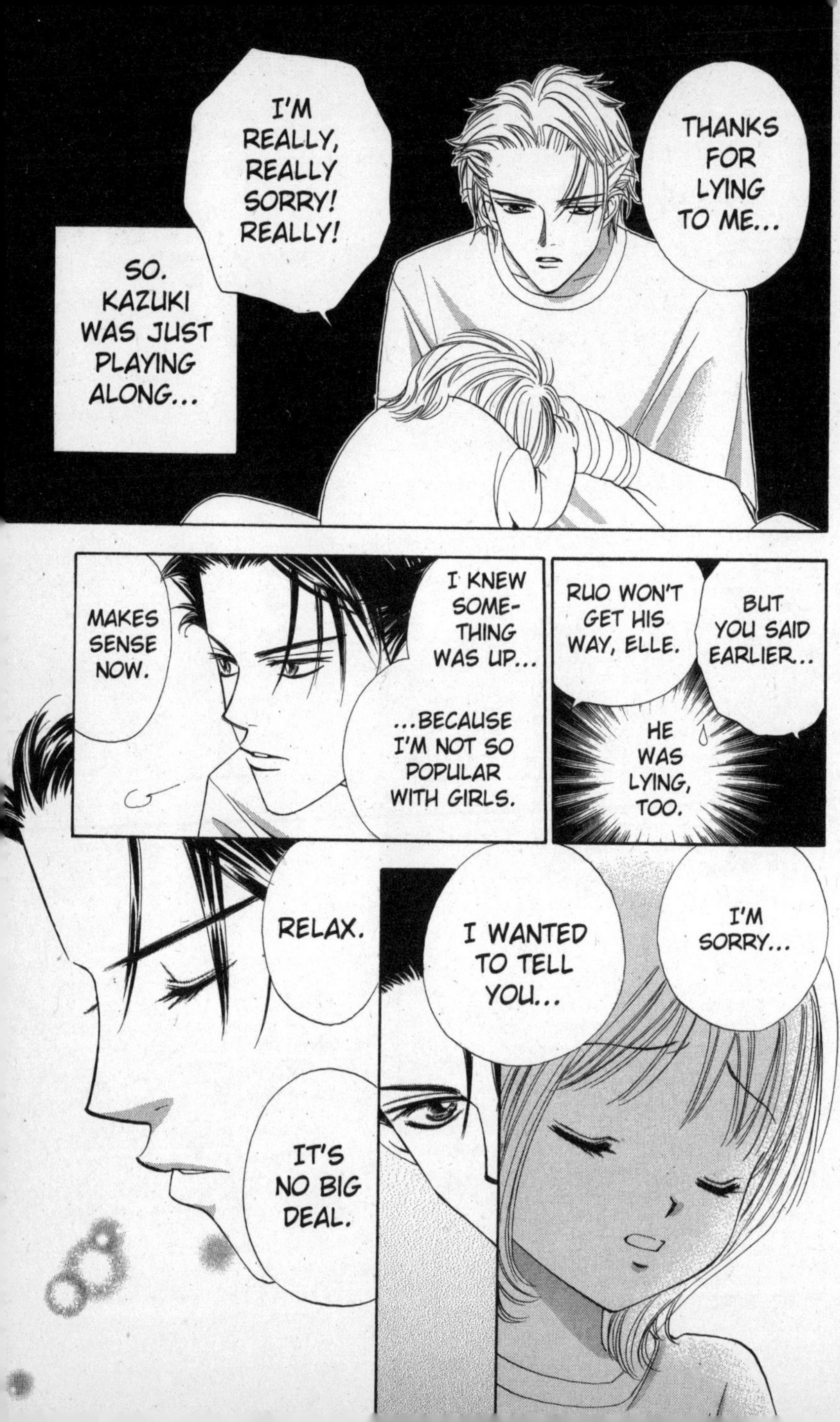
THANKS FOR LYING TO ME...
I'M REALLY, REALLY SORRY! REALLY!
SO. KAZUKI WAS JUST PLAYING ALONG...
BUT YOU SAID EARLIER...
RUO WON'T GET HIS WAY, ELLE.
HE WAS LYING, TOO.
I KNEW SOME-THING WAS UP...
MAKES SENSE NOW.
...BECAUSE I'M NOT SO POPULAR WITH GIRLS.
I'M SORRY...
I WANTED TO TELL YOU...
RELAX.
IT'S NO BIG DEAL.

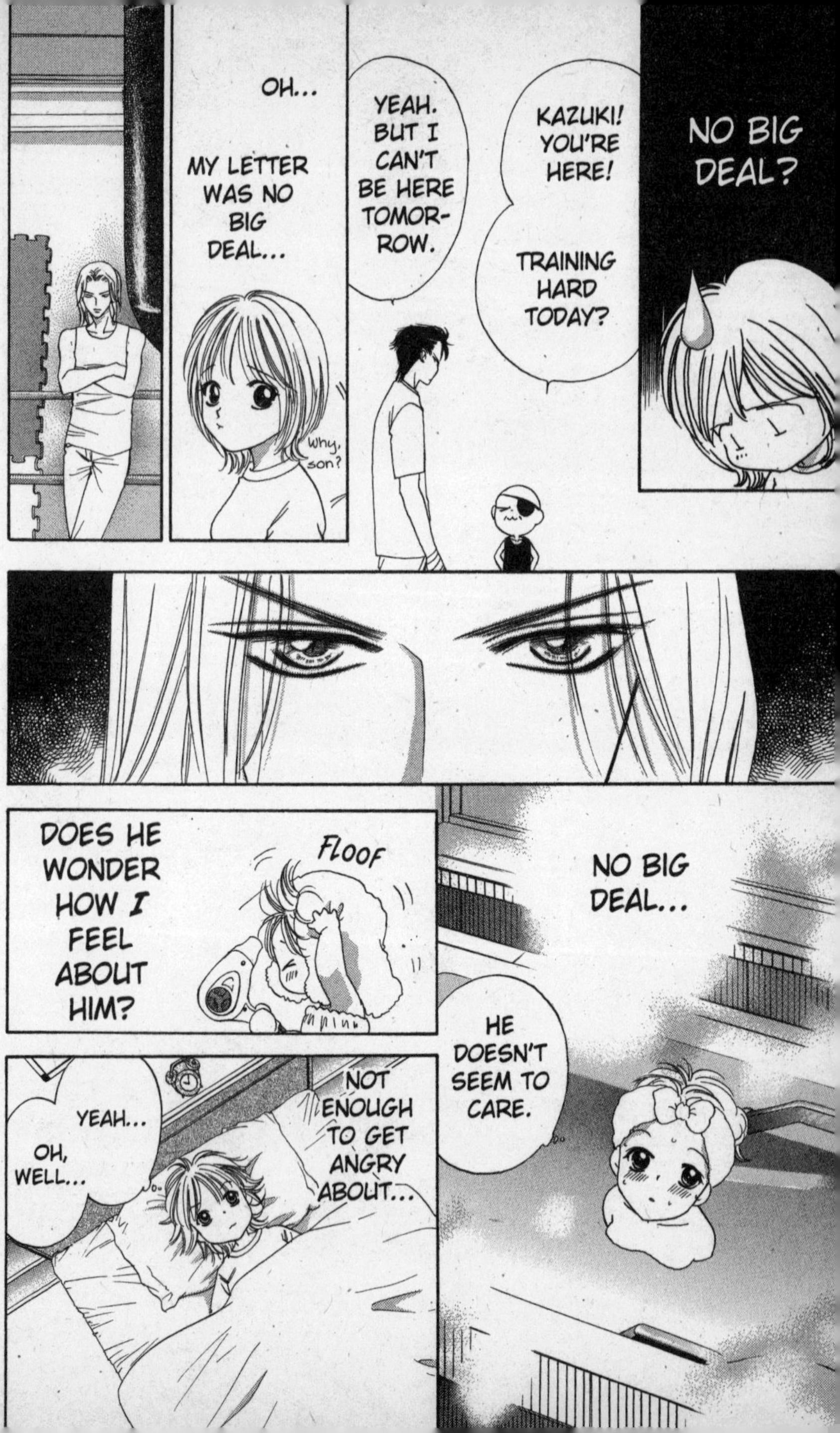
NO BIG DEAL?
KAZUKI! YOU'RE HERE!
TRAINING HARD TODAY?
YEAH. BUT I CAN'T BE HERE TOMORROW.
Why, son?
OH...
MY LETTER WAS NO BIG DEAL...
NO BIG DEAL...
HE DOESN'T SEEM TO CARE.
DOES HE WONDER HOW I FEEL ABOUT HIM?
FLOOF
NOT ENOUGH TO GET ANGRY ABOUT...
YEAH...
OH, WELL...

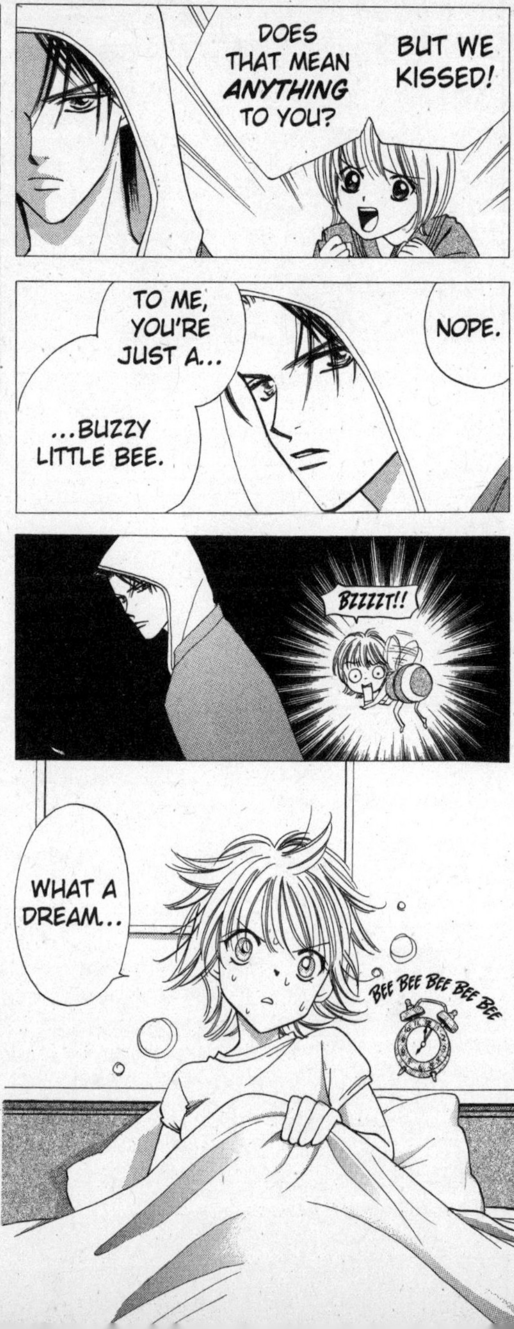
BUT WE KISSED!
DOES THAT MEAN ANYTHING TO YOU?
NOPE.
TO ME, YOU'RE JUST A...
...BUZZY LITTLE BEE.
BZZZZT!!
WHAT A DREAM...
BEE BEE BEE BEE BEE

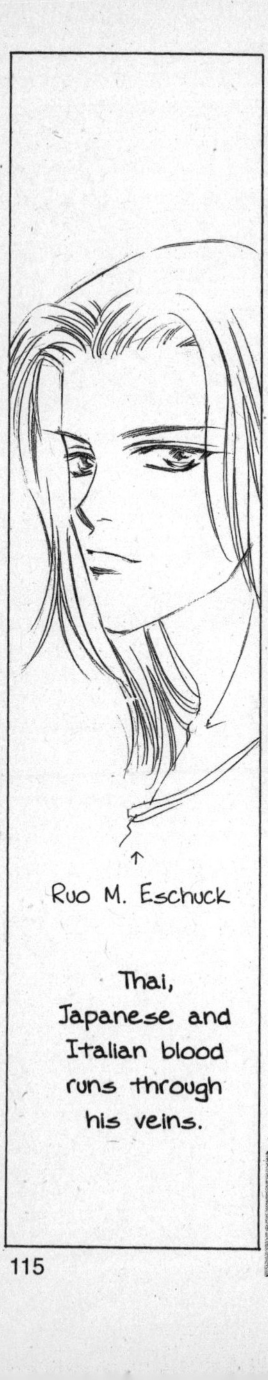

↑
Ruo M. Eschuck

Thai, Japanese and Italian blood runs through his veins.

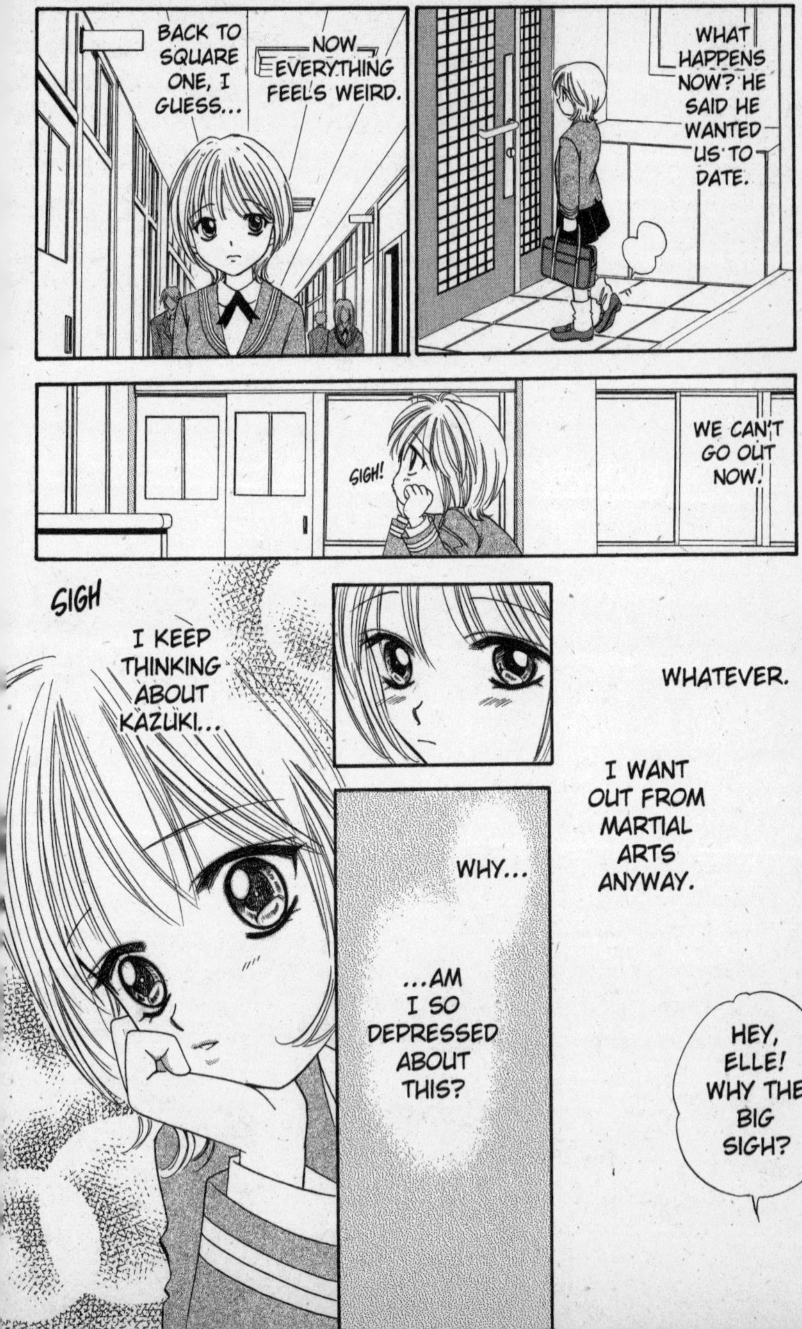
WHAT HAPPENS NOW? HE SAID HE WANTED US TO DATE.
NOW EVERYTHING FEELS WEIRD.
BACK TO SQUARE ONE, I GUESS...
WE CAN'T GO OUT NOW.
SIGH!
WHATEVER.
I WANT OUT FROM MARTIAL ARTS ANYWAY.
WHY...
...AM I SO DEPRESSED ABOUT THIS?
HEY, ELLE! WHY THE BIG SIGH?
SIGH
I KEEP THINKING ABOUT KAZUKI...

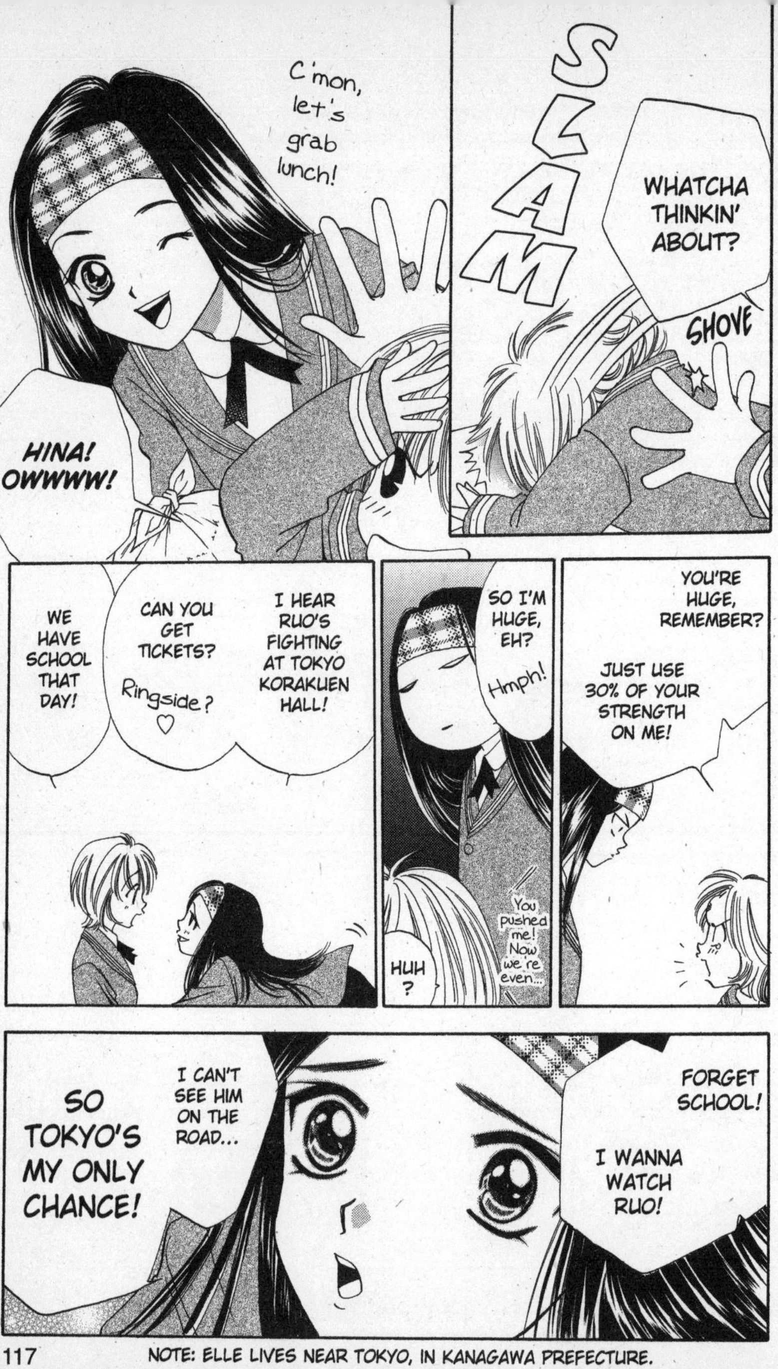
SLAM
WHATCHA THINKIN' ABOUT?
SHOVE
C'mon, let's grab lunch!
HINA! OWWWW!
YOU'RE HUGE, REMEMBER?
JUST USE 30% OF YOUR STRENGTH ON ME!
SO I'M HUGE, EH?
Hmph!
You pushed me! Now we're even...
HUH?
I HEAR RUO'S FIGHTING AT TOKYO KORAKUEN HALL!
CAN YOU GET TICKETS?
Ringside? ♡
WE HAVE SCHOOL THAT DAY!
FORGET SCHOOL!
I WANNA WATCH RUO!
I CAN'T SEE HIM ON THE ROAD...
SO TOKYO'S MY ONLY CHANCE!

NOTE: ELLE LIVES NEAR TOKYO, IN KANAGAWA PREFECTURE.

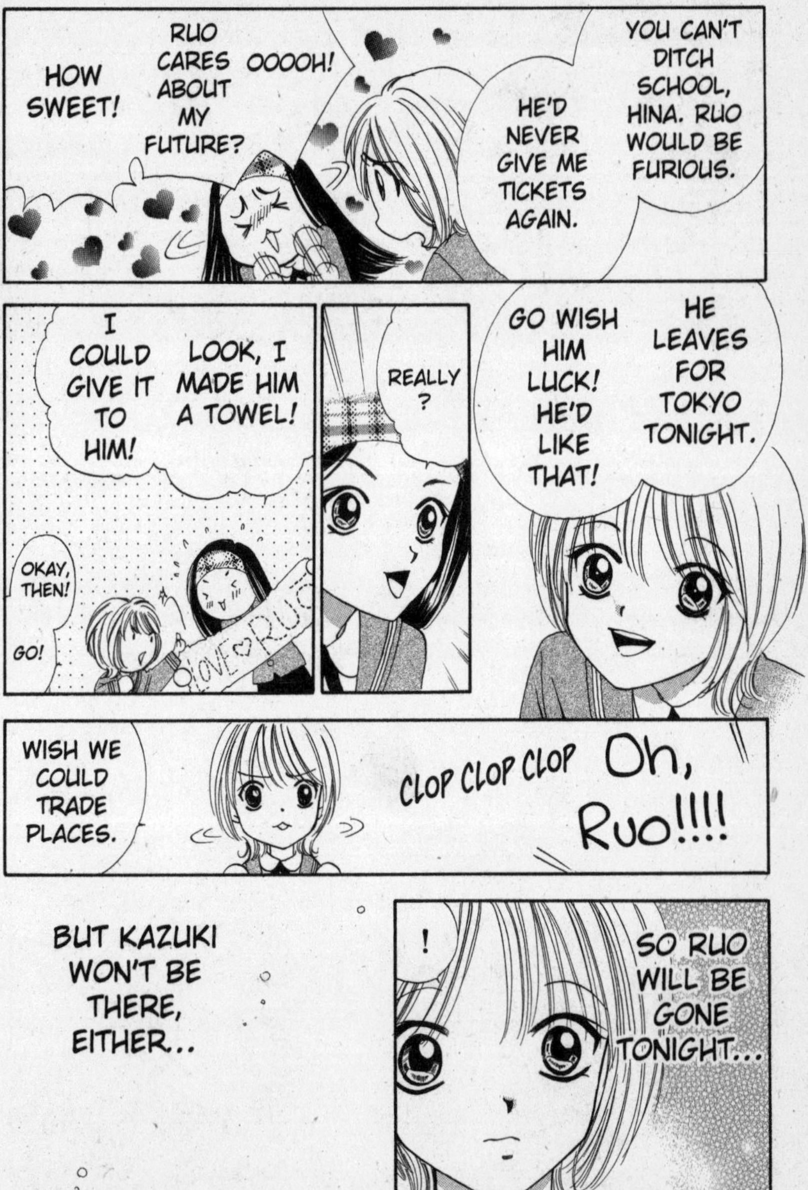
YOU CAN'T DITCH SCHOOL, HINA. RUO WOULD BE FURIOUS.
HE'D NEVER GIVE ME TICKETS AGAIN.
OOOOH!
RUO CARES ABOUT MY FUTURE?
HOW SWEET!
HE LEAVES FOR TOKYO TONIGHT.
GO WISH HIM LUCK! HE'D LIKE THAT!
REALLY?
LOOK, I MADE HIM A TOWEL!
I COULD GIVE IT TO HIM!
LOVE♡RUO
OKAY, THEN!
GO!
Oh, Ruo!!!!
CLOP CLOP CLOP
WISH WE COULD TRADE PLACES.
SO RUO WILL BE GONE TONIGHT...
!
BUT KAZUKI WON'T BE THERE, EITHER...

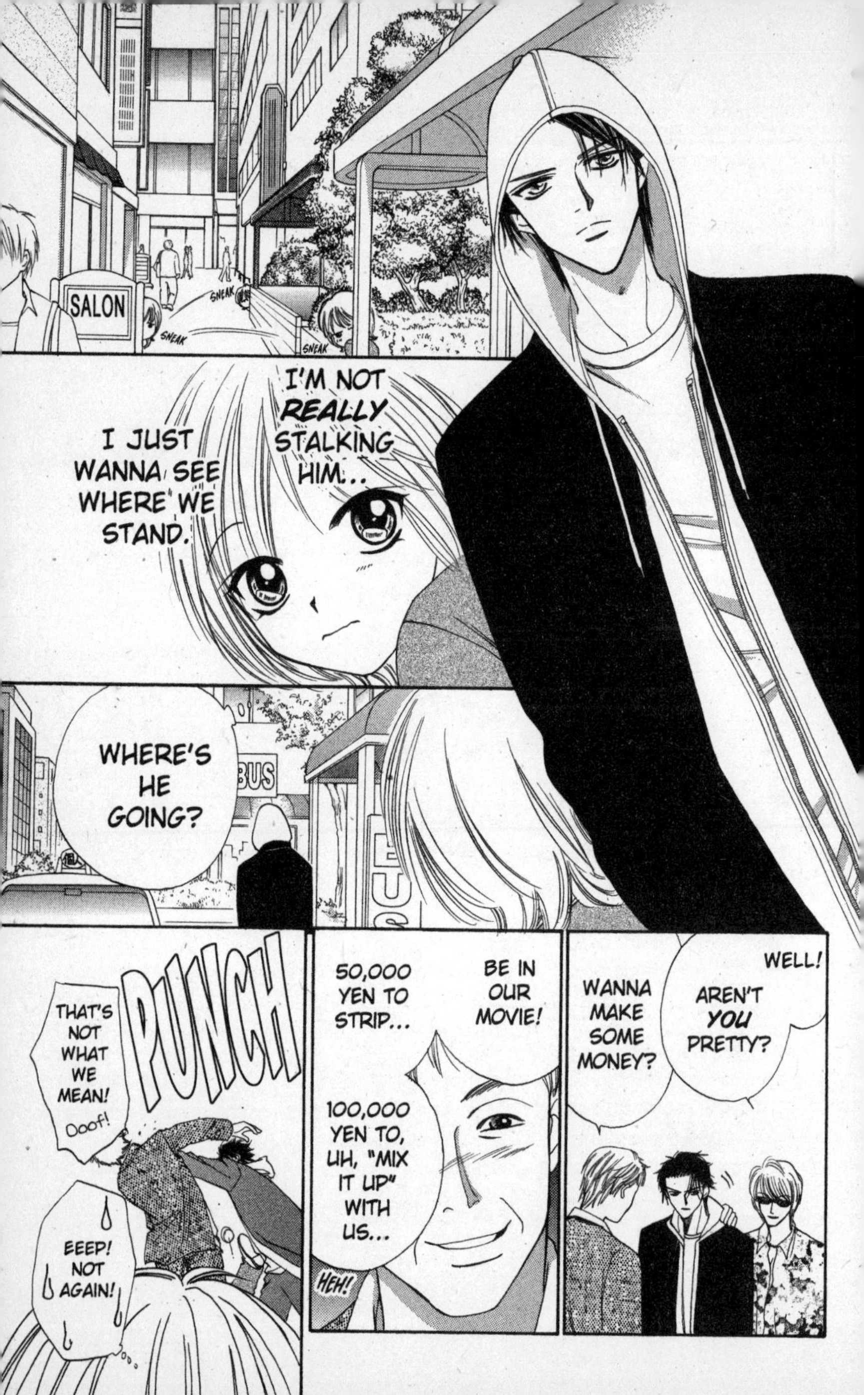
SNEAK
SNEAK
SNEAK
I'M NOT *REALLY* STALKING HIM...
I JUST WANNA SEE WHERE WE STAND.
WHERE'S HE GOING?
SALON
BUS
WELL! AREN'T *YOU* PRETTY?
WANNA MAKE SOME MONEY?
BE IN OUR MOVIE!
50,000 YEN TO STRIP...
100,000 YEN TO, UH, "MIX IT UP" WITH US...
HEH!
PUNCH
THAT'S NOT WHAT WE MEAN!
Oof!
EEEP! NOT AGAIN!

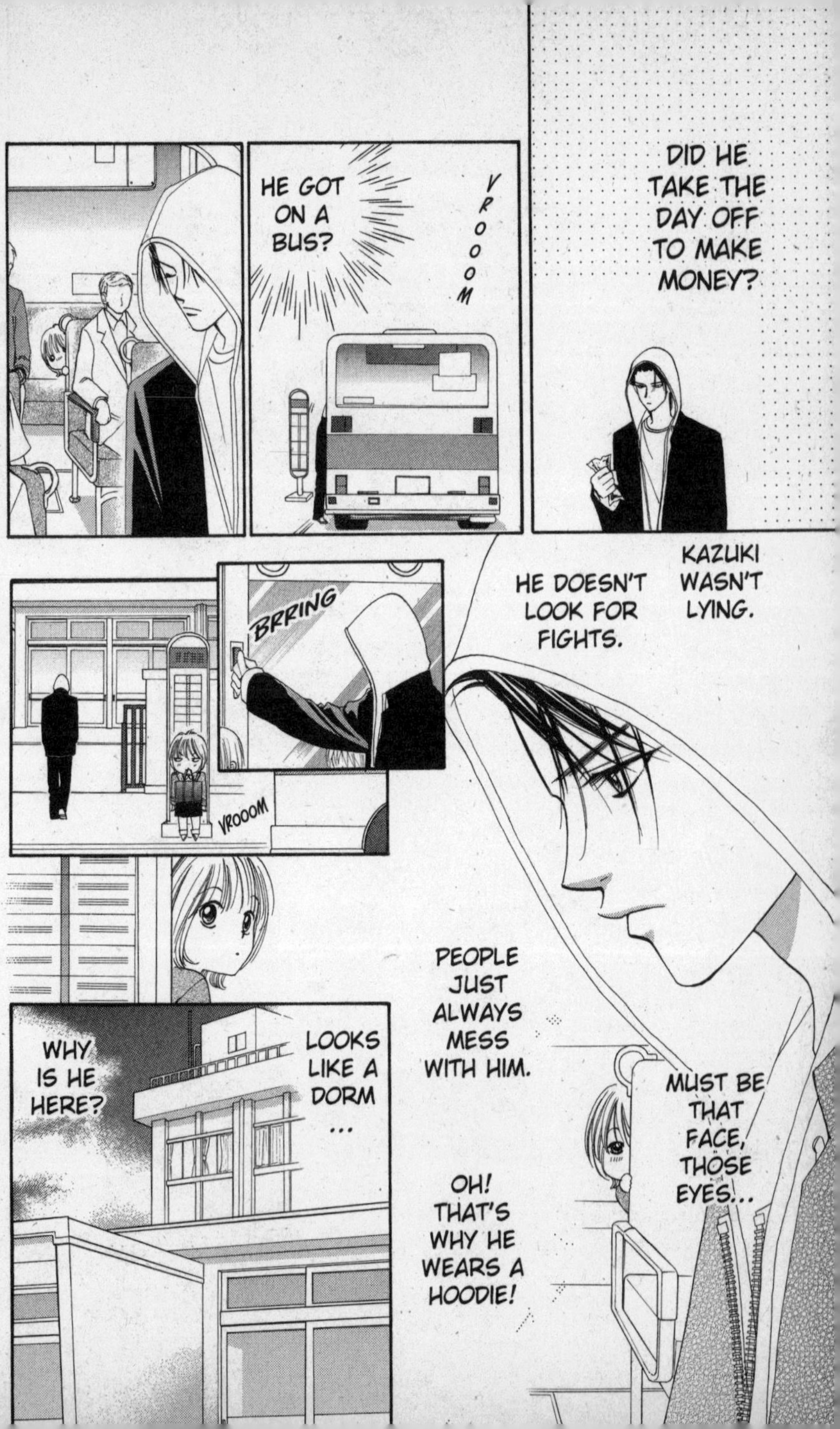
DID HE TAKE THE DAY OFF TO MAKE MONEY?
HE GOT ON A BUS?
VROOOOM
KAZUKI WASN'T LYING.
HE DOESN'T LOOK FOR FIGHTS.
PEOPLE JUST ALWAYS MESS WITH HIM.
MUST BE THAT FACE, THOSE EYES...
OH! THAT'S WHY HE WEARS A HOODIE!
BRRING
VROOOM
LOOKS LIKE A DORM...
WHY IS HE HERE?

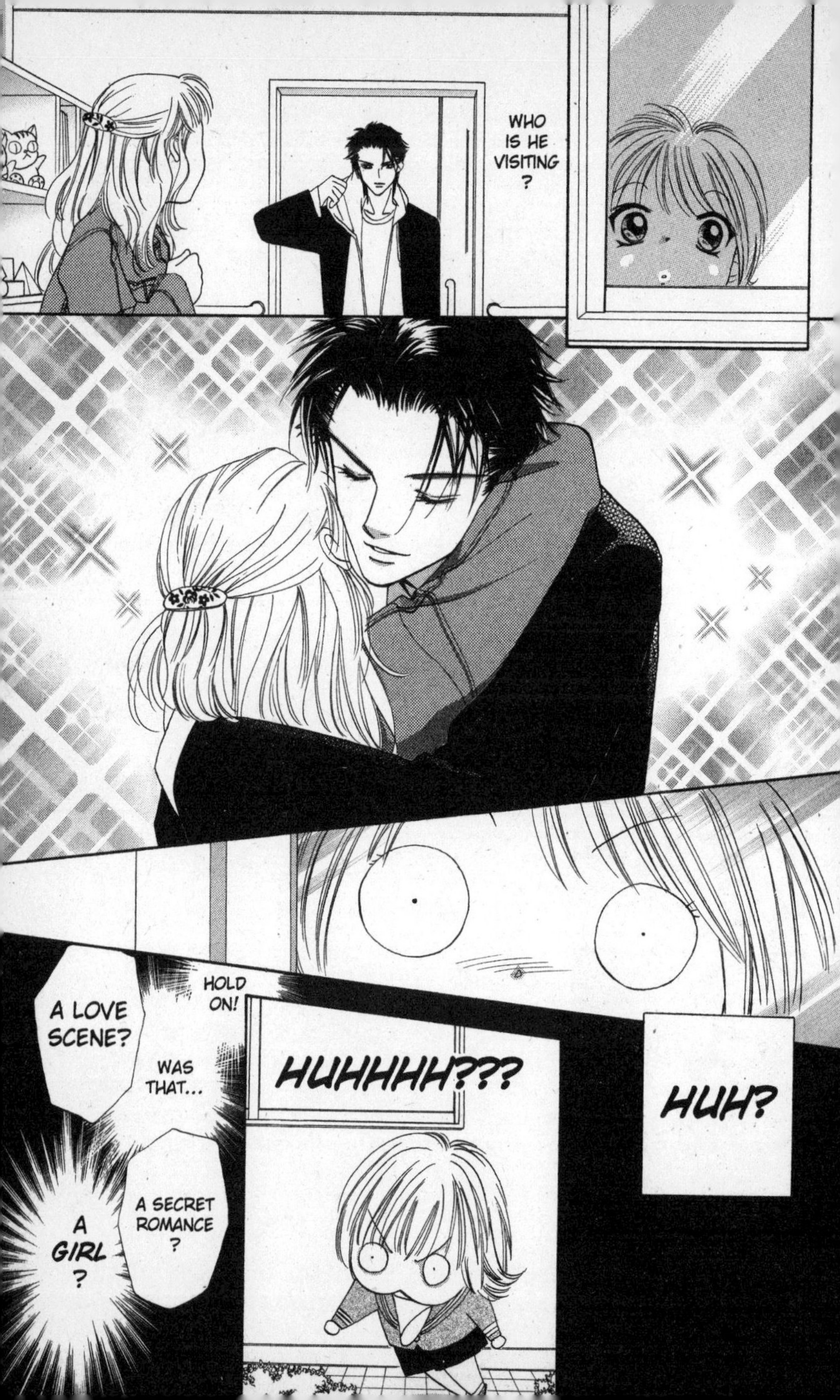
WHO IS HE VISITING ?
HUH?
HUHHHH???
HOLD ON!
WAS THAT...
A LOVE SCENE?
A SECRET ROMANCE ?
A GIRL ?

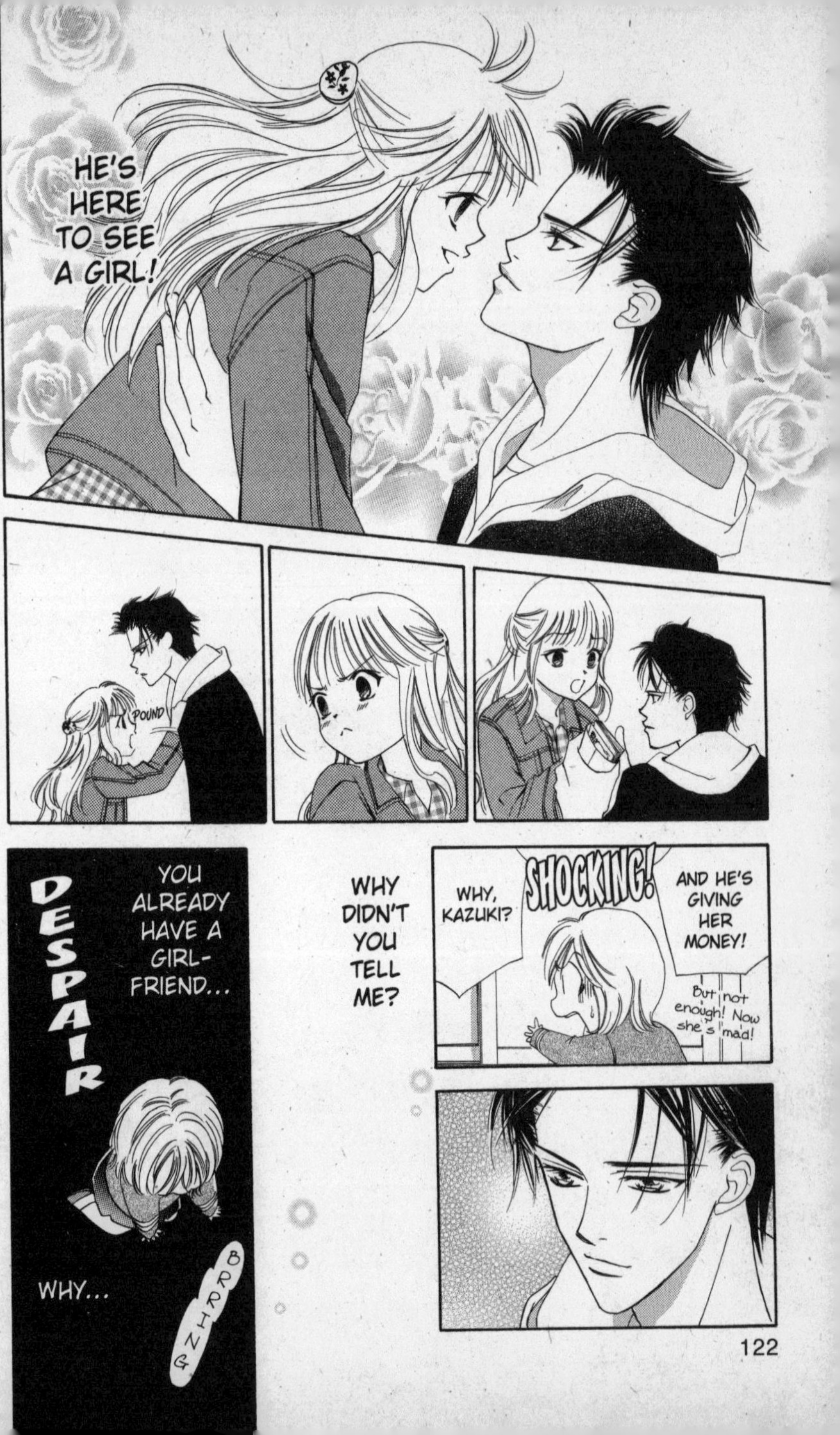

HE'S HERE TO SEE A GIRL!
POUND
AND HE'S GIVING HER MONEY!
SHOCKING!
WHY, KAZUKI?
But not enough! Now she's mad!
WHY DIDN'T YOU TELL ME?
YOU ALREADY HAVE A GIRL-FRIEND...
DESPAIR
WHY...
BRRING

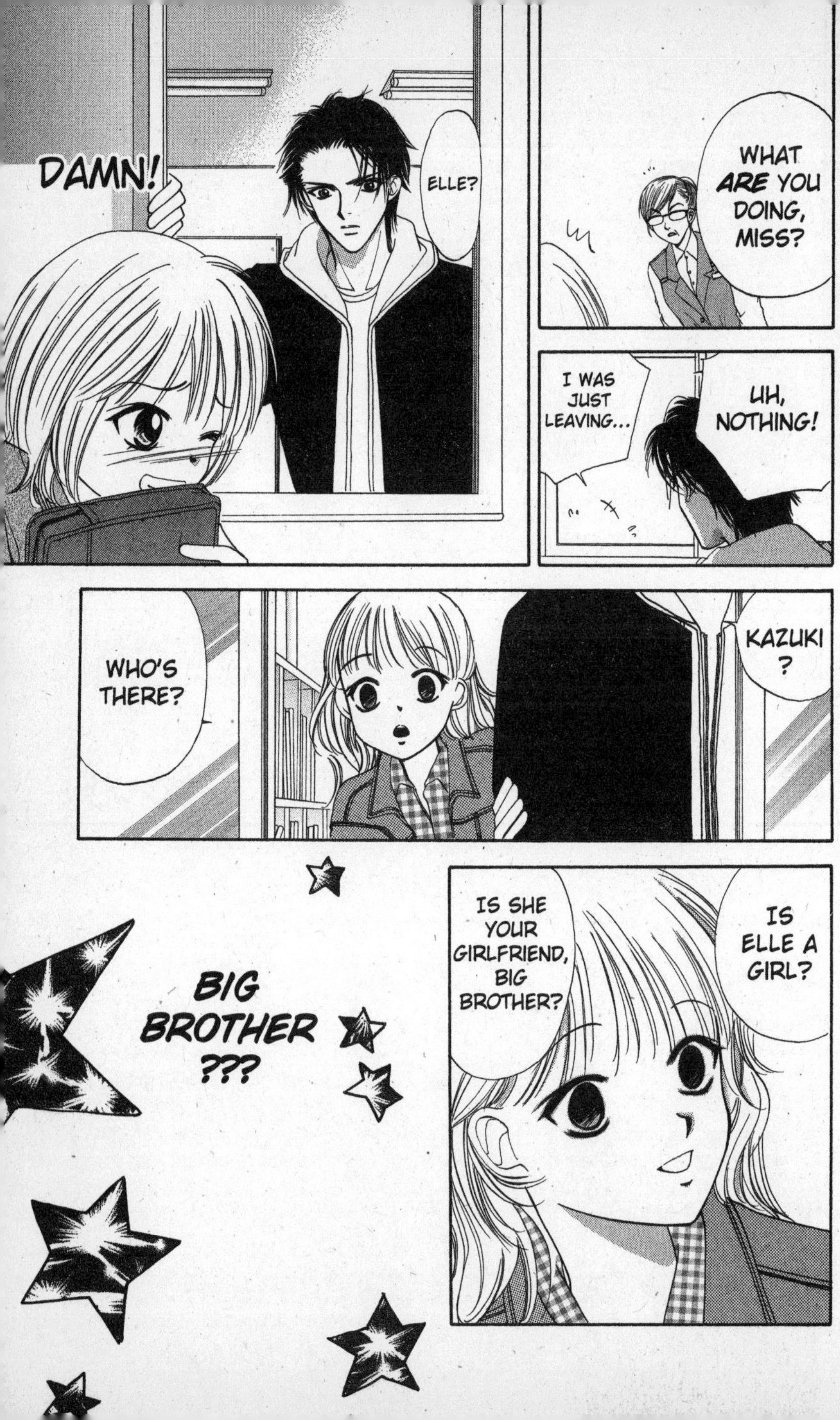
WHAT ARE YOU DOING, MISS?
UH, NOTHING!
I WAS JUST LEAVING...
ELLE?
DAMN!
KAZUKI ?
WHO'S THERE?
IS ELLE A GIRL?
IS SHE YOUR GIRLFRIEND, BIG BROTHER?
BIG BROTHER ???

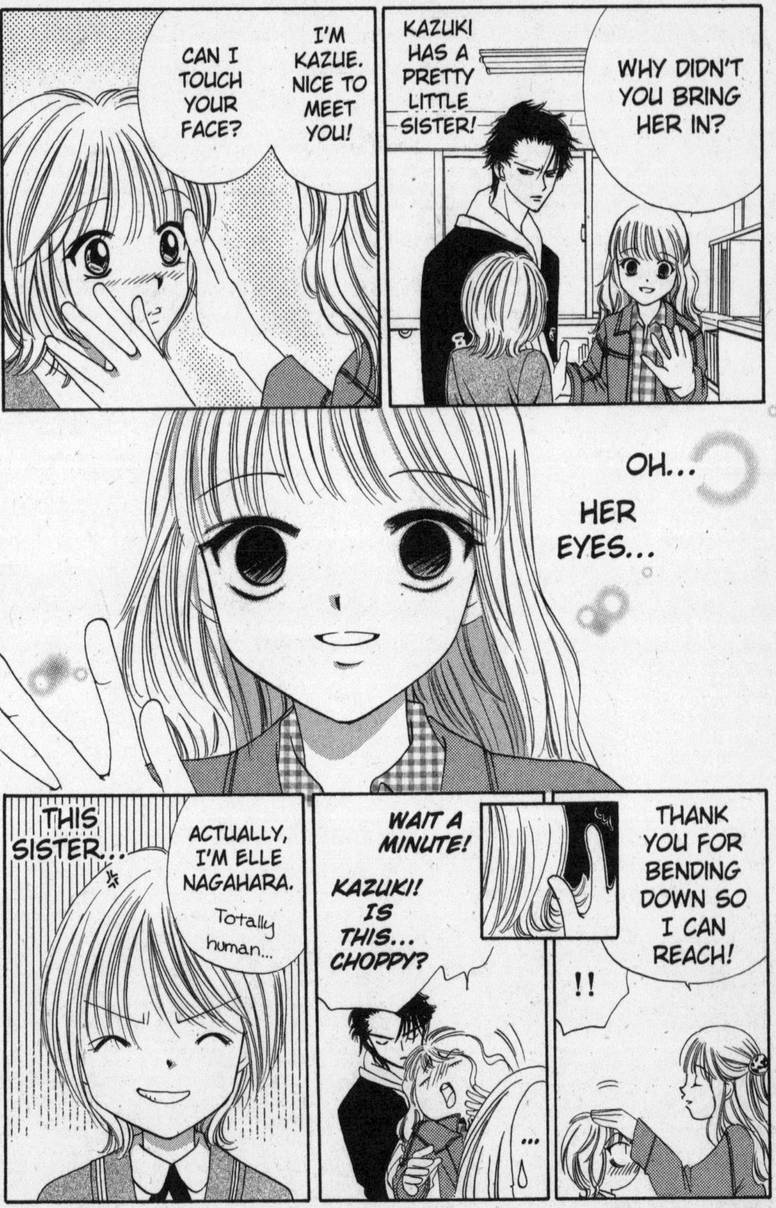
WHY DIDN'T YOU BRING HER IN?
KAZUKI HAS A PRETTY LITTLE SISTER!
I'M KAZUE. NICE TO MEET YOU!
CAN I TOUCH YOUR FACE?
OH...
HER EYES...
THANK YOU FOR BENDING DOWN SO I CAN REACH!
!!
WAIT A MINUTE!
KAZUKI! IS THIS... CHOPPY?
...
ACTUALLY, I'M ELLE NAGAHARA.
Totally human...
THIS SISTER...

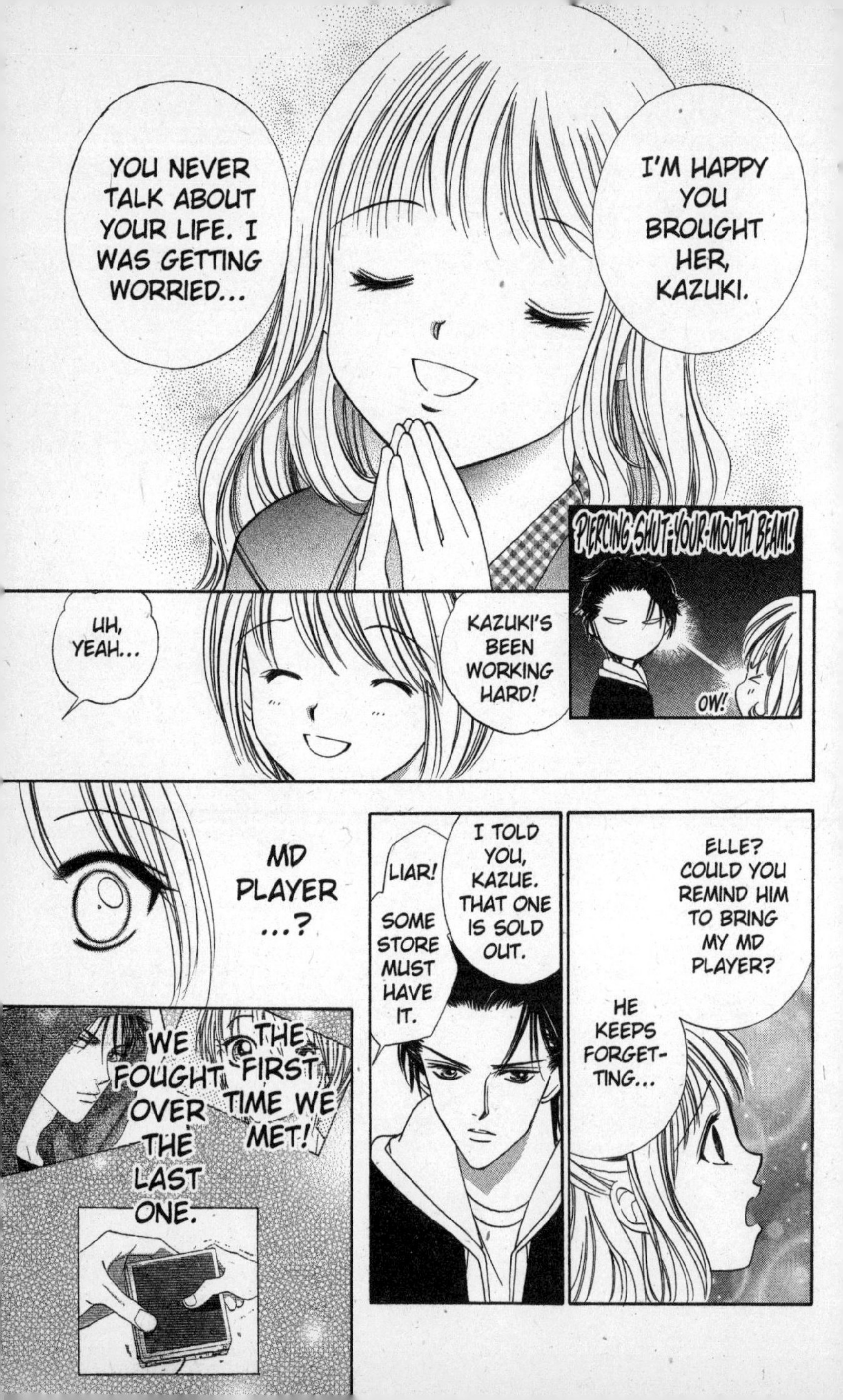
I'M HAPPY YOU BROUGHT HER, KAZUKI.
YOU NEVER TALK ABOUT YOUR LIFE. I WAS GETTING WORRIED...
KAZUKI'S BEEN WORKING HARD!
UH, YEAH...
PIERCING-SHUT-YOUR-MOUTH BEAM!
OW!
ELLE? COULD YOU REMIND HIM TO BRING MY MD PLAYER?
HE KEEPS FORGET-TING...
I TOLD YOU, KAZUE. THAT ONE IS SOLD OUT.
LIAR! SOME STORE MUST HAVE IT.
MD PLAYER ...?
THE FIRST TIME WE MET!
WE FOUGHT OVER THE LAST ONE.

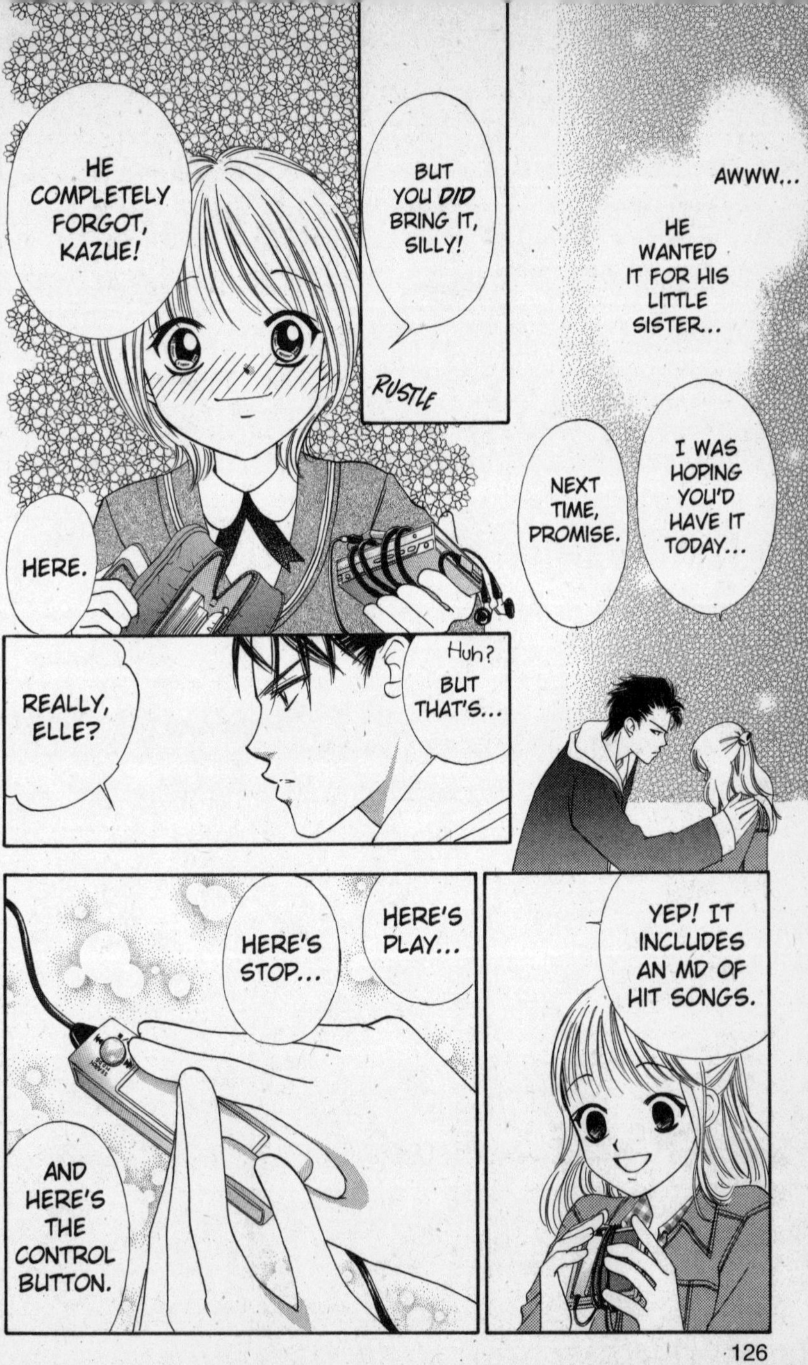
AWWW...
HE WANTED IT FOR HIS LITTLE SISTER...
I WAS HOPING YOU'D HAVE IT TODAY...
NEXT TIME, PROMISE.
BUT YOU *DID* BRING IT, SILLY!
RUSTLE
HE COMPLETELY FORGOT, KAZUE!
HERE.
Huh?
BUT THAT'S...
REALLY, ELLE?
YEP! IT INCLUDES AN MD OF HIT SONGS.
HERE'S PLAY...
HERE'S STOP...
AND HERE'S THE CONTROL BUTTON.

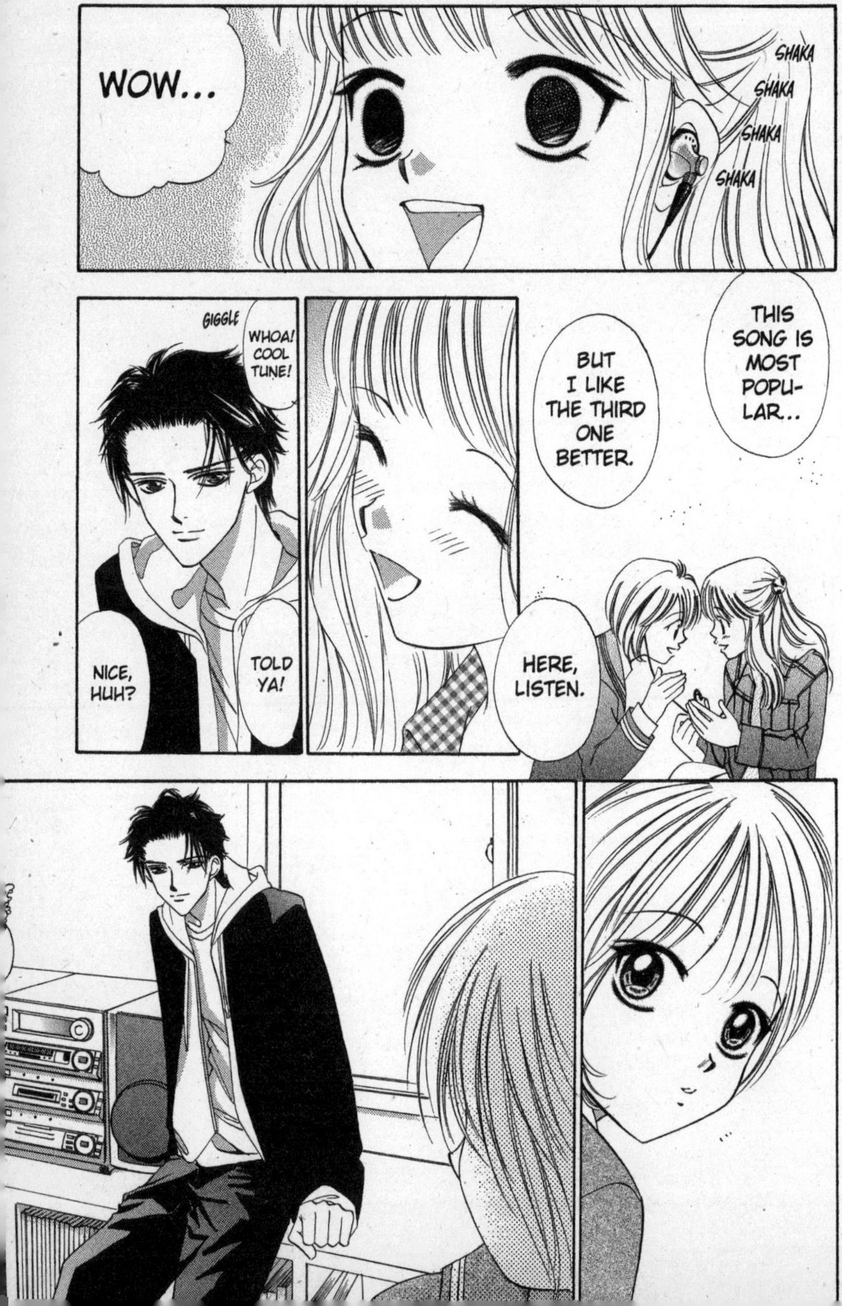
SHAKA
SHAKA
SHAKA
SHAKA
WOW...
THIS SONG IS MOST POPU-LAR...
BUT I LIKE THE THIRD ONE BETTER.
HERE, LISTEN.
WHOA! COOL TUNE!
GIGGLE
TOLD YA!
NICE, HUH?

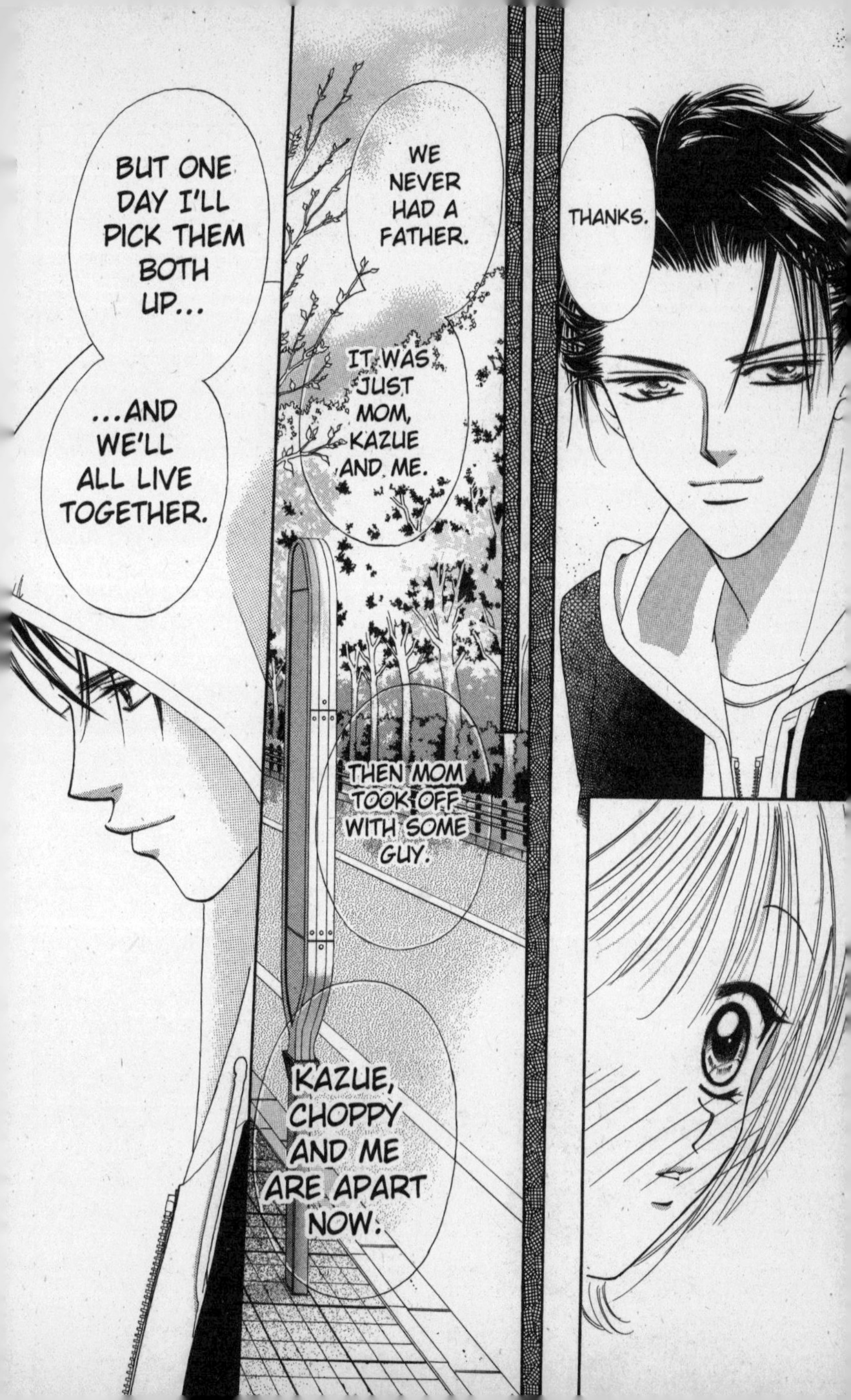
THANKS.
WE NEVER HAD A FATHER.
IT WAS JUST MOM, KAZUE AND ME.
THEN MOM TOOK OFF WITH SOME GUY.
KAZUE, CHOPPY AND ME ARE APART NOW.
BUT ONE DAY I'LL PICK THEM BOTH UP...
...AND WE'LL ALL LIVE TOGETHER.

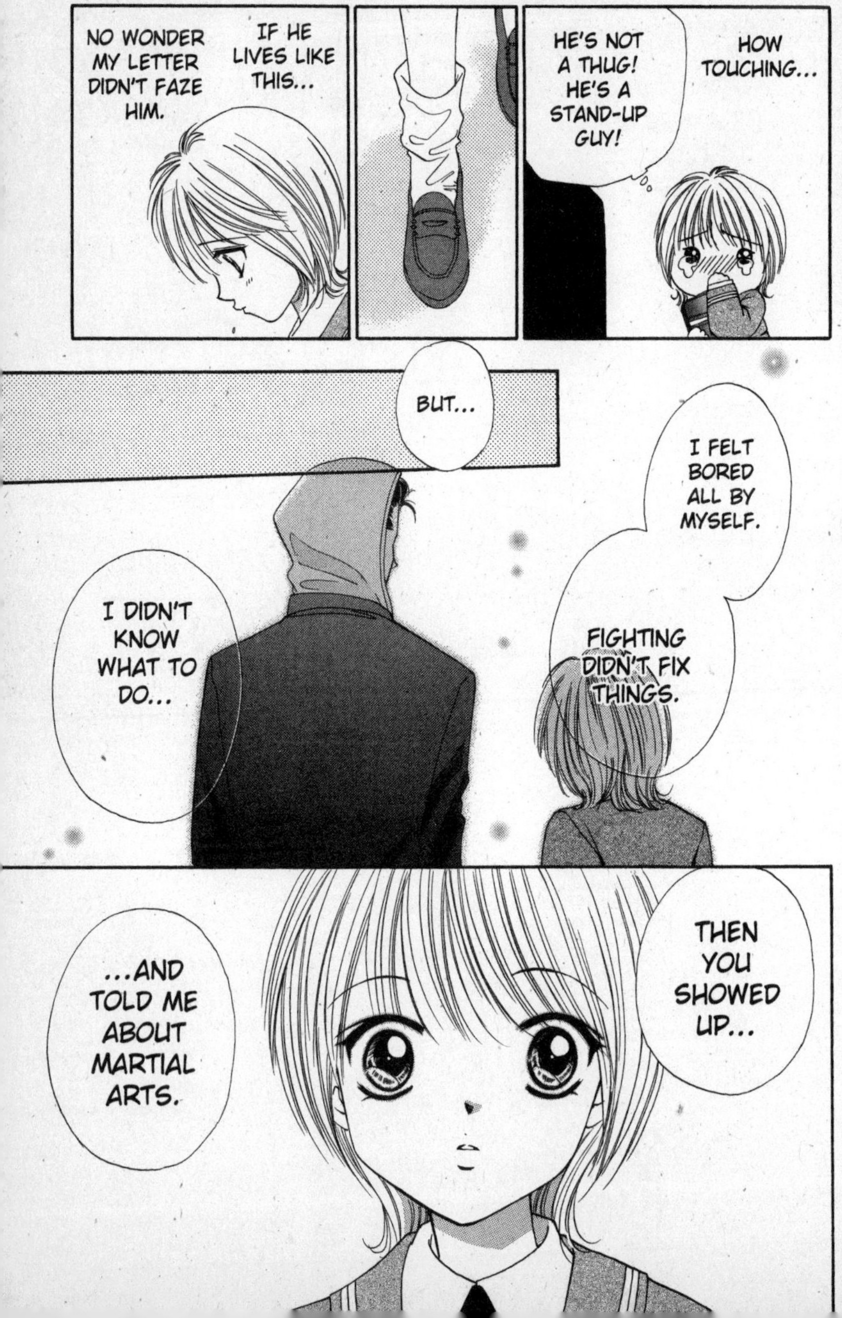
HOW TOUCHING...
HE'S NOT A THUG! HE'S A STAND-UP GUY!
IF HE LIVES LIKE THIS...
NO WONDER MY LETTER DIDN'T FAZE HIM.
BUT...
I FELT BORED ALL BY MYSELF.
FIGHTING DIDN'T FIX THINGS.
I DIDN'T KNOW WHAT TO DO...
THEN YOU SHOWED UP...
...AND TOLD ME ABOUT MARTIAL ARTS.

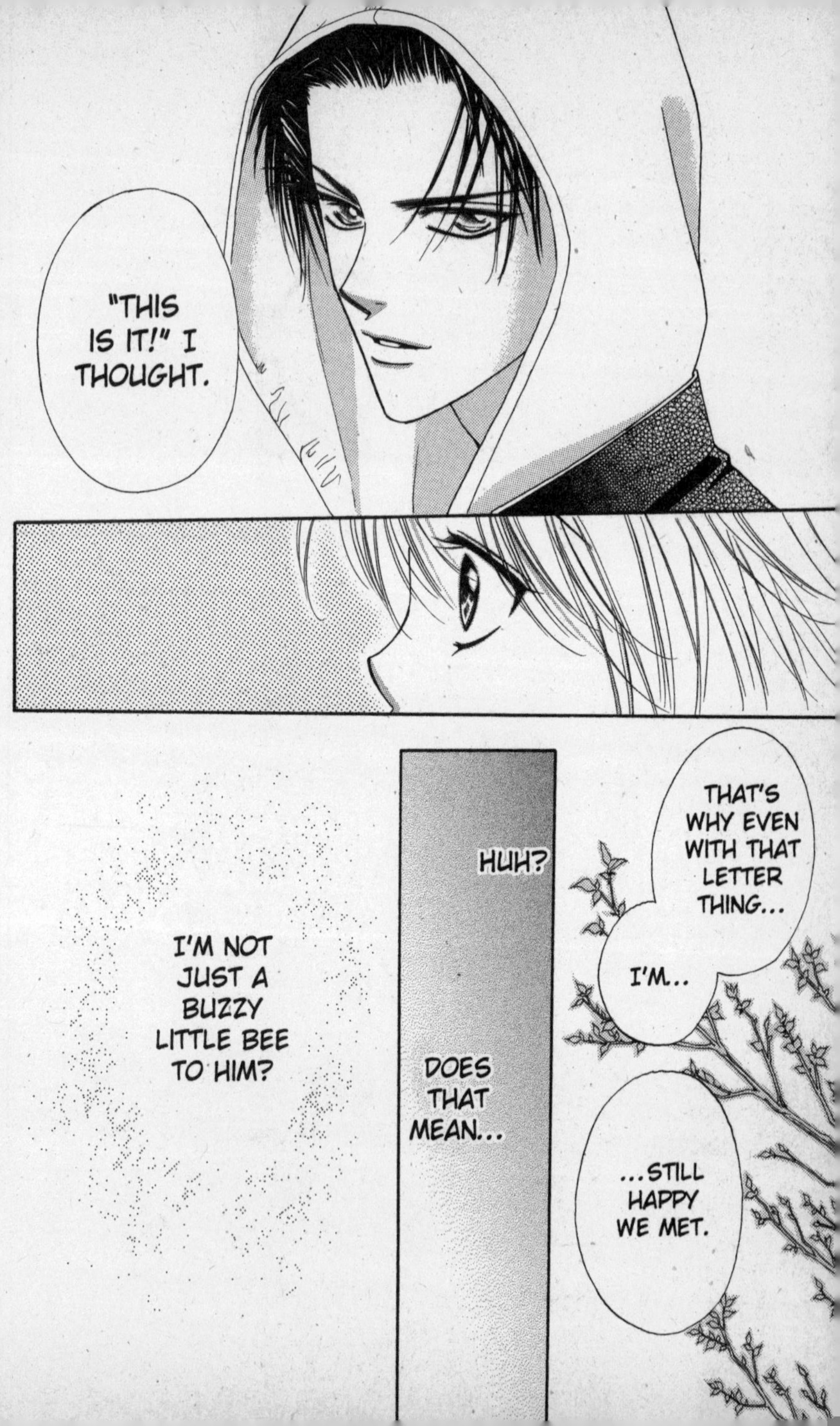
"THIS IS IT!" I THOUGHT.
THAT'S WHY EVEN WITH THAT LETTER THING...
I'M...
...STILL HAPPY WE MET.
HUH?
DOES THAT MEAN...
I'M NOT JUST A BUZZY LITTLE BEE TO HIM?

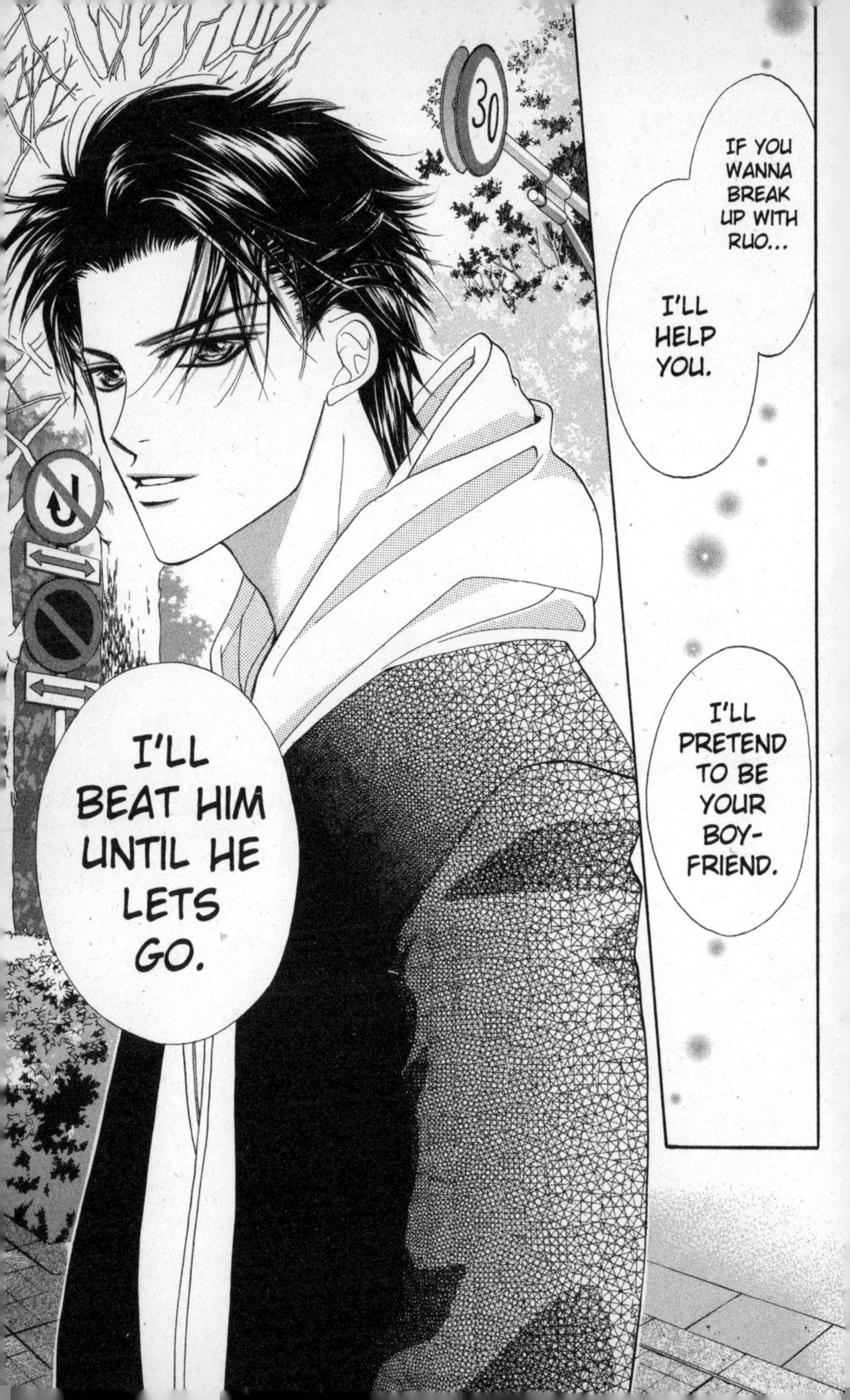
IF YOU WANNA BREAK UP WITH RUO...
I'LL HELP YOU.
I'LL PRETEND TO BE YOUR BOY-FRIEND.
I'LL BEAT HIM UNTIL HE LETS GO.

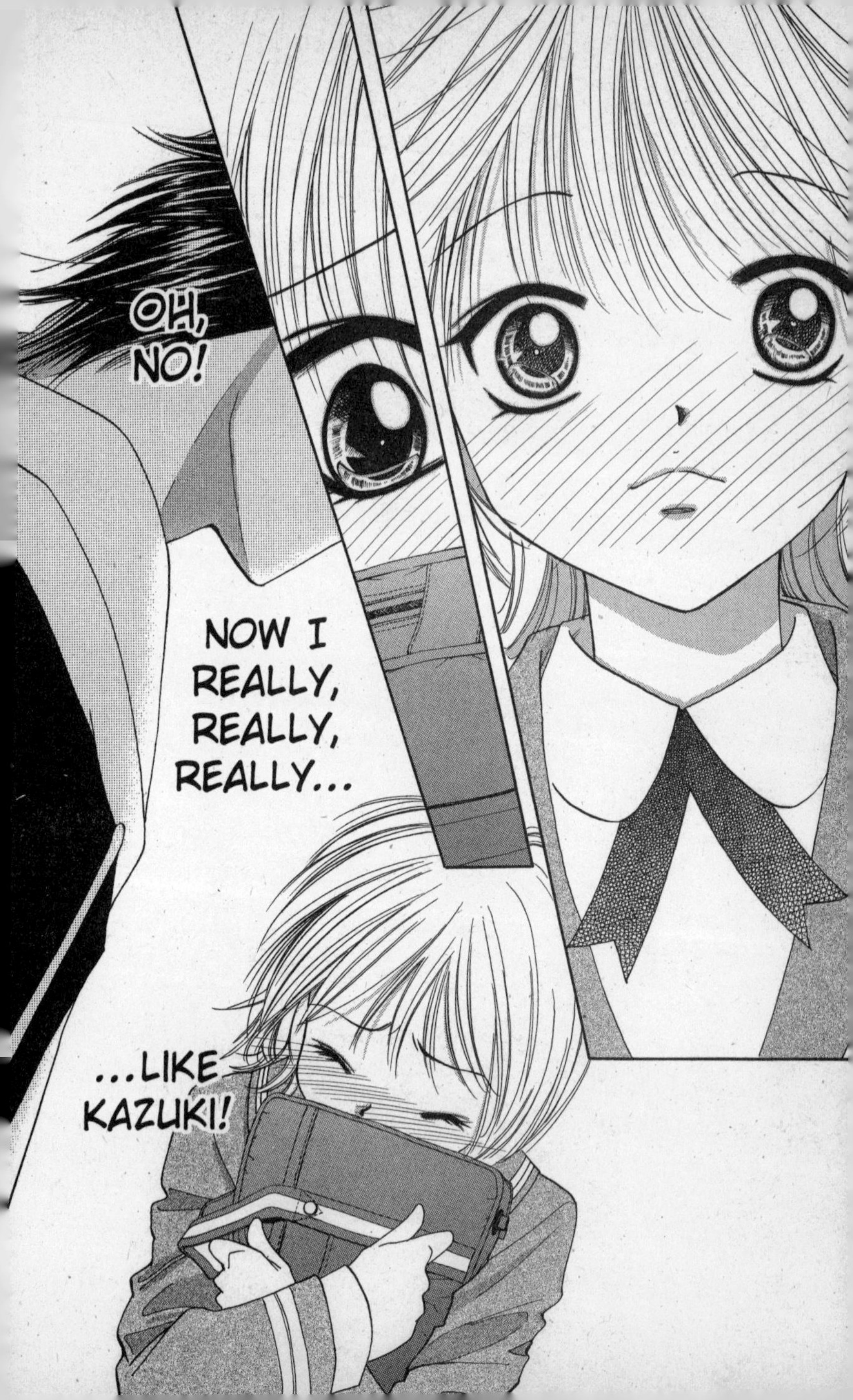
OH, NO!
NOW I REALLY, REALLY, REALLY...
...LIKE KAZUKI!

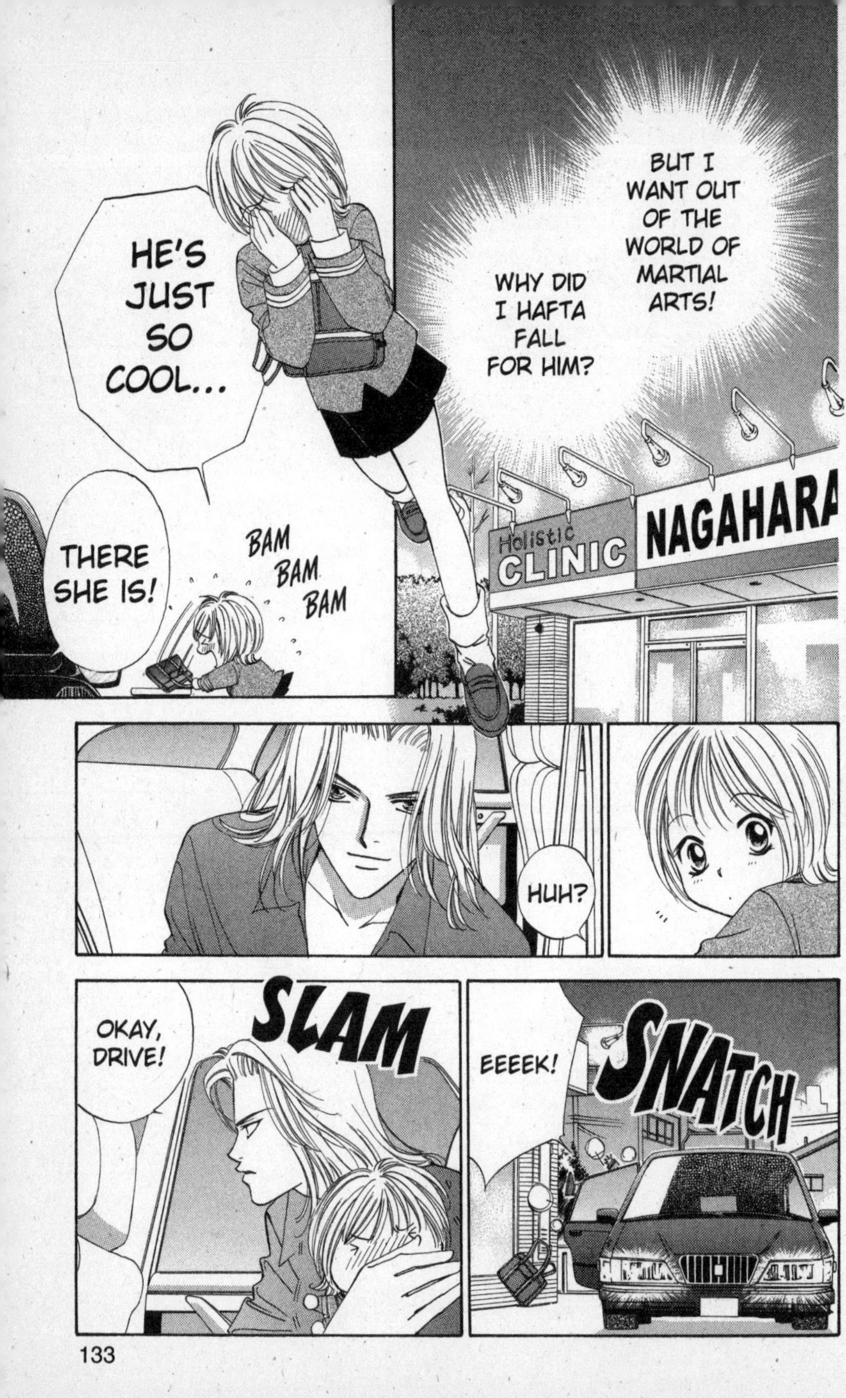
BUT I WANT OUT OF THE WORLD OF MARTIAL ARTS!
WHY DID I HAFTA FALL FOR HIM?
Holistic CLINIC
NAGAHARA
HE'S JUST SO COOL...
THERE SHE IS!
BAM BAM BAM
HUH?
SNATCH
EEEEK!
SLAM
OKAY, DRIVE!

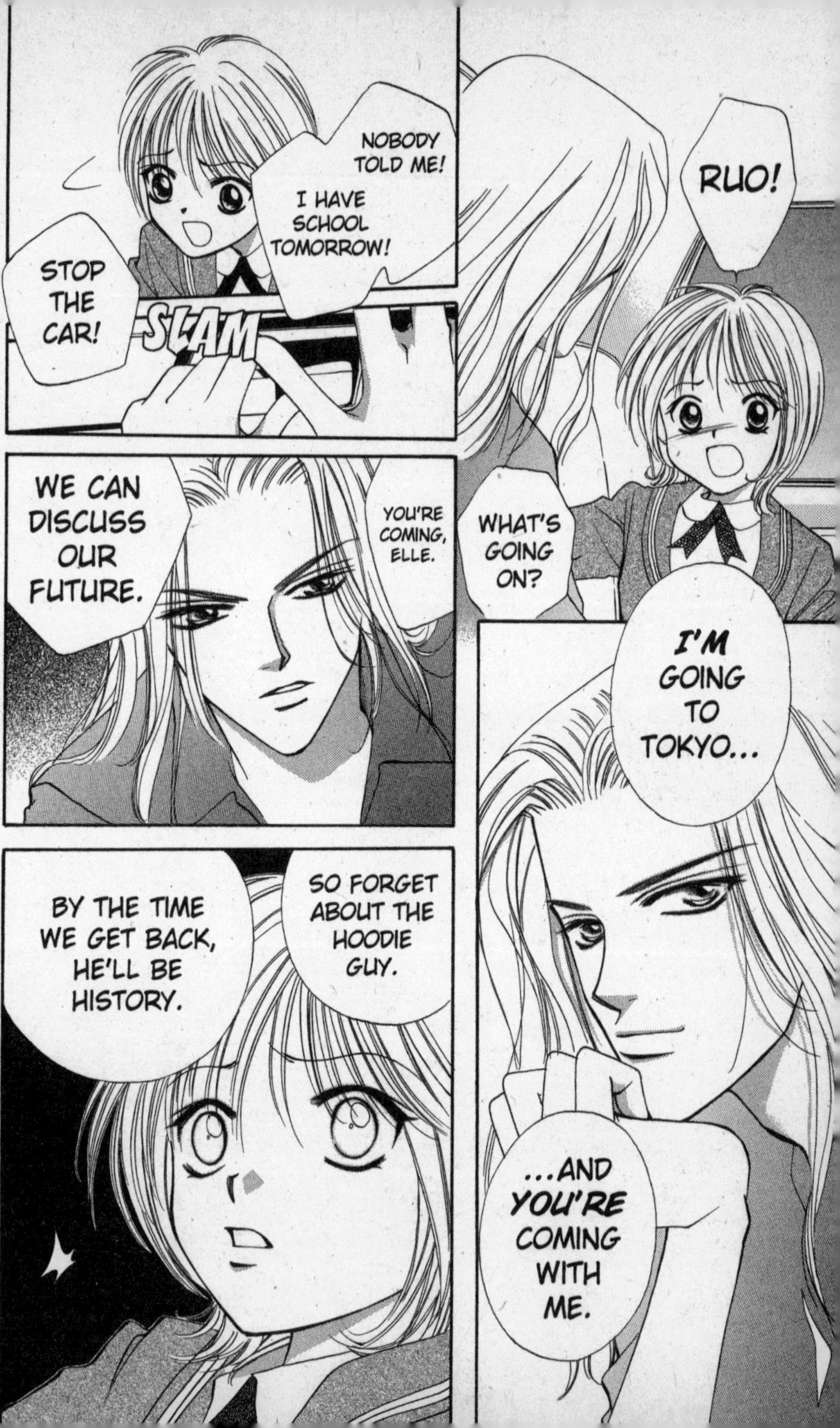
RUO!
WHAT'S GOING ON?
I'M GOING TO TOKYO...
...AND YOU'RE COMING WITH ME.
NOBODY TOLD ME!
I HAVE SCHOOL TOMORROW!
STOP THE CAR!
SLAM
YOU'RE COMING, ELLE.
WE CAN DISCUSS OUR FUTURE.
SO FORGET ABOUT THE HOODIE GUY.
BY THE TIME WE GET BACK, HE'LL BE HISTORY.

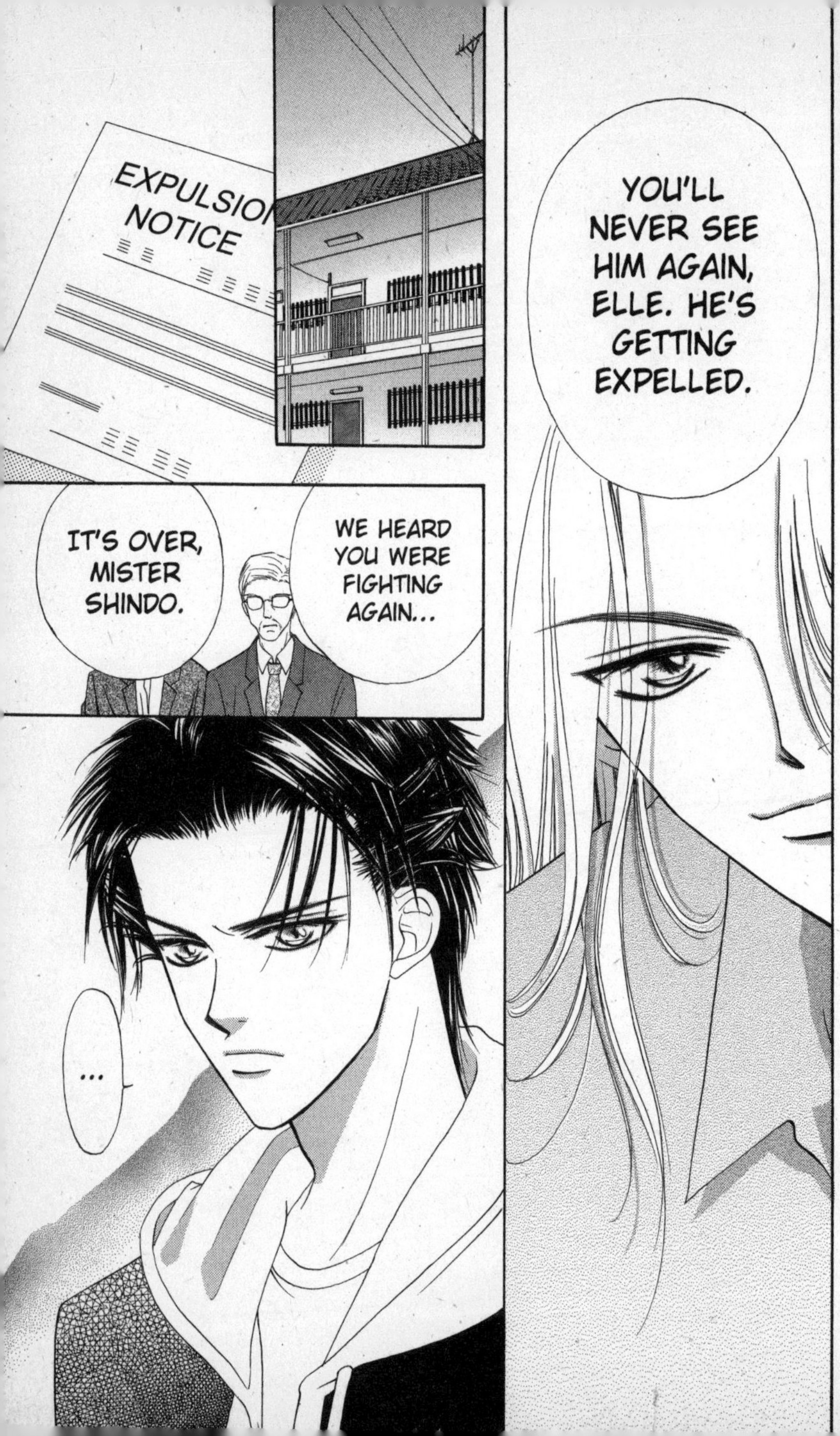
YOU'LL NEVER SEE HIM AGAIN, ELLE. HE'S GETTING EXPELLED.
EXPULSIO
NOTICE
WE HEARD YOU WERE FIGHTING AGAIN...
IT'S OVER, MISTER SHINDO.
...

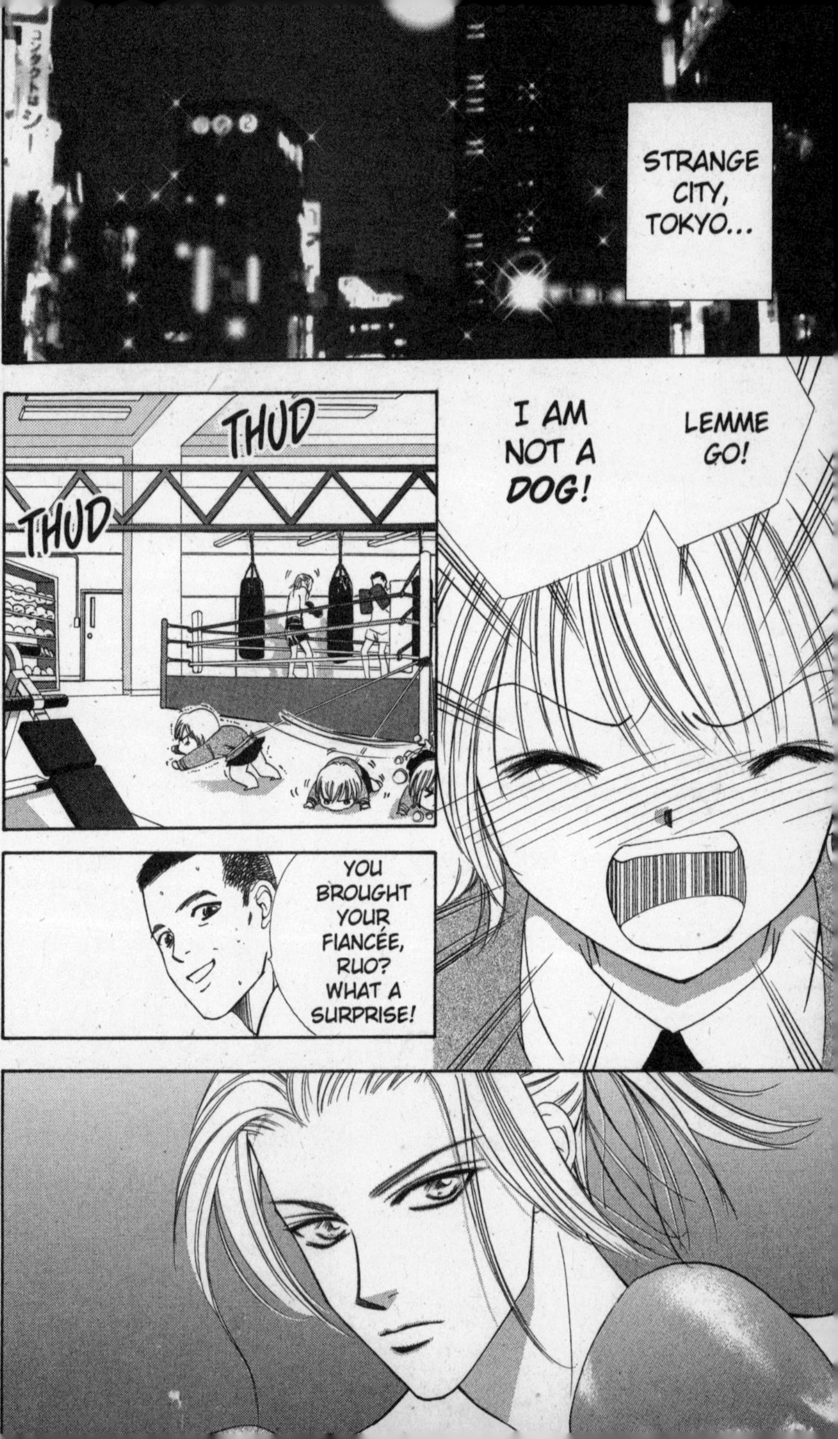
STRANGE CITY, TOKYO...
LEMME GO!
I AM NOT A DOG!
THUD
THUD
YOU BROUGHT YOUR FIANCÉE, RUO? WHAT A SURPRISE!

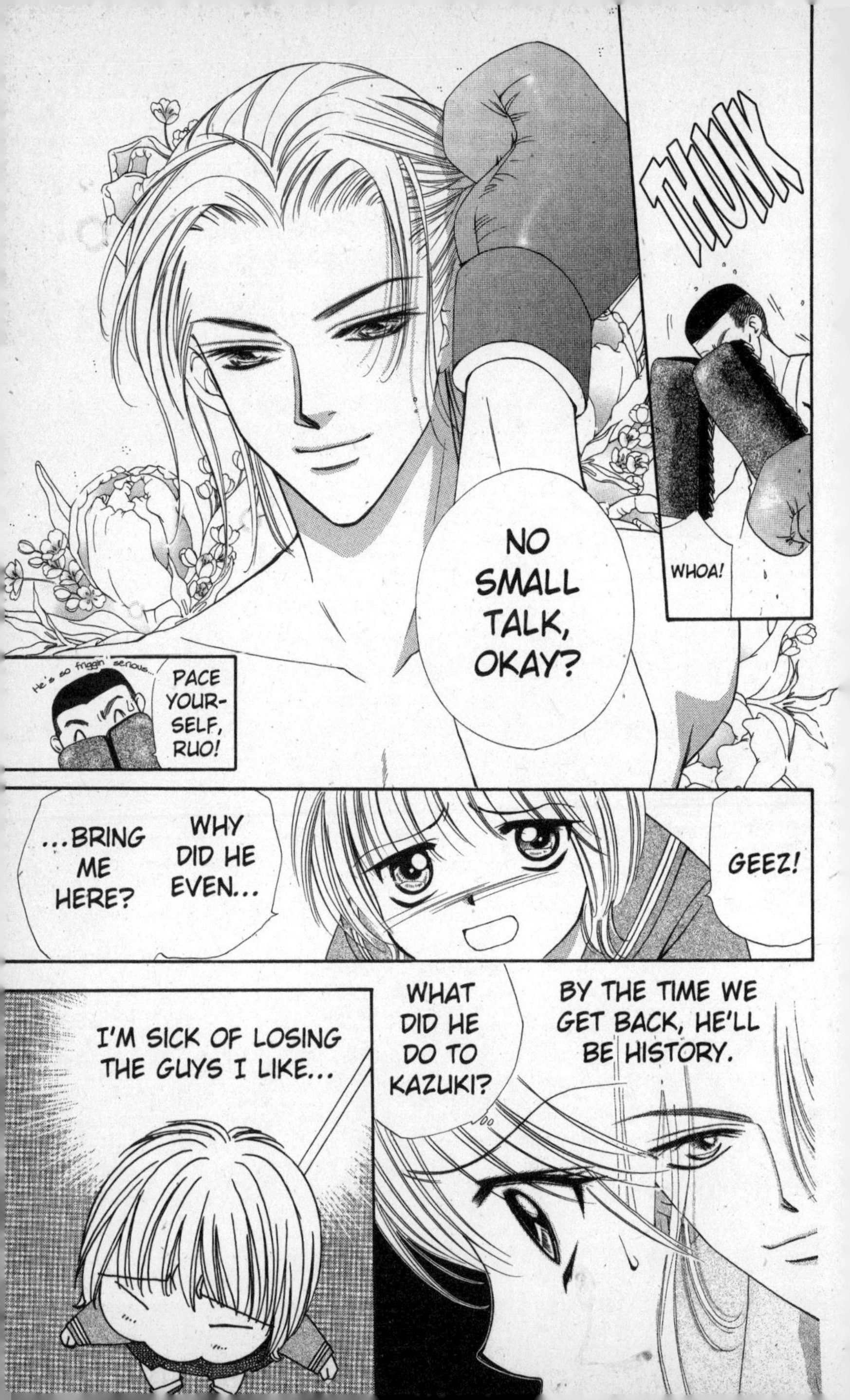
THUNK
WHOA!
NO SMALL TALK, OKAY?
He's so friggin' serious...
PACE YOURSELF, RUO!
GEEZ!
WHY DID HE EVEN...
...BRING ME HERE?
BY THE TIME WE GET BACK, HE'LL BE HISTORY.
WHAT DID HE DO TO KAZUKI?
I'M SICK OF LOSING THE GUYS I LIKE...

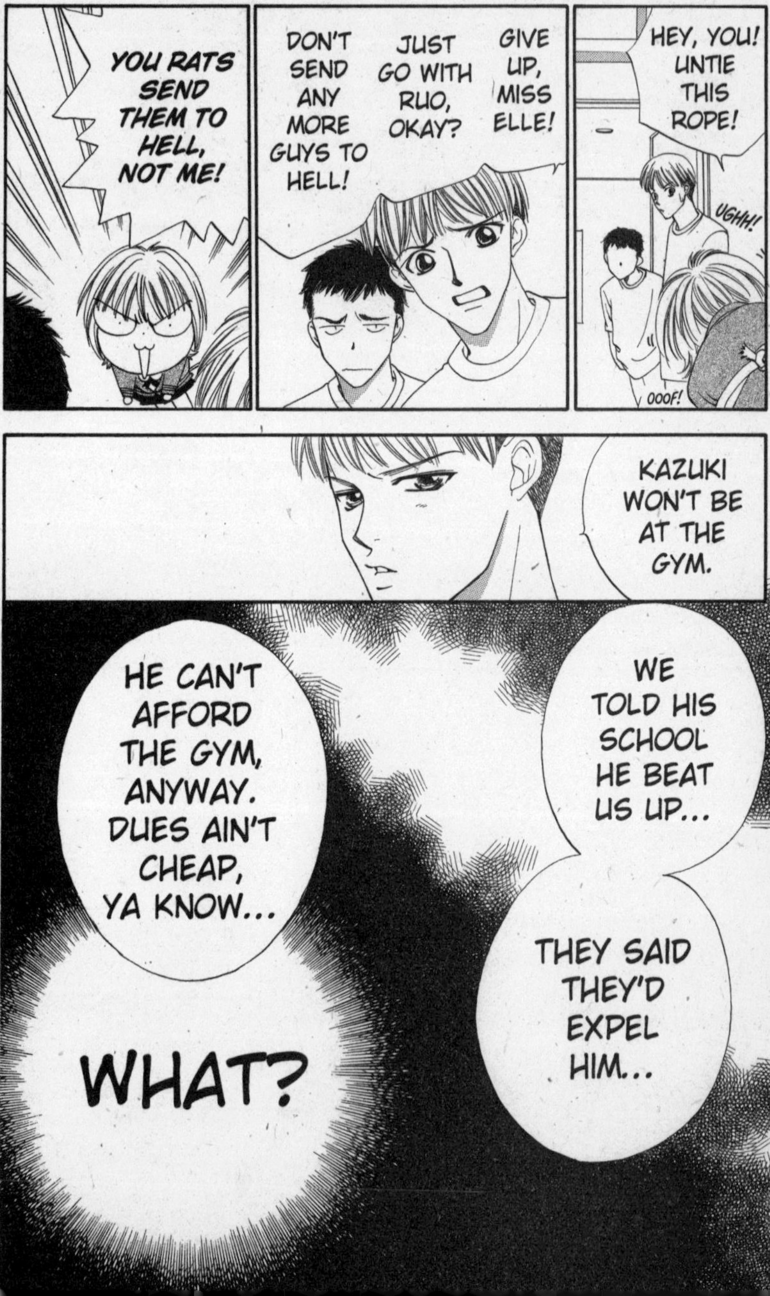
HEY, YOU! UNTIE THIS ROPE!
UGHH!
OOOF!
GIVE UP, MISS ELLE!
JUST GO WITH RUO, OKAY?
DON'T SEND ANY MORE GUYS TO HELL!
YOU RATS SEND THEM TO HELL, NOT ME!
KAZUKI WON'T BE AT THE GYM.
WE TOLD HIS SCHOOL HE BEAT US UP...
THEY SAID THEY'D EXPEL HIM...
HE CAN'T AFFORD THE GYM, ANYWAY. DUES AIN'T CHEAP, YA KNOW...
WHAT?

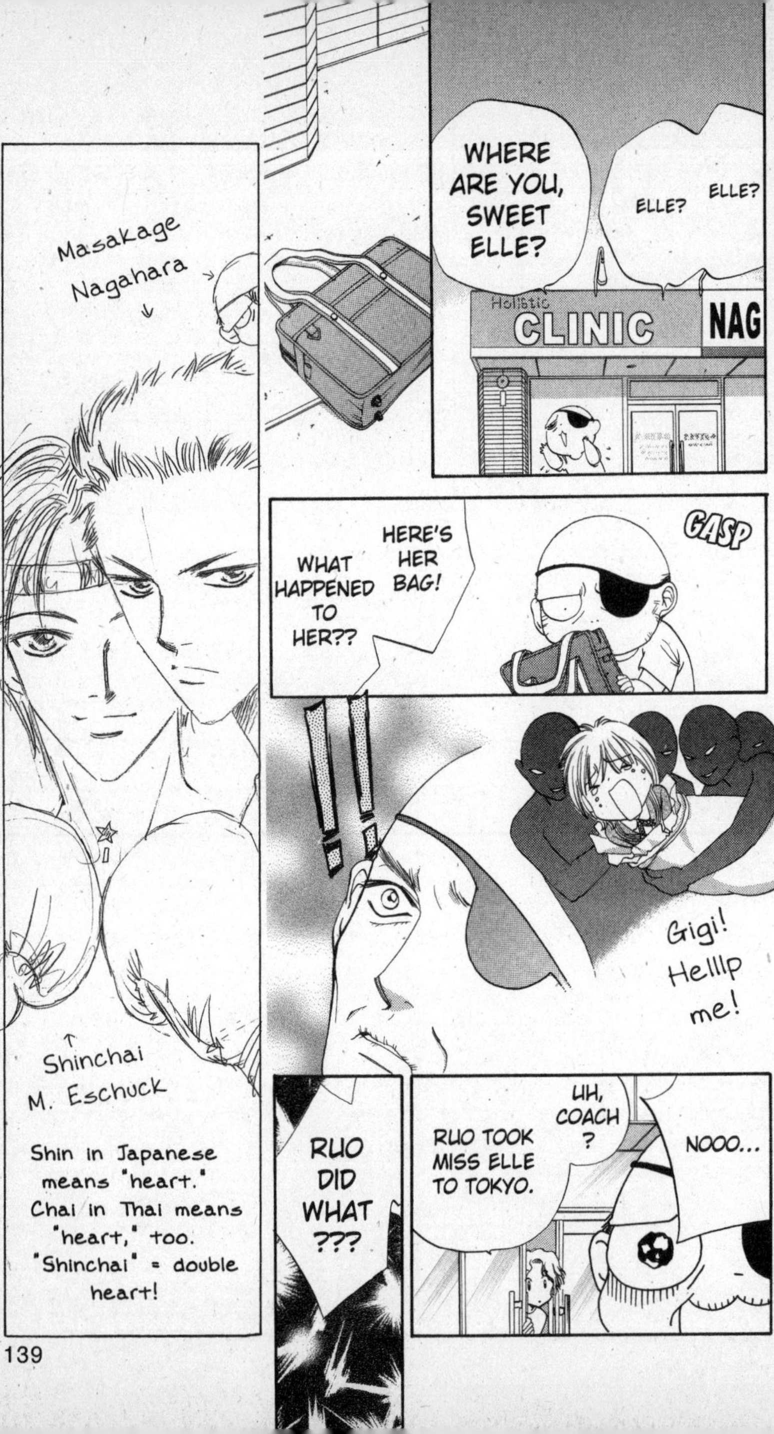
ELLE? ELLE?
WHERE ARE YOU, SWEET ELLE?
Holistic CLINIC
NAG
GASP
HERE'S HER BAG!
WHAT HAPPENED TO HER??
Gigi! Helllp me!
NOOO...
UH, COACH?
RUO TOOK MISS ELLE TO TOKYO.
RUO DID WHAT???
Masakage Nagahara
Shinchai M. Eschuck
Shin in Japanese means "heart." Chai in Thai means "heart," too. "Shinchai" = double heart!

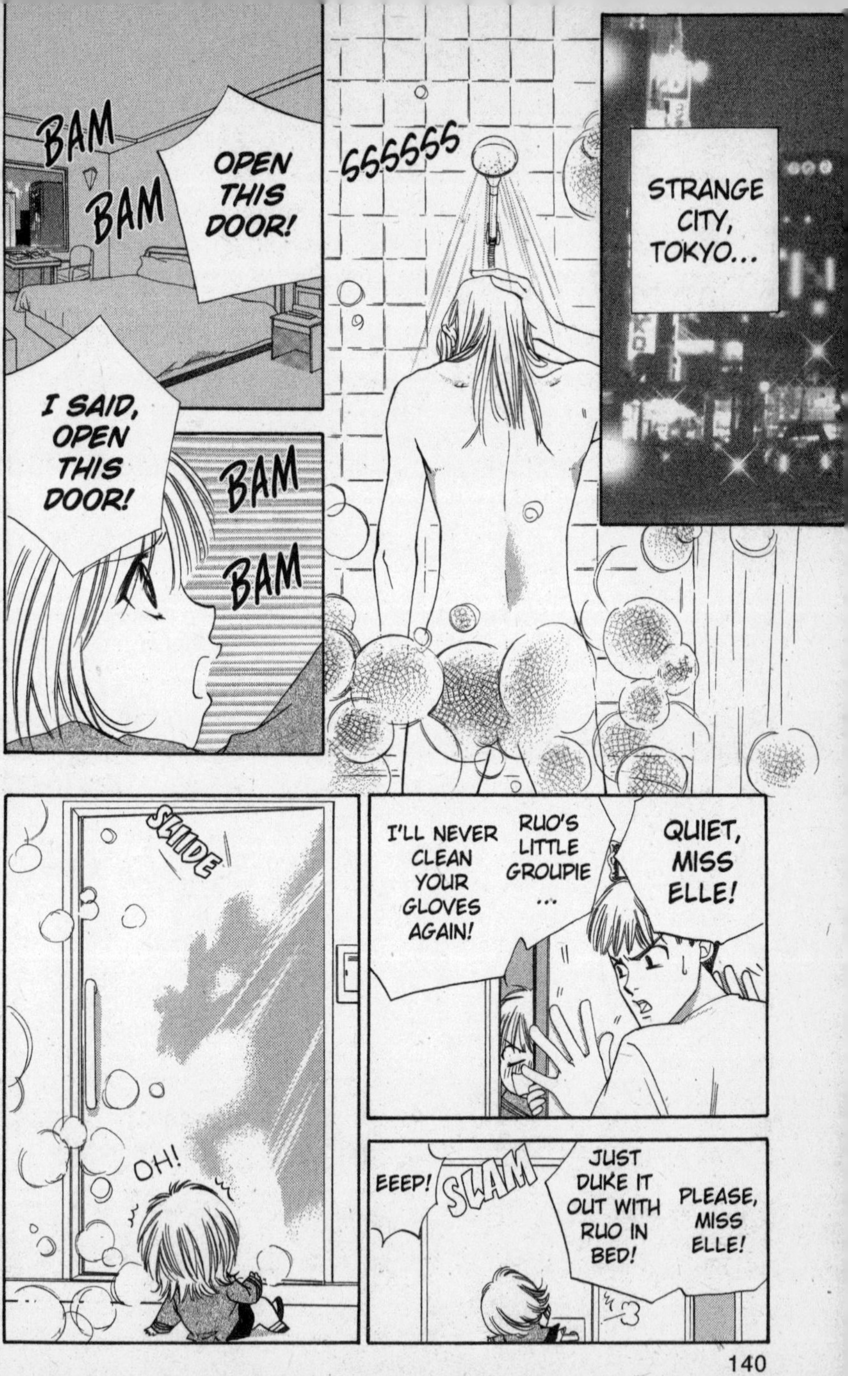

STRANGE CITY, TOKYO...
SSSSSS
BAM
BAM
OPEN THIS DOOR!
I SAID, OPEN THIS DOOR!
BAM
BAM
QUIET, MISS ELLE!
RUO'S LITTLE GROUPIE ...
I'LL NEVER CLEAN YOUR GLOVES AGAIN!
PLEASE, MISS ELLE!
JUST DUKE IT OUT WITH RUO IN BED!
SLAM
EEEP!
SLIDE
OH!

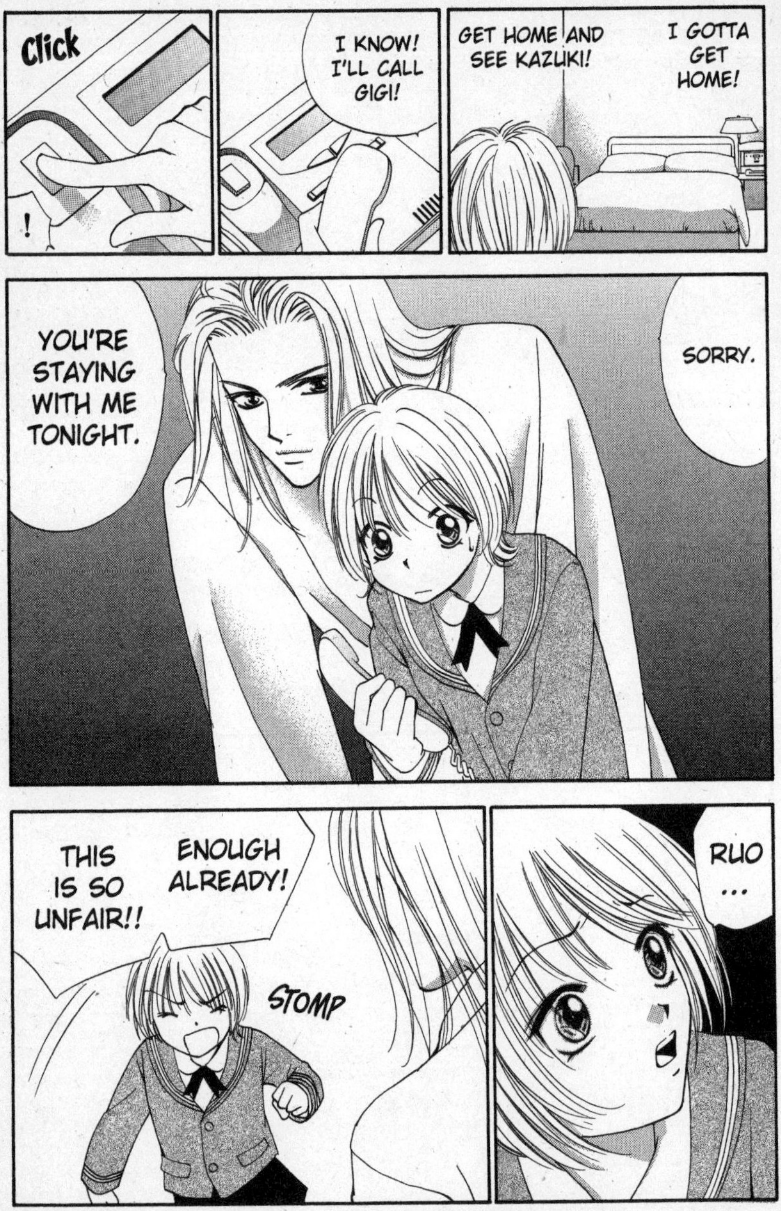
I GOTTA GET HOME!
GET HOME AND SEE KAZUKI!
I KNOW! I'LL CALL GIGI!
Click
!
SORRY.
YOU'RE STAYING WITH ME TONIGHT.
RUO ...
ENOUGH ALREADY!
THIS IS SO UNFAIR!!
STOMP

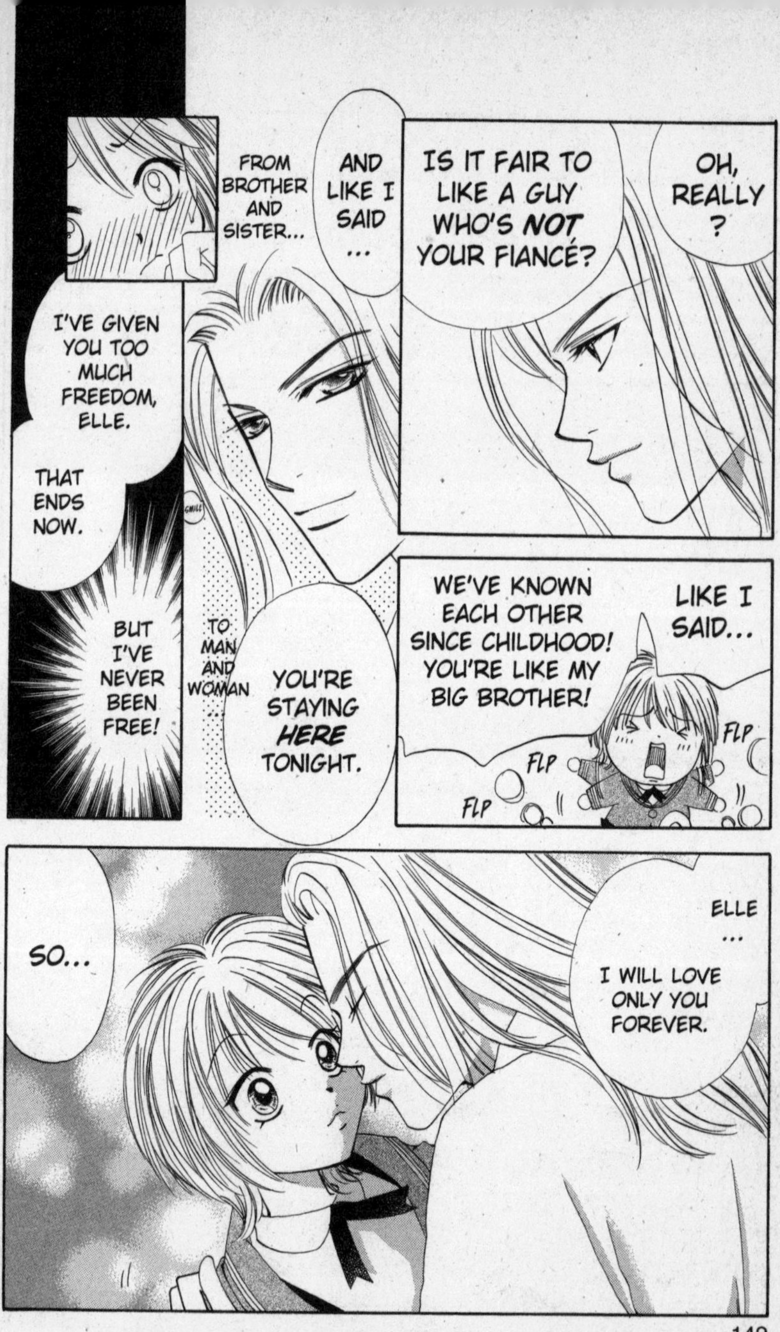
OH, REALLY?
IS IT FAIR TO LIKE A GUY WHO'S **NOT** YOUR FIANCÉ?
LIKE I SAID...
WE'VE KNOWN EACH OTHER SINCE CHILDHOOD! YOU'RE LIKE MY BIG BROTHER!
FLP
FLP
FLP
AND LIKE I SAID...
FROM BROTHER AND SISTER...
SMILE
TO MAN AND WOMAN...
YOU'RE STAYING ***HERE*** TONIGHT.
I'VE GIVEN YOU TOO MUCH FREEDOM, ELLE.
THAT ENDS NOW.
BUT I'VE NEVER BEEN FREE!
ELLE...
I WILL LOVE ONLY YOU FOREVER.
SO...

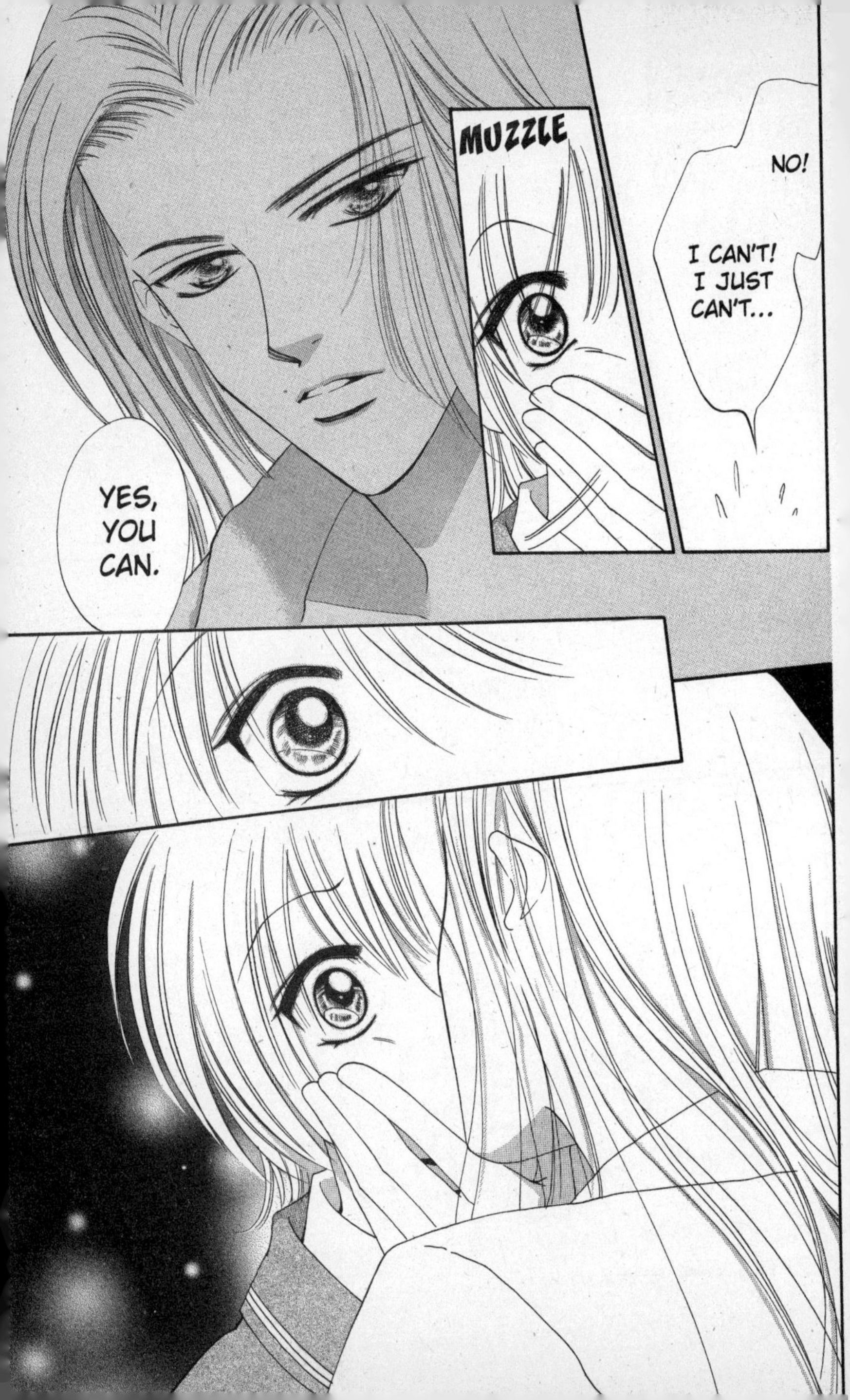
NO!
I CAN'T! I JUST CAN'T...
MUZZLE
YES, YOU CAN.

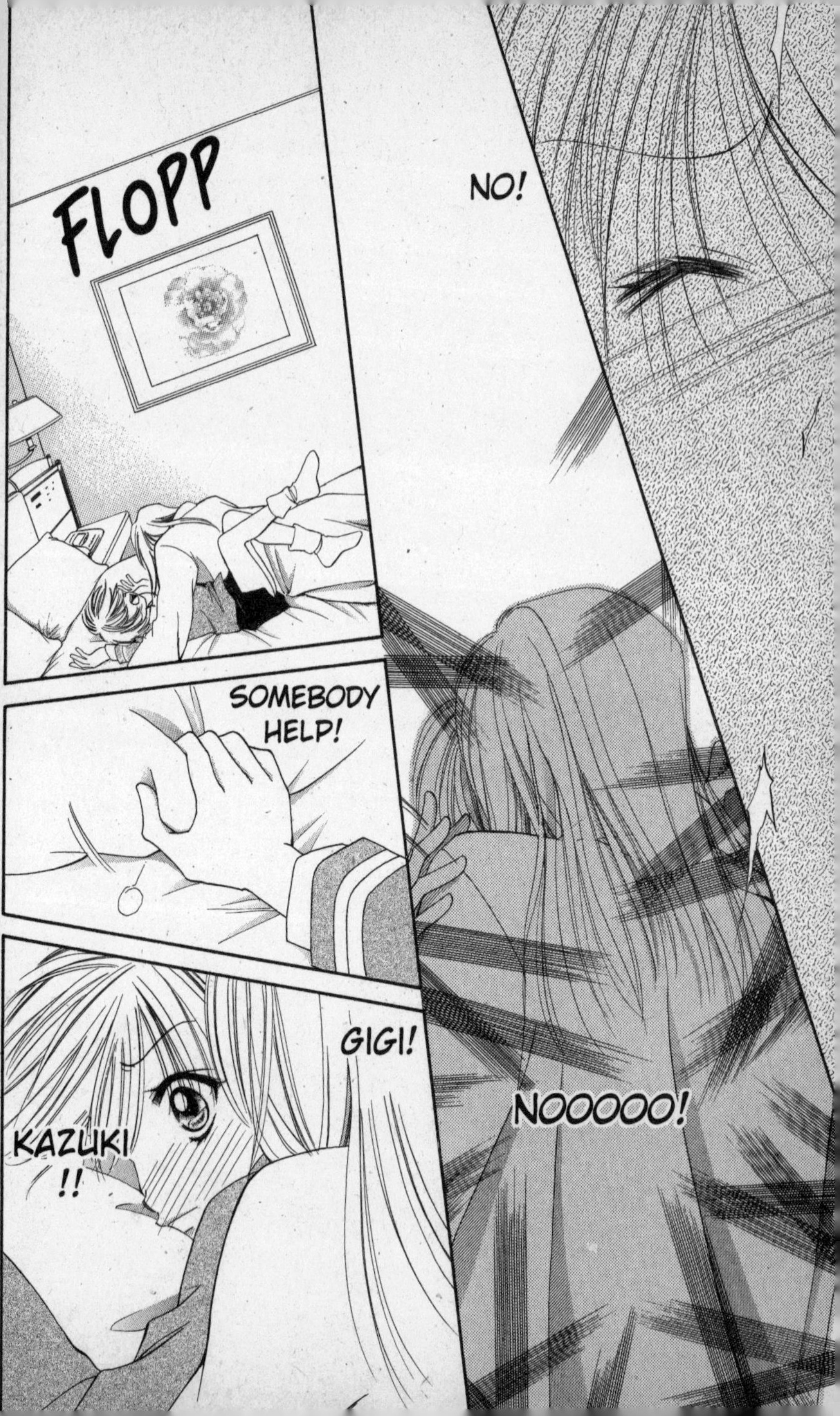
NO!
NOOOOO!
FLOPP
SOMEBODY HELP!
GIGI!
KAZUKI !!

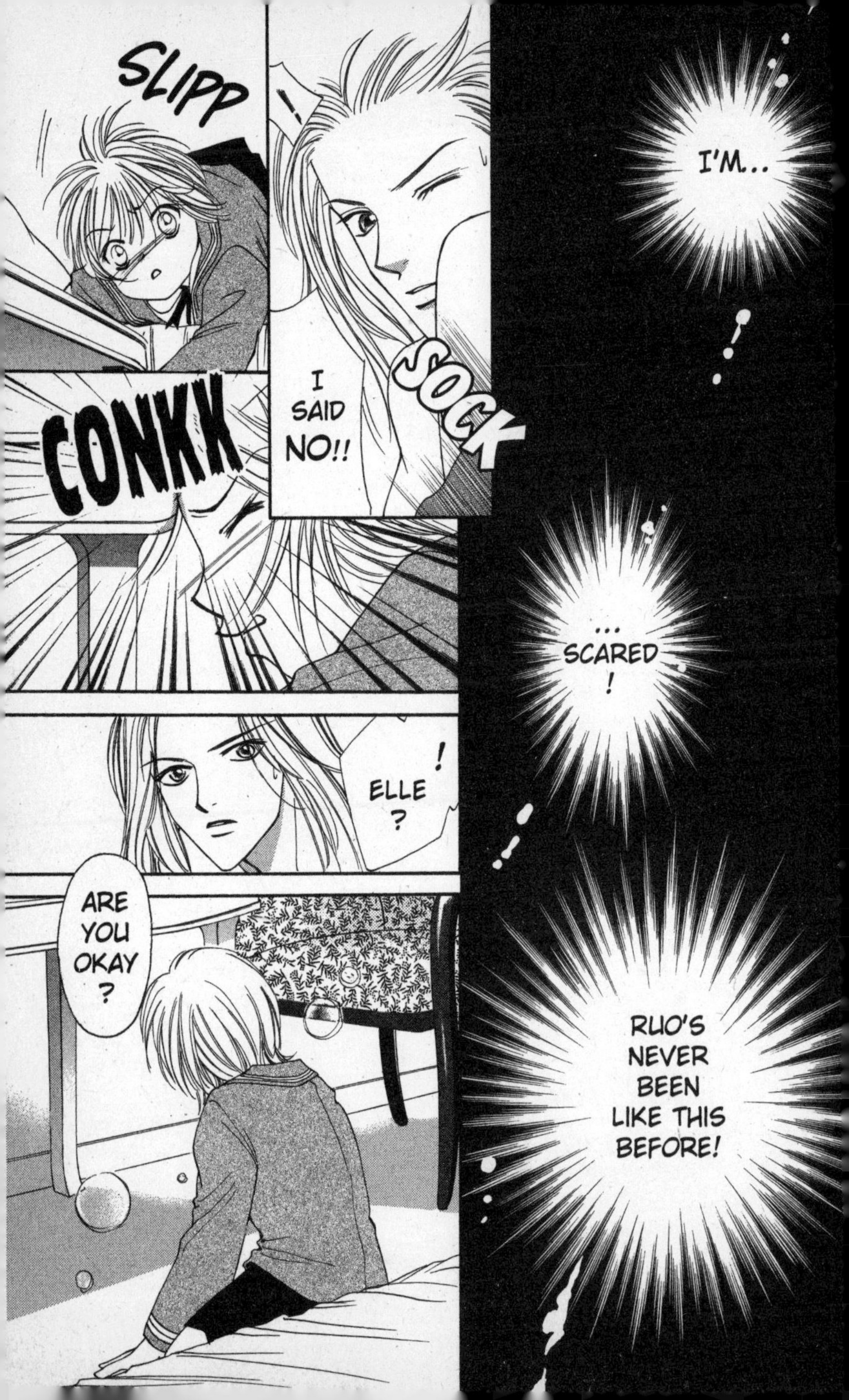
I'M...
... SCARED!
RUO'S NEVER BEEN LIKE THIS BEFORE!
I SAID NO!!
SOCK
SLIPP
CONKK
!
ELLE?
ARE YOU OKAY?

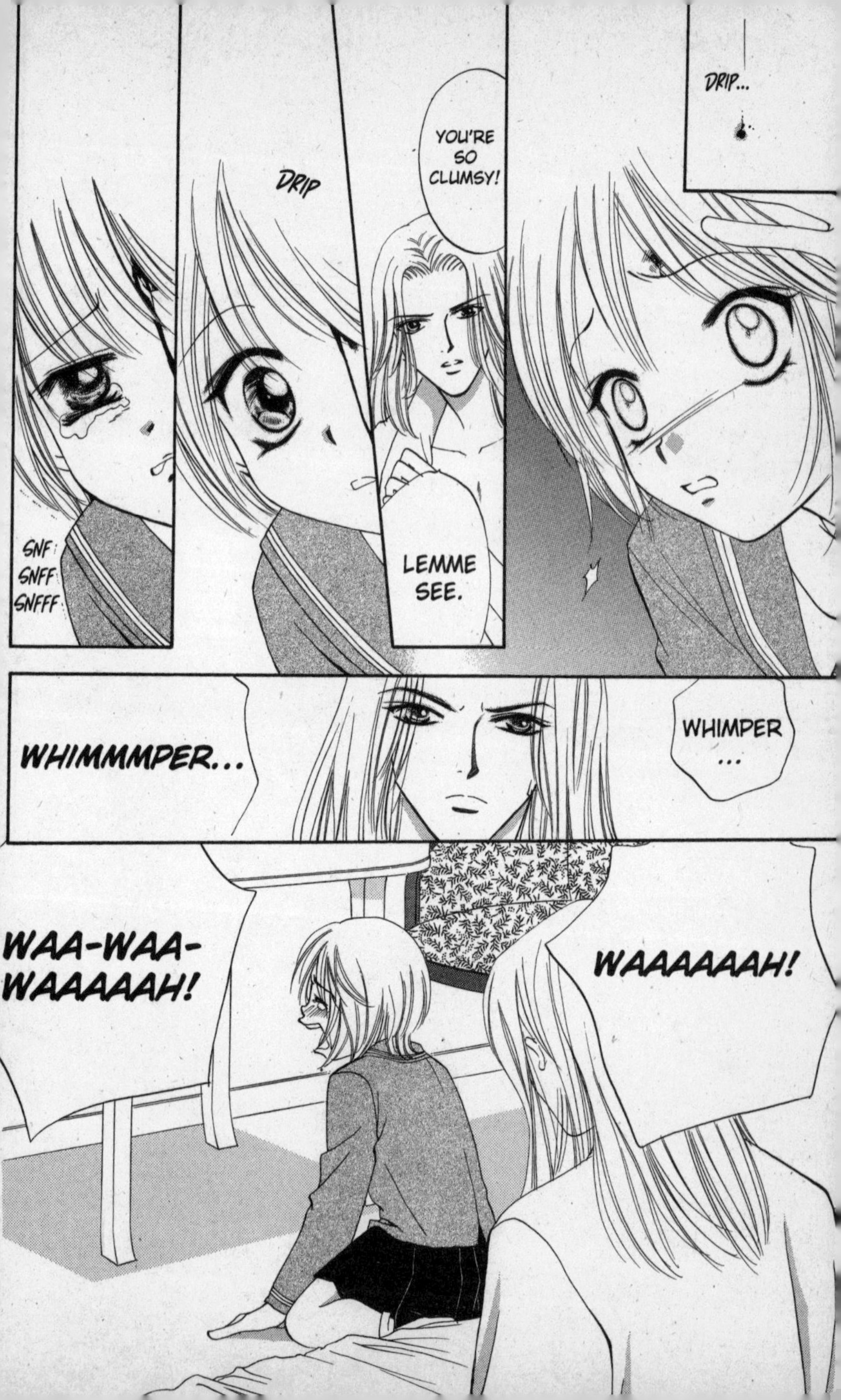
DRIP...
YOU'RE SO CLUMSY!
LEMME SEE.
DRIP
SNF SNFF SNFFF
WHIMPER ...
WHIMMMPER...
WAAAAAAH!
WAA-WAA-WAAAAAAH!

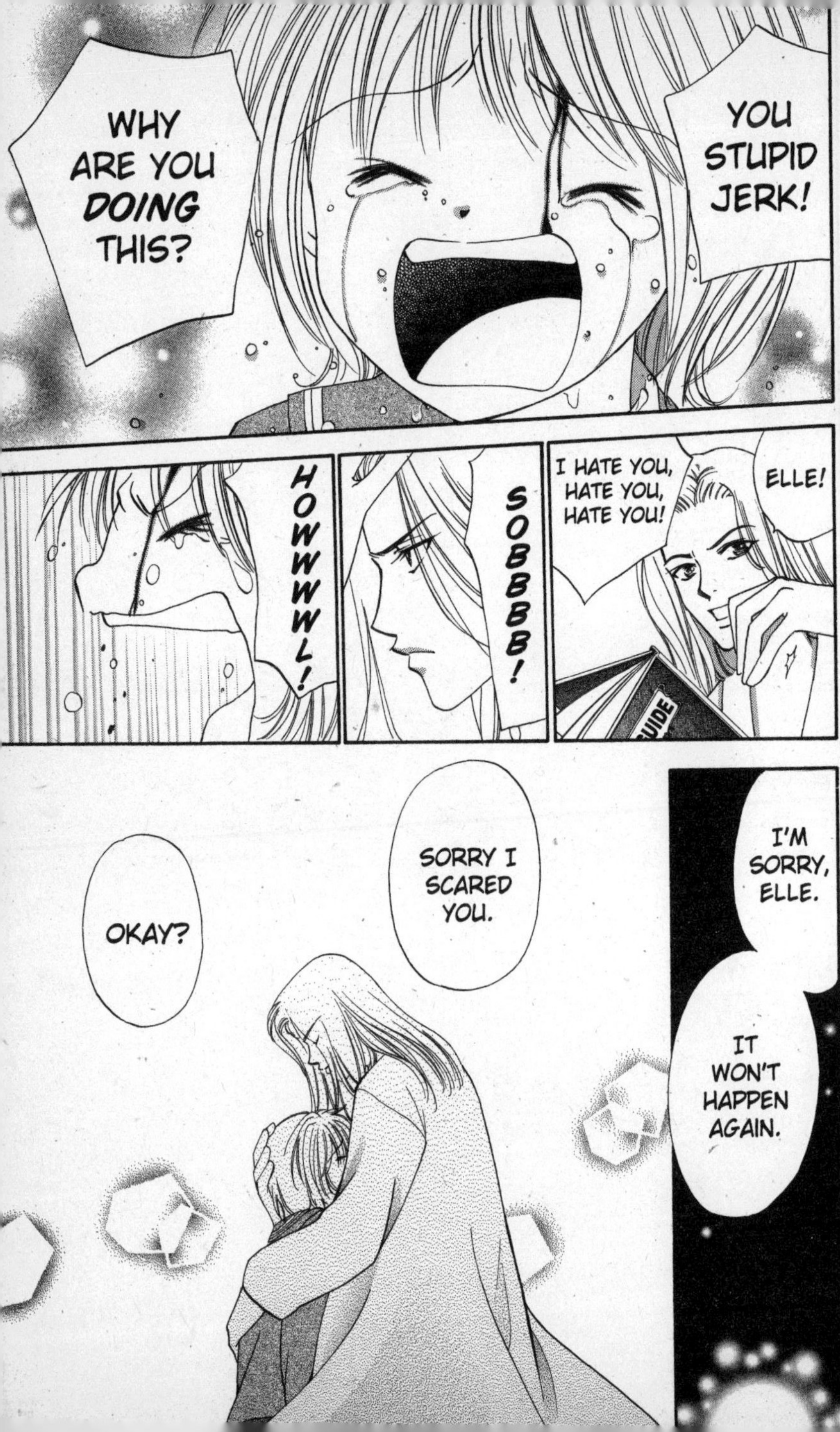
YOU STUPID JERK!
WHY ARE YOU DOING THIS?
ELLE!
I HATE YOU, HATE YOU, HATE YOU!
GUIDE
SOBBBBB!
HOWWWWWL!
I'M SORRY, ELLE.
IT WON'T HAPPEN AGAIN.
SORRY I SCARED YOU.
OKAY?

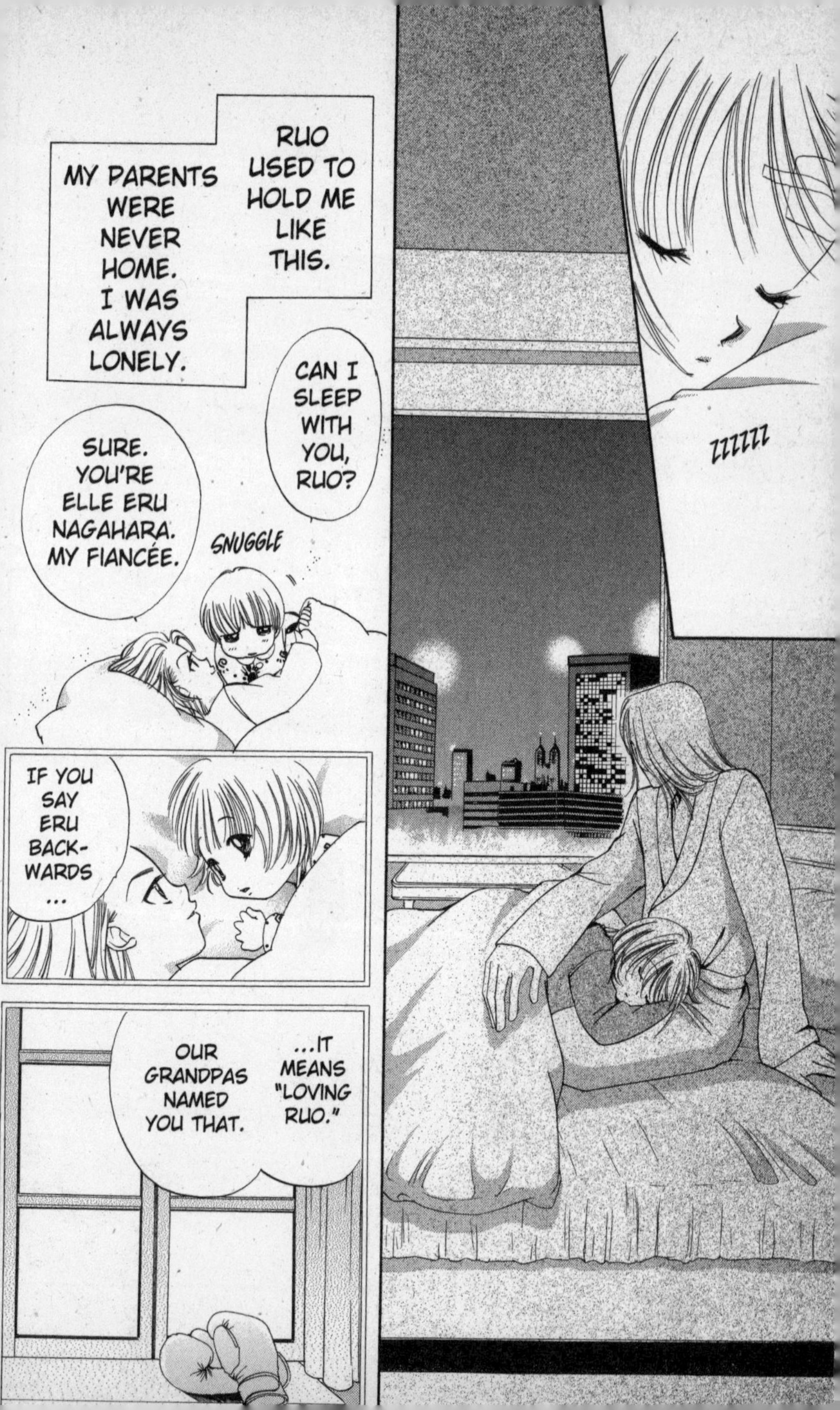
ZZZZZZ
RUO USED TO HOLD ME LIKE THIS.
MY PARENTS WERE NEVER HOME. I WAS ALWAYS LONELY.
CAN I SLEEP WITH YOU, RUO?
SURE. YOU'RE ELLE ERU NAGAHARA. MY FIANCÉE.
SNUGGLE
IF YOU SAY ERU BACKWARDS...
...IT MEANS "LOVING RUO."
OUR GRANDPAS NAMED YOU THAT.

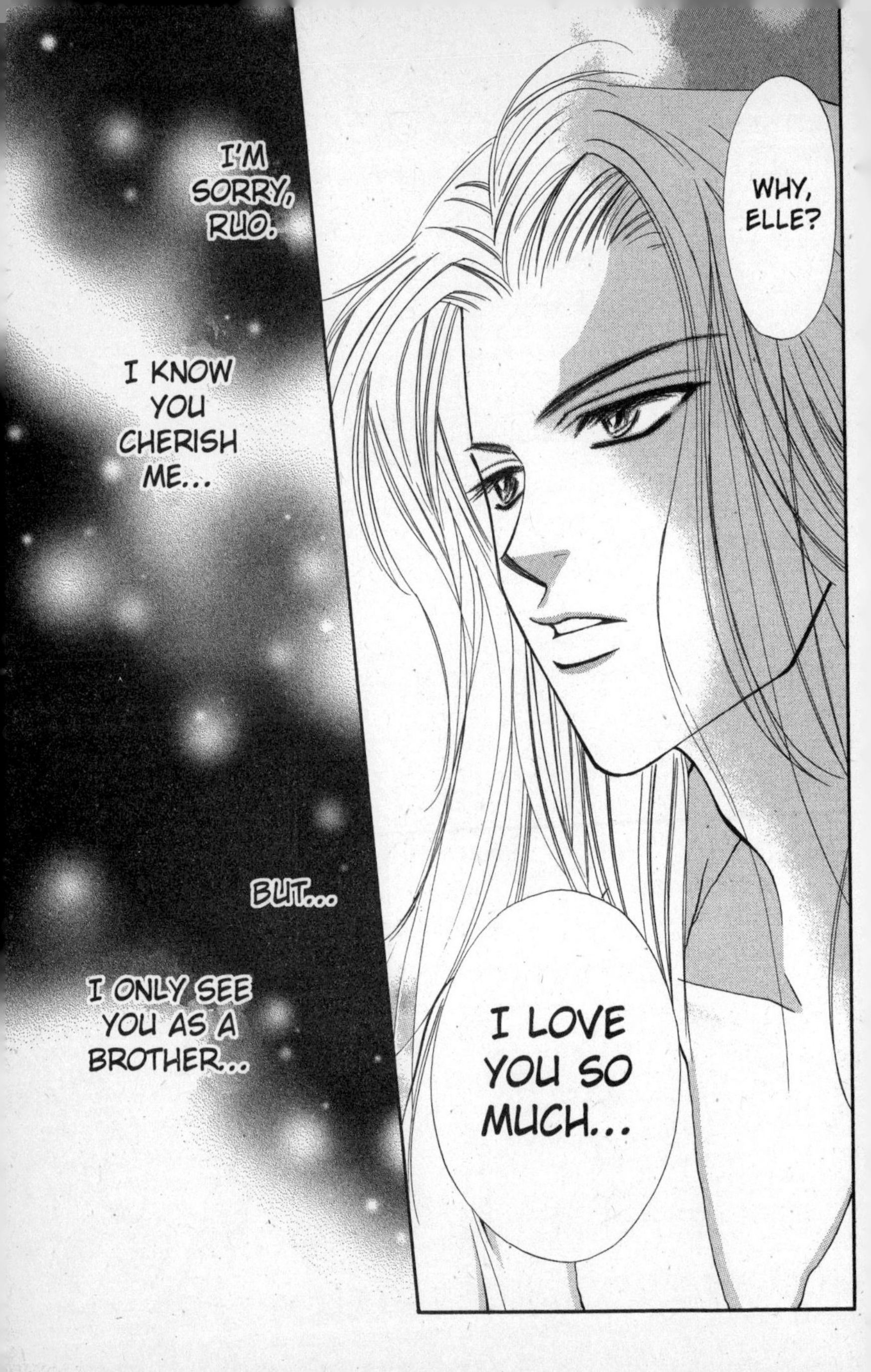
WHY, ELLE?
I LOVE YOU SO MUCH...
I'M SORRY, RUO.
I KNOW YOU CHERISH ME...
BUT...
I ONLY SEE YOU AS A BROTHER...

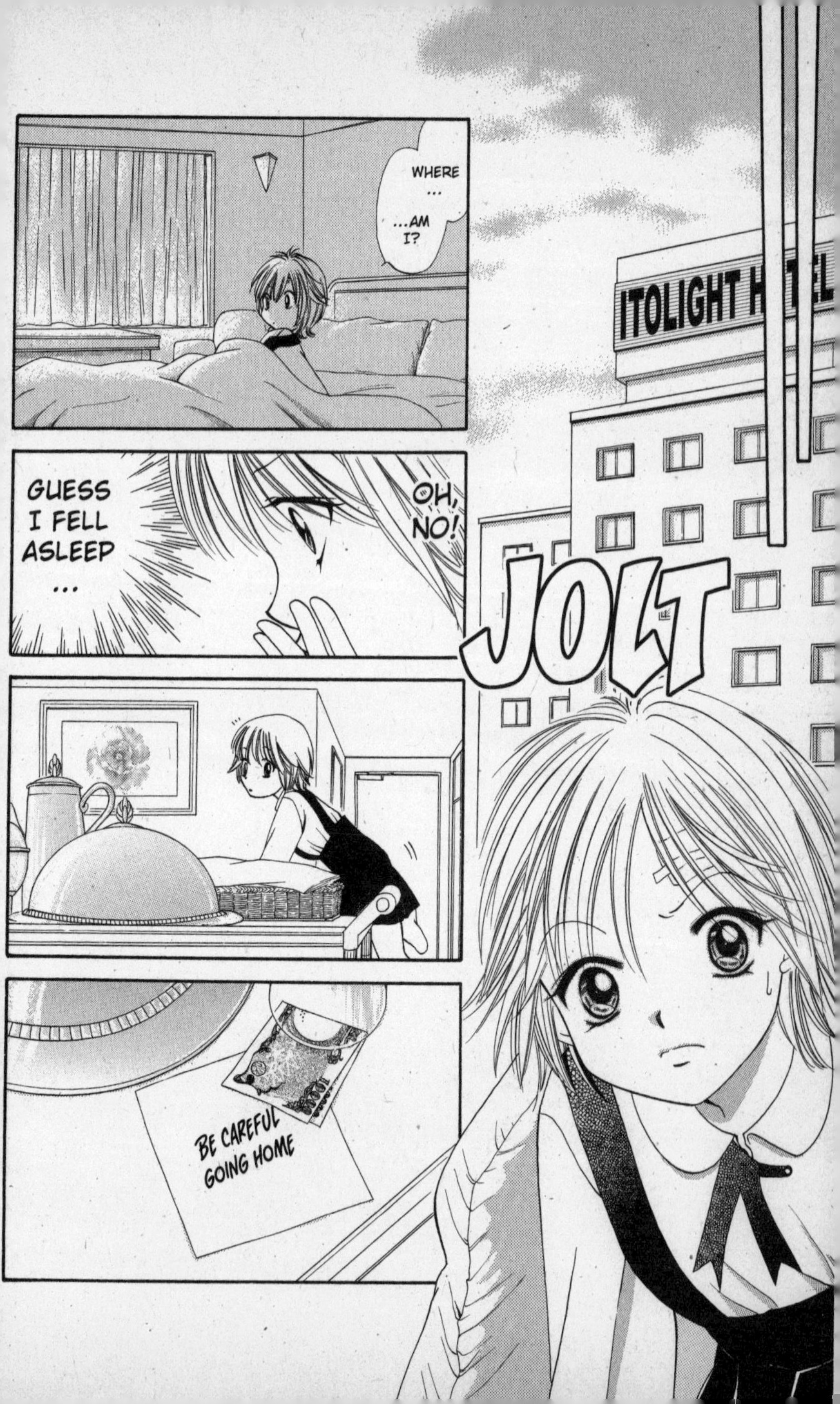
ITOLIGHT H TEL
JOLT
WHERE ...
...AM I?
OH, NO!
GUESS I FELL ASLEEP ...
BE CAREFUL GOING HOME

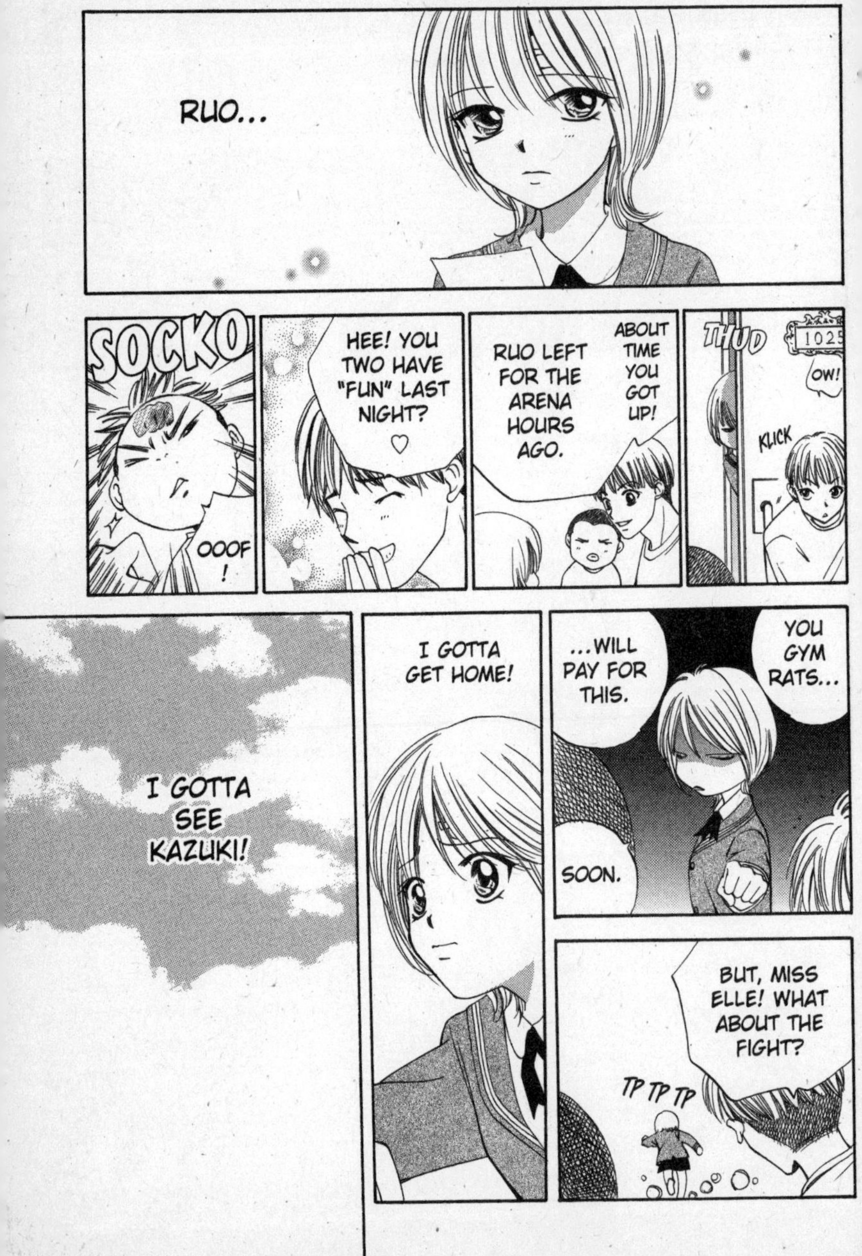
RUO...
THUD
1025
OW!
KLICK
ABOUT TIME YOU GOT UP!
RUO LEFT FOR THE ARENA HOURS AGO.
HEE! YOU TWO HAVE "FUN" LAST NIGHT? ♡
SOCKO
OOOF!
YOU GYM RATS...
...WILL PAY FOR THIS.
SOON.
BUT, MISS ELLE! WHAT ABOUT THE FIGHT?
TP TP TP
I GOTTA GET HOME!
I GOTTA SEE KAZUKI!

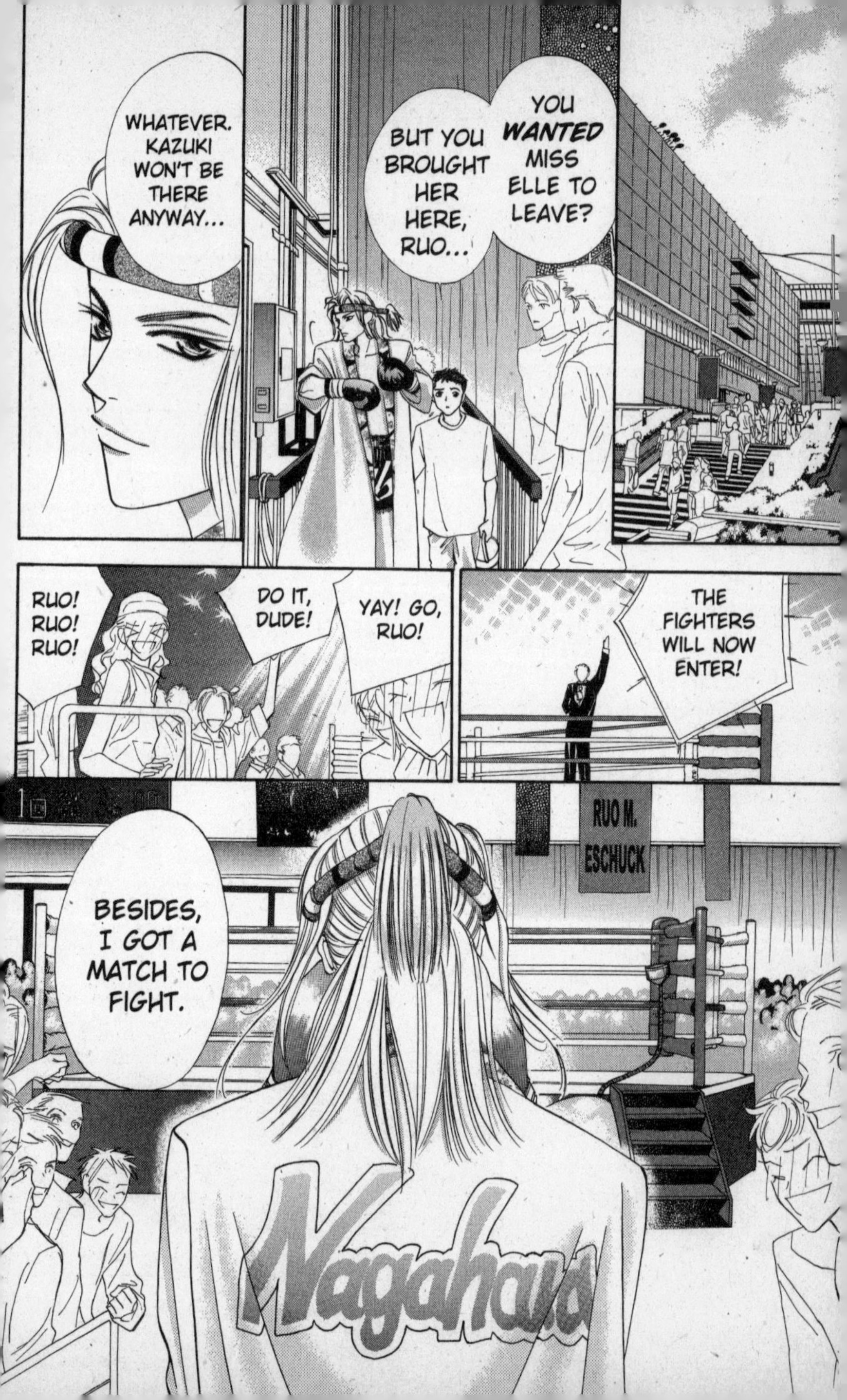
YOU *WANTED* MISS ELLE TO LEAVE?
BUT YOU BROUGHT HER HERE, RUO...
WHATEVER. KAZUKI WON'T BE THERE ANYWAY...
THE FIGHTERS WILL NOW ENTER!
YAY! GO, RUO!
DO IT, DUDE!
RUO! RUO! RUO!
RUO M. ESCHUCK
BESIDES, I GOT A MATCH TO FIGHT.
Nagahara

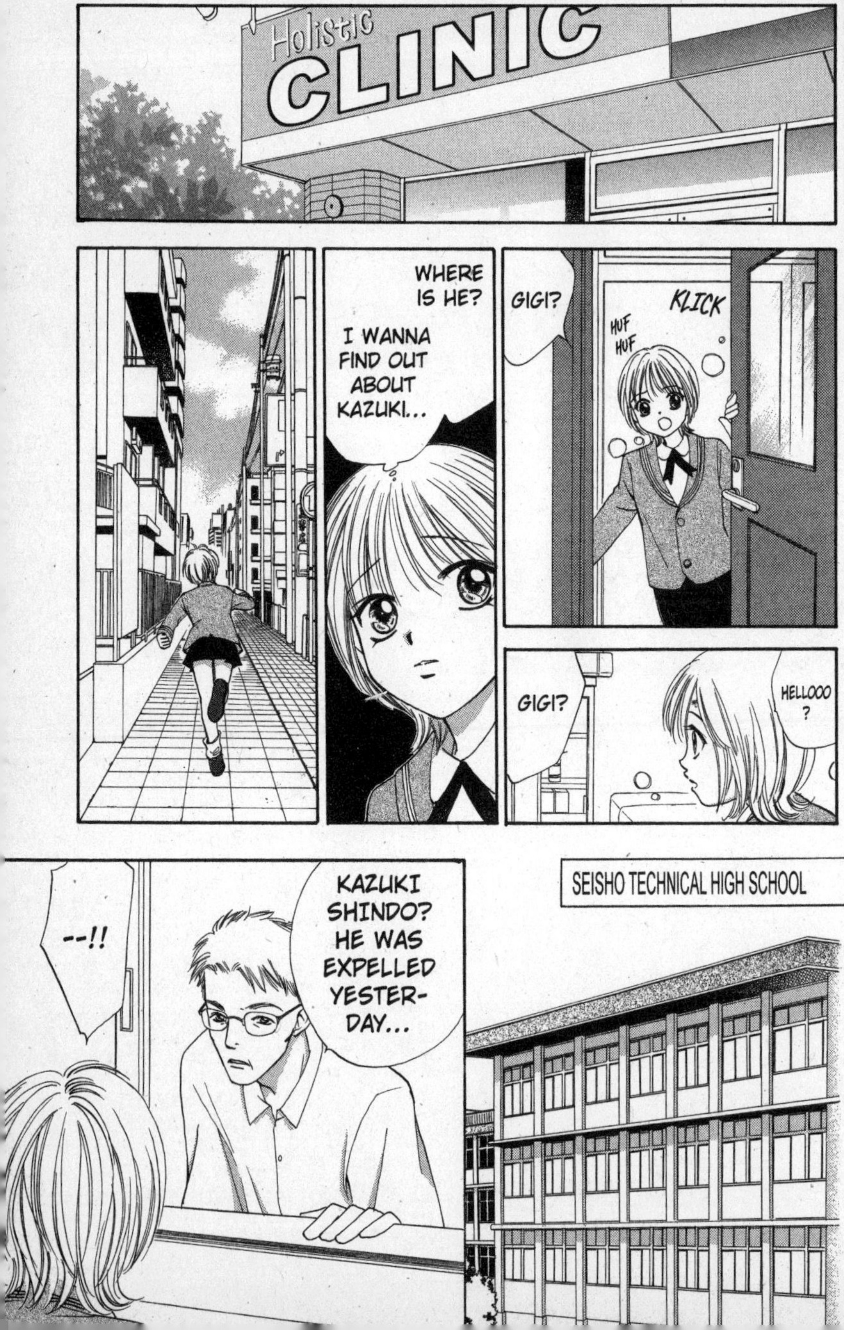
Holistic
CLINIC
KLICK
HUF HUF
GIGI?
HELLOOO ?
GIGI?
WHERE IS HE?
I WANNA FIND OUT ABOUT KAZUKI...
SEISHO TECHNICAL HIGH SCHOOL
KAZUKI SHINDO? HE WAS EXPELLED YESTER-DAY...
--!!

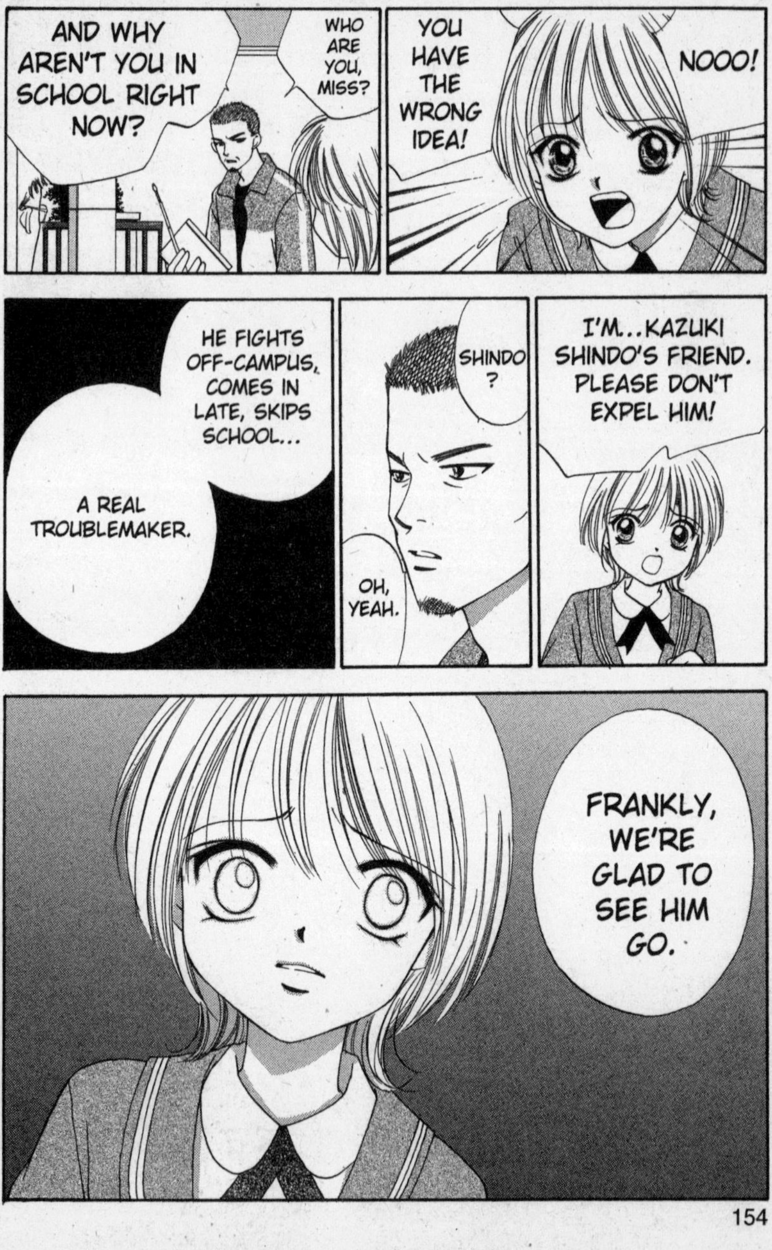
NOOO!
YOU HAVE THE WRONG IDEA!
WHO ARE YOU, MISS?
AND WHY AREN'T YOU IN SCHOOL RIGHT NOW?
I'M...KAZUKI SHINDO'S FRIEND. PLEASE DON'T EXPEL HIM!
SHINDO?
OH, YEAH.
HE FIGHTS OFF-CAMPUS, COMES IN LATE, SKIPS SCHOOL...
A REAL TROUBLEMAKER.
FRANKLY, WE'RE GLAD TO SEE HIM GO.

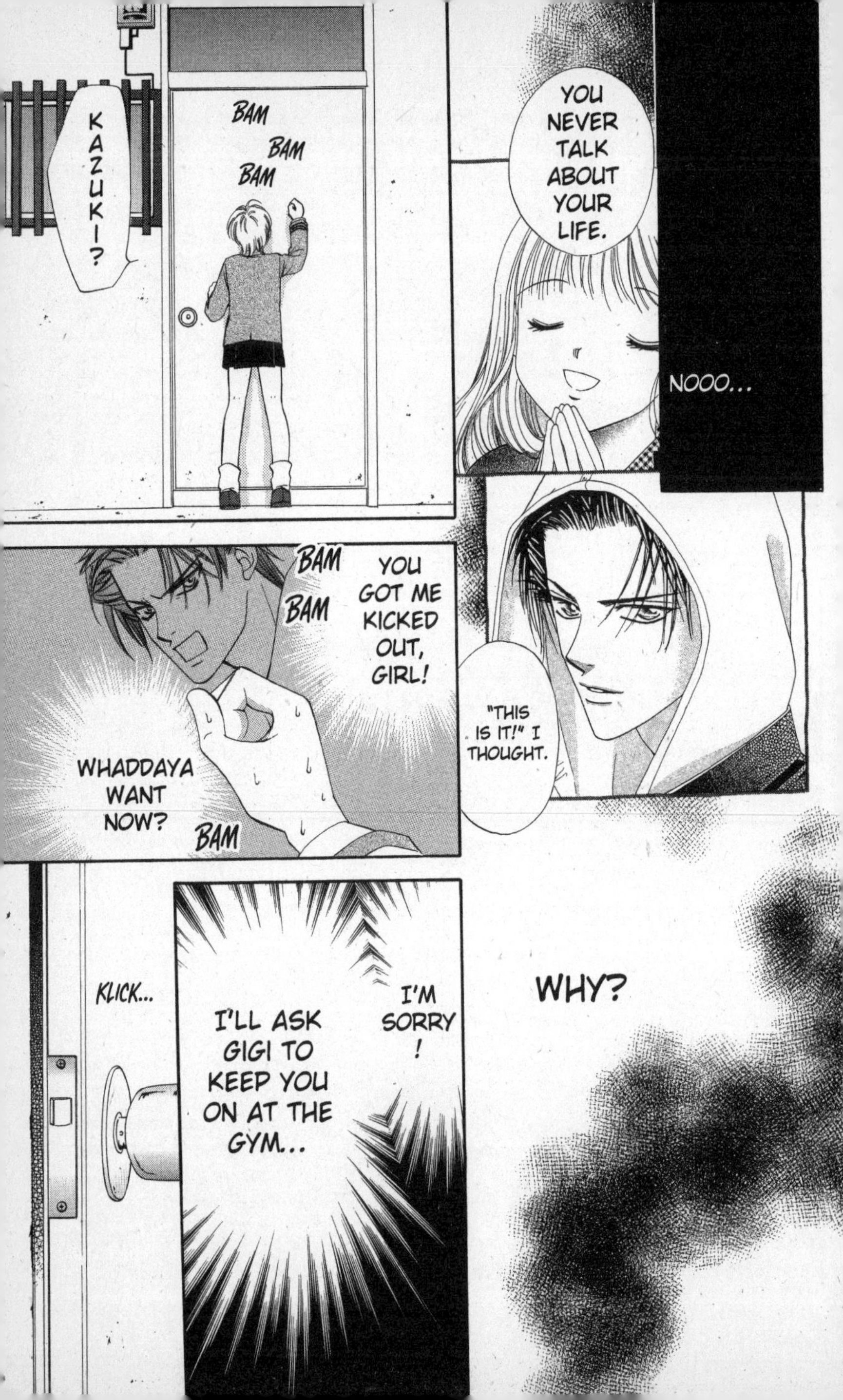
YOU NEVER TALK ABOUT YOUR LIFE.
NOOO...
"THIS IS IT!" I THOUGHT.
KAZUKI?
BAM
BAM
BAM
YOU GOT ME KICKED OUT, GIRL!
BAM
BAM
WHADDAYA WANT NOW?
BAM
WHY?
I'M SORRY!
I'LL ASK GIGI TO KEEP YOU ON AT THE GYM...
KLICK...

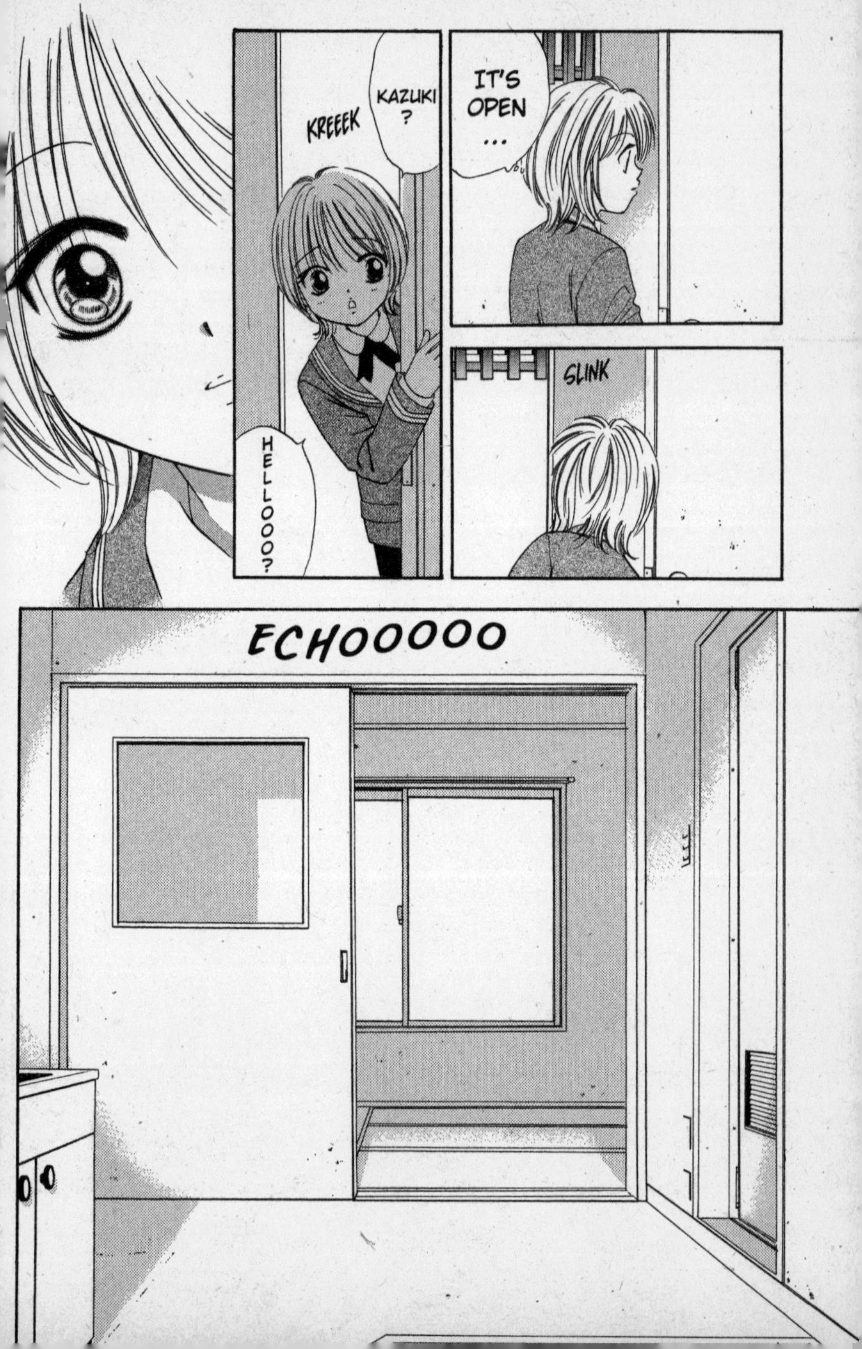
IT'S OPEN ...
SLINK
KAZUKI ?
KREEEK
HELLOOO?
ECHOOOOO

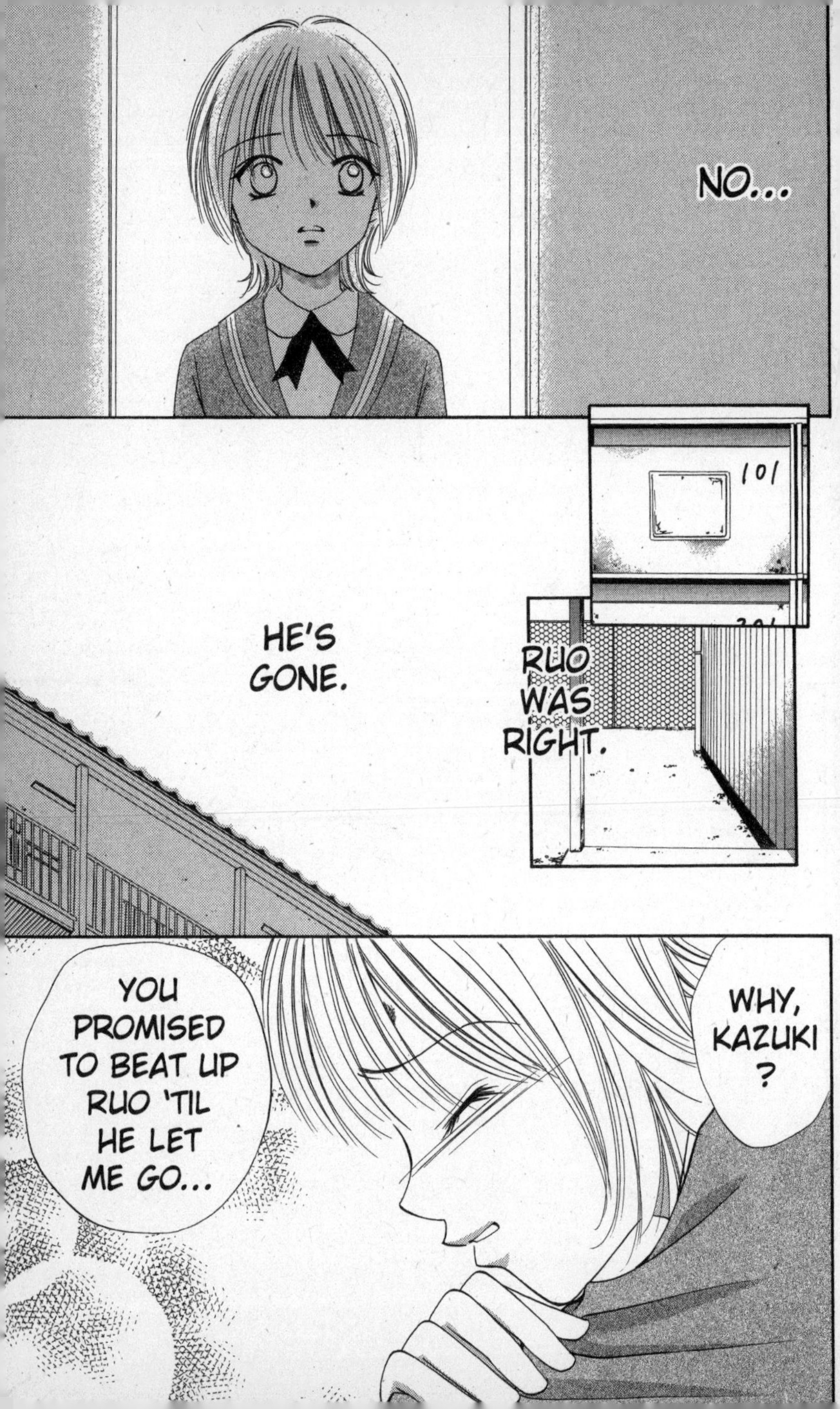
NO...
101
RUO WAS RIGHT.
HE'S GONE.
WHY, KAZUKI?
YOU PROMISED TO BEAT UP RUO 'TIL HE LET ME GO...

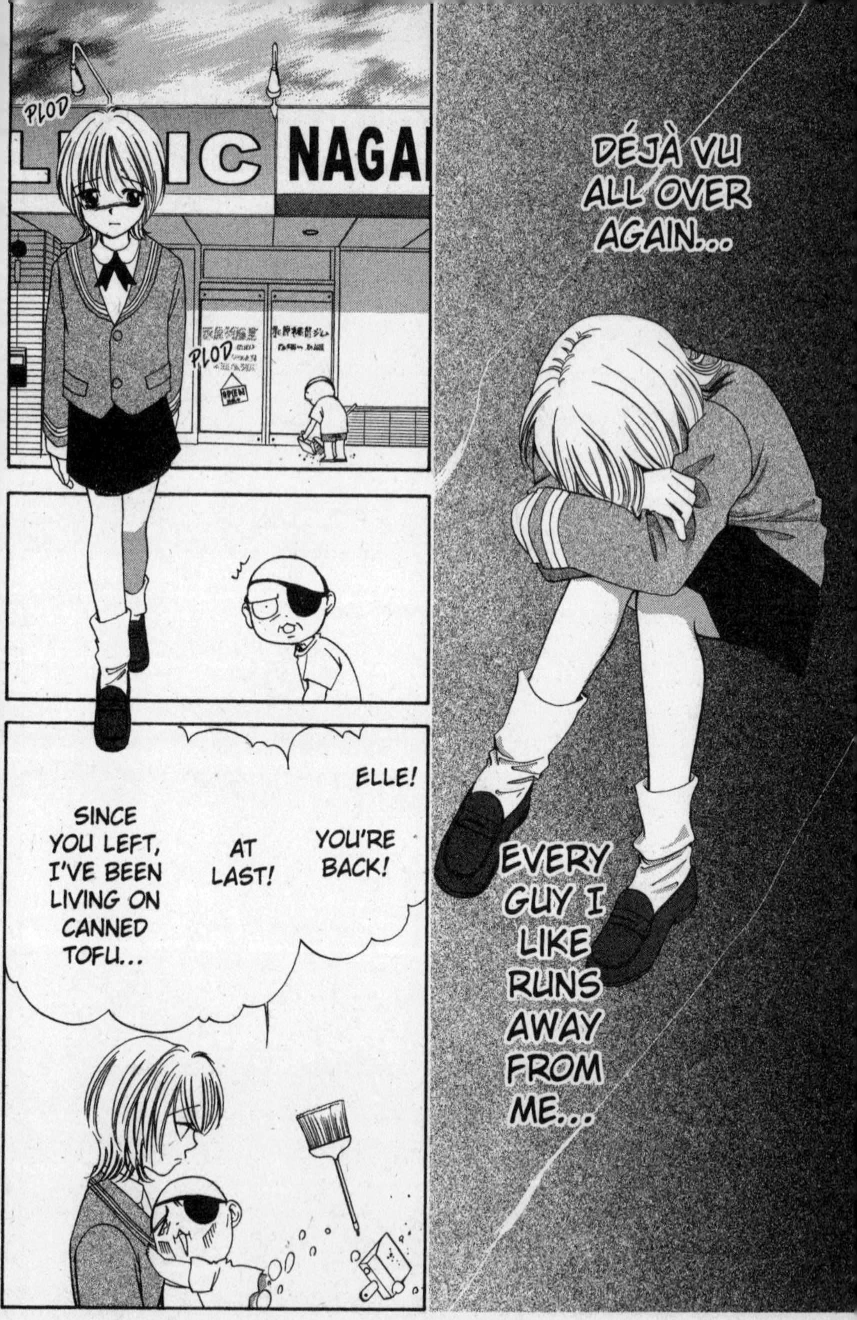
DÉJÀ VU ALL OVER AGAIN...
EVERY GUY I LIKE RUNS AWAY FROM ME...
PLOD
PLOD
ELLE!
YOU'RE BACK!
AT LAST!
SINCE YOU LEFT, I'VE BEEN LIVING ON CANNED TOFU...

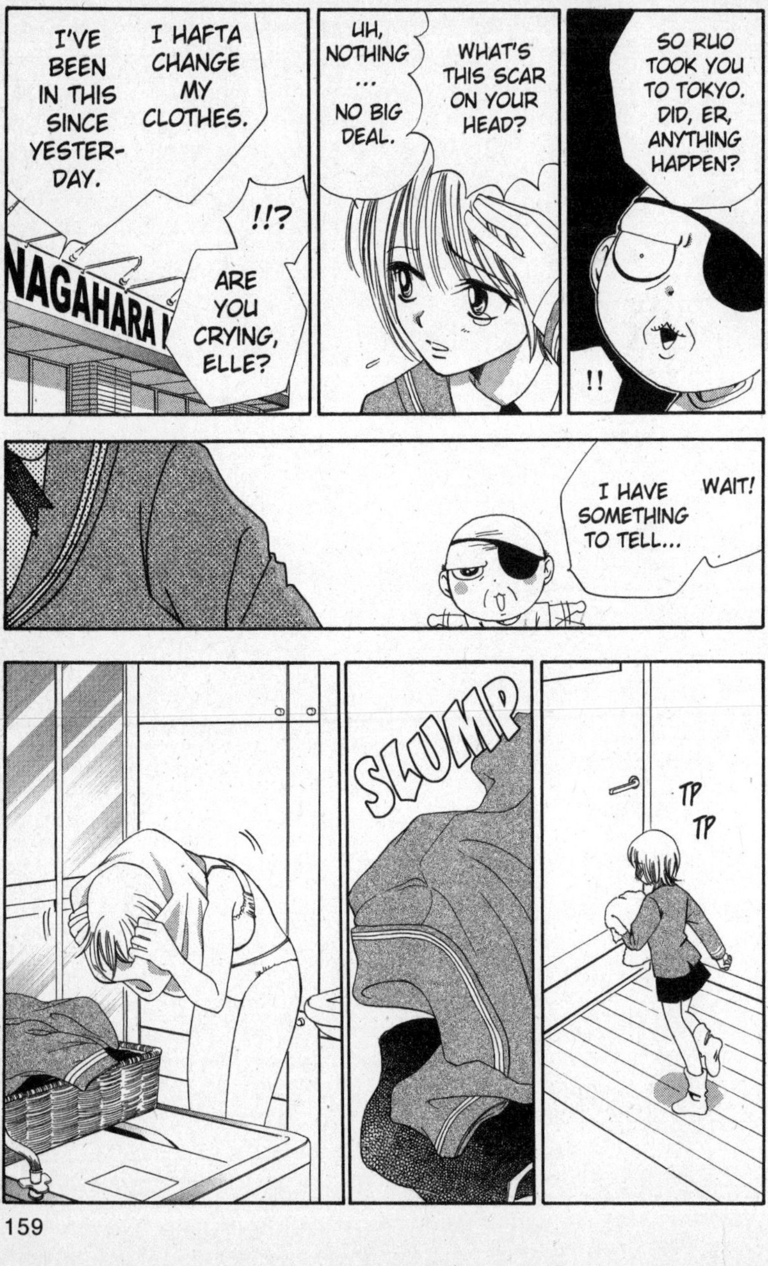
SO RUO TOOK YOU TO TOKYO. DID, ER, ANYTHING HAPPEN?
!!
WHAT'S THIS SCAR ON YOUR HEAD?
UH, NOTHING ... NO BIG DEAL.
I HAFTA CHANGE MY CLOTHES.
I'VE BEEN IN THIS SINCE YESTER-DAY.
!!?
ARE YOU CRYING, ELLE?
NAGAHARA
WAIT!
I HAVE SOMETHING TO TELL...
TP
TP
SLUMP

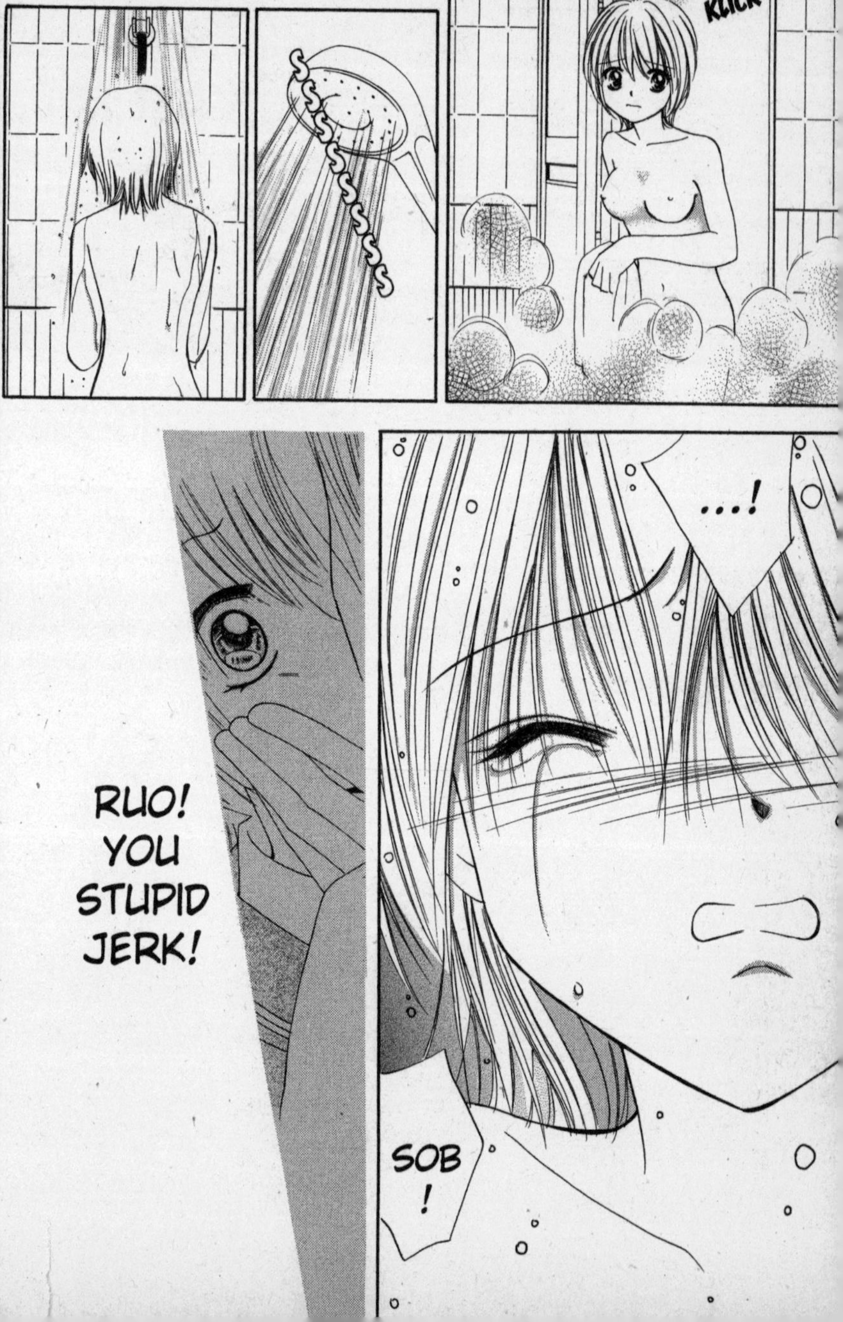
KLICK
SSSSSSSS
...!
SOB!
RUO! YOU STUPID JERK!

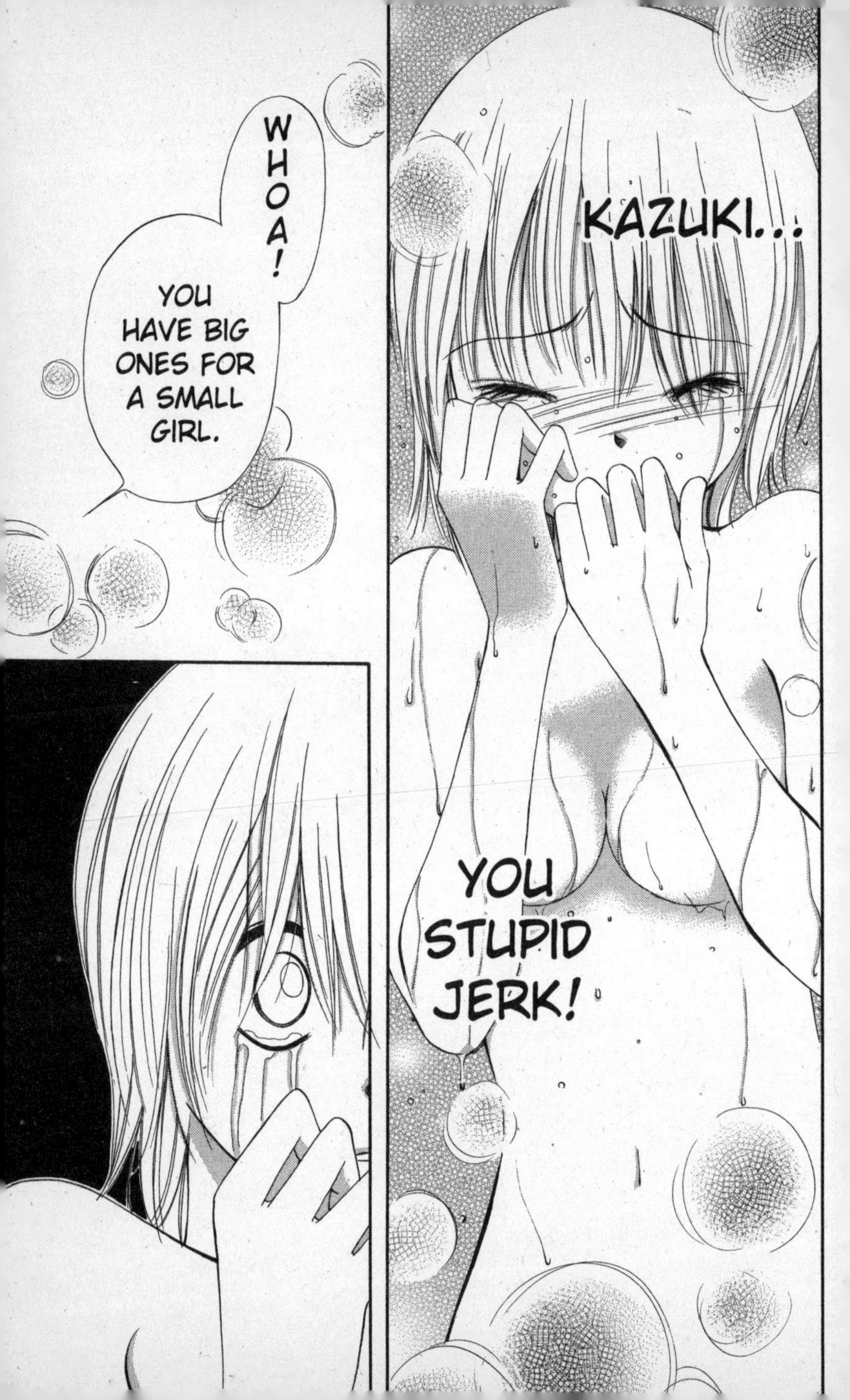
KAZUKI...
YOU STUPID JERK!
WHOA!
YOU HAVE BIG ONES FOR A SMALL GIRL.

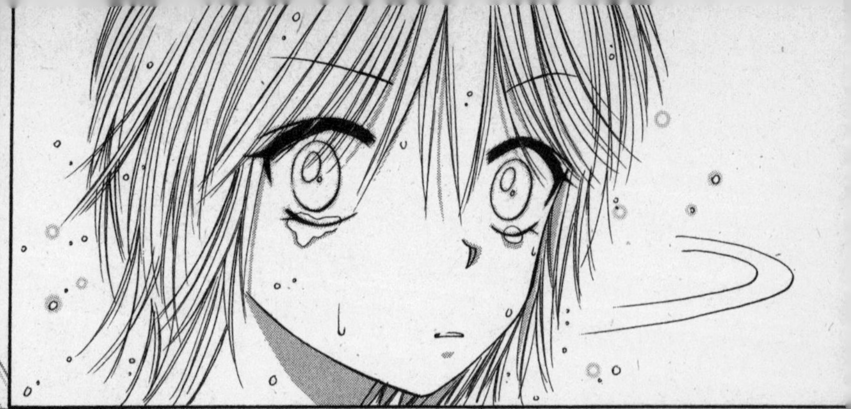
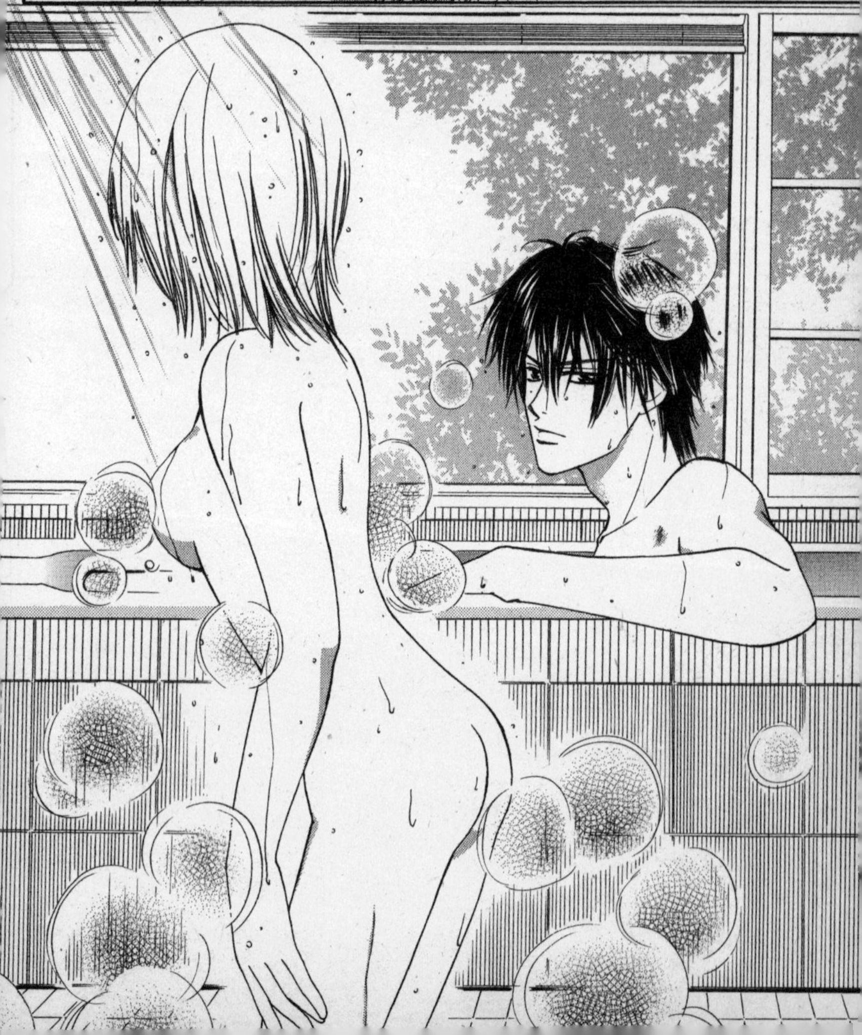

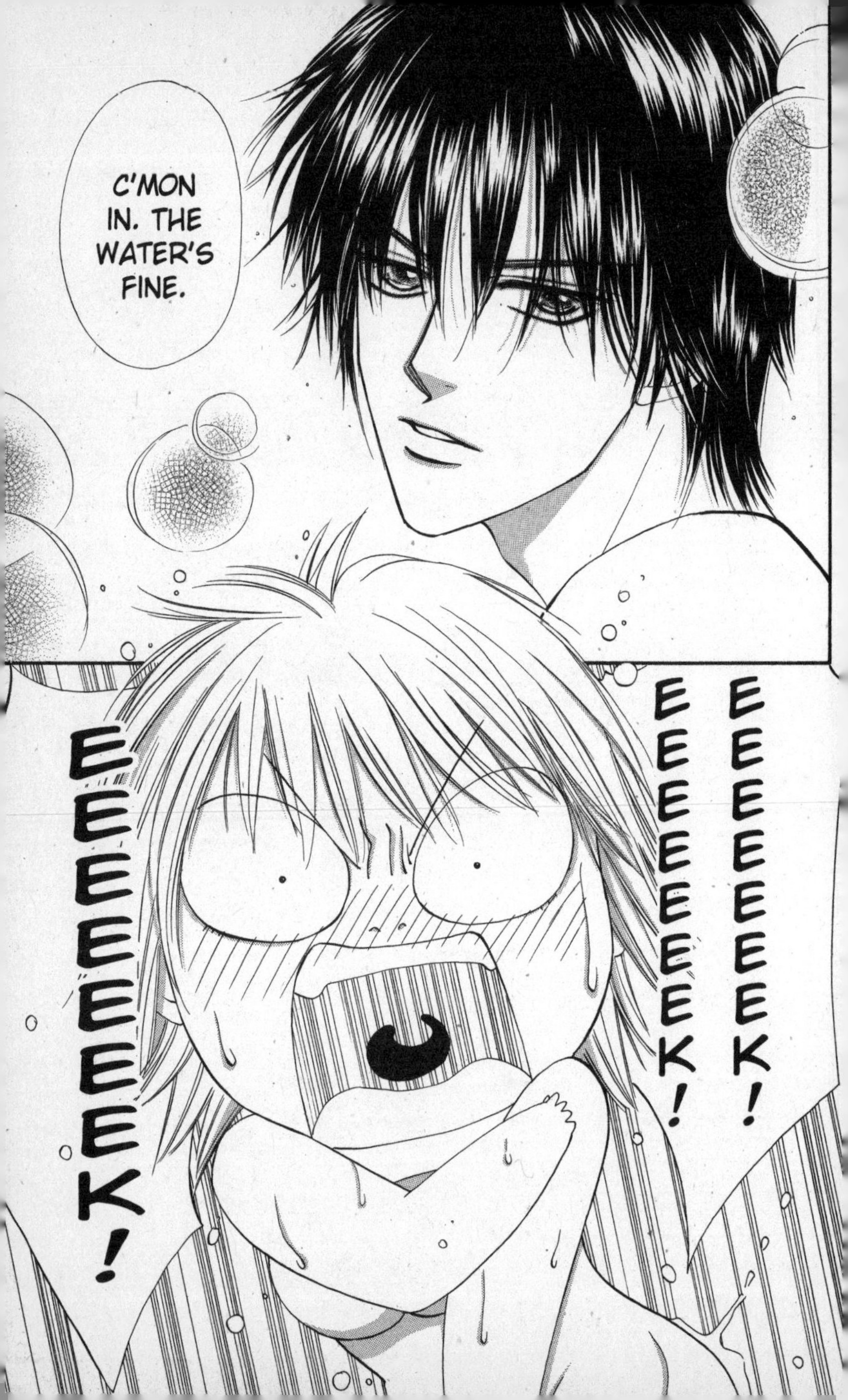
C'MON IN. THE WATER'S FINE.
EEEEEEEK!
EEEEEEEK!
EEEEEEEK!

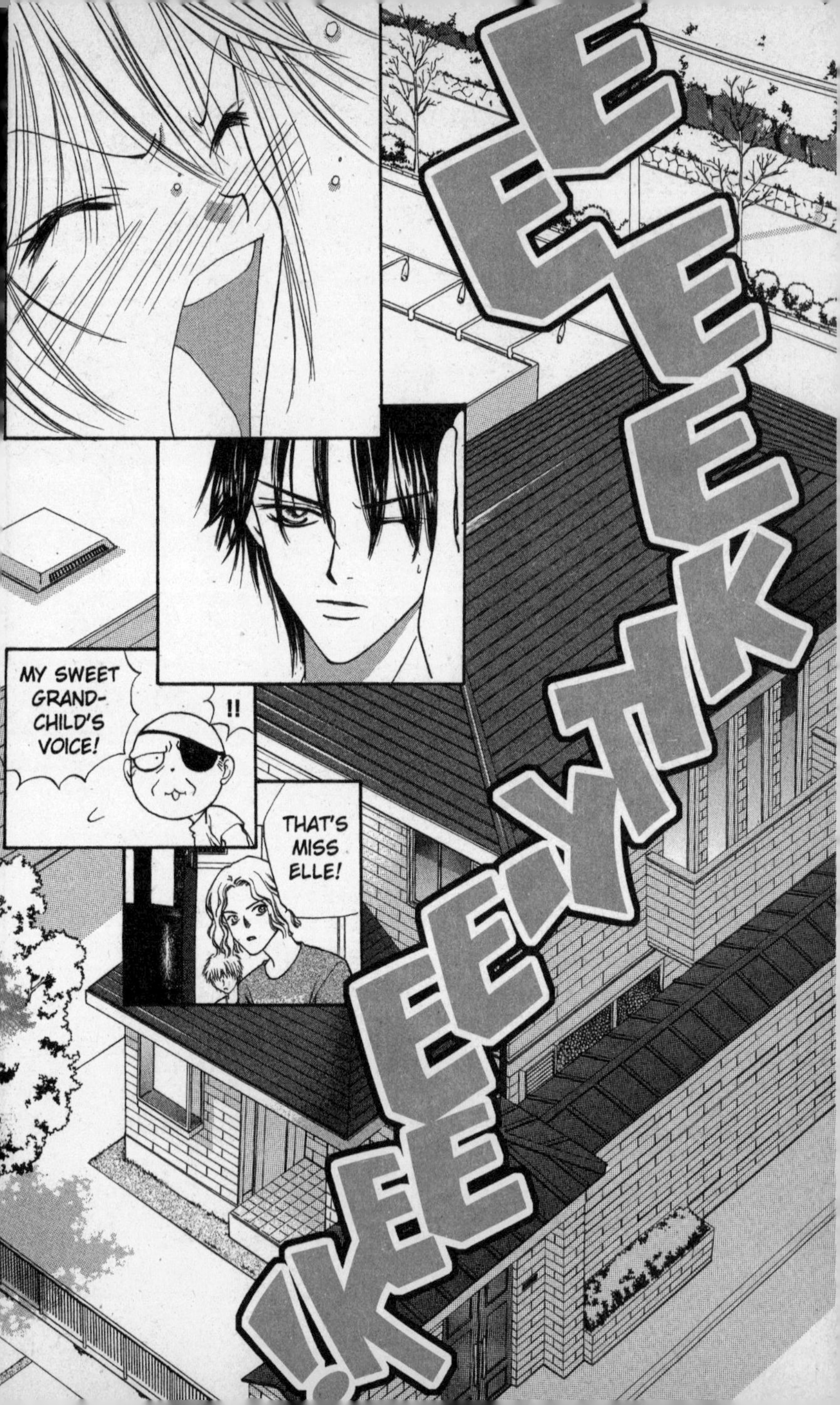
EEEEEK!
MY SWEET GRAND-CHILD'S VOICE!
!!
THAT'S MISS ELLE!

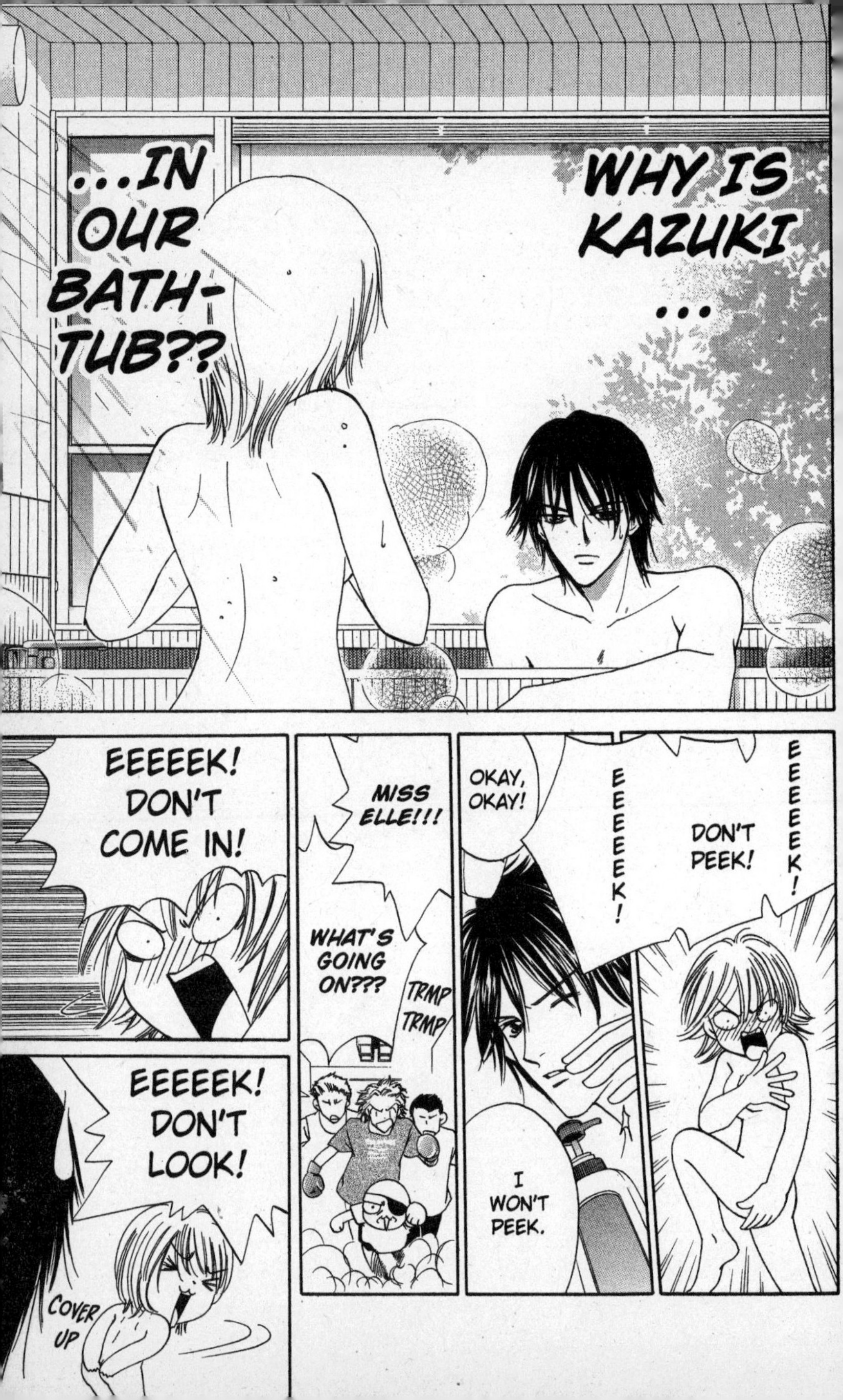
WHY IS KAZUKI ...
...IN OUR BATH-TUB??
EEEEEK!
DON'T PEEK!
EEEEEK!
OKAY, OKAY!
I WON'T PEEK.
MISS ELLE!!!
WHAT'S GOING ON???
TRMP TRMP
EEEEEK! DON'T COME IN!
EEEEEK! DON'T LOOK!
COVER UP

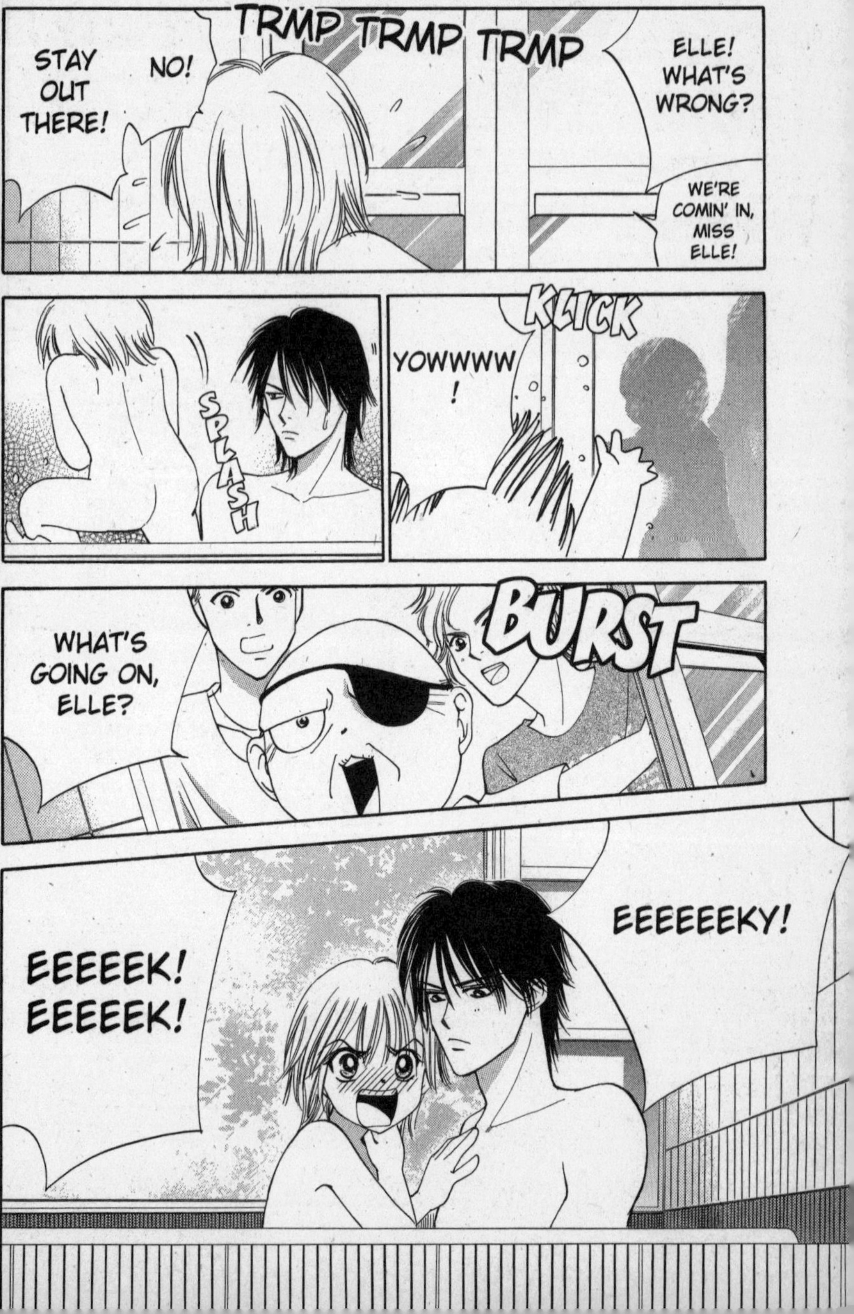
ELLE! WHAT'S WRONG?
TRMP TRMP TRMP
NO!
STAY OUT THERE!
WE'RE COMIN' IN, MISS ELLE!
KLICK
YOWWWW!
SPLASH
BURST
WHAT'S GOING ON, ELLE?
EEEEEEKY!
EEEEEK! EEEEEK!

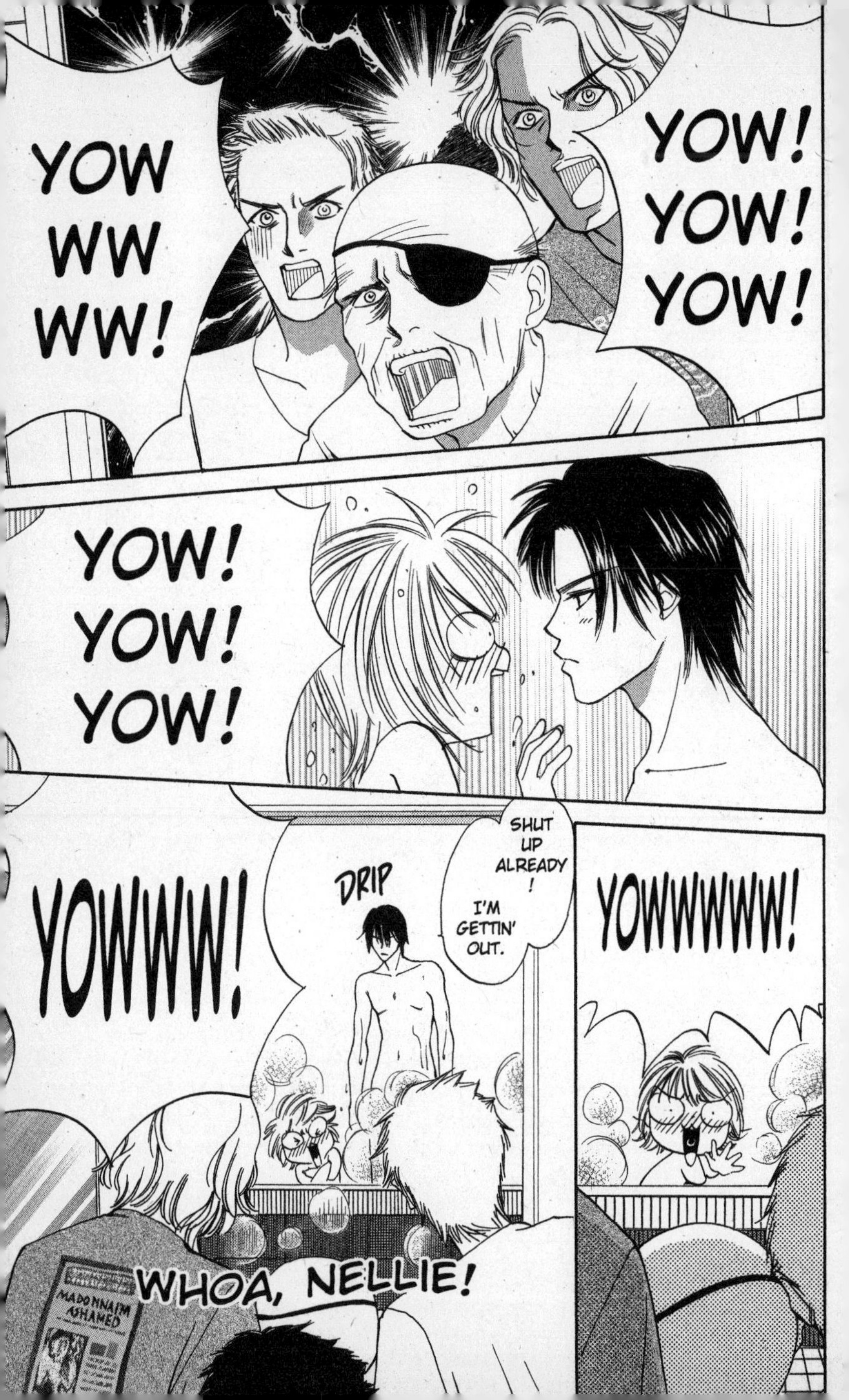
YOW! YOW! YOW!
YOW WW WW!
YOW! YOW! YOW!
YOWWWWW!
SHUT UP ALREADY!
I'M GETTIN' OUT.
DRIP
YOWWW!
MADONNAIM ASHAMED
WHOA, NELLIE!

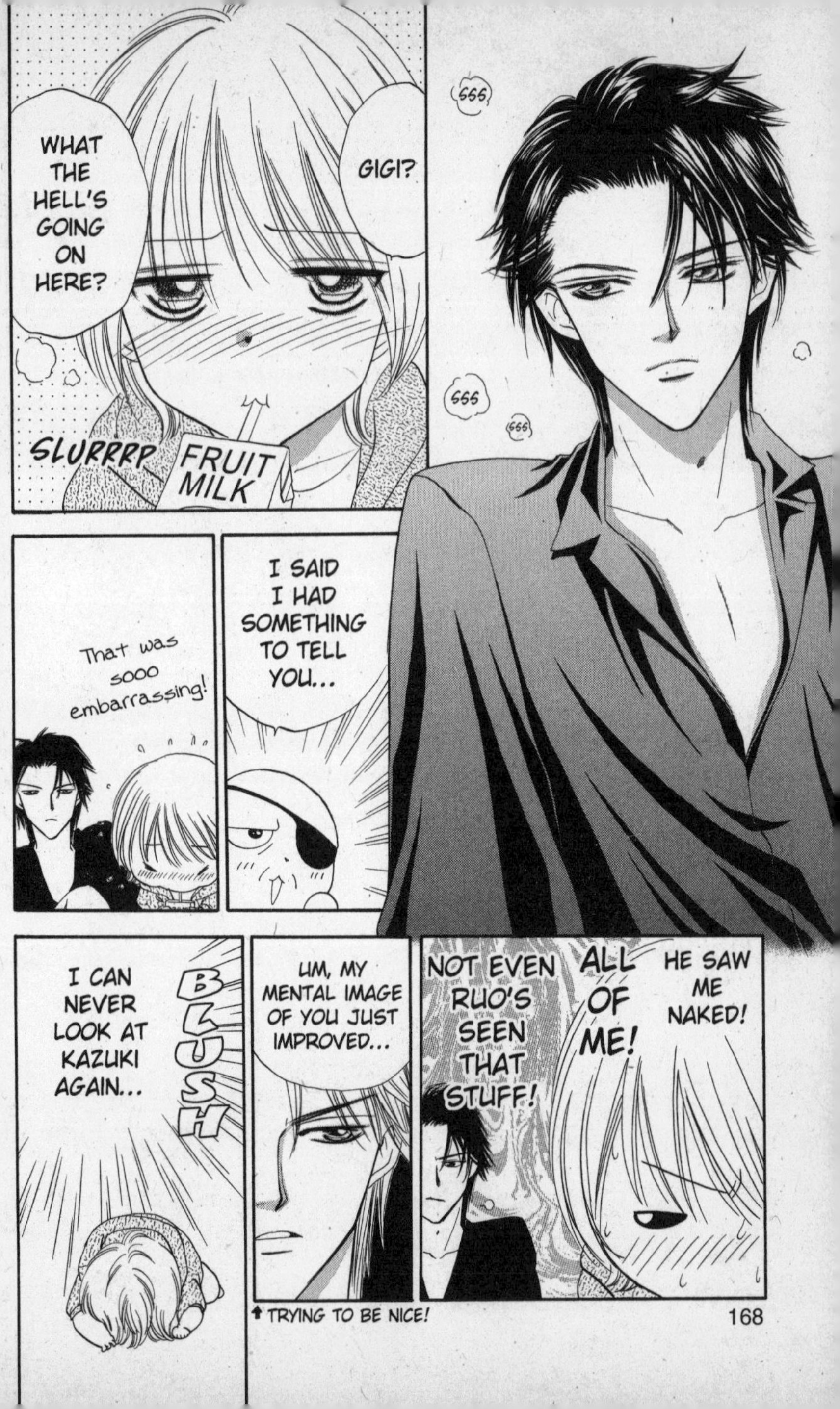
SSS
SSS
SSS
GIGI?
WHAT THE HELL'S GOING ON HERE?
SLURRRP
FRUIT MILK
I SAID I HAD SOMETHING TO TELL YOU...
That was sooo embarrassing!
HE SAW ME NAKED!
ALL OF ME!
NOT EVEN RUO'S SEEN THAT STUFF!
UM, MY MENTAL IMAGE OF YOU JUST IMPROVED...
TRYING TO BE NICE!
BLUSH
I CAN NEVER LOOK AT KAZUKI AGAIN...

WHY ARE YOU HERE?

THOUGHT YOU GOT EXPELLED...

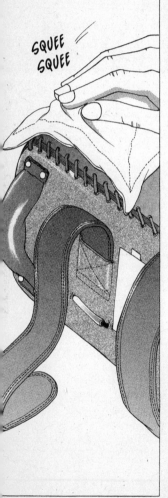

SQUEE SQUEE

YEAH ...

AFTER YESTERDAY...

I THOUGHT I'D HAFTA LEAVE THE GYM FOR A WHILE.

SO I CAME HERE TO TELL THE OLD MAN.

YUP! HE DID!

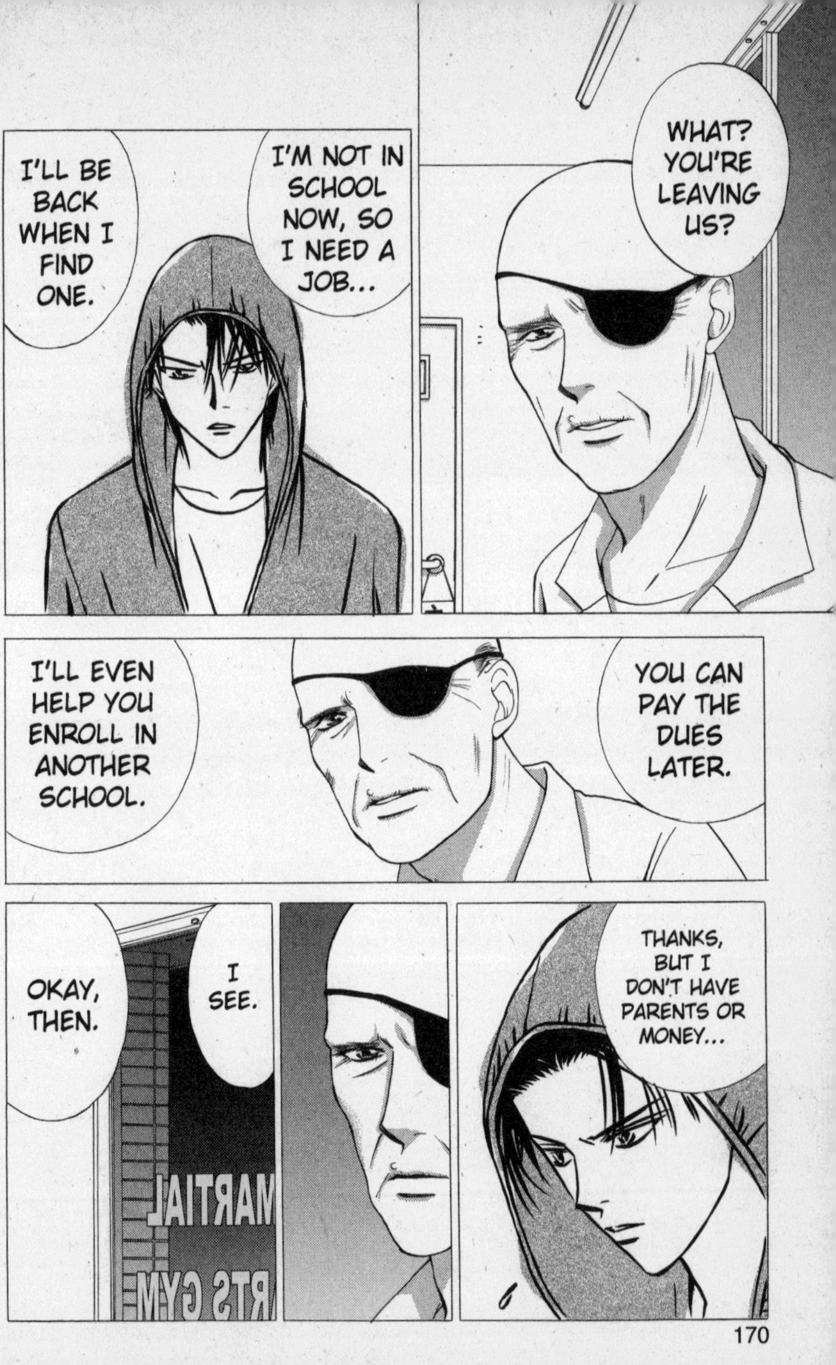
WHAT? YOU'RE LEAVING US?
I'M NOT IN SCHOOL NOW, SO I NEED A JOB...
I'LL BE BACK WHEN I FIND ONE.
YOU CAN PAY THE DUES LATER.
I'LL EVEN HELP YOU ENROLL IN ANOTHER SCHOOL.
THANKS, BUT I DON'T HAVE PARENTS OR MONEY...
I SEE.
OKAY, THEN.
MARTIAL
RTS GYM

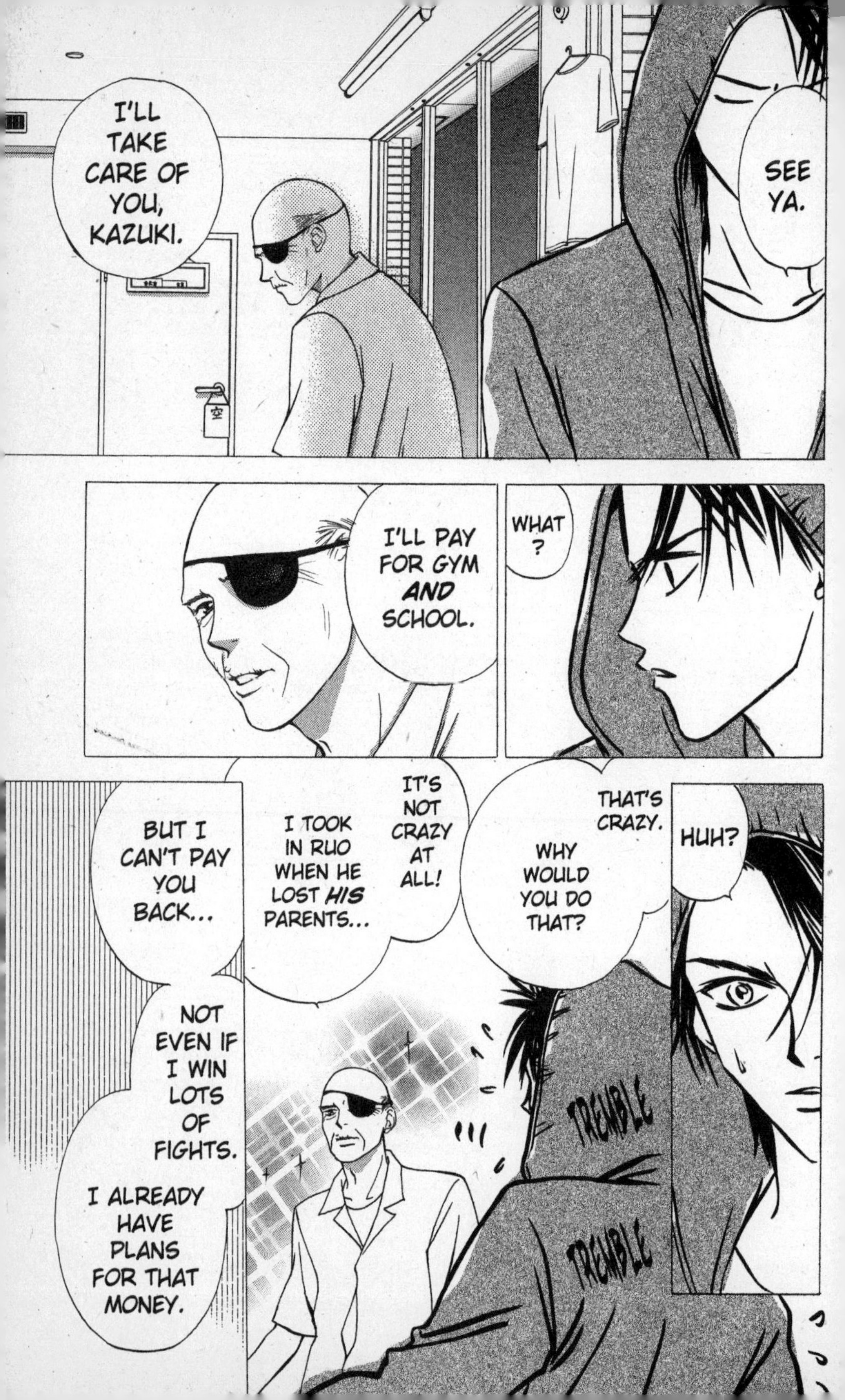
SEE YA.
I'LL TAKE CARE OF YOU, KAZUKI.
WHAT ?
I'LL PAY FOR GYM *AND* SCHOOL.
HUH?
THAT'S CRAZY.
WHY WOULD YOU DO THAT?
IT'S NOT CRAZY AT ALL!
I TOOK IN RUO WHEN HE LOST *HIS* PARENTS...
BUT I CAN'T PAY YOU BACK...
NOT EVEN IF I WIN LOTS OF FIGHTS.
I ALREADY HAVE PLANS FOR THAT MONEY.
TREMBLE
TREMBLE

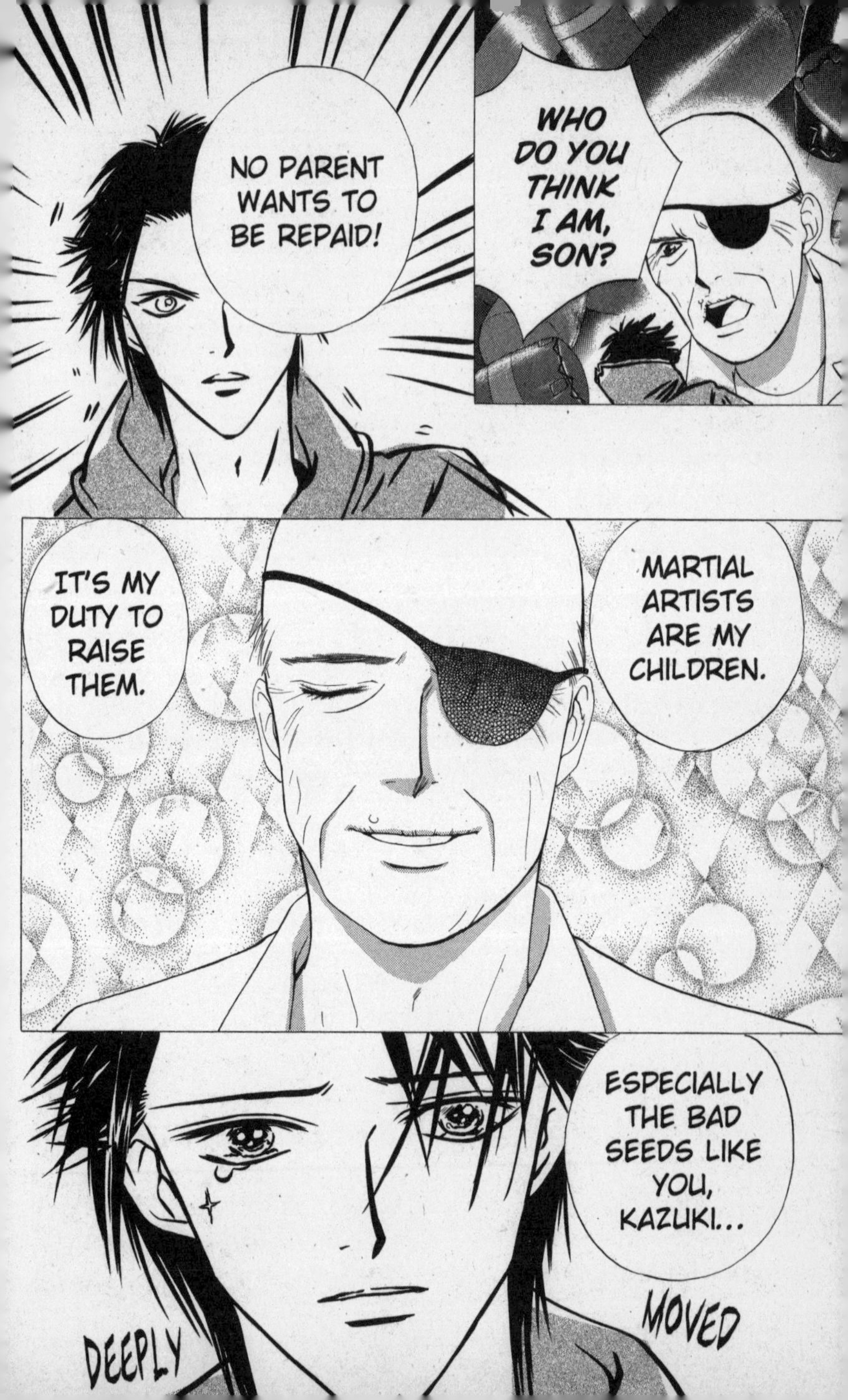
WHO DO YOU THINK I AM, SON?
NO PARENT WANTS TO BE REPAID!
MARTIAL ARTISTS ARE MY CHILDREN.
IT'S MY DUTY TO RAISE THEM.
ESPECIALLY THE BAD SEEDS LIKE YOU, KAZUKI...
MOVED
DEEPLY

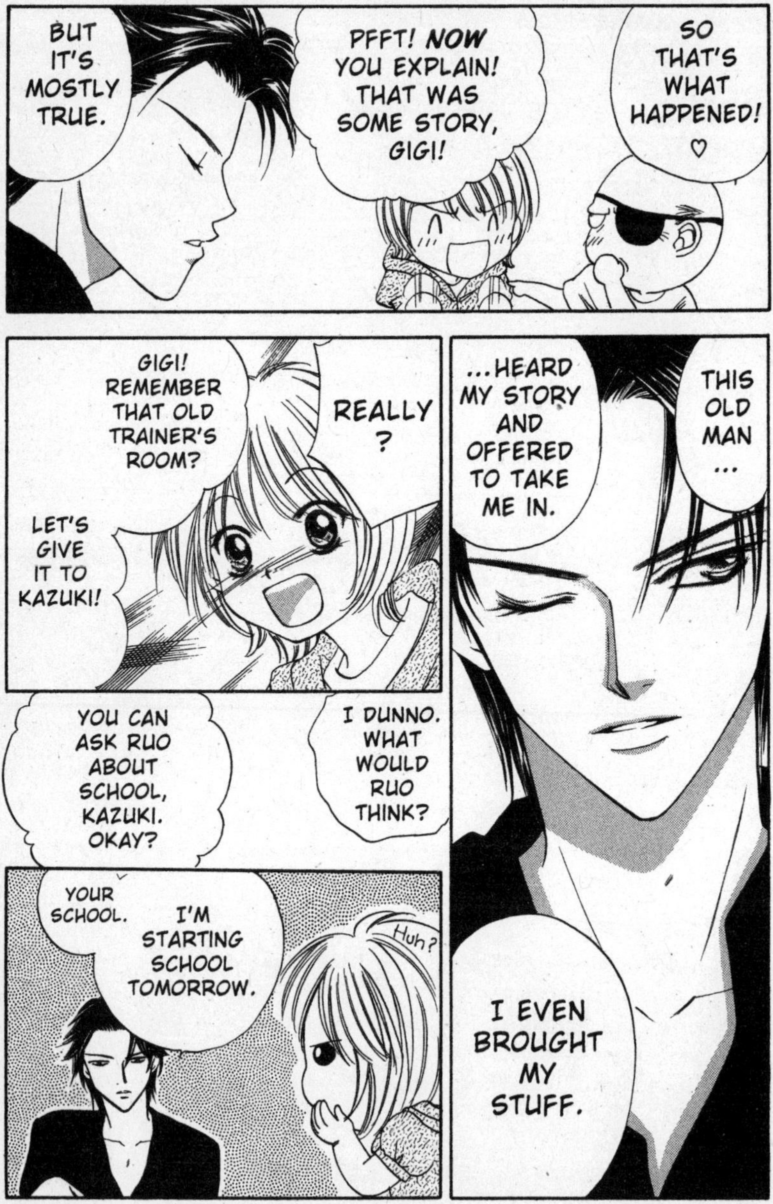
SO THAT'S WHAT HAPPENED! ♡
PFFT! *NOW* YOU EXPLAIN! THAT WAS SOME STORY, GIGI!
BUT IT'S MOSTLY TRUE.
THIS OLD MAN ...
...HEARD MY STORY AND OFFERED TO TAKE ME IN.
I EVEN BROUGHT MY STUFF.
REALLY ?
GIGI! REMEMBER THAT OLD TRAINER'S ROOM?
LET'S GIVE IT TO KAZUKI!
I DUNNO. WHAT WOULD RUO THINK?
YOU CAN ASK RUO ABOUT SCHOOL, KAZUKI. OKAY?
Huh?
I'M STARTING SCHOOL TOMORROW.
YOUR SCHOOL.

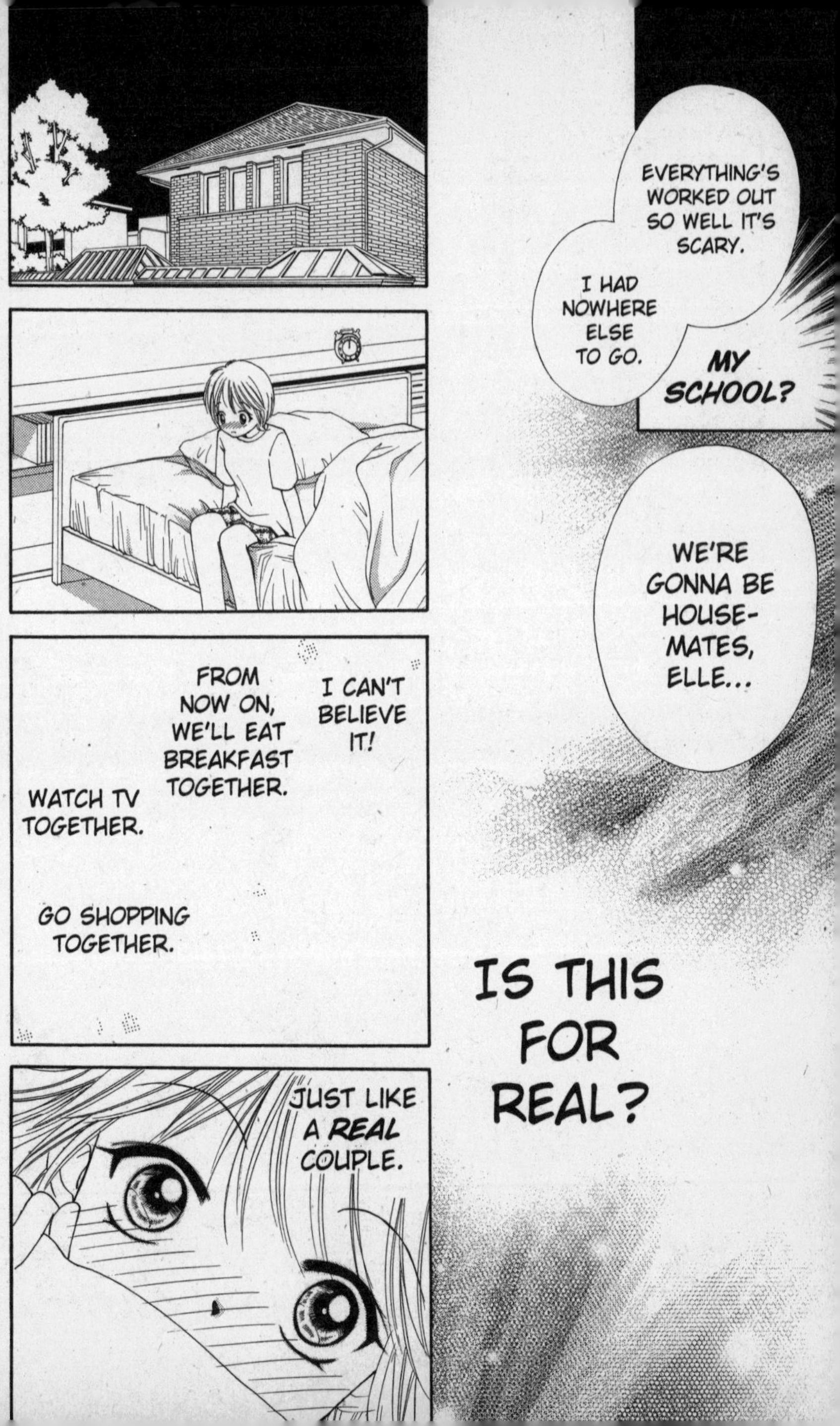
EVERYTHING'S WORKED OUT SO WELL IT'S SCARY.
I HAD NOWHERE ELSE TO GO.
MY SCHOOL?
WE'RE GONNA BE HOUSE-MATES, ELLE...
IS THIS FOR REAL?
I CAN'T BELIEVE IT!
FROM NOW ON, WE'LL EAT BREAKFAST TOGETHER.
WATCH TV TOGETHER.
GO SHOPPING TOGETHER.
JUST LIKE A REAL COUPLE.

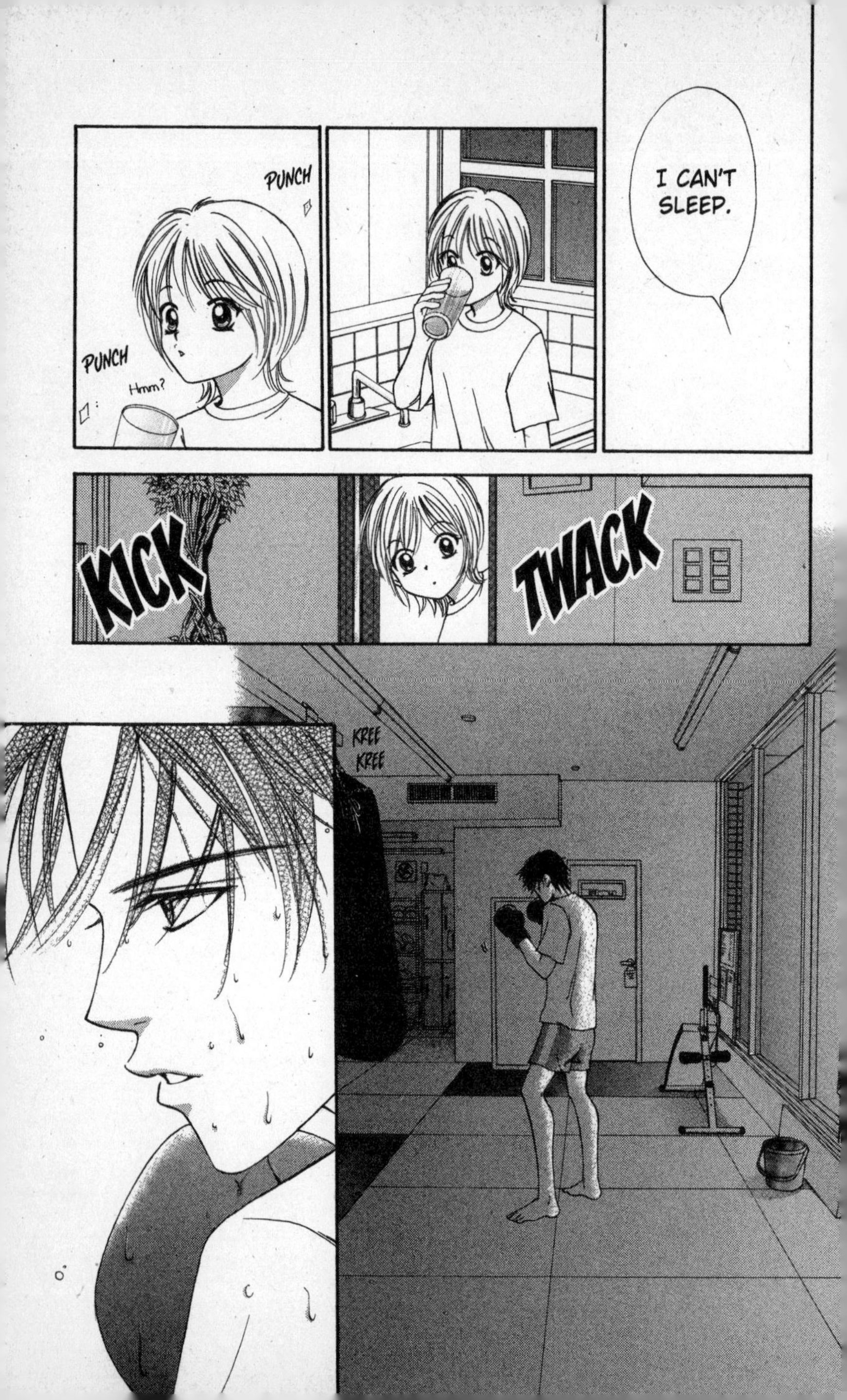

I CAN'T SLEEP.
PUNCH
PUNCH
Hmm?
TWACK
KICK
KREE KREE

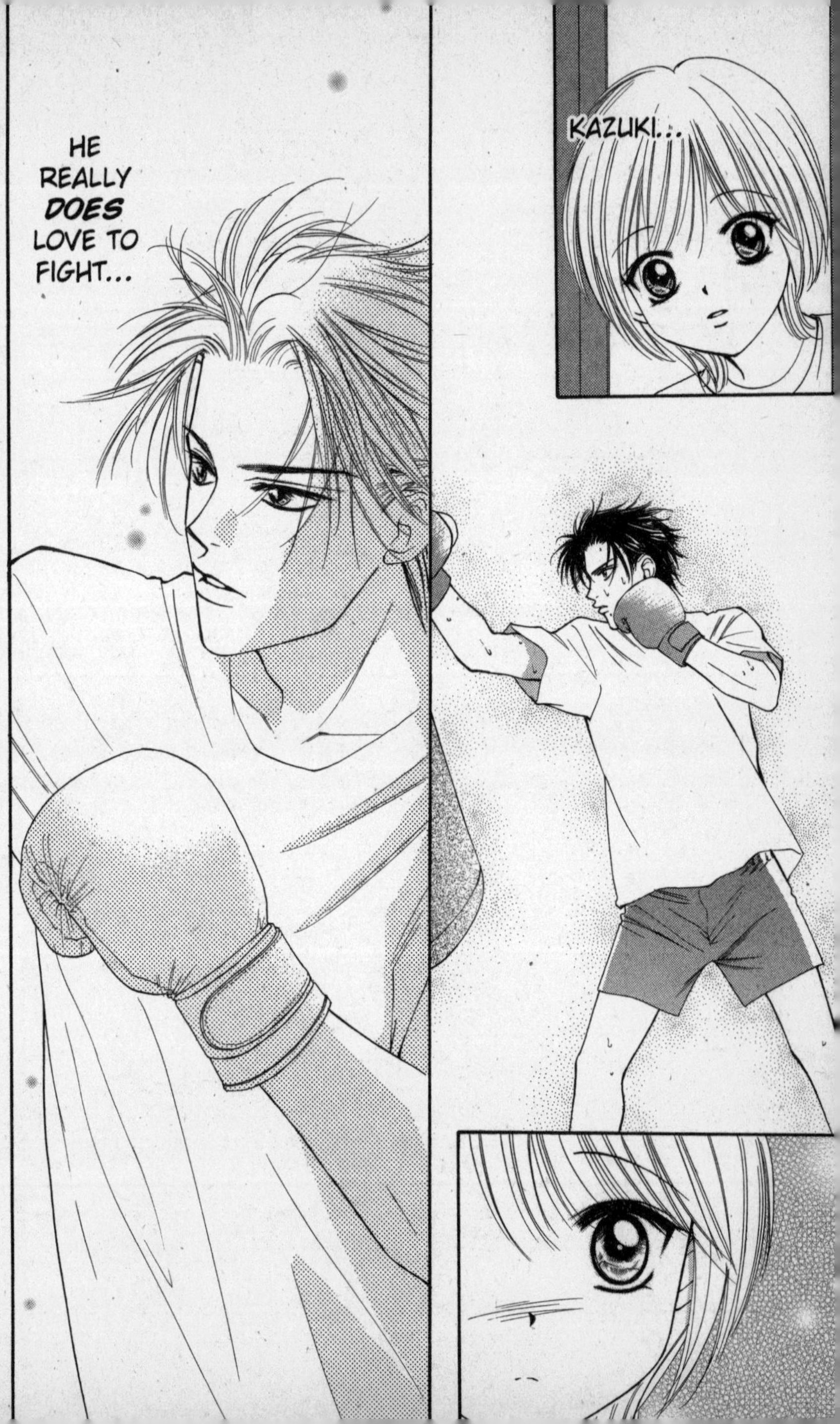
KAZUKI...
HE REALLY *DOES* LOVE TO FIGHT...

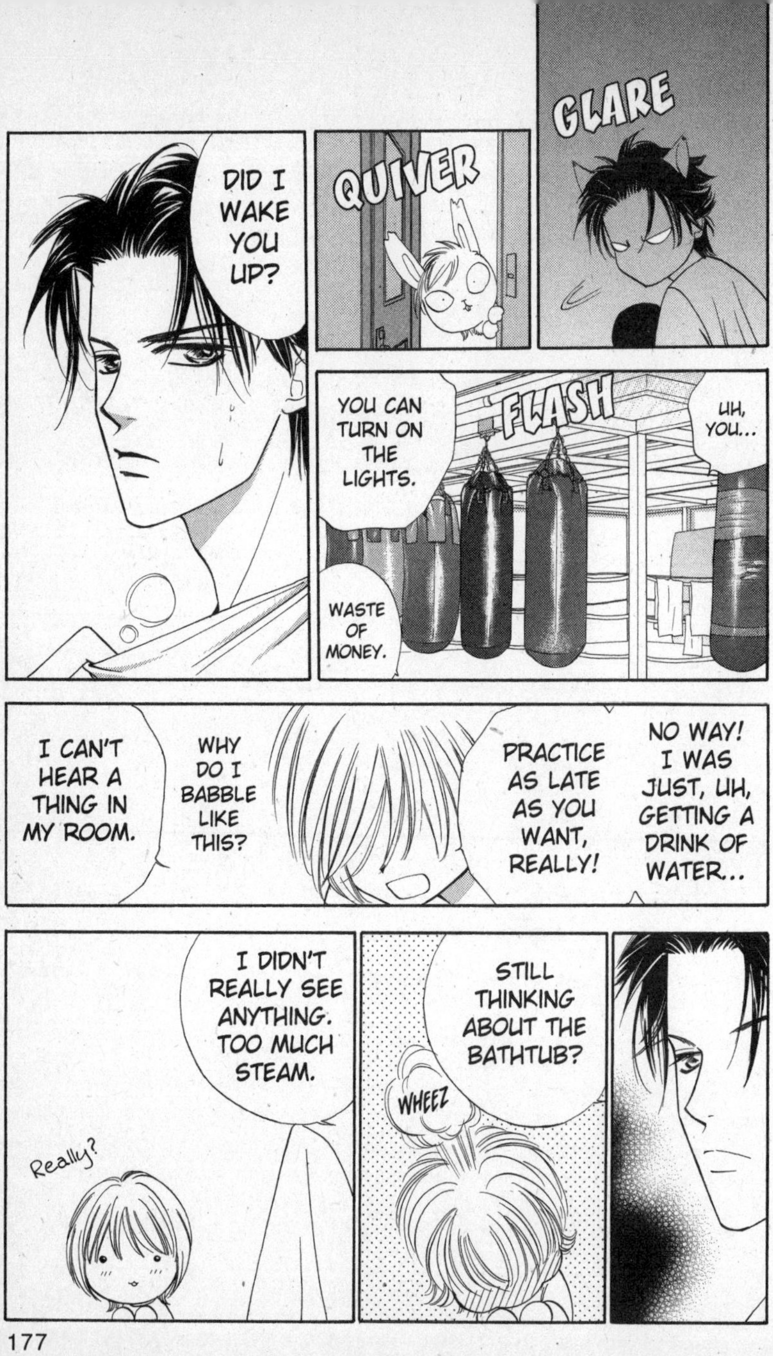
GLARE
QUIVER
UH, YOU...
FLASH
YOU CAN TURN ON THE LIGHTS.
WASTE OF MONEY.
DID I WAKE YOU UP?
NO WAY! I WAS JUST, UH, GETTING A DRINK OF WATER...
PRACTICE AS LATE AS YOU WANT, REALLY!
WHY DO I BABBLE LIKE THIS?
I CAN'T HEAR A THING IN MY ROOM.
STILL THINKING ABOUT THE BATHTUB?
WHEEZ
I DIDN'T REALLY SEE ANYTHING. TOO MUCH STEAM.
Really?

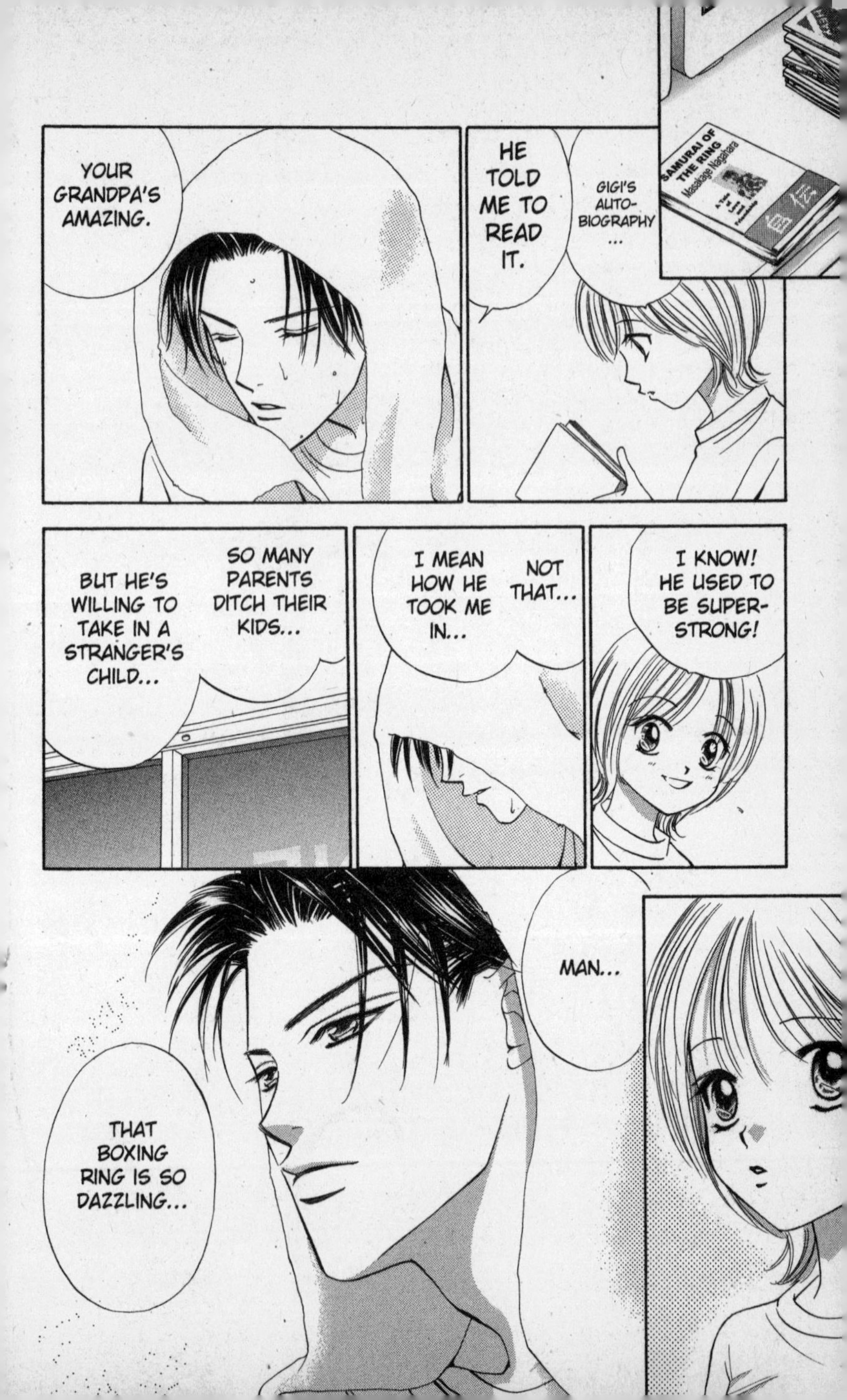
SAMURAI OF THE RING
Masakage Nagahara
GIGI'S AUTO-BIOGRAPHY ...
HE TOLD ME TO READ IT.
YOUR GRANDPA'S AMAZING.
I KNOW! HE USED TO BE SUPER-STRONG!
NOT THAT...
I MEAN HOW HE TOOK ME IN...
SO MANY PARENTS DITCH THEIR KIDS...
BUT HE'S WILLING TO TAKE IN A STRANGER'S CHILD...
MAN...
THAT BOXING RING IS SO DAZZLING...

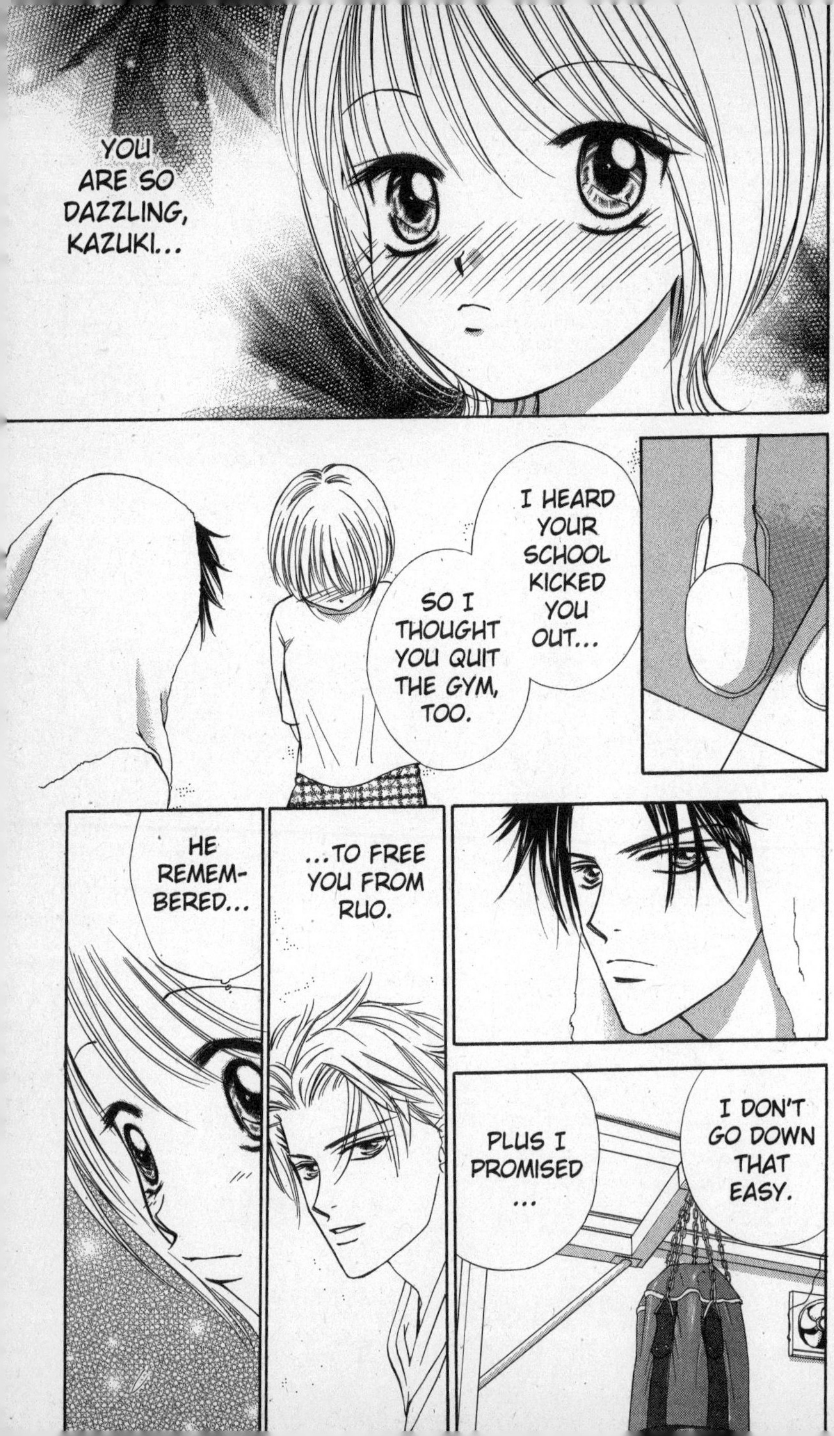
YOU ARE SO DAZZLING, KAZUKI...
I HEARD YOUR SCHOOL KICKED YOU OUT...
SO I THOUGHT YOU QUIT THE GYM, TOO.
I DON'T GO DOWN THAT EASY.
PLUS I PROMISED ...
...TO FREE YOU FROM RUO.
HE REMEM-BERED...

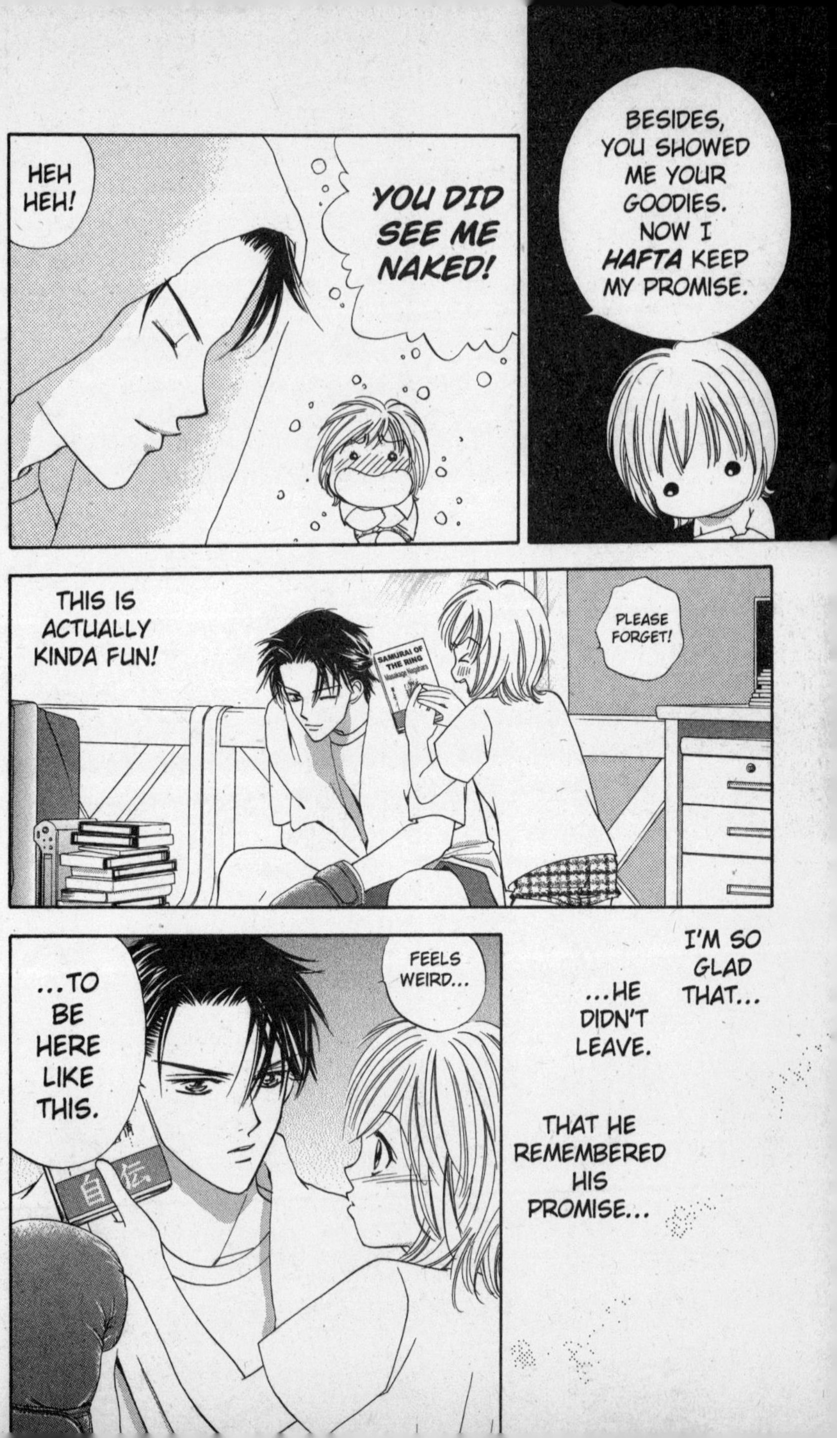
BESIDES, YOU SHOWED ME YOUR GOODIES. NOW I *HAFTA* KEEP MY PROMISE.
YOU DID SEE ME NAKED!
HEH HEH!
PLEASE FORGET!
SAMURAI OF THE RING
THIS IS ACTUALLY KINDA FUN!
I'M SO GLAD THAT...
...HE DIDN'T LEAVE.
THAT HE REMEMBERED HIS PROMISE...
FEELS WEIRD...
...TO BE HERE LIKE THIS.
自伝

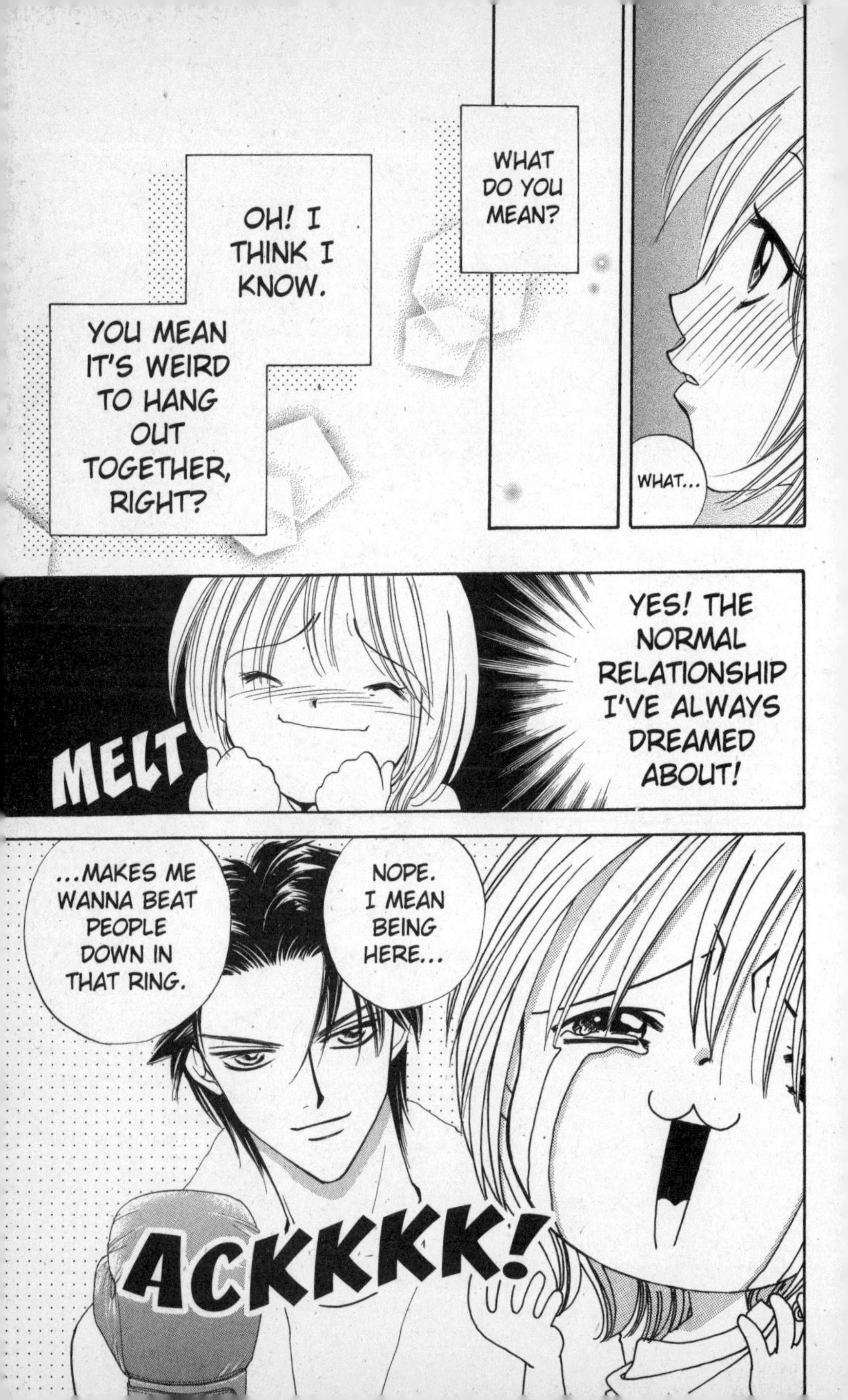
WHAT...
WHAT DO YOU MEAN?
OH! I THINK I KNOW.
YOU MEAN IT'S WEIRD TO HANG OUT TOGETHER, RIGHT?
YES! THE NORMAL RELATIONSHIP I'VE ALWAYS DREAMED ABOUT!
MELT
NOPE. I MEAN BEING HERE...
...MAKES ME WANNA BEAT PEOPLE DOWN IN THAT RING.
ACKKKK!

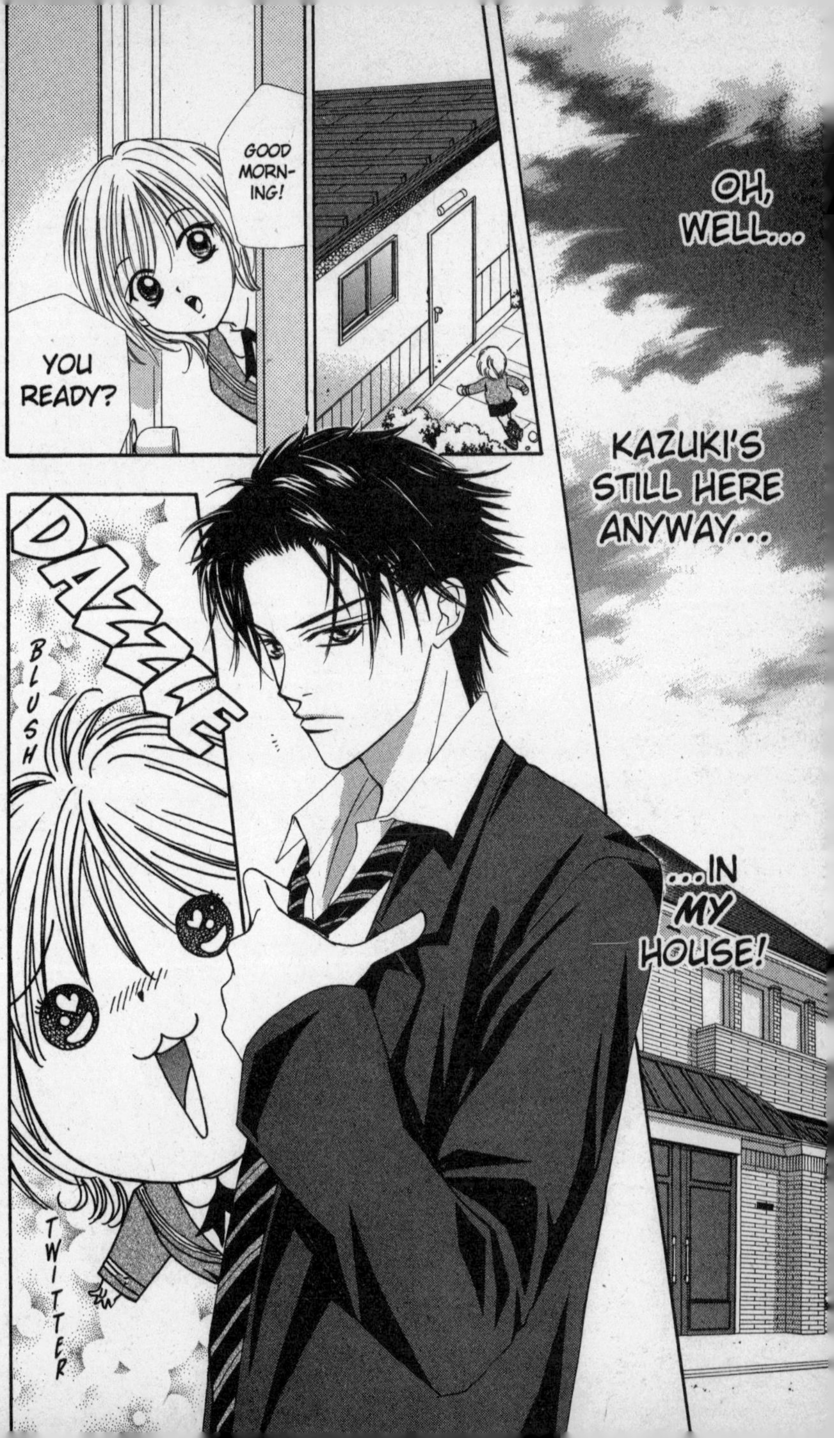
GOOD MORNING!
YOU READY?
OH, WELL...
KAZUKI'S STILL HERE ANYWAY...
...IN MY HOUSE!
DAZZLE
BLUSH
TWITTER

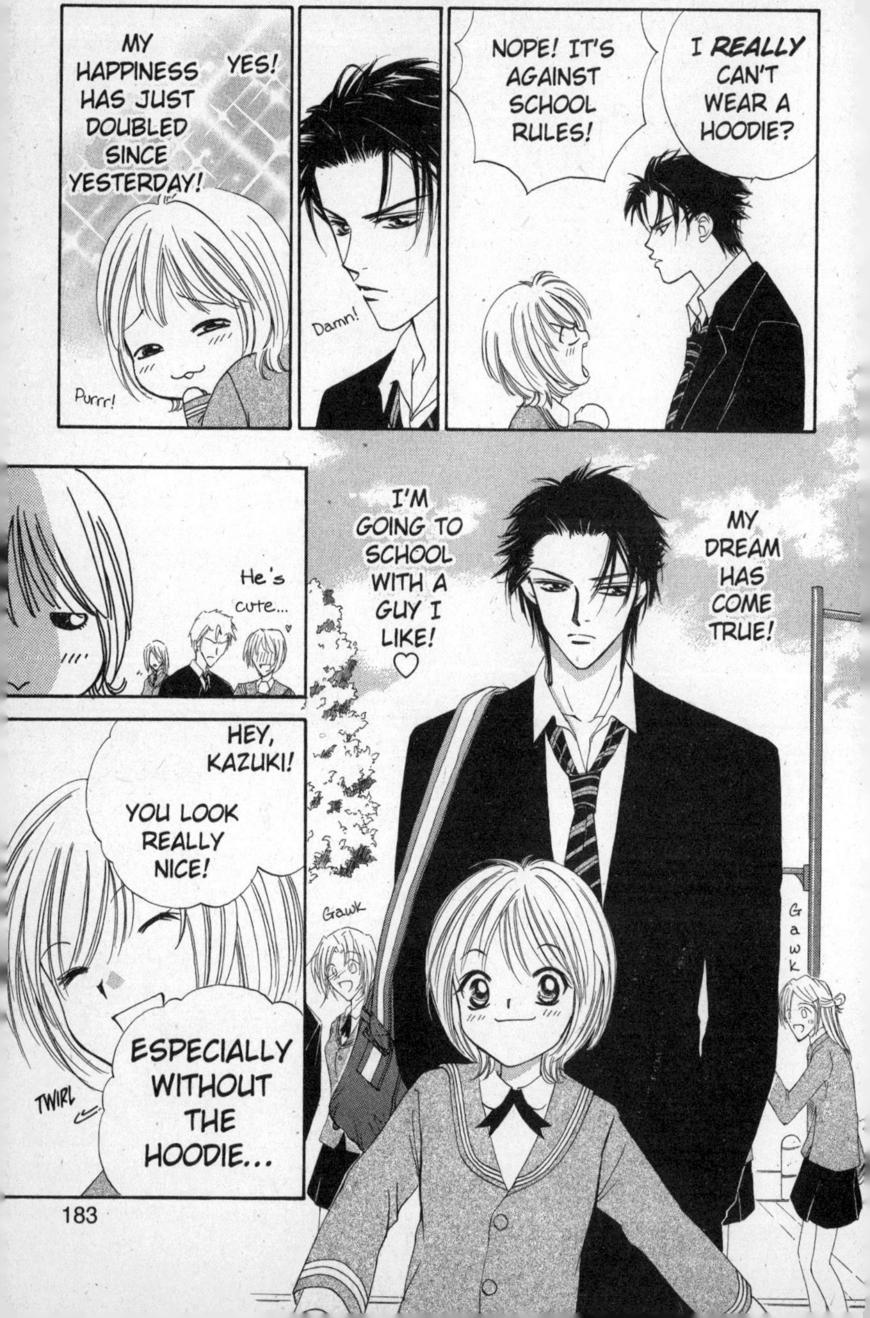
I REALLY CAN'T WEAR A HOODIE?
NOPE! IT'S AGAINST SCHOOL RULES!
Damn!
YES!
MY HAPPINESS HAS JUST DOUBLED SINCE YESTERDAY!
Purrr!
MY DREAM HAS COME TRUE!
I'M GOING TO SCHOOL WITH A GUY I LIKE! ♡
Gawk
Gawk
He's cute...
HEY, KAZUKI!
YOU LOOK REALLY NICE!
ESPECIALLY WITHOUT THE HOODIE...
TWIRL

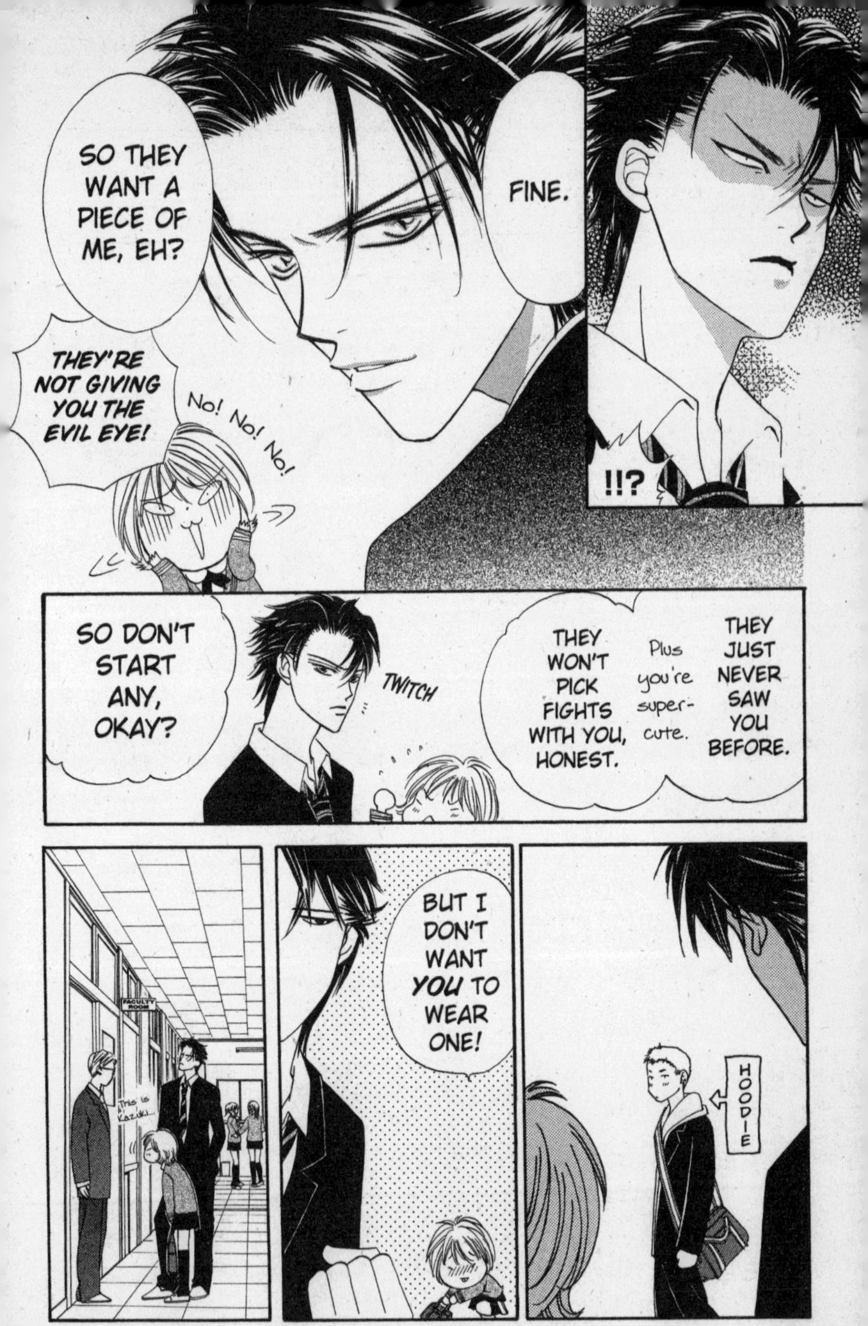
!!?
FINE.
SO THEY WANT A PIECE OF ME, EH?
No! No! No!
THEY'RE NOT GIVING YOU THE EVIL EYE!
THEY JUST NEVER SAW YOU BEFORE.
Plus you're super-cute.
THEY WON'T PICK FIGHTS WITH YOU, HONEST.
TWITCH
SO DON'T START ANY, OKAY?
HOODIE
BUT I DON'T WANT YOU TO WEAR ONE!
FACULTY ROOM
This is Kazuki...

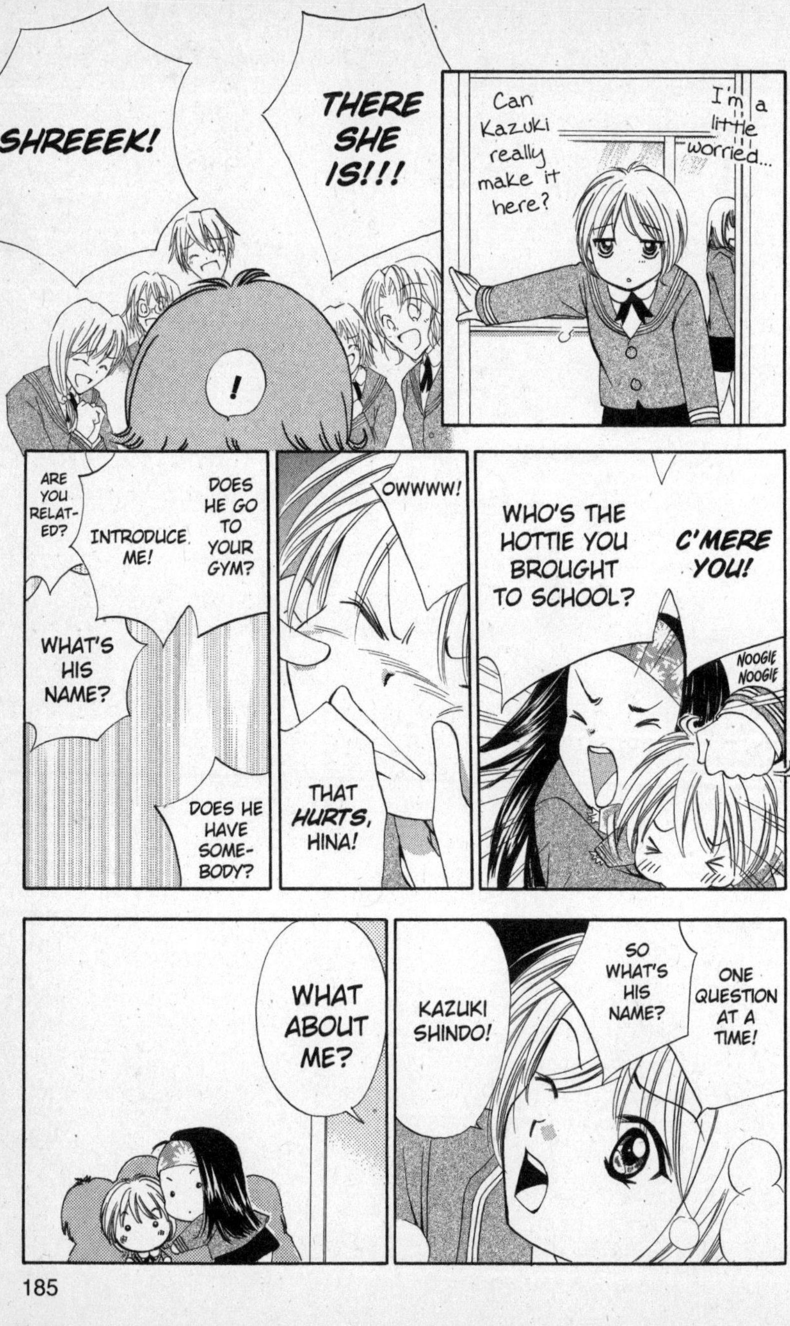
I'm a little worried...
Can Kazuki really make it here?
THERE SHE IS!!!
SHREEEK!
!
C'MERE YOU!
WHO'S THE HOTTIE YOU BROUGHT TO SCHOOL?
NOOGIE NOOGIE
OWWWW!
THAT HURTS, HINA!
DOES HE GO TO YOUR GYM?
INTRODUCE ME!
ARE YOU RELAT-ED?
WHAT'S HIS NAME?
DOES HE HAVE SOME-BODY?
ONE QUESTION AT A TIME!
SO WHAT'S HIS NAME?
KAZUKI SHINDO!
WHAT ABOUT ME?

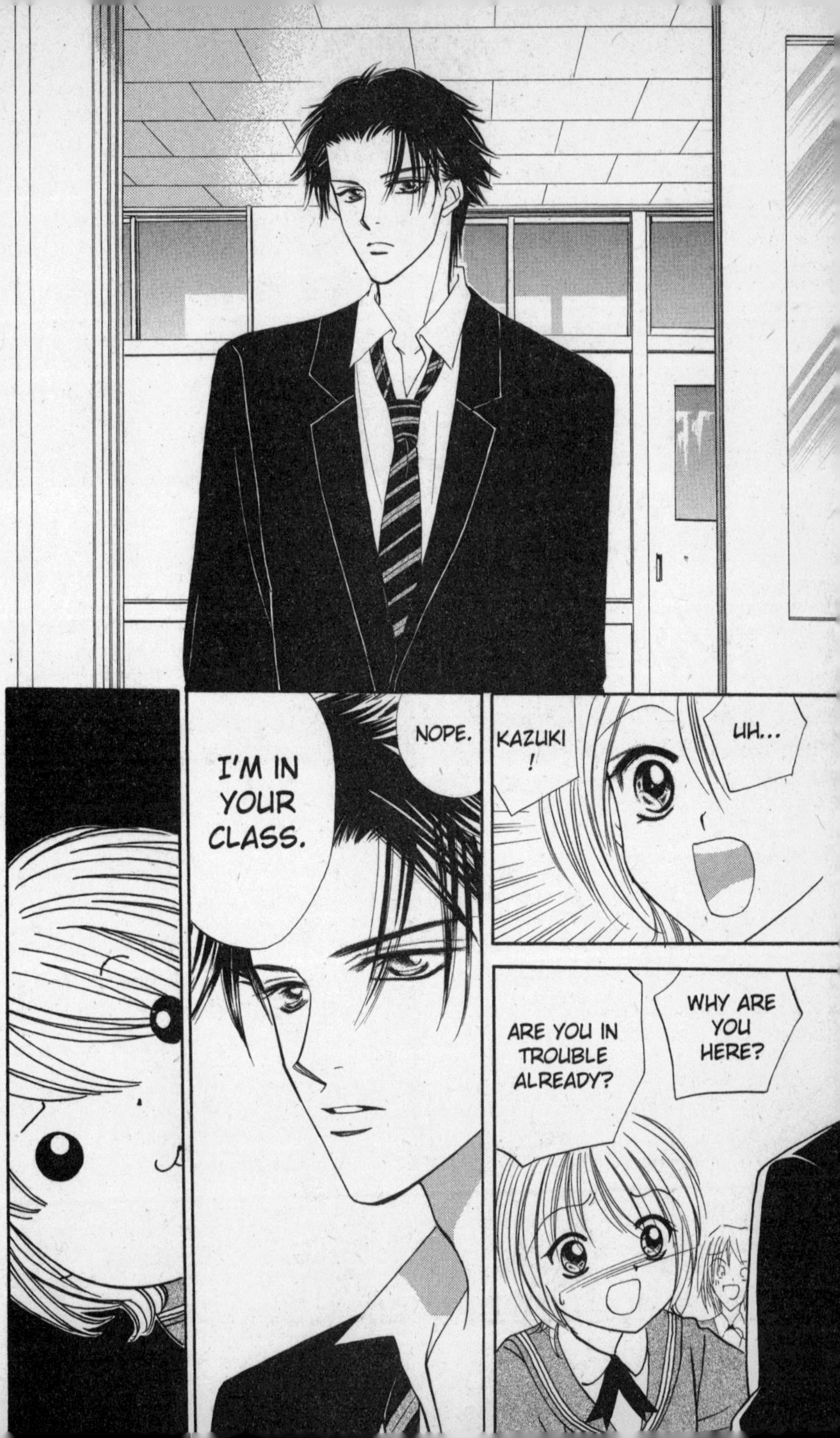
UH...
KAZUKI!
WHY ARE YOU HERE?
ARE YOU IN TROUBLE ALREADY?
NOPE.
I'M IN YOUR CLASS.

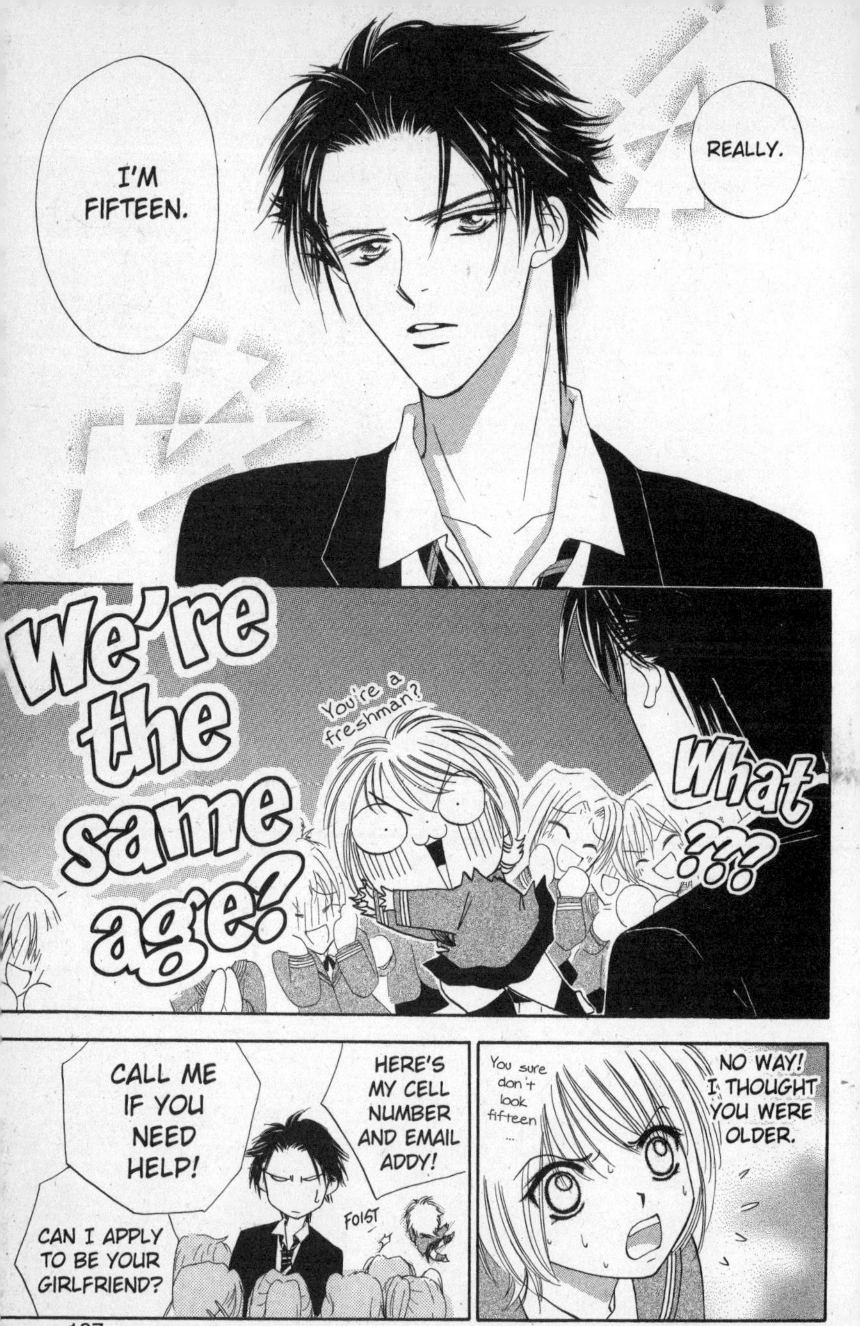
REALLY.
I'M FIFTEEN.
What ???
You're a freshman?
We're the same age?
NO WAY! I THOUGHT YOU WERE OLDER.
You sure don't look fifteen ...
HERE'S MY CELL NUMBER AND EMAIL ADDY!
CALL ME IF YOU NEED HELP!
FOIST
CAN I APPLY TO BE YOUR GIRLFRIEND?

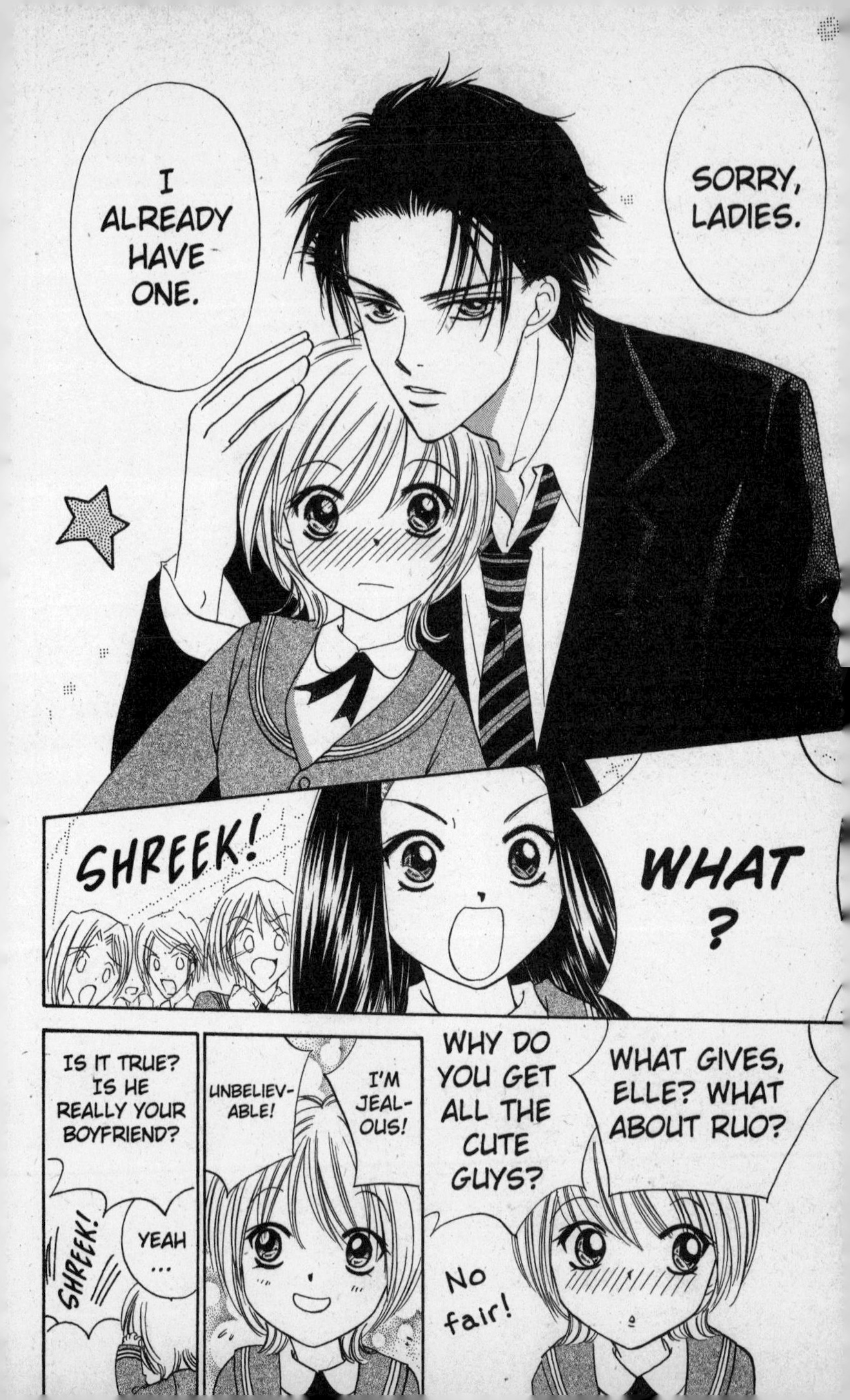
SORRY, LADIES.
I ALREADY HAVE ONE.
WHAT?
SHREEK!
WHAT GIVES, ELLE? WHAT ABOUT RUO?
WHY DO YOU GET ALL THE CUTE GUYS?
No fair!
I'M JEAL-OUS!
UNBELIEV-ABLE!
IS IT TRUE? IS HE REALLY YOUR BOYFRIEND?
YEAH ...
SHREEK!

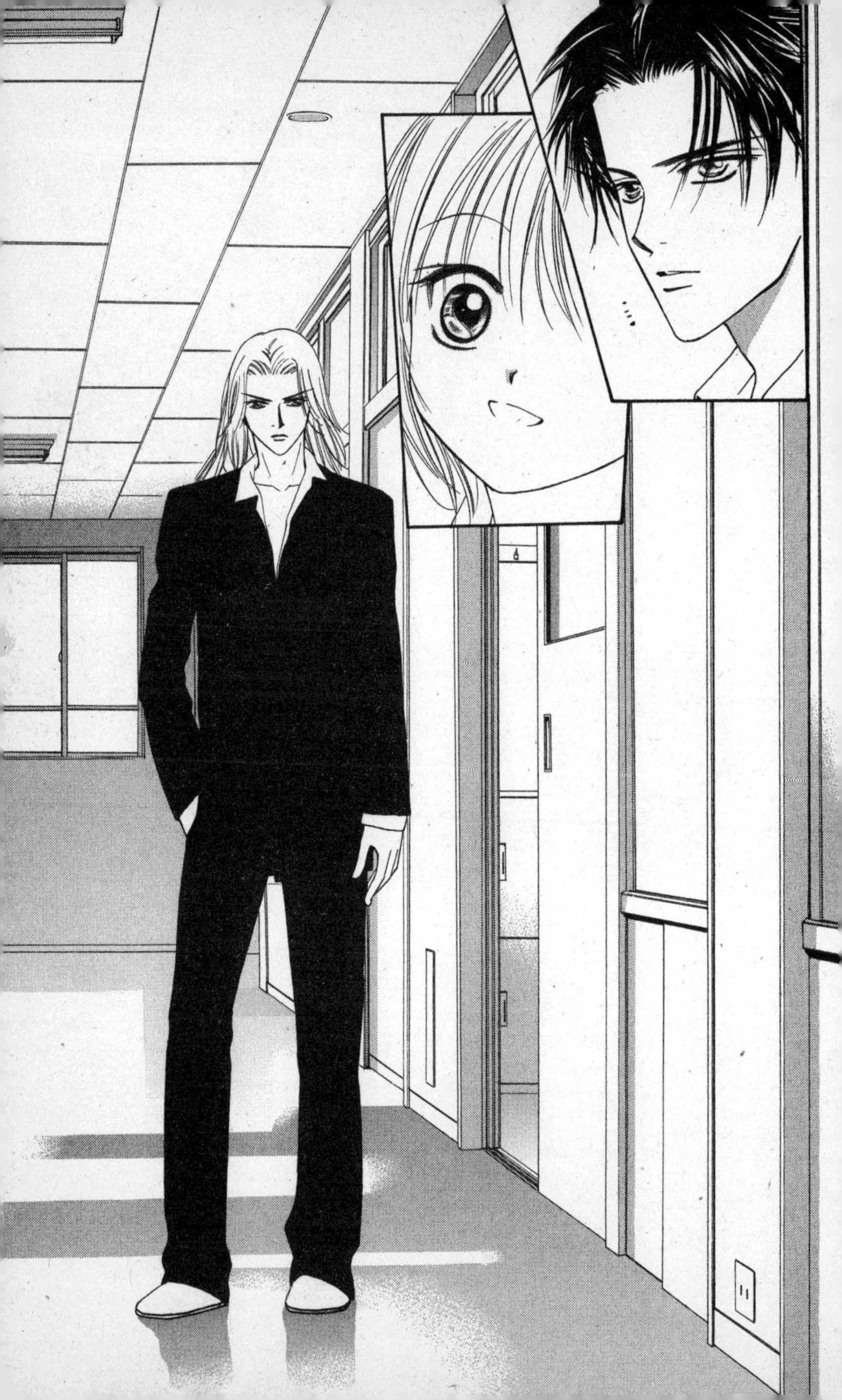

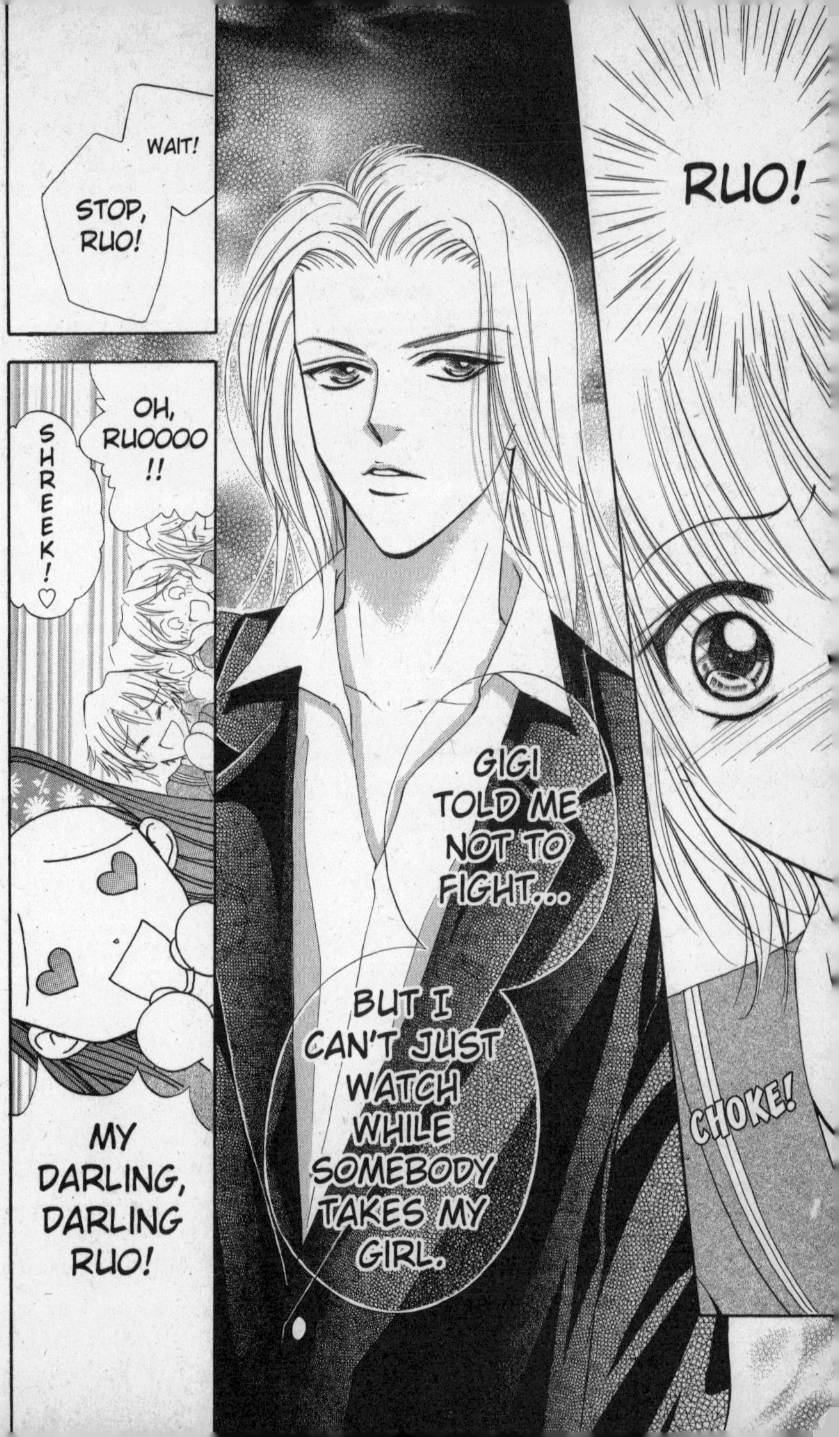
RUO!
CHOKE!
GIGI TOLD ME NOT TO FIGHT...
BUT I CAN'T JUST WATCH WHILE SOMEBODY TAKES MY GIRL.
WAIT!
STOP, RUO!
OH, RUOOOO!!
SHREEK!♡
MY DARLING, DARLING RUO!

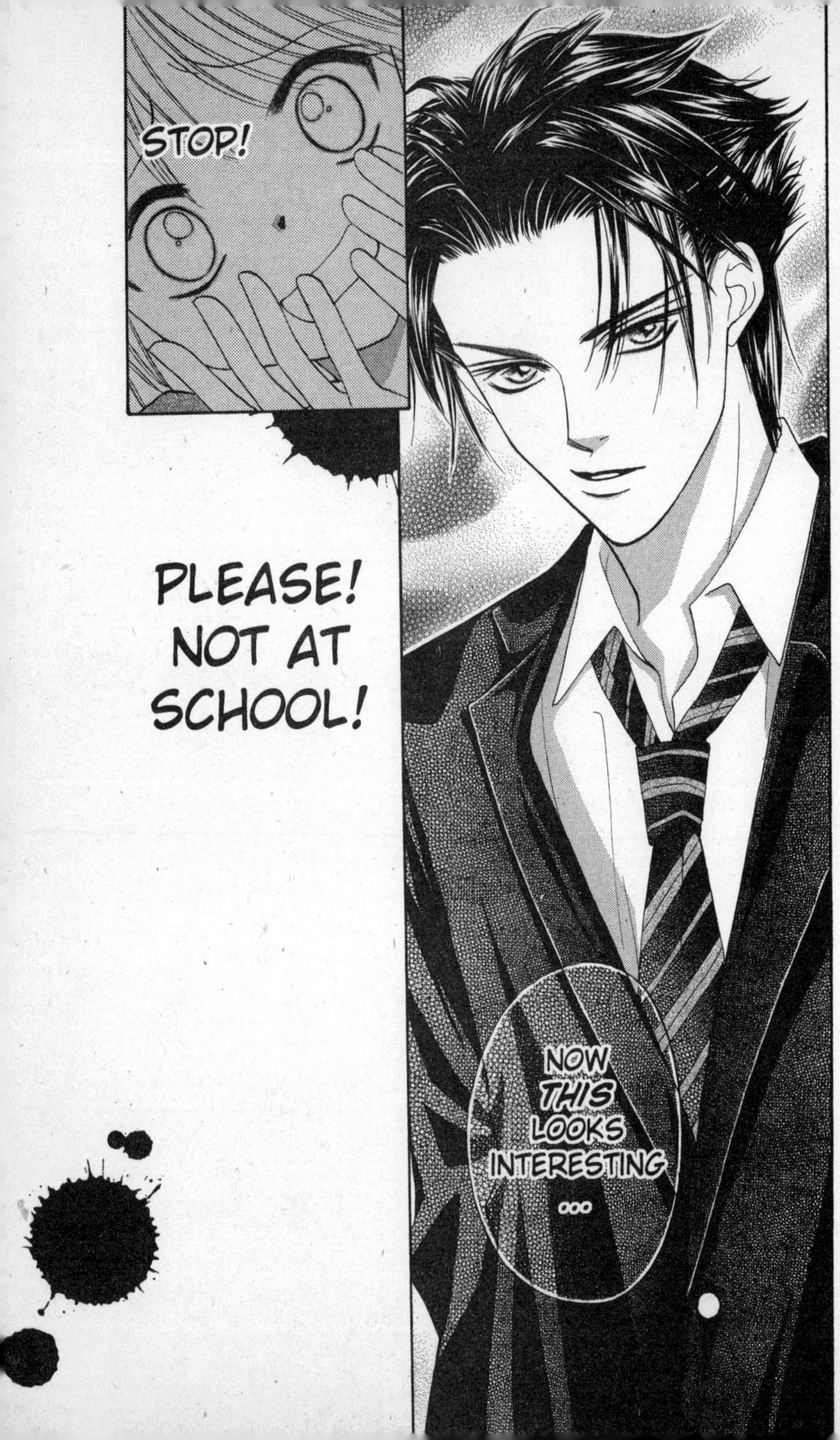
NOW THIS LOOKS INTERESTING...
STOP!
PLEASE! NOT AT SCHOOL!

RIE TAKADA

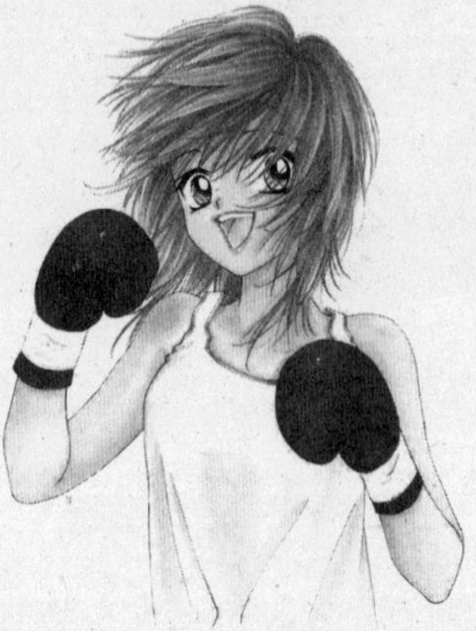

★Born August 10th in Hokkaido. Leo. Blood type O.
★Made her debut with *SP Girl* in 1990's Shojo Comic issue 17.
★Currently publishing in Shojo Comic.

I am able to write this comic with help and guidance from a lot of people. Especially Chairman Okabayashi and everybody at the gym. Thank you very much. I hope I can express how great martial arts is through *PUNCH!*. Oh, and this is a work of fiction–there are no relations to any group or individuals.

Rie Takada, 2005

Shojo Beat

PUNCH!
VOL. 1
The Shojo Beat Manga Edition

STORY & ART BY
RIE TAKADA

English Adaptation/Janet Gilbert
Translation/Joe Yamazaki
Touch-up Art & Lettering/Primary Graphix
Design/Izumi Hirayama
Editor/Urian Brown

Managing Editor/Megan Bates
Editorial Director/Elizabeth Kawasaki
Vice President & Editor in Chief/Yumi Hoashi
Sr. Director of Acquisitions/Rika Inouye
Sr. VP of Marketing/Liza Coppola
Exec. VP of Sales & Marketing/John Easum
Publisher/Hyoe Narita

Printed in Canada

Published by VIZ Media, LLC
P.O. Box 77010
San Francisco, CA 94107

Shojo Beat Manga Edition
10 9 8 7 6 5 4 3 2 1
First printing, November 2006

VIZ media

store.viz.com

RATED T+ FOR OLDER TEEN

PARENTAL ADVISORY
PUNCH is rated T+ for Older Teen and is recommended for ages 16 and up. This volume contains strong language and sexual themes.

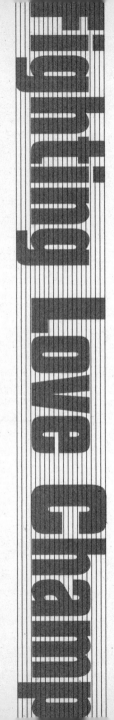

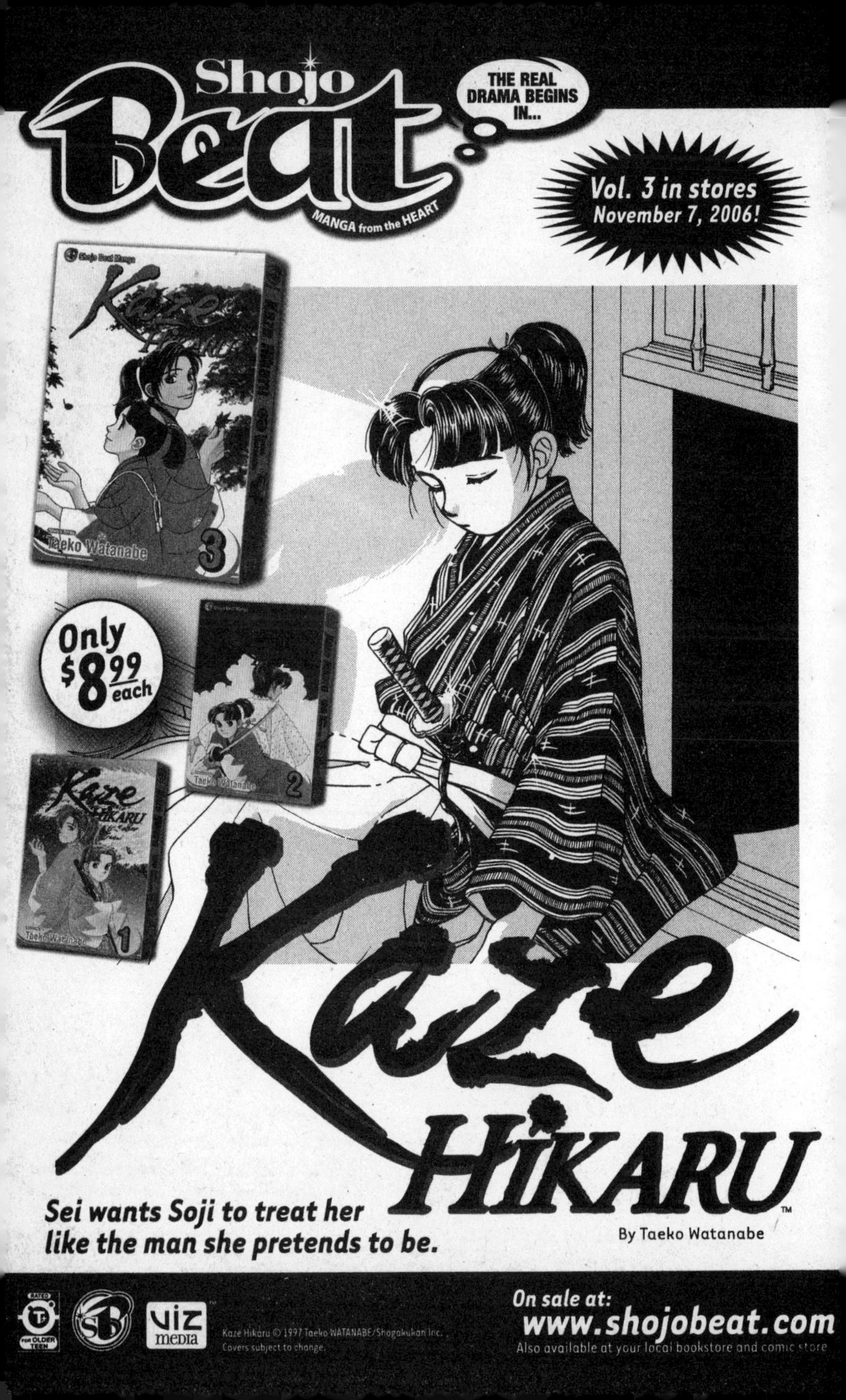

Shojo Beat
MANGA from the HEART
THE REAL DRAMA BEGINS IN...
Vol. 3 in stores November 7, 2006!
Only $8.99 each
Kaze Hikaru
By Taeko Watanabe
Sei wants Soji to treat her like the man she pretends to be.
RATED T+ FOR OLDER TEEN
VIZ media
Kaze Hikaru © 1997 Taeko WATANABE/Shogakukan Inc.
Covers subject to change.
On sale at:
www.shojobeat.com
Also available at your local bookstore and comic store

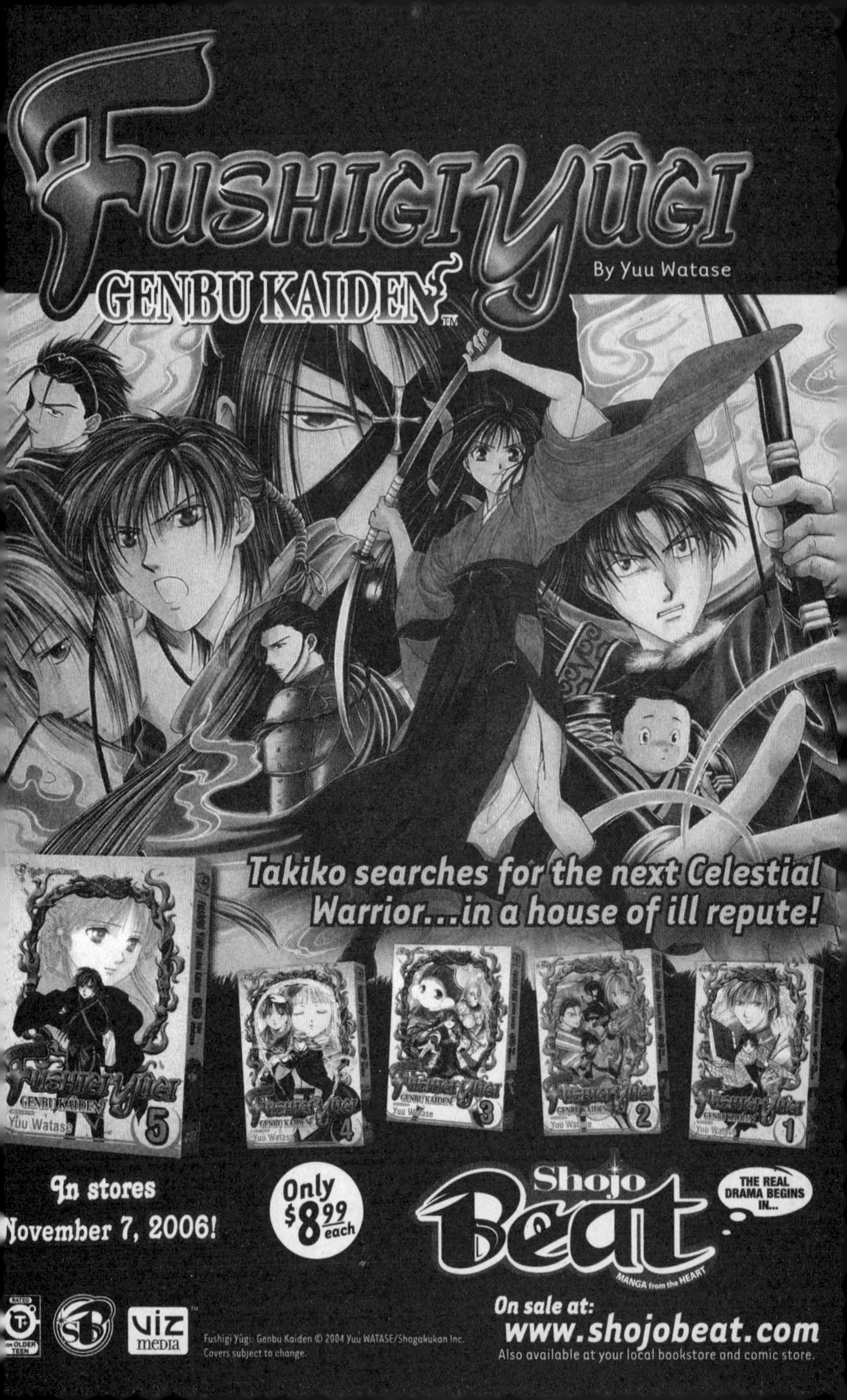
FUSHIGI YÛGI
GENBU KAIDEN™
By Yuu Watase
Takiko searches for the next Celestial Warrior...in a house of ill repute!
Fushigi Yûgi Genbu Kaiden Yuu Watase 5
Fushigi Yûgi Genbu Kaiden Yuu Watase 4
Fushigi Yûgi Genbu Kaiden Yuu Watase 3
Fushigi Yûgi Genbu Kaiden Yuu Watase 2
Fushigi Yûgi Genbu Kaiden Yuu Watase 1
In stores November 7, 2006!
Only $8.99 each
Shojo Beat MANGA from the HEART
THE REAL DRAMA BEGINS IN...
RATED T+ FOR OLDER TEEN
viz media
Fushigi Yûgi: Genbu Kaiden © 2004 Yuu WATASE/Shogakukan Inc.
Covers subject to change.
On sale at:
www.shojobeat.com
Also available at your local bookstore and comic store.

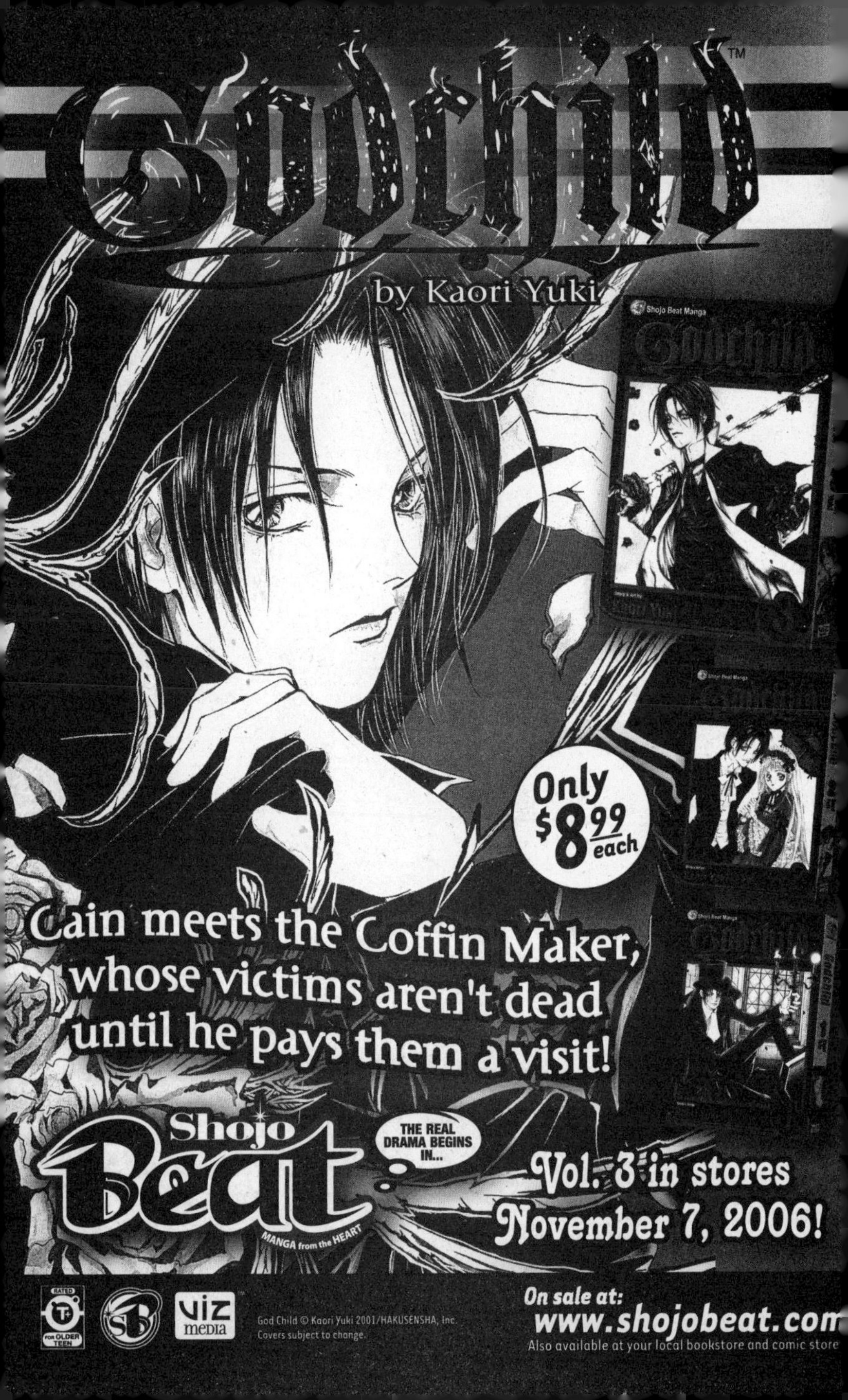
Godchild™
by Kaori Yuki
Only $8.99 each
Cain meets the Coffin Maker, whose victims aren't dead until he pays them a visit!
Shojo Beat
THE REAL DRAMA BEGINS IN...
MANGA from the HEART
Vol. 3 in stores November 7, 2006!
RATED T+ FOR OLDER TEEN
viz media
God Child © Kaori Yuki 2001/HAKUSENSHA, Inc.
Covers subject to change.
On sale at:
www.shojobeat.com
Also available at your local bookstore and comic store

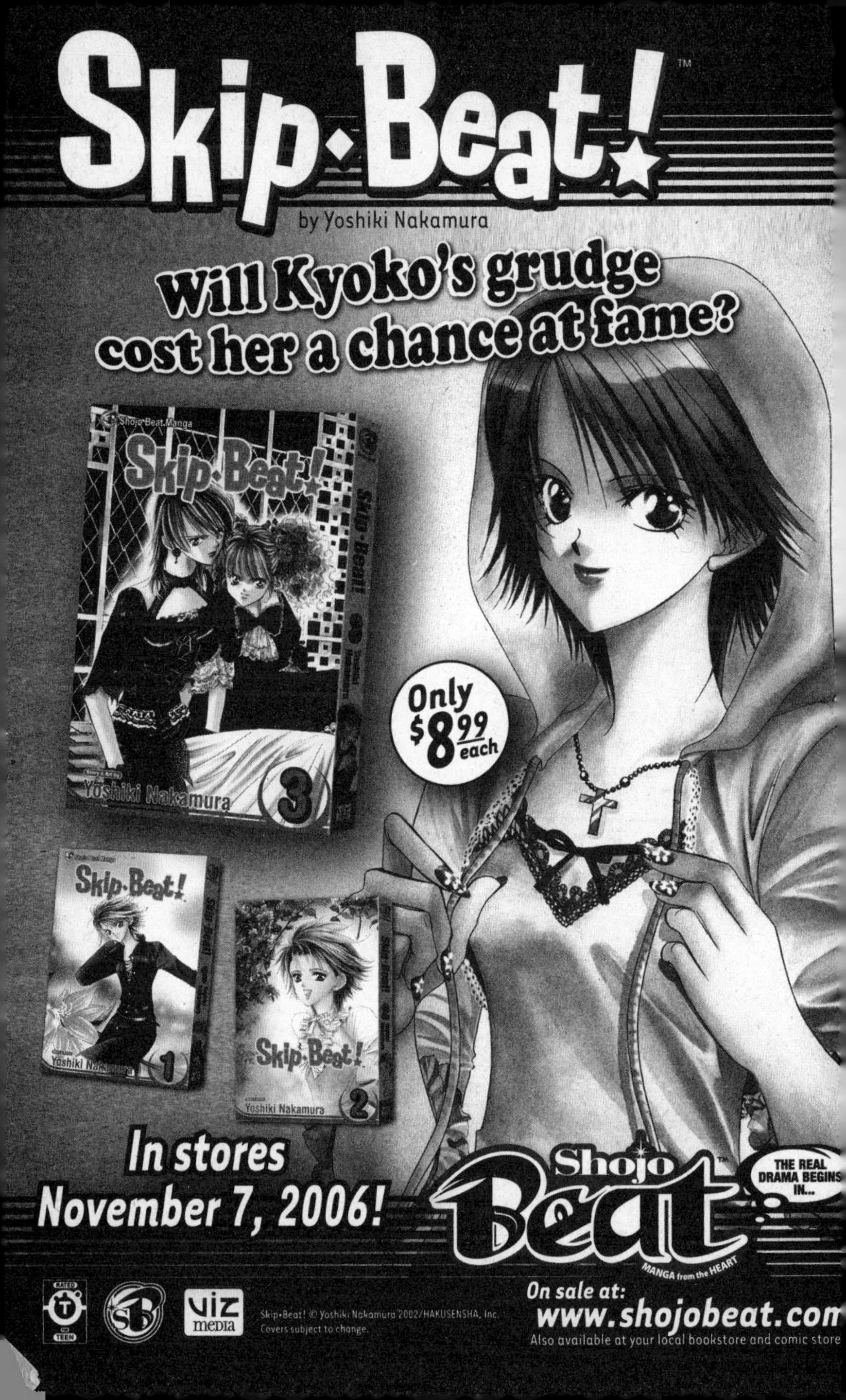
Skip·Beat!™
by Yoshiki Nakamura
Will Kyoko's grudge cost her a chance at fame?
Only $8.99 each
In stores November 7, 2006!
Shojo Beat™
MANGA from the HEART
THE REAL DRAMA BEGINS IN...
On sale at:
www.shojobeat.com
Also available at your local bookstore and comic store
Skip·Beat! © Yoshiki Nakamura 2002/HAKUSENSHA, Inc.
Covers subject to change.

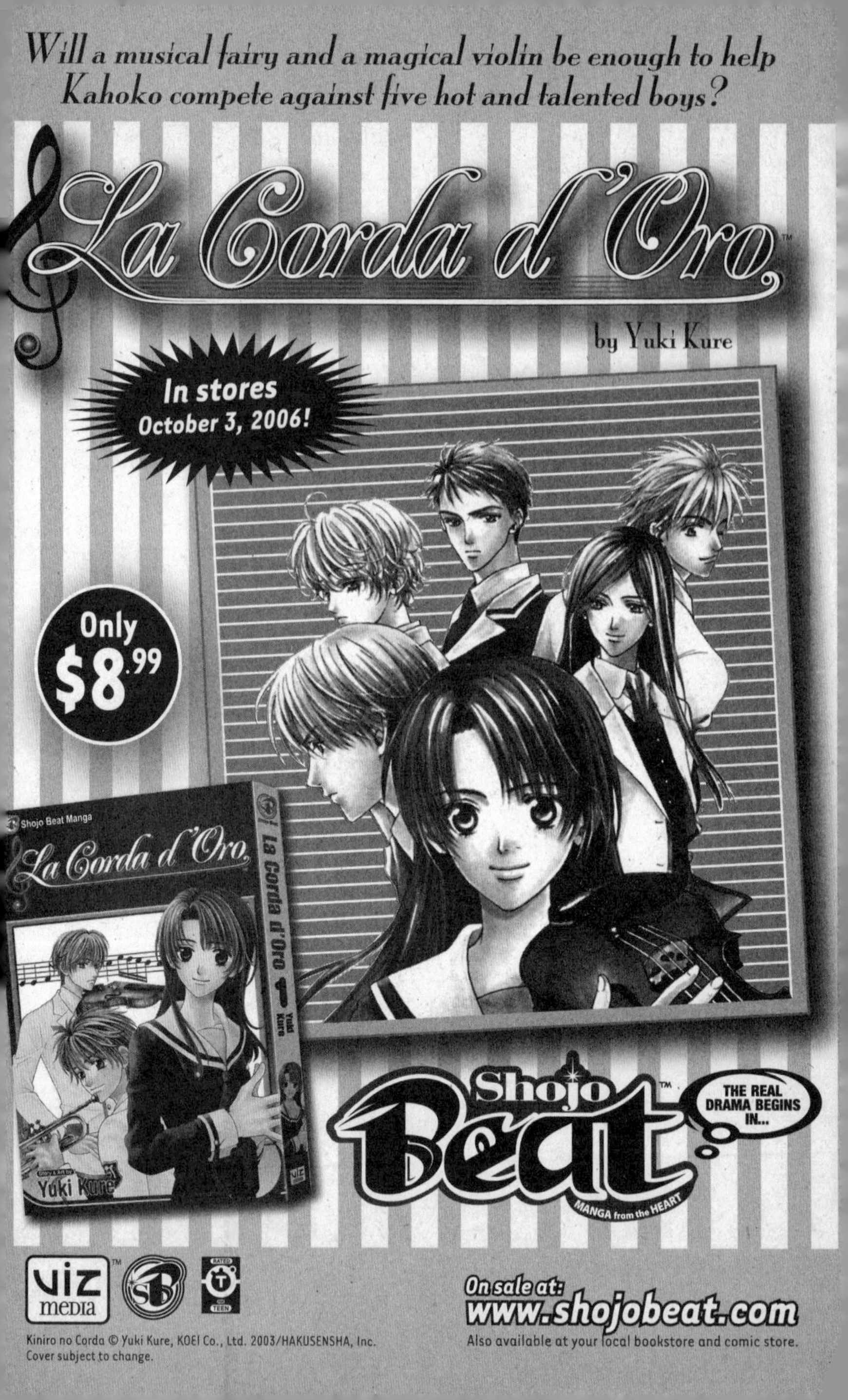
Will a musical fairy and a magical violin be enough to help Kahoko compete against five hot and talented boys?
La Corda d'Oro™
by Yuki Kure
In stores October 3, 2006!
Only $8.99
Shojo Beat Manga
La Corda d'Oro
La Corda d'Oro 1 Yuki Kure
Yuki Kure
Shojo Beat™
MANGA from the HEART
THE REAL DRAMA BEGINS IN...
viz media™
RATED T TEEN
On sale at:
www.shojobeat.com
Also available at your local bookstore and comic store.
Kiniro no Corda © Yuki Kure, KOEI Co., Ltd. 2003/HAKUSENSHA, Inc.
Cover subject to change.

Find the Beat online!
Check us out at

www.shojobeat.com!

COMPLETE OUR SURVEY AND LET US KNOW WHAT YOU THINK!

☐ Yes, I am interested in receiving information, advertising andpromotional materials related to VIZ Media, Shojo Beat and/or theirbusiness partners as well as any related products, services, news, events, contests, promotions and special offers <u>via email</u>.

☐ Yes, I am interested in receiving information, advertising andpromotional materials related to VIZ Media, Shojo Beat and/or theirbusiness partners as well as any related products, services, news, events, contests, promotions and special offers <u>via postal mail</u>.

Name: _____

Address: _____

City: _____ **State:** _____ **Zip:** _____

E-mail: _____

☐ **Male** ☐ **Female** **Date of Birth** (mm/dd/yyyy): ___/___/___ $\left(\begin{array}{c}\text{Must be 13}\\\text{and over.}\end{array}\right)$

❶ Do you purchase *Shojo Beat* magazine?

☐ Yes   ☐ No **(if no, skip the next two questions)**

If **YES**, do you subscribe?

☐ Yes   ☐ No

If you do **NOT** subscribe, why? **(please check one)**

☐ I prefer to buy each issue at the store.   ☐ I prefer to buy the manga volumes instead.

☐ I share a copy with my friends/family.   ☐ It's too expensive.

☐ My parents/guardian won't let me.   ☐ Other _____

❷ Which particular Shojo Beat Manga did you purchase? **(please check one)**

☐ Aishiteruze Baby ★★   ☐ Beauty Is the Beast   ☐ Beauty Pop

☐ Full Moon   ☐ Fushigi Yûgi: Genbu Kaiden   ☐ Godchild

☐ Kaze Hikaru   ☐ MeruPuri   ☐ Ouran High School Host Club

☐ Skip•Beat!   ☐ Tokyo Boys & Girls   ☐ Ultra Maniac

☐ Other _____

Will/did you purchase subsequent volumes?

☐ Yes   ☐ No   ☐ Not Applicable

❸ How did you learn about this title? **(check all that apply)**

☐ Advertisement   ☐ Article   ☐ Favorite creator/artist

☐ Favorite title   ☐ Gift   ☐ Recommendation

☐ Read a preview online and wanted to read the rest of the story

☐ Read introduction in *Shojo Beat* magazine   ☐ Special offer

☐ Website   ☐ Other _____

4 Will/did you purchase Shojo Beat Manga volumes of titles serialized in *Shojo Beat* magazine?

☐ Yes ☐ No

If **YES**, which one(s) will/did you purchase? (check all that apply)

☐ Absolute Boyfriend ☐ Baby & Me ☐ Backstage Prince
☐ Crimson Hero ☐ Nana ☐ Vampire Knight

If **YES**, what are your reasons for purchasing? (please pick up to 3)

☐ Favorite title ☐ Favorite creator/artist
☐ I want to read the full volume(s) all at once ☐ I want to read it over and over again
☐ There are extras that aren't in the magazine ☐ Recommendation
☐ The quality of printing is better than the magazine ☐ Other ______________

If **NO**, why would you not purchase it? (check all that apply)

☐ I'm happy just reading it in the magazine ☐ It's not worth buying the graphic novel
☐ All the manga pages are in black and white ☐ There are other graphic novels that I prefer
☐ There are too many to collect for each title ☐ It's too small
☐ Other ______________

5 Of the titles NOT serialized in the magazine, which ones have you purchased? (check all that apply)

☐ Aishiteruze Baby ★★ ☐ Beauty Is the Beast ☐ Beauty Pop
☐ Full Moon ☐ Fushigi Yûgi: Genbu Kaiden ☐ Godchild
☐ Kaze Hikaru ☐ MeruPuri ☐ Ouran High School Host Clu
☐ Skip•Beat! ☐ Tokyo Boys & Girls ☐ Ultra Maniac
☐ Other ______________

If you did purchase any of the above, what were your reasons for purchase?

☐ Advertisement ☐ Article ☐ Favorite creator/artist
☐ Favorite title ☐ Gift ☐ Recommendation
☐ Read a preview online and wanted to read the rest of the story
☐ Read introduction in *Shojo Beat* magazine ☐ Special offer
☐ Website ☐ Other ______________

Will you purchase subsequent volumes, if available?

☐ Yes ☐ No

6 Optional: What race/ethnicity do you consider yourself? (please check one)

☐ Asian/Pacific Islander ☐ Black/African American ☐ Hispanic/Latino
☐ Native American/Alaskan Native ☐ White/Caucasian ☐ Other
☐ I'd rather not say

THANK YOU! Please send the completed form to:

Shojo Survey
42 Catharine St.
Poughkeepsie, NY 12601

VIZ media

All information provided will be used for internal purposes only. We promise not to sell or otherwise divulge your information.